Jesus, the Voice, and the Text

JESUS, THE VOICE, AND THE TEXT
Beyond The Oral and the Written Gospel

---※---

TOM THATCHER
EDITOR

BAYLOR UNIVERSITY PRESS

© 2008 by Baylor University Press
Waco, Texas 76798-7363

All Rights Reserved. No part of this publication may be reproduced, stored in a retrieval system, or transmitted, in any form or by any means, electronic, mechanical, photocopying, recording or otherwise, without the prior permission in writing of Baylor University Press.

Scripture quotations, where not an author's own translation, are from the New Revised Standard Version Bible, copyright 1989, Division of Christian Education of the National Council of the Churches of Christ in the United States of America. Used by permission. All rights reserved.

Cover Design by Stephanie Blumenthal

Library of Congress Cataloging-in-Publication Data

Jesus, the voice, and the text : beyond the oral and the written gospel / Tom Thatcher, editor.
    p. cm.
   Includes bibliographical references and index.
   ISBN 978-1-932792-60-7 (pbk. : alk. paper)
   1. Kelber, Werner H. Oral and the written Gospel. 2. Bible. N.T. Gospels--Criticism, interpretation, etc. 3. Oral tradition. I. Thatcher, Tom, 1967-

BS2555.52.J48 2008
225.6'63--dc22
                       2008010625

Printed in the United States of America on acid-free paper with a minimum of 30% pcw recycled content.

This book is dedicated to
Rudolf Bultmann
and
Birger Gerhardsson,
who each, in his own way,
enriched our understanding of Christian origins.

TABLE OF CONTENTS

1	Beyond Texts and Traditions: Werner Kelber's Media History of Christian Origins Tom Thatcher	1
2	"It's Not Easy to Take a Fresh Approach": Reflections on *The Oral and the Written Gospel* (An Interview with Werner Kelber) Werner H. Kelber and Tom Thatcher	27
3	Oral Performance and Mark: Some Implications of *The Oral and the Written Gospel*, Twenty-Five Years Later Richard A. Horsley	45
4	The Gospel of Mark as Oral Hermeneutic Joanna Dewey	71
5	Storytelling in Oral and Written Media Contexts of the Ancient Mediterranean World Holly E. Hearon	89
6	Vice Catalogues as Oral-Mnemonic Cues: A Comparative Study of the Two-Ways Tradition in the *Didache* and Parallels from the Perspective of Oral Tradition Jonathan A. Draper	111
7	Human Memory and the Sayings of Jesus: Contemporary Experimental Exercises in the Transmission of Jesus Traditions April D. DeConick	135

8	The Gospel of Trajan *Arthur J. Dewey*	181
9	The Scar of the Cross: The Violence Ratio and the Earliest Christian Memories of Jesus *Chris Keith and Tom Thatcher*	197
10	Manuscript Tradition as a *Tertium Quid*: Orality and Memory in Scribal Practices *Alan Kirk*	215
11	The Oral-Scribal-Memorial Arts of Communication in Early Christianity *Werner H. Kelber*	235

Notes	263
Works Cited	273
Contributors	295
Index of Biblical Books and Other Ancient Works	299
Index of Authors	302
Index of Subjects	306

1

BEYOND TEXTS AND TRADITIONS
WERNER KELBER'S MEDIA HISTORY OF CHRISTIAN ORIGINS

TOM THATCHER

[T]he nature of the medium helps determine the form and kind of knowledge preserved.

—*Kelber 1983, 90*

Our premise is furthest removed from the notion that language and different linguistic embodiments are comprehensible as neutral carriers of ideational freight.... [M]odes of communication were themselves potential embodiments of cognition and shapers of consciousness.

—*Kelber 1995a, 443*

I am persuaded that the integration of issues such as speech and the oral matrix of chirographic life, media interfaces, and the human sensorium—issues that have clearly not been given their due—matters considerably for a more adequate, indeed different, understanding of our religious tradition.

—*Kelber 1995b, 163*

In February of 1983, Werner Kelber released a short book with a long title and the ambitious aim of exposing the media dynamics of early Christianity: *The Oral and the Written Gospel: The Hermeneutics of Speaking and Writing in the Synoptic Tradition, Mark, Paul, and Q*. Essentially, *Oral and Written Gospel* (OWG) sought to demonstrate that biblical scholars had overlooked a key element in their conceptions of early Christianity: the impact of communications media on the structure of life and thought. Of course, all scholars recognize that the extant written sources for Jesus were based on early Christian preaching, and that Paul's letters were normally read aloud in community gatherings. Kelber, however, sought to show that the dynamics of orality are so different from those of textuality—that speech is so different from writing—that the gospels cannot be viewed as the inevitable product of Jesus traditions and that Paul's theology cannot be comprehended apart from his media milieu. Rather, when viewed from the perspective of first-century media culture, the books of the New Testament are best understood as attempts to harness and control the forces of orality.

Obviously, any thesis so sweeping cannot be met with indifference, and Kelber's claims immediately drew criticism as well as praise.[1] But while many of the specific points of *OWG* have been disputed, time has shown that the book was a milestone in biblical studies, significant less for the answers it gave than for the questions it raised. Most substantially, *OWG* dared to ask what would happen if scholars began to wrestle with the fact that the early Christian documents (canonical and noncanonical) were written in a media milieu very different from our own, a world where orality was the dominant mode of cognition and communication, and no more than ten percent of the population could read (see Bar-Ilan 1992, 54–55; Harris 1989, 1–24; Hezser 2001, 496). The present volume seeks to assess the state of research into this question at the twenty-fifth anniversary of *OWG*'s publication and to point the way to future avenues of exploration.

This introduction will contextualize the programmatic essays to follow by surveying several major themes of Werner Kelber's research. In both *OWG* and subsequent essays, Kelber has focused on three sets of interrelated issues, each of which represents a distinct theme in the recent study of the media dynamics of early Christianity. First, Kelber has discussed in detail the hermeneutics of speaking and writing, and the interfaces between them, on a theoretical level. Oral and written words generate and communicate meaning in different ways, and the implications of these differences are significant for our understandings of speech and texts. Second, Kelber has applied his theoretical model to a variety of issues in Christian origins and to developmental trajectories in the history of Western thought. These first two facets of Kelber's work intersect in his sophisticated readings of the gospels, Paul, and noncanonical Christian texts (most notably Q and the *Gospel of Thomas*). Taken as a whole, Kelber's exegetical studies, beginning with *OWG* and continuing to the present time, have gradually taken the form of a media history of Christian origins.[2] Third, building on his media model, Kelber frequently critiques conventional conclusions of biblical scholarship. In these moments, Kelber calls for sweeping changes in both the methods and anticipated results of form criticism, source criticism, and the study of the historical Jesus.

The remainder of this essay will review Kelber's conclusions in each of these three areas: the hermeneutics of orality and writing, the media history of Christian origins, and the inevitable clash between a media-sensitive approach and traditional text-based models of biblical interpretation. Because *OWG* essentially inaugurated the sustained study of these issues, this review will in many respects summarize the current state of research into the media dynamics of the New Testament and early Christianity.

The Voice and the Text: The Hermeneutics of Speech and Writing

At least since the writing of *OWG,* Kelber's research has been driven by the premise that "artistic creativity is tied to terms dictated by the chosen medium" (Kelber 1983, xv). Following this maxim, Kelber attempts to describe and to differentiate between the unique psychological, sociological, and hermeneutical implications of the various media outlets that Christians have used to communicate their beliefs about Jesus. Three such media are particularly relevant to the evolution of Christian thought: orality, chirographs, and printed books.[3] The earliest Christians proclaimed Jesus by word of mouth, and the crucial, initial stages of the development of Jesus material were shaped by the possibilities and limitations of the oral medium. Within fifty years of Jesus' death, however, some early Christians had begun to write books and letters, allowing them to harness the rhetorical and cognitive potential of writing. These handwritten texts ("chirographs") were first published orally (read aloud to groups of believers) alongside the ongoing oral tradition, but as time passed they became the primary authorities for Christian belief and practice. The status of Scripture was further enhanced by the invention of movable type, a technology that gave written words a stability they had never before enjoyed and that offered new possibilities for mass distribution of ideas. Studies of the media history of Christian thought are particularly concerned, then, with two technological shifts: the shift from orality to handwritten texts in the first and second centuries and the shift from multiple manuscripts to printed books in the fifteenth and sixteenth centuries. Kelber has commented extensively on the social and hermeneutical dynamics of all three media, with particular attention to the implications of the two major shifts from one medium to another.[4]

> *"The sounding of words, the gestures of the speaker, facial contact between speaker and hearers, as well as an environment shared by speaker and hearers alike are all crucial aids in conveying meaning without saying it."*
>
> —Kelber 1983, 62

Oral Words Are Events

In Kelber's view, any adequate understanding of the hermeneutics of orality must focus on two aspects of spoken words: their event character and the immediate physical presence of their audience. As events in time, oral words have no existence beyond the moment in which they are uttered (Kelber 1983, 1; 1988a, 34–35). As transactions between people, oral words draw their meanings from the larger social and physical context of their utterance. At the moment of oral performance, the speaker and audience achieve what Kelber calls a "homeostatic balance" or "oral synthesis" through "a continuous process of adjustment of language to communal expectations, of social to linguistic realities" (Kelber 1983, 19, 92).[5] Speakers consider what they want to say, remember how others have said such things before, evaluate how they can communicate their point most effectively, and reflect on how the audience is reacting (or might react) to their words. The "meaning" of an utterance lies at the intersection of all these considerations. Kelber refers to this interactive speech environment as a "biosphere in which speaker and hearers live . . . an invisible nexus of references and identities from which people draw sustenance . . . and in relation to which they make sense of their lives" (Kelber 1995b, 159). The social biosphere thus serves as a sort of human intertext, the referential field from which spoken words derive their meaning (Kelber 1990, 77–78).

Kelber's "biosphere" model raises three significant implications for the understanding of oral tradition in general and early Christian Jesus traditions in particular. First, the observable style of oral speech, and of documents based on oral traditions, entirely reflects the needs of listening audiences. Second, there can be no real "transmission of content" in an oral milieu, for every telling of a story is a discrete speech act operating within the dynamics of its own unique situation. An "oral tradition" should therefore be conceived as a loosely connected series of individual oral performances, not as a process by which fixed texts are handed down from one generation to the next, more or less intact. Third, the hermeneutical potentials of orality shape and limit the ideological cargo of spoken words. In Kelber's view, any adequate model of early Christian proclamation must account for these three realities.

First, because speech is always shaped by the needs and interests of a listening audience, the stylistic features of traditional tales and sayings may be viewed as byproducts of the oral medium. Aphorisms, for example, are characterized by "brevity, rhythmic patterning, and focal intensity" with "a distinct topicality, a rhetorically impressive style, and a sharp focus"; all these features are "closely attuned to the sensibilities of . . . hearing recipients" (Kelber 1990, 71). Oral bards typically utilize plot techniques that can hold the active attention of a listening audience, such as triad patterns, direct discourse, the historical present tense, the use of third-person plural verbs rather than the passive ("they did" rather than "it was done"), and "progressive duplication" (the repetition of a theme with slight variations to move the story forward; Kelber 1983, 66–68). Kelber places particular emphasis on the fact that oral plots are cumulative and paratactic rather than programmatic, so that "knowledge is gathered and multiplied more than critically developed" (Kelber 1983, 80). Oral storytellers, in other words, do not create cause-and-effect narratives that unify many discrete episodes. Instead, they tend to string together stories that emphasize a single point by viewing it from a variety of angles. Finally, the characters in oral stories tend to be "poorly developed" and are often treated collectively and stereotypically, with emphasis on their actions rather than their personalities (Kelber 1983, 68–69). All these features of traditional tales, widely documented by folklorists, reflect the storyteller's need to capture and hold the attention of his or her listening audience.

A second major implication of Kelber's "biosphere" model relates to the problem of "tradition." Any comparison of several renditions of a folk story or wisdom saying will immediately reveal three trends: "plurality, uniformity, and variability" (Kelber 1983, 51). In Kelber's idiom, "plurality" means that each utterance—each version of the story or saying—is independent and unique. Because every oral performance draws its meaning and energy from its own peculiar biosphere (a unique social context and moment), three very similar renderings of a traditional saying should be viewed as three completely autonomous texts (Kelber 1983, 30). In his more recent work, Kelber has referred to this quality of oral speech as "equiprimordiality": "each rendition [of an oral saying/story] was an original version, and in fact *the original version*" (Kelber 1995b, 151, emphasis original; see also 2002a, 64; 2005, 237).[6] The biosphere model also resists any notion of a "transmission," more or less accurate, of the content of a traditional saying or story. Rather, an "oral tradition" is a series of "discrete acts of speech, separated by intervals of nonspeaking, and unconnectable by temporal or spatial tracts" (Kelber 1987a, 99). Oral words, like atoms, can jump from one state to another "without actually occupying an intermediate position"; it is therefore impossible to speak of "originals" and "variants" in an oral milieu (Kelber 1990, 74).

"*In the beginning were the words.*"

—Kelber 1990, 74

The equiprimordiality of oral speech events informs Kelber's understanding of the complicated interplay between "uniformity" and "variability" in a performance tradition. When considering several renditions of a traditional story—such as the tale of Red Riding Hood or the parable of The Sower/Soils—one generally observes a certain continuity in basic structural features alongside an inevitable variability in details and language. Both the similarities and the differences between the various versions may be explained through the biosphere model: to the extent that two performance situations are similar, they will produce similar texts; conversely, differences in the texts reflect differences in the respective performance contexts. For example, when an early Christian preacher told the familiar parable of The Good Samaritan, the expectations and beliefs of the immediate audience "imposed artistic and ideological constraints upon the speaker" (Kelber 1990, 71). The audience has heard this story, and/or others like it, before and holds certain beliefs about the proper way to communicate its content; the preacher must respond to these expectations in order to maintain the oral synthesis. Versions of an oral story are thus the same to the extent that their performance contexts are similar and different to the extent that those contexts differ.

Third and finally, the fact that the form and meaning of speech are intertwined with performance settings must impact not only our conception of oral style and transmission but also our interpretation of oral texts. Specifically, literate interpreters should not expect an oral story to carry the same ideological freight as a written philosophical treatise. The preacher asks his audience to accept his story and live within its claims; he does not invite his audience to interpret the content of his words, for the words and their contents can never be differentiated. Indeed, "spoken words discourage reflection on meaning as something apart from utterance" simply because they have no meaning apart from the moment of their utterance (Kelber 1983, 99). For example, the "oral Christology" of the pre-Markan Jesus tradition was "disinclined, and perhaps not able to reflect on the nature of Jesus and the essence of redemption," because such abstract concepts are alien to the oral way of thinking about things (Kelber 1983, 55). In the same way, pronouncement stories were not told with a view to philosophical elaboration; the ethical proposition was embedded in a hypothetical situation that made the principle vivid, but the principle could not be separated from that situation. Indeed, "only a mind removed from oral

> "Oral life is not merely embellished by rhetorical conventionalities, but [rather]it lives from them."
> —Kelber 1983, 27

mentality would probe stories and narrators with a curiosity about the *nature* of justice, piety, morality, social and civic responsibility" (Kelber 1983, 57, emphasis original). Oral words are tied to the concrete human situations from which they draw their shape, meaning, and energy and do not aspire to transcend those situations or point to abstract concepts.

Manuscripts and Machined Texts

In Kelber's view, "readers confronted with texts find themselves in a hermeneutical situation quite different from that of hearers of words" (Kelber 1990, 86). This is the case because writing differs from orality in three key respects. First, whereas oral speech is shaped by the dialogic interaction between speaker and audience, authors work in isolation from readers and are not immediately accountable to them. Second, written texts do not derive meaning from unique performance biospheres. As such, they are not equipromordial, a fact that makes it possible to speak of "originals," "sources," and "variants." Third, writing objectifies language by fixing words in a stable form and thus opens new possibilities for interpretation and abstraction. Overall, whereas oral words are *events* that draw their meaning from human interactions, written words are *things* that exist independently of the people who use them.

"[W]riting is deconstructive to the vital concerns of orality."
—Kelber 1987b, 111

On the first point above, while oral storytellers need an audience, writers work alone and normally are not present when their texts are read. There is, therefore, no "homeostatic balance" or "oral synthesis" between the author and the reader—in fact, there is often no relationship at all beyond common contact with the document in question. "[O]rality manages to synchronize composition and communication, whereas in writing the production of the text is always separate from the actual transmission of information" (Kelber 1990, 86). The oral storyteller is constrained to a large degree by people who can affirm or reject his words, but the author enjoys "a sense of emancipation from communal pressures" (Kelber 2005, 227; cf. 1983, 14–15, 115). This physical/temporal distance between the author and the reader initiates a significant "shift in contextuality" when oral words are committed to writing (Kelber 1983, 109). As noted earlier, speech derives meaning from the human biosphere in which it is produced—the relationships between speaker, audience, message content, and performance tradition function as the "informing context of

"Texts fossilize."
—Kelber 1987a, 101

symbolic reference" from which oral words derive their meaning (Kelber 1990, 86). Written words, by contrast, are enmeshed in a textual web and derive meaning from their fixed relationship with other words in the book (Kelber 1983, 109–10). When speech is written down, words lose their "mündlichen Aktionscharakters" simply because "Distanz, Entfremdung und eine Aufschiebung des Signifikationsprozesses unauflöslich mit der Verschriftlichung mündlicher Traditionen verbunden sind" (Kelber 1988a, 36–37, 40).[7]

A second major difference between orality and writing relates to the problem of the relationship between multiple texts. As noted above, oral words are events in time; as a result, each telling of a tale is discrete and equiprimordial. Documents, however, are objects in space; as a result, written words enjoy a permanence and stability that allows them to move from one text to another in the same way that furniture might be moved from an old house to a new one. Writing thus makes it possible to speak of an "original text" and to distinguish between multiple variants of this original. Orality is characterized by plurality and temporality: many utterances coexist, each a product of its own moment. Written words, by contrast, are characterized by singularity and spatiality: a single author places words side by side on a page, each of which could be reproduced elsewhere (see Kelber 1983, 94–95).

Third and finally, writing introduces new possibilities for the interpretation of words. In Kelber's view, the invitation to interpret is one of the most significant hermeneutical implications of the shift from speech to text. The author, free from the pressures of spontaneous performance and the whims of the audience, can reflect on the material in a much more sustained way than the oral storyteller; the reader, free from the need to follow the story, can revisit the text to speculate about underlying themes and transcendental meanings. Because writing fosters interpretation, authors and readers may safely adopt a critical posture that orality cannot tolerate. Audiences can silence speakers through protest or physical restraint and can suppress heretical interpretations simply by forbidding their verbalization. Writers, however, stand at a safe distance from their readers, enjoying "the kind of alienation that will prove productive for creative reassessments of tradition" (Kelber 2002a, 57). As a result, while both preachers and authors can "appeal to and reinforce group identity," authors alone have the option "to challenge and reshape it" (Kelber 2005, 228). Whether interpretation affirms group values or displaces them, "in textuality, reflection on words takes priority over mere perpetuation of them" (Kelber 1983, 109).

While *OWG* focused on the implications of the shift from orality to literacy in the early church, Kelber's more recent work shows greater sensitivity to the differences between ancient and modern experiences of written texts. Specifically, because ancient manuscripts differed significantly from modern books in both their production and their reception, it is relevant to distinguish between "scribality" (handwritten manuscripts) and "print" (texts produced with mechanical type). Ancient and medieval handwritten manuscripts, or *chirographs,* were different from modern printed books in two important respects, both of which reflect their embeddedness in oral culture. First, in the ancient world, texts were almost always read aloud and in public; manuscripts were thus "closely allied with recitation and auditory apperception" (Kelber 1995b, 153; 1997, xxii). Ancient authors were therefore more conscious of the mnemonic and stylistic demands of a listening audience than are their modern counterparts, and "texts were likely to be composed in conformity with a phenomenology of sound more than sight" (Kelber 1997, xxiii–xxiv). Second, in ancient manuscript culture, texts "were not perceived as having permanently fixed boundaries"—certainly not boundaries limited by any notion of a single author's creative genius (Kelber 1995b, 155; 1987b, 122; 1995a, 432). "Oral and orally dependent texts were tradition-bound, variously interfacing with orality and other texts, and deriving meaning from extra-textual signifieds no less than from internal signification" (Kelber 1995a, 410, 433). The notion that words are fixed, self-sustaining entities that give "the appearance of autosemantic objectivity" did not arise until the invention of mechanical type, which made it possible to copy and distribute the words of individual authors in unprecedented fashion (Kelber 1987b, 123). Scribality, then, is a more complex phenomenon than print, and the hermeneutical differences between these two media must be comprehended for an adequate understanding of ancient literacy and the history of pre-Gutenberg Christian thought.

> "The ancient world of communications exemplifies the unbound nature of all language," oral and written.
> —Kelber 1995b, 155

In one of his most recent essays, a paper delivered at the University of Glasgow in 2007, Kelber critiques the foundational premises of modern textual criticism from the perspective of a media-sensitive approach to ancient biblical manuscripts. Here, Kelber extends his earlier discussions of the orality/literacy interface to characterize manuscript production as a form of oral memory performance. A review of the physical evidence

> "Both in terms of compositional intent and audience adjustment, the early scribal tradition of Jesus' sayings still operates according to oral dynamics."
> —Kelber 2007

suggests that chirographic texts paralleled orality in at least four ways: a) variation in expression was the norm, not the exception; b) there were no single "originals" but rather a plurality of original and independent compositions; c) Jewish and Christian scribes attempted to keep texts relevant to the needs of their immediate audiences; d) in view of points a, b, and c, the early "manuscript tradition" should be understood as a series of active recompositions rather than as simple transmission and copying. This conclusion calls for a complete rethinking of the status of the Masoretic Text (MT) and the Greek *textus receptus*. Just as the written gospels should not be viewed as the sea into which all oral traditions were inevitably flowing, the Masoretic Hebrew text should not be viewed as the center of the manuscript universe. Recent research into the Dead Sea Scrolls, ancient Samaritan documents, the Septuagint (LXX), and Josephus suggests that the notion of a single, "standard" text—or even of a fixed canon of sacred books—was alien to late Second Temple and early rabbinic Jewish thought. Certainly, the MT cannot be used to evaluate or "correct" earlier manuscripts as if this standardized text somehow represents an "original" that was only waiting to emerge. The same fluidity is evident in the manuscript history of the gospels, not because the early Christians had a careless disinterest in Jesus' words but rather because these words were considered vitally important to the church's ongoing life and thought.

Hot and Cold Running Memory

Any consideration of the workings of "tradition" carries with it a theory of memory, a model for understanding how people retain, recall, and transmit information about the past. Kelber's research includes reflections on two major dimensions, or two major types, of memory. In his earlier works, including *OWG*, Kelber focused on what might be called "performance memory," mnemonic techniques that oral speakers use to structure their speech in memorable ways. More recently, however, Kelber has begun to conceptualize "tradition" as "cultural memory," the broader set of social frameworks that guide the composition of both oral and written texts that refer to the past.[8] Kelber thus understands "memory" both as a structural element of

> "But this much does seem clear to me: memory and manuscript are the twin categories that are critical for our understanding of the gospels and their narrative compositions."
> —Kelber 2002a, 81

oral speech (mnemotechnique) and as the human context in which words about the past become meaningful (memory frameworks).

Oral audiences rely on memory much more than do readers, and successful storytellers are sensitive to this fact. Readers can go back and review; hearers can only move on to the next point. The oral composer therefore "has no choice but to enter into a binding contract with a mnemonically structured language" (Kelber 2005, 227). According to the terms of this memory covenant, storytellers must telegraph their intentions with familiar themes and formulaic clichés; they must also abide by the principle of applicability, following the logic that people are more likely to remember material that seems relevant to life. Both aspects of performance memory—formulaic style and relevant content—may be conveniently illustrated by early Christian mnemotechnique. For example, the traditional sayings of Jesus that are now preserved in written gospels "abound" with the "earmarks of mnemonics" such as "alliteration, appositional equivalence, proverbial and aphoristic diction, contrasts and antitheses, synonymous, antithetical, and tautological parallelisms, rhythmic structures, and so forth" (Kelber 2005, 233). Preachers made stories about Jesus more memorable by using simple plots with "scenic duality" (no more than two characters are involved at once), by focusing on individual instances rather than general situations, and by charging dialogues with an agonistic tone that gives them "mnemonic advantages over the daily grind and routine" (Kelber 1983, 51–54). Ultimately, oral materials are always shaped with memorability in mind.[9]

In his more recent work, Kelber has expanded his model of the interface between media and memory to comprehend the implications of social/cultural memory studies. Social memory theorists argue that "memory" has two essential functions that work together in constant tension: "to resurrect the images of the past so as to transport them into the present, and to reconstruct the images of the past so as to integrate them into the present context" (Kelber 2005, 234). Memory, in other words, is concerned both with the preservation and recall of past events ("to resurrect") and with the presentation of the past in ways that are relevant to, and meaningful within, present circumstances ("to integrate"). In any specific act of remembering, the actual past defines the scope of what can be remembered, while present circumstances shape what is evoked so as to make it useful here and now. Kelber refers to the repetitive, preservative element of memory as "cold memory" and calls the integrative, situational element of memory "hot memory" (Kelber 2002a, 61; 2005, 228–29, 232).

While manuscripts obviously do a better job of preserving hard data than orality, it is important to stress that Kelber views both early Christian

> *"I venture the suggestion that the Gospel composition is unthinkable without the notion of cultural memory, which serves ultimately not the preservation of remembrances per se but the preservation of the group, its social identity and self-image."*
> —Kelber 1997, xxiii

preaching and the written gospels as forms of hot memory, invoking the past in service of present needs. All statements about the past—oral and written—are expressed in words and exchanged between human beings; therefore, memory is always already intertwined with human interactions and is thus ultimately social in nature. Because memory is a social phenomenon, "the process of remembering does not work purely for the benefit of what is deemed worthy of recollection; that is to say, it is not primarily fed by needs for preservation of the past in a state of authenticity." Instead, memory "selects and modifies subjects and figures of the past in order to make them serviceable to the image the community wishes to cultivate of itself" (Kelber 2002a, 56). Whether through oral preaching or writing and reading gospels, early Christians remembered Jesus in ways that would help them make sense of themselves and their current situations.

If both oral Jesus tradition and written gospels are hot memory, how does one conceptualize the shift from orality to literacy in early Christianity? Why, in other words, did early Christians feel compelled to record their memories of Jesus in books? Kelber finds the answer to this question in Jan Assmann's theory of *Traditionsbruch*. Assmann notes that a group's communicative memory of a significant event enters a critical phase after about forty years, when a new generation must begin to carry recollections of the past in order to preserve the group's sense of heritage and identity (see Assmann 1992, 101–3, 212–22). At these transitional moments, the production of written texts "may facilitate a degree of forgetfulness—distortion even—of prior memories, in the interest of retaining/constructing a particular version of them" (Kelber 2005, 245). As noted earlier, documents can sustain revisionist interpretations of tradition in ways that orality cannot, allowing authors to preserve important information while also suppressing certain facts and reconfiguring what they choose to protect. In the process, authors can strategically reshape a group's past and, consequently, its self-image.

The Gospel of Mark, the first attempt to strategically transfer oral memories of Jesus to a written narrative, is a prime example of *Traditionsbruch*. Throughout his career, Kelber has argued that Mark should be dated in the early 70s, some forty years after the cross and just after the destruction of Jerusalem (see Kelber 1974, 1; 1979, 91–93). At this point in time, the church was wrestling with "a threefold crisis: the death of Jesus, the devastation of Jerusalem, . . . and the cessation of a generation of memories and memory carriers." Mark wrote a gospel not so much to preserve living memories of Jesus as to construct a new Christian identity that in many respects represented a "corrective gesture vis-à-vis tradition." The Gospel of Mark, in other words, is not cold memory seeking to archive the primitive apostolic witness in a more durable medium. Rather, Mark is hot memory that reaches into the past to resurrect Jesus as "an *Erinnerungsfigur* [memory figure] for the benefit of solidifying present group identity" (Kelber 2005, 244).

In one of his most recent essays, a forthcoming article titled "Memory and Violence" for the Edith Wyschogrod *Festschrift,* Kelber discusses several specific ways that the canonical Evangelists appropriated the past to construct identities for their respective audiences. Focusing on the passion narratives, Kelber notes that groups filter traumatic events through the symbolic resources of collective memory, which reduces the apparent randomness of violent events and gives meaning and value to death. Following this pattern, the Evangelists rationalized Jesus' violent demise by connecting the cross to established memorial frameworks. Kelber highlights three such assimilation techniques that are readily evident in the gospels: situating the events of Calvary within familiar "memory places," particularly the well-known Jewish *topos* of the "innocent sufferer"; "keying" details of Jesus' death story to themes and texts from the Hebrew Bible; and contextualizing the passion within larger stories of Jesus' career, stories that give the crucifixion a distinct rationale and meaning. By tying the value of Jesus' death to the immediate context of his life story and the broader contexts of Scripture and Jewish martyr stories, the Evangelists allowed their communities to remember the horrors of the cross in a way that established not only the identity of Christ but also of the emerging Christian movement.

But, as "Memory and Violence" points out, the memorial potential of the gospels was not exhausted on their first readers. The symbols and themes that made the gospels hot memory continued to simmer long after the situations envisioned by their authors. Most notably, all four canonical Evangelists clearly sought to define Christian identity over against Judaism, while also insisting that the claims of the church were not in conflict with the interests of Rome. As a result, the gospels tend to portray Jews as being hostile to Christ, resistant to God's truth, and worthy of divine judgment, while essentially exonerating the Romans of any responsibility for Jesus' death or the destruction of Jerusalem. Because words and symbols draw their meaning from the human contexts in which they are exchanged, the gospels—at once products and catalysts of social memory—have been readily serviceable to anti-Semitic readings that rationalize the most insane acts of violence against Jewish people. As history has shown, hot memory is difficult to turn off.

"Whoever Hears You Hears Me": Speech, Writing, and Power in Early Christianity

Kelber has applied his model of orality, scribality, and memory to a variety of problems in early Christianity. Viewed as a whole, these studies take the shape of a media history of Christian origins. Early Christians communicated their recollections of Jesus through three distinct channels—"orality, the sayings genre, and the narrative gospel" (Kelber 1987b, 116; 1990, 74)—each of which balanced the tension between orality and writing in its own unique way to achieve specific rhetorical and ideological effects. While all early Christian discourse about Jesus (including written gospels and letters) was subject to the needs of listening audiences, *orality* refers here particularly to the rhetorical dynamics of prophetic utterances. The authors of *sayings and dialogue gospels*—such as Q, the *Gospel of Thomas*, and the *Apocryphon of James*—attempted to capture the persuasive power of live speech while also encouraging the deeper interpretive moves that writing supports. These first two modes of Jesus tradition were, however, ultimately rejected by canonical Christianity, which preferred *narrative gospels* that fix the meaning of Christ's words and actions in thematic stories. In Kelber's view, all early Christian documents can be situated at some point on this media spectrum.

The Power of Presence: Paul and the Prophets

The original mode of Christian memory was oral proclamation, the preferred media outlet of early prophets and the Apostle Paul. As noted earlier, oral words draw their meaning from the human biosphere in which they are uttered. The speaker and the audience are always physically present to one another, so that "consummating presence" is a key feature of oral language. Early Christian prophets could exploit this peculiar dynamic of oral hermeneutics by uttering sayings of the risen Lord in the first person; from this platform, they "spoke as representatives of Jesus and embodied in this manner his very authority" (Kelber 1983, 99). As John 6:68 indicates, Jesus' spoken words have "power to deliver life," save from death, and effect judgment; to reject the prophetic utterance, then, is to reject the salvation that Christ himself offers (Kelber 1990, 75). While this rhetorical posture would give the prophet's audience a strong sense of Christ's powerful, living presence, it obviously could not tolerate theological notions that highlight Jesus' absence from the community. "Wo man die Herrenworte als eine sich auf den lebendigen Christus gründende und lebenspendende Autorität verstand, da hatten Jesu längst vergangene, irdische Existenz und sein Tod, wie auch eine zukünftige Auferstehung der Gläubigen samt aller Eschatologie ihren Sinn verloren" (Kelber 1988a, 32–33).[10] The communicative strategy of these charismatic prophets is summarized by their slogan at Q 10:16//John 13:20—"Whoever hears/receives you [the prophet] hears/receives me [Jesus]" (Kelber 1983, 99; 1990, 74).

Like the charismatic prophets, Paul was "an oral traditionalist whose commitment to faith is based on oral, rhetorical grounds" (Kelber 1997, xx; 1983, 164, 177; 1987a, 99).[11] Paul's commitment to the media dynamics of orality is particularly evident in two of the most distinctive elements of his theology: his conception of "the gospel" and his ambiguous posture toward the Law of Moses. At the same time, however, Paul's letters reveal that he often found it necessary to disassociate himself from "the enthusiastic employment of oral words in some of his communities" (Kelber 1997, xx). Paul, then, was a transitional figure in early Christianity, a preacher and writer who variously affirmed and critiqued both orality and scribality.

While Paul wrote many of the books of the New Testament, several pieces of evidence suggest that his thought was primarily driven by oral sensibilities. Paul's media preferences are particularly evident in his "master metaphor," "the gospel." "The gospel he [Paul] writes about bears the indelible imprint, or more accurately, echoes the voiceprints of an oral authority" (Kelber 1983, 144). When spoken and proclaimed, the gospel word is an expression of divine power that effects salvation as it enters the ears and hearts of those who listen. For this reason, whenever Paul speaks of "the gospel," he is not so much concerned with the content of his proclamation as with its impact on the audience (Kelber 1983, 144–45). Paul's oral sensibilities are also the hermeneutical key to his notoriously difficult posture on the Law. Passages such as 2 Corinthians 3 and Galatians 3 do not reflect a concern that people might use the Law to achieve righteousness through works but rather reveal Paul's dissatisfaction with "the grammatological nature of the Law," the fact that the Law freezes God's revelatory word in fixed form (Kelber 1983, 158). While preaching draws its power from the oral biosphere, writing "lacks the quality of immediacy" that is an essential feature of the active proclamation of the gospel; with the Law, interpretation of God's revelation supersedes existential experience of that revelation

> "But rhetoric, not logic, is the key to Paul."
>
> —Kelber 1995a, 421

(Kelber 1983, 153, 163). Overall, Paul's posture on the gospel, the Law, and other key theological issues reveals that his "theology is . . . animated by complex orality-literacy interfaces" (Kelber 1997, xx).[12]

But while Paul was committed to oral synthesis and generally suspicious of texts, he was sometimes forced to harness the power of writing to silence prophetic voices that opposed his own message and authority. This tactic is particularly evident in 1 Corinthians. "The unusual increase in sayings attributed to the Lord in 1 Corinthians, Paul's relative freedom toward them, and the singular reference to the lack of a saying of the Lord [1 Cor. 7:25] will all be features mirroring the apostle's engagement with authorities who are themselves in the habit of invoking sayings of the Lord" (Kelber 1983, 175). Of course, Paul himself sometimes quotes or alludes to Jesus' words, including several references in this very letter. Yet he "takes a critical attitude toward a certain use of sayings"—specifically, toward any proclamation of the words of the risen Lord that would authorize pronouncements contrary to his own teaching. To gain control of the situation, Paul urges the Corinthians not to "go beyond what has been written" (1 Cor 4:6), a remarkable statement in view of his general attitude toward the Law. Ironically, "when faced with the extreme consequences of oral wisdom, Paul, preacher of the oral gospel, is here compelled to reconsider his hermeneutical priorities and to invoke the norm of Scripture" (Kelber 1983, 177).

Writing the Voice of Jesus: Prophetic Speech, Sayings Gospels

Sayings gospels such as Q and *Thomas* represent a "second order of operation" in early Jesus tradition. Kelber views the sayings and dialogue gospels as a hybrid genre that sought to manipulate both oral and literate sensibilities. Public readings of these first-person sayings would evoke the powerful presence of the risen Lord, while the fixation of Jesus' words in writing would offer new possibilities for interpretation.

Like all other ancient texts, sayings collections were published through oral recitation in community gatherings, allowing them to exploit the hermeneutics of presence that was so appealing to the early Christian prophets. In fact, the goal of these collections was "to retain the living voice of Jesus and to extend it into the communal present" (Kelber 1987b, 118). The desire to sustain this rhetorical effect explains the most notable literary feature of the sayings gospels: their failure to comment on Jesus' death. It only stands to reason that "a tradition that focuses on the continuation of Jesus' words cannot simultaneously bring to consciousness what put an end to his speaking" (Kelber 1983, 201). At the same time, while sayings gospels play on the hermeneutical dynamics of oral speech, they are "unthinkable without the technology of writing" (Kelber 1990, 79). The *Gospel of Thomas* in particular betrays a "tension between its chirographic existence and Jesus' speaking posture" (Kelber 1995b, 157). In terms of form, additive lists of sayings are not typical of oral discourse. "One does not speak in lists"; rather, "the clustering of like items is entirely the achievement of writing" (Kelber 1990, 79). Further, while *Thomas*' prologue indicates that the words of Jesus give life, they do so only through acts of interpretation that would expose their deeper meaning (Kelber 1987b, 118; 1990, 80; 1995b, 157). Overall, "what one observes in the case of the *Gos. Thom.* [and Q] is a genre at once produced by the technology of writing and yet still faithful to oral interests and sensibilities" (Kelber 1990, 78).

Narrative Gospels: The "Eclipse of Voices and Sound"[13]

The narrative gospels of the New Testament represent a "third order of operation" in early Christian tradition. Kelber's research in Christian origins is characterized by an ongoing commitment to the thesis that the canonical gospels adopt a corrective posture toward orality. Indeed, "the very genre of the written [narrative] gospel may be linked with the intent to provide a radical alternative to a preceding tradition" (Kelber 1997, xvii). "Bei der Absicht des Evangelientextes kann es sich deshalb kaum um eine originalgetreue Wiedergabe mündlicher Traditionen handeln. Vielmehr darf man bei der Umsetzung in das schriftliche Medium eine bewußte Absetzung von mündlichen Interessen, vielleicht sogar eine Korrektur mündlicher Hermeneutik vermuten" (Kelber 1988a, 37).[14] Matthew, Mark, Luke, and John all attempted to manage the power of prophetic speech by contextualizing Christ's words in stories that sharply distinguish the earthly Jesus from the living Lord. "In the oral genre, Jesus was essentially a figure of the present with a view toward the future and minimal roots in the past. It is only with writing that a true sense of pastness is possible. The one dimension least developed in orality has become constitutive for written Christology" (Kelber 1983, 209). It is fair to say, then, that the narrative gospels are distinguished from their oral predecessors primarily by their retrospective posture.

While all four canonical gospels embraced historical consciousness as the cure for prophetic presence, the Evangelists adopted different strategies for managing Jesus' powerful words. Mark suppressed the prophetic voice in three ways: first, by simply refusing to include any significant amount of sayings material in his gospel; second, by portraying those people who would typically function as authoritative guardians of oral tradition—Jesus' disciples, his family, and Christian prophets—in an extremely negative light; third, by excluding resurrection stories from his narrative, thereby leaving Jesus absent from the tomb rather than risen and present to the community.[15] Obviously, Matthew and Luke did not follow Mark's example—their narratives include detailed resurrection accounts and large blocks of sayings. This was possible, however, only because Mark had already leveled the path for them. "Once the written form of a gospel existed, Matthew and Luke could relax and even reverse some aspects of Mark's anti-oral bias" (Kelber 1983, 209). This relaxed posture allowed them to adopt a different strategy for managing Jesus' words: while Mark ignored Q, Matthew and Luke harnessed some of its potency by fixing Q sayings in written narratives that reduced the urgency of these utterances and limited their potential meaning (Kelber 1983, 203). Thus, "once the Markan outline was established, it could in the hands of Matthew and Luke serve to deactivate and then absorb the very materials [Q] whose oral hermeneutics the form of Mark's gospel had been designed to overcome" (Kelber 1983, 209–10).

The Gospel of John adopts a third narrative strategy for the *Depotenzierung* of prophetic speech. At first glance, John seems to fully embrace the dynamic potential of Jesus' words. Quite the opposite of Mark, sayings and dialogues occupy approximately three-fourths of the total text of the Fourth Gospel (Kelber 1990, 82). Further, John, like the sayings gospels, capitalizes on the metaphysics of presence. John's oral interests emerge in the version of Q 10:16 at John 13:20, in the commission formula at John 20:21, in the first-person "I Am" sayings, in Jesus' claims that his words effect life and judgment, in the obviously post-resurrectional perspective of much of Jesus' discourse, and finally in the motif of Jesus' secret self-disclosure to a select group of followers (Kelber 1990, 82–85; 1988a, 34–36). Overall, "die johanneischen Herrenworte zeichen sich viele durch eine pneumatisch-orale Wirkungskomponente aus"; indeed, "Worte werden hier [in the Fourth Gospel] primär als Wirkungskräfte eingeschätzt und weniger als Ideen- oder Informationsträger." One could therefore fairly say that the Johannine Jesus speaks "wie ein frühchristlicher Prophet" (1988a, 34–35).[16] In many respects, then, the audience of an oral recitation of the Fourth Gospel would experience the same hermeneutics of presence that was so highly valued in the Q and Thomasine communities.

John's obvious exploitation of the media dynamics of sayings collections might seem to undermine Kelber's thesis that narrative gospels work against the hermeneutics of orality. Yet John differs from, and ultimately subverts, the sayings genre at two key points. First, John situates the powerful words of Jesus in a story that ends with an unusually graphic depiction of his death. This has the effect of binding Jesus "to historicized time and space" so that "the generic identity the sayings had attained in the form of a discourse gospel was thereby overruled by the narrative form" (Kelber 1990, 85–87). "Henceforth, Jesus' words are no longer those of a disembodied figure clinging to the present," such as they would be in Q or, especially, in *Thomas*. Second, John defies the equiprimordiality of oral speech events through a *Logos* Christology that presents Jesus as the single, archetypal "Word" (see especially John 1:1-18). "Orality, we saw, traffics in a plurality of authentic *logoi*. It cannot justify itself in reference to an *arche-Logos*, let alone conceptualize the notion of *Urwort*" (Kelber 1990, 91). John's *Logos* Christology thus reduces the plurality of the discourse genres, the *logoi* of Jesus, to a single, definitive *Logos* locked in a written narrative that cannot be challenged.[17] Through this ingenious move, the risen Jesus can speak directly to the Johannine community but can only say what John wants him to say.

Overall, when one considers the broad spectrum of early Christianity, the canonical gospels clearly represent an "elementary disorientation" of oral sensibilities (Kelber 1983, 94). While Matthew, Mark, Luke, and John all absorbed, in varying degrees, the stylistic features of oral Jesus tradition, the fixing of hot memories in cold texts represented a dramatic hermeneutical shift. "Strictly speaking, therefore, the gospel [genre] arises not from orality *per se*, but out of the debris of deconstructed orality" (Kelber 1983, 94–95).

The Challenge: Escape from Paper World

Obviously, Kelber's media history of Christian origins departs from conventional perspectives at a number of points. Quite aware of this fact, Kelber unapologetically warned potential readers of *OWG* that "I have written this book out of a concern for what seemed to me a disproportionately print-oriented hermeneutic in our study of the Bible" (Kelber 1983, xv). In Kelber's view, this general misconception of the media dynamics of early Christianity is supported by faulty research tools and fatal flaws in several foundational assumptions of New Testament criticism.

The Great Deception

Reflecting upon the erudition of Kelber's arguments, one wonders why his perspective has not become the majority view. Kelber explains this phenomenon by noting "the tendency among biblical scholars to think predominantly, or even exclusively, in literary, linear, and visual terms" (Kelber 1983, 2). While the biblical texts are "chirographically produced" documents attuned to the hermeneutics of ancient orality and scribality, the modern scholar is "a child of the typographic age," mesmerized by the chimera of individual authors, fixed texts, and original meanings (Kelber 2002a, 70). Dazed by the glare of books and models of oral tradition based on textuality, biblical scholars "have grown accustomed to operating in a scholarly orbit, which, while uncannily depopulated and barren of emotive significance, is crowded with texts that seem to commune only with one another in the absence of human mediation" (Kelber 1995b, 141; 1987a, 97–98). To escape from this world of paper communication, scholars must "wean [themselves] from the notion that texts constitute the center of gravity in tradition" (Kelber 1995b, 163).

In order to break the spell of documents and documentary models, biblical scholars must seriously reevaluate two of their most cherished and well-worn methodological tools: the Two/Four Source Theory of the composition of the canonical gospels, and the use of gospel parallels to reconstruct primitive Christian tradition. The typographical logocentrism of modern biblical studies is particularly well illustrated by the Two Source Theory, which uses linear diagrams to explain Matthew and Luke as redactional compilations of other written texts. "There is no room in this model for orality, for memorial processes, for social engagement, for mental compositional activities, and for extratextual sensibilities of any kind." One must therefore conclude that the Two Source Theory "is inadequate at best and seriously misleading at most" (Kelber 2002a, 71–72; 2005, 240–41). Scholars must also discard their copies of Kurt Aland's *Synopsis of the Four Gospels*, a device that creates "a mental image of a closed system of gospel relations" and implies that each gospel is only comprehensible when taken apart and laid alongside the others. While gospel parallels have supported many interesting readings, they project a hologram of early Christian tradition that "in no way corresponds to the oral and chirographic dynamics of the ancient marketplace of communications" (Kelber 2002a, 72). Kelber's own research testifies to the fact that "once we have taken full cognizance of the compositional artistry and respective narrative autonomy of each canonical gospel, we are bound to acknowledge that gospel parallels and source diagrams are at best formalistic propositions that beg, indeed cover up, vital questions about the nature of the gospels" (Kelber 2002a, 78).[18]

Having critically examined these foundational tools, Kelber proceeds to question several of the most significant working assumptions of New Testament scholarship: that it is possible to recover the single, original version of Jesus' words; that early Christian tradition moved from Jesus' speech to the written gospels along inevitable trajectories; and that the Evangelists played a passive role in the traditioning process. Kelber's critique of these principles has largely taken the form of a running dialogue with the research of Rudolf Bultmann, Birger Gerhardsson, and John Dominic Crossan. In his interaction with these individuals, Kelber attempts to dismantle the methodological supports of form and source criticism and the methods and rationale of the quests for a historical Jesus.

Which Historical Jesus?

Kelber's media approach to Christian origins raises serious doubts about several foundational premises of historical Jesus studies. These problems may be conveniently illustrated by his ongoing dialogue with the work of John Dominic Crossan.[19] In Kelber's view, Crossan's research is notable for its erudition, precision of method, and serious attempt to engage recent theories of orality and memory. Following the form critics, Crossan attempts to identify layers of tradition both within and behind the gospel texts; within each layer, "the logic of quantification is set into motion," with an emphasis on multiple attestations (Kelber 1995b, 144–45). While such an approach is fairly typical of Jesus research, Crossan's method is unique in that he does not seek to discover the *ipsissima verba* of Jesus, but rather his *ipsissima structura*, the rhetorical formulas Jesus utilized to generate specific sayings. Once these core structures are identified in the earliest layers of tradition, Crossan proceeds to contextualize the latent meaning of each structure within Jesus' cultural milieu. It is therefore fair to say that Crossan seeks to determine the original sense of Jesus' words rather than the precise words themselves (Kelber 2005, 237).

In Kelber's view, Crossan is to be commended for his departure from the notion that Jesus' exact words can be reconstructed from written texts. As noted earlier, oral speech is equiprimordial, a fact that makes it impossible to conceive of Jesus tradition in terms of "originals" and "variants." Yet Crossan fails to perceive that equiprimordiality was not only a characteristic of the Jesus tradition, but also an essential feature of Jesus' own discourse. "When the charismatic speaker pronounced a saying at one place and subsequently chose to deliver it elsewhere, neither he nor his hearers could have understood this other rendition as a secondhand version of the first one. And when the second rendition, delivered before a different audience, was at variance with the first one, neither the speaker nor his audience would have thought of differentiating between the primary, original wording and its secondary, derivative version" (Kelber 2005, 238). This being the case, it is futile to compare written

> "Every word spoken by Jesus was equiprimordial with every other one."
> —Kelber 1990, 74

sources in hopes of reconstructing the "original" of Jesus' words, whether at the textual or the structural level. Ten instances of the parable of The Good Samaritan cannot be reduced to a single, original structural outline with a consistent core meaning; each time Jesus performed the parable, it became meaningful within the confines of its immediate oral biosphere, and the essential features of these ten individual biospheres cannot be reconstructed. Therefore, "Würde man sie [the principle of equiprimordiality] ernst nehmen, müßte sie sich in der Tat fatal auf die ewige Suche nach der *ipsissima vox* Jesu bzw. der *ipsissima structura* seiner Worte auswirken" (Kelber 1988a, 37).[20] In the end, Crossan's work does not fail to follow the canons of logic; rather, it forces us to consider whether the logic of writing is relevant to the study of Jesus. "The principle question it raises is whether Jesus, the oral performer, and the early tradition that delivered him unto writing have played by our rules" (Kelber 1995b, 145).

No Trajectories

In Kelber's view, research in Christian origins has been crippled by an essential misunderstanding of oral transmission. The depth of this problem is illustrated by the widely divergent theories of Rudolf Bultmann and Birger Gerhardsson. Bultmann's form-critical project was built on the principle of intrinsic causation, the theory that oral Jesus materials naturally tended toward expansion, conflation, and amalgamation through processes that cannot now be explained. In Bultmann's view, the development of tradition "was a process as natural as that of biological evolution: simplicity grew into complexity" (Kelber 1983, 4–5). In sharp contrast to Bultmann, Birger Gerhardsson based his model of oral transmission on the early rabbinic documents, leading him to argue that the first Christians memorized Jesus material through rote repetition and passed sayings and stories almost verbatim from generation to generation. Gerhardsson postulated that Jesus tradition was characterized "by fixity, stability, and continuity, and the primary purpose of transmission was the deliberate act of communicating information for its own sake" (Kelber 2002a, 59). Despite their significant differences, then, Bultmann and Gerhardsson were agreed that the word *tradition* refers to those processes by which Jesus' original utterances were passed from one oral audience to another until their inevitable inclusion in written gospels.

Reflecting on Bultmann's paradigm, Kelber is compelled to confess that "this model of the tradition's evolutionary ascent from simplicity to complexity, propelled by the law of intrinsic causation, suggests a thought pattern so utterly persuasive to the human imagination, so conveniently logical (not to say intellectually seductive), and so deeply comforting and diagrammatically visualizable that it may seem difficult to imagine any other mode of tradition." Yet, despite its appeal, this approach "is burdened with significant problems stemming from a lack of understanding of orality, gospel narrativity, and, last but not least, memory" (Kelber 2002a, 63–64). In the first place, as noted earlier, the notion of "the original version" of Jesus' words is itself a misconception: "the relationship between Jesus and tradition is not, therefore, imaginable in terms of stability versus change" (Kelber 2005, 238). Second, the "transmission" model of oral tradition labors against the fact that "there is no spatial directionality inherent in speech." Spoken words are not handed from one person to the next like a baton, more or less intact; rather, an "oral tradition" is a series of "discrete [equiprimordial] acts of speaking, separated by intervals of non–speaking and silence" (Kelber 2002a, 64). It is therefore incorrect to imagine that Jesus' original words were passed down from person to person, whether through carefully controlled rote memorization or with accretions and variations along the way. Rather, each and every performance, whether by Jesus himself or by later Christian preachers, was unique, original, and ultimately discontinuous with every other.

> "I emphatically deconstruct the paradigm of the tradition's evolutionary ascent."
> —Kelber 1997, xxi

Gospels as Hot Memory

Both Bultmann and Gerhardsson portrayed early Christian tradition as an anonymous and inevitable process of transmission. Consistent with this approach, both also assigned the Evangelists a passive role in the traditioning process. In Bultmann's view, the Gospel of Mark was simply the river into which all streams of oral tradition were flowing, a product of the intrinsic laws of tradition and the theological tendencies of the Hellenistic churches. Bultmann therefore portrayed Mark merely as an editor of materials that had already developed before him and without him; to admit otherwise would have threatened Bultmann's foundational premise that the Two Source Theory can serve as a model for the oral phase of gospel tradition (Kelber 1983, 5–6).[21] In Gerhardsson's view, Mark's primary sources were memorized traditions and written notes, which the Evangelist simply compiled for purposes of preservation. A solid chain of rote memory anchored Mark's gospel in the witness of the Apostles and, ultimately, in the deeds of Jesus himself (Kelber 1983, 11; 2002a, 59). Neither Bultmann nor Gerhardsson attributed any "constructive powers" to the Evangelists, preferring instead to see the written gospels essentially as the inevitable outcome of the forces of tradition (Kelber 2002a, 64; 2005, 230). In Kelber's view, the notion of intrinsic development was at least partially responsible for what Hans Frei—writing some ten years before the release of *OWG*—had called "the eclipse of biblical narrative" in nineteenth-century scholarship (Frei 1974). By focusing on inevitable laws of development and disregarding the creative input of the Evangelists, form and source critics essentially atomized the gospel texts. "[T]he essential core [of tradition] was extrapolated from what was downgraded to an inessential [narrative] frame" (Kelber 2002a, 67–70, quote 67).

Against this notion of passive Evangelists, Kelber everywhere insists that "the written gospel cannot be properly perceived as the logical outcome of oral proclivities and forces inherent in orality" (Kelber 1983, 90). First, such an approach fails to account for the compositional unity and peculiar emplotment of each individual gospel (Kelber 2005, 231).[22] Second, as noted earlier, Kelber has often argued that the narrative gospels were written "as a counterform to oral speech and not as an evolutionary progression of it" (Kelber 1983, 210). Matthew, Mark, Luke, and John were not seeking to preserve and perpetuate the voices of their oral predecessors, but rather to silence them. Finally, in his more recent work, Kelber has questioned the validity of Gerhardsson's cold memory approach to early Christian tradition. "The issue raised by Gerhardsson comes down to the question of whether early Christian memorial culture transpired as passive transmission under the aegis of cold memory, or as hot memory, propelled by active remembering and socialization" (Kelber 2002a, 61; 2005, 232). In Kelber's view, the written gospels, like the oral performances that preceded them, are "hot memory," the Evangelists' active attempts to reshape the past in view of present needs and realities.

Postscript: The Five Pillars of The Oral and the Written Gospel

Although Kelber has published numerous essays in the twenty-five years since the release of *The Oral and the Written Gospel,* many of which reveal substantial developments in his thinking, the major premises of his research are still fairly summarized by five key principles that are outlined in the final chapter of *OWG*. First, oral speech is "diffusive" and "multidirectional." "Oral traditions do not move through a gradually widening tunnel, showing, as it were, the way toward the light of textuality." Second, because there are "multiple oral links between the written gospel and primary forms of oral speech," scholars must acknowledge that the canonical gospels were "rooted in and surrounded by orality." Third, the gospels absorbed but also transformed the traditions that preceded them, and these transformations reflect points of tension between the Evangelists and their oral predecessors. Fourth, Paul's hermeneutics focus on "the oral power of words" and betray an "aversion to written objectification." Fifth and finally, the canonical texts should be viewed as "a counterform to, rather than an extension of, oral hermeneutics" (Kelber 1983, 184–85).

If these assertions seem somewhat less novel today than they did in 1983, it is only because *OWG* has initiated a project that has grown to be much larger than the vision of its own author. The programmatic essays to follow in this volume will press the current boundaries of this project and chart a course for its future. As will become clear, the authors of these articles generally take an eclectic approach, combining at least two or several of the theoretical approaches that have driven Kelber's research in an effort to understand the complex interfaces between memory, orality, and manuscripts in early Christianity. Because this is the case, the book has not been divided into distinct "parts." Instead, the articles are presented in a sequence that reflects their primary methodological emphasis. Richard Horsley's essay provides a general overview of the implications of Kelber's research for the study of early Christianity, the New Testament, and the historical Jesus. Joanna Dewey interacts closely with several of the key presuppositions of *OWG* to describe the media context of the Gospel of Mark. The essay by Holly Hearon explores the nature of "story" and "history" in the ancient Mediterranean world, and Jonathan Draper uses a model of performance memory to explain the parallels and differences between several early Christian texts. The last four articles explore issues that emerge from Kelber's most recent area of interest: the relationship between memory, performance, and manuscripts. April DeConick offers groundbreaking psychological research on the cognitive processes that undergird performance memory; Arthur Dewey and Chris Keith and Tom Thatcher apply social/collective memory models to explain the relationship between memory, tradition, and texts in the ancient world; Alan Kirk offers a new, media-sensitive approach to the problems of textual criticism, seeking to conceptualize scribal activity as a form of performance. The flow of this volume thus reflects the broad chronological movement of Kelber's own career, from an emphasis on orality and textuality to performance and collective memory and, most recently, early Christian manuscript culture. The book will close with a reflective essay by Kelber himself on the state of research at the twenty-fifth anniversary of *The Oral and the Written Gospel*.

> I am searching for a way out of what I perceive to be an impasse in historical biblical scholarship, which, notwithstanding its stunning accomplishments, is empowered by an inadequate theory of the art of communication in the ancient world.
> —*Kelber 1997, xxviii*

> The oral medium ... handles information differently from the written medium.... This axiom forms the premise of my work.
> —*Kelber 1983, xv*

2

"IT'S NOT EASY TO TAKE A FRESH APPROACH"
Reflections on *The Oral and the Written Gospel*
(An Interview with Werner Kelber)

Werner H. Kelber and Tom Thatcher

In the conceptual phase of the present volume, I (Tom Thatcher) met with Werner Kelber to discuss Kelber's current views on key issues in the media culture of early Christianity and also his reactions to various criticisms of his work. A transcript of this conversation follows. The abbreviation *OWG* throughout refers to Kelber's *The Oral and the Written Gospel* (1983).

Thatcher: Professor Kelber, let's begin with a general overview of your current thinking about the differences between oral words and written texts. I'll throw out a few questions and/or statements, and you can respond to them however you like. First, in the most general sense, how does oral speech work? And how do written words work differently from oral words? What's the essential, critical difference between the two?

In the same vein, in your earlier work you focused on the divide between orality and literacy, but more recently you've added a third element to the discussion, what you call "scribality/chirography." It seems that there are three issues here or three modes of communication that we need to account for: oral speech, chirographs, and mechanical type. What are the essential differences between these different modes of communication?

Kelber: In the oral medium of communication, the verbalization takes place face to face, person to person. Spoken words are not visible or permanent in any material sense of the word. Walter Ong stressed this point many times: words transpire at the moment of speaking, and their continued existence is retained only in the mind, the heart, and the memory.

There is therefore a sense of union, an essential union, between speaker, audience, and words transacted in each performance. But the act of performance changes when scribality is introduced: it is changed by the scribal medium. For now the writer is distant from the audience, and the audience is no longer a direct participant in the performance. The writer does not feel the pressure of the audience, who are always there with the oral performer. Also, we must stress that written words take on a new visual authority that it is impossible to conceive of in orality. Impossible. This is a basic and totally elementary statement about these two media [orality and writing].

Going further ahead now to the question of scribality, and of mechanically-produced type. It is interesting to see that print media was a contributing factor, a factor that cannot be overrated, in the religious revolution of the sixteenth century, the Reformation. Here we see very essentially different processes of duplication coming into consideration. To copy a manuscript, scribes had to write laboriously, an exceptionally grueling task—note here that "manuscript" and "chirograph" both come from the words for "hand," *manus* from the Latin and *cheir* from the Greek. The early texts were produced by hand by individuals. But mechanical type more easily produces an infinite number of copies, even more and more so as the technological processes were refined over time. The issue here is now the reproduction of *identical* copies, identical. Both the mechanism of production and the resultant identity of the copies are new with mechanical type: identical texts now existed in multiplicity for rapid dissemination across Europe and the Western world.

The typographical medium, as a result of mechanization processes, makes each letter exactly the same in every document, thus creating an objectification of speech that words did not have—and never could have had—in manuscript culture. Hence, the sense of the authority of the biblical text increases, and at the same time we see the division of the text into paragraphs and chapters. This is, of course, aesthetically pleasing, but much more significant is the sense of power that is conveyed. Now the sacrality of the text, its religious authority, is further enhanced. Of course, many of the chirographs were also aesthetically pleasing, and Gutenberg himself used manuscripts as models when he produced his typographic characters. So I am not saying that the chirographs could not have a certain appeal in their appearance. But at the same time, the mechanically produced text gives the words a sense of perfection that is divine—that seems to be divine—so that the text itself more than ever before takes on divine authority.

Now, the chirographs also had a divine authority, to some degree, an authority that came partly from the very fact that most people couldn't read them. In actuality, if a large number of people cannot read a text, this fact in and of itself can enhance the mysterious quality of the sacred book. Ultimately, mechanical type contributes to democratization, because now more people can have the text, and more people can learn to read it. And ultimately, the authority of print laid the ground for historical criticism and eventually literalism, finally in the modern sense of fundamentalism. All of this is possible because printed words are fixed and permanent.

I would also argue that media transitions, as we observe them in the shift from chirography to type, bring about a displacement of meaning, identity, and authority. With the introduction of print we see, from a historical perspective, a shift in authority from the Pope and the Vulgate to the typographic authority of vernacular Bibles. So the shift from scribally produced manuscripts to mechanical type was no small thing.

Thatcher: Professor Kelber, an ongoing criticism of your work relates to the problem of what is sometimes called "the Great Divide" between orality and literacy in early Christianity, the notion that there is a vast difference between these two forms of communication. Many of your critics have stated that you stressed this point too sharply in OWG. In subsequent essays, you have said that you don't want to overstate the differences between spoken words and the gospel texts and that you emphasized the issue in OWG mainly because it was necessary to do so in order to break the prevailing paradigm. Yet, you have often used metaphors that posture the written text as a hostile takeover of orality. Much of your writing on this topic gives a sense of a process of natural selection, where the strong devours the weak. So do you like the notion of "the Great Divide" or not?

Kelber: Yes, one major objection all along has been "the Great Divide." I would stress first that this term was imposed on my work later. I have described the media shift from orality to chirography in the synoptic tradition in very stark and radical and sometimes polemical terms. That is very true. Yet I never used this term, "the Great Divide," myself and I would also say that no one was using it in the late 1970s and early 1980s, at the time when the book [OWG] was written.

First, readers of OWG often have not considered that my basic theory is not just one of a "Great Divide," but also one of coherence between orality and writing. At the end of OWG, I stressed this unity and am very fond of the conclusion at the very end: that in Mark "the parabolist has become parable"—Jesus the teller of parables has become parable—by which I mean that the basic functions of the parable have now become structural features for the written gospel. This gives a sense of unity between Jesus as speaker of parables and Mark's parabolic presentation. I would stress that this is the *last* word of that book [*OWG*], not the second to last word. So even there, I noted that there was this unity between the oral and written processes.

But there is more to it now. I am now aware, possibly much more than when I was writing *OWG*, that there were manifold and complex interactions between orality and writing in the ancient world. Foley stresses this in *How to Read an Oral Poem,* where he emphasizes that there are multiple ways in which the oral and the written interface (see Foley 2002). I would stress that both I and my critics—I *and* my critics—have to take this reality seriously, because it does not rule out the possibility of a *conflictual* relationship between oral and written. Some would argue that any kind of conflictual relationship between the two is impossible; it is in fact very possible. So that when we acknowledge that the working relationship between orality and literacy is complex, we do not thereby rule out the possibility of a conflictual relationship between them. This complexity in fact makes the question of a conflictual relationship possible. The argument against my position is usually made that "everywhere in the ancient world, writing comes from and is embedded in orality"—that texts are both drawn from and published as, and alongside of, oral speech, which is of course the case, because people read them out loud. But there are still many possible interfaces between the two, and a conflictual relationship is certainly one of these possibilities. I think that my critics need to take this possibility quite seriously, just as I need to take other possibilities seriously.

Maybe one last thought. In part, my argument [in *OWG*] was based on my own interpretive observations of the role that the disciples, Jesus' family, and the prophets play in Mark. Of course, one can question my interpretation of this, specifically as to whether Mark's narrative presentation of these three authority figures or groups can reasonably be viewed as a sort of distancing from oral authorities. One could certainly question this, although I would be prepared to defend my interpretation. But in truth, few of my detractors have actually entered into any sustained argument about my position on the disciples, family, and prophets. It is not sufficient to simply say that it would be impossible for Mark to do this—to criticize these authority figures—without actually addressing the narrative data, as I have done. One cannot simply say that no one in Mark's time could conceivably call these figures into question. If Mark himself has done this, of course it is conceivable.

Thatcher: Why do people want to rule out conflict? Why do you think people don't want to allow any real difference between orality and literacy?

Kelber: Let me think about that. We are now talking here about other people's motives, and I can only speculate about the motives of other people. Let me think. I can only speculate that there may be two motives. First, a sincere historical understanding that orality and scribality never worked in antiquity in the way that I describe—essentially the argument made by some that I have projected two thousand years of media development back onto the ancient context. Second, a more theological objection, that feels uneasy about the negativity that I describe [in Mark] toward the oral authorities, and a certain theological concept of the function of tradition as associated with these figures. But again, I am speculating.

Thatcher: OK, let's continue on that same theme of "the Great Divide" for a second, but take it in a little bit different direction. This question pertains directly to your view of Mark, but I will state it first in terms of Eric Havelock's reading of Plato, which you cite with approval in numerous articles.

According to Havelock, Plato straddled the great divide between orality and literacy—as the first really literate philosopher, he lived at a moment when ideas and rhetoric suddenly came under a much higher level of interpretive scrutiny. Havelock argues that Plato was able to do much of what he did because of the cognitive strategies that writing supports—because he could take advantage of writing, he was able to develop more complex arguments and to apply greater scrutiny to ideas that had developed before him, in the oral period (see Havelock 1963). But for Plato to write a book that reflects a revisionist approach to oral thought, speech, and tradition, he must have been capable of some high-level revisionist thinking *before* he produced his works; otherwise, he couldn't have written them in the first place, because you have to be able to think something before you can write it down. But if Plato was able to think that way *before* he wrote his books, doesn't that mean that other people in his oral culture would also be capable of thinking this way whether or not they could read and write? What would be your response to that issue, and then we'll move on to how it would relate to Mark and John.

Kelber: Havelock's example of Plato's ambivalent attitude toward both the oral poets and to writing is an example of the continuum of orality and writing in the ancient world, one which here reveals Plato's deep consciousness of the conflictual problematics between the two. Here again, we see that both the oral–scribal interfacing and the conflictual relationship between orality and writing cannot be ruled out altogether as a matter of principle. It is clearly a possibility.

Now, in the case of Plato and Mark both, in terms of their similar media situations—which is really perhaps the only point where we can say that they are similar—I would suggest that the people who argue the interface between orality and literacy in terms of blurring between the two do have a point that something like distancing oneself from one's own oral legacy is not possible unless and until one also shares in—and is made a beneficiary of—the scribal medium and its implications for thinking. This distance from one's own orality becomes possible largely because of what writing makes possible. So I agree that a sense of the interface between orality and writing is a media precondition for the possibility of the "Great Divide." It is very plausible that Mark is familiar with, for example, the Septuagint and thus with the Law as a written law, that he is at home both in writing and in the oral medium at the particular moment in history when he wrote his book—and I have talked about that moment in a number of places. Mark has the media and cognitive ability to distance himself and to reconceptualize the tradition, and this ability comes through writing.

But now I should also stress that I don't think that Mark—and I need to define here in just a moment what I mean by "Mark"—I don't think that Mark is essentially a literary person, nor would I say that he rejects the tradition. I would not say that. I would feel more comfortable saying that he reconceptualizes and reshapes the oral tradition; he obviously does not reject it. I have written a chapter on Mark's oral legacy [in *OWG*]. Mark is thoroughly at home in orality and he is also a writer. Educated people, both in that time and in our world today, can live in both worlds at once. Most of us live in two or three media worlds at once nowadays. It is precisely this ability to communicate in both orality and writing at once that creates Mark's reflective posture, and I would say the same for Plato as well.

Thatcher: Sir, let me focus the discussion on Mark for a moment. You characterize the oral mode of Jesus tradition as episodic: individual stories and sayings were performed on multiple occasions with little sense of a larger story arc. At the same time, you characterize Mark's narrative gospel as a substantial reflection upon, and rejection of, the oral mode of performance, as evident from a number of well-known, and quite sophisticated, literary features of his story (lack of resurrection, absence of sayings, failure of the disciples, and so forth). How could it be that Mark, himself so engrossed in the sensitivities of an oral world and with a faith built on the oral mode of speaking about Jesus, could develop such a thorough critique of the oral mode *before* he wrote a book about Jesus? And since you seem to think that Mark was the first person to write a gospel, this essentially means that he was able to critique the oral mode before anyone else had written a book about Jesus, either. What is your thinking on that issue?

Kelber: On this particular point—on the issue of isolated items in the tradition over against a more developed narrative—I am now more cautious, and I would express this caveat: to make far-reaching assumptions about pre-written gospel traditions, we may now base our arguments on a better understanding—certainly a much better understanding than was evident in the first half of the twentieth century—of the narrative poetics of the gospels. Sensitivity to the narrative rationality/causality/coherence is an eminently important hallmark of modern study of the gospels, very important. I think that what I regret is that those of us who have worked in narrative criticism and narratology have been so absorbed with narrative criticism and have not reflected with greater sophistication on the implications of narrative criticism for our broader conceptions of history and the tradition. In this regard, Stephen Moore's *Literary Criticism and the Gospels* is superb, simply superb, but I don't find it mentioned all that frequently (see Moore 1989).

One of the many important implications of narrative criticism is that—as we are coming to know better all the time—it becomes more and more difficult to extrapolate from the texts of the gospels individual chapters, speeches, sayings, signs, the miracle stories, and postulate pre-gospel trends. I see this as nearly impossible in view of the fact that these individual pieces are now united in, and entirely shaped by, our written gospels on the principle of narrative causality. So the shift from redaction criticism to narrative criticism has taught us that we have put the cart before the horse in fundamental ways. We have made many assumptions about pre-gospel traditions on the basis of form criticism without having first studied the narrative nature of the gospels as we have them, which is where we encounter the traditional material about which form criticism concerns itself. I think we should consider the narratives before we begin to speak of tradition—of course, I cannot conceive of tradition without orality—but to extract something from Mark or John and say that it exists in that form because it was orally shaped, we must be much more cautious than we have been. It has been shaped in Markan and Johannine ways, regardless of what we think it may have looked like in the tradition. I am now much more cautious on this point.

I am very cautious now about making such statements, to the effect that in the tradition there were only episodic stories and sayings. What I would now like to say is that there need to be several shifts in the way we approach this. The first shift, which I just mentioned, is that we must start with the gospels as narratives and analyze their narrative elements before we think about whatever tradition may have been in existence before them. That is imperative.

The second shift, another shift that must occur in the way we approach this—I now turn to text criticism. As has so often been the case, text criticism remains the domain of experts in what is perceived to be a specialized field requiring special expertise. We should try to overcome this compartmentalization of knowledge. There is absolutely no reason, no reason at all, why narrative critics and rhetorical critics should not be interested in text criticism. The different domains into which biblical studies has been divided need to be unified so that the fields can better work together.

In any case, for the longest period of time, textual criticism has been conducted with an interest in the "original text," which can be reconstructed through proper rules and analogies and the like. That is to say, textual evidence was collected, classified, and evaluated with respect to the contribution it could make to "the original text." The concern of textual criticism was, therefore, for the most part, with reconstructing the most reliable text of the New Testament. Recently, textual criticism has taken a new turn, and this is due to the work of people like Eldon Epp and David Parker, who have taught us to understand and appreciate the plurality, the inherent multiplicity, of textual relations in and of themselves; who have taught us to look at this plurality of manuscripts not as contributors to an "original text" but rather as witnesses to the tradition (see Epp 1999; 2004; Parker 1997). Parker's *The Living Text of the Gospels* describes case-by-case situations where the textual evidence manifests multiple traditions of passages in the gospels. So when we consider this evidence, we must now imagine early Christian situations where portions of the gospels exist in plural form. It is one thing to analyze these plural forms, as we see them in the existing manuscripts, in order to perceive what we want to call "the oldest form" or "the original form," but quite another thing to acknowledge that the manuscript tradition, if it is to be taken seriously, is not interested in "the original form." To take the tradition seriously, we must take it seriously in its multiformity, especially in its earliest parts—the first, second, and third centuries—and especially in respect to the core area of the Jesus tradition, Jesus' words in particular. These manuscripts are not taking us back in some way to a single original of Jesus' words. This is a second shift that must occur in our thinking: there simply are no "single originals."

Thatcher: Professor Kelber, do you still believe that Mark was the first Christian, at least in his branch of the church, to produce a coherent narrative about Jesus' life and/or death? Did people before Mark have any sense of a larger story arc behind all these individual sayings and episodes?

Kelber: I cannot answer directly but I think that certainly I must restate the question with greater caution than I used to. What do we mean when we say "Mark," in referring to either the text or to the Evangelist himself, in view of the new assessments of the manuscript tradition? In doing narrative criticism, many of us have gotten into the habit of using "Mark" as a cipher. I think we have to be more forthright and give much deeper thought to the notion of "Who is Mark?" There is, on the one hand, the problem that one ought to be careful with the concept of the solitary genius of a writer, especially in the situation and time period that we are talking about. On the other hand, there is the textual problem of the Greek text of the gospels, which, as we have it today, is a composite, voted into existence by a committee on the basis of the so-called "best evidence." It is a construct of a kind of typographic mentality, and we have based far-reaching source-critical theories and methods on this "reconstructed" Greek text of Mark.

So who is Mark? There are, as I now see it, three problematics, and this turns out to be a very difficult question to answer: the problematic of singular authorship; the problematic of the Greek text as we have it reconstructed; the third problematic aspect to be taken into consideration is the text-critical observation that texts of Mark are clearly shown to have existed in multiform. Different copies of the same text are in existence, and they are in existence side by side all at once. With the *Secret Gospel of Mark*, it looks more like a Markan textual tradition than a single text of Mark, as though no single so-called "Markan text" ever existed in one version. Who is Mark? Or which one of these texts? The present text before us is the Nestle–Aland construction, which is an abstract constructed from the many texts of Mark. To think through the multiplicity of these texts of Mark, these *texts* and not *the text*, to think through the multiplicity of these textual traditions and the ways we have gone about constructing the single text of Mark, we need to take all these problematics into deep consideration.

Thatcher: Professor Kelber, for sake of clarification: Wasn't one of the major achievements of the Parry/Lord/Ong/Foley school of tradition, the Anglo–American school, the notion of the singularity of the author? Before this approach, wasn't the dominant notion the idea that folk traditions developed from anonymous communities rather than through the specific words of individuals? Are you saying that we should not think of "Mark" in terms of a single person and text?

Kelber: I would disagree with your understanding of Ong and Foley. As knowledgeable as they are about oral speech and tradition, they would also question the notion of individual, solitary authorship. This is the foundation of the solution to the Homeric question: the songs are based on centuries of oral recitation and rendering. It's a tricky thing, because I have also argued that there is such a thing as narrative competence and there is, not a moment, but a process, where, in a community setting, this narrative evaluation and reevaluation of the gospel tradition—this composing/writing of the gospels—takes place. It's difficult to determine the precise dynamics. It's not the tradition alone that provides impetus for the gospels but rather a narrative will. But to think of that in terms of an individual author seems to me to be a too-modern concept. We need to bring to bear on this problem not a single compositional method but a combination of oral–scribal interfaces, memory culture, memorial traditions, rituals, the whole notion of "memory." These aspects ought to be brought together and these could possibly be a breakthrough for the conventional, established concepts of "the author and text of Mark."

Thatcher: So who is Mark? Is Mark a single person, or should we be thinking of a group of writers who produced similar texts that could ultimately be combined into what we call "Mark" today?

Kelber: In the end, individuals cannot be excluded, but the scribal situation was so different from what our typographic mindset will allow or can conceive. Scribes can be merely copyists or they can be active contributors to the composition. We need to reflect carefully on the possible interactions between the dictator and the scribe. The old, romantic notion of a single author, Mark or John or someone, as portrayed in the old paintings—someone sitting at a desk surrounded by books or scrolls and copying or writing a text while some angel, or a dove representing the Holy Spirit, sits at his shoulder whispering into his ear—these are all medieval and modern concepts. We have to move far more deeply into the crucial media world of what Gerald Downing calls "word processing" (Downing 1996). I'm not the only person who has questioned the notion of a single person, like Mark, producing a single text.

Thatcher: So how do you understand the early Christian traditions that would point toward single authors for the gospels? Peter working with Mark, Luke the Physician, John the Apostle. Are we seeing here early attempts to fix the textual tradition by naming a single author?

Kelber: As you say, very early on there is a notion that the authority of the gospels is enhanced by attributing them to single authorship. But your own [Thatcher's] work on John shows that there are sophisticated memorial traditions and processes embedded in John's gospel (see Thatcher 2006). Luke's Prologue [Luke 1:1-4] envisions a fairly complicated process of traditioning, which includes both oral and written materials, and it also suggests that Luke is written not simply to reproduce material. Here we have an instance of a critical reflection on tradition, so that one must not say, as I said several times earlier, that critical reflection is not possible in the early stages of the Christian tradition. In the last analysis, I do not rule out the notion of an "author"—of course, there has to be a human being who produces the text. But the whole problem of "the author of the text," especially in the case of the gospels, needs to be addressed in terms of a communal tradition and not just of an individual genius. This notion of the individual genius seems to me to be especially rooted in the Protestant tradition.

I am dissociating myself from any modern conception of "authorship." I rule out any notion of an individual working in isolation. It's got to be collaborative.

Thatcher: This leads to my next question: When we speak of Mark "writing a gospel," what process do you envision? If we could travel back in time and watch Mark at work, what exactly would we see happening, and where is it taking place? Was he talking to an audience, or to a scribe, or to a piece of paper, or was he silent when he wrote this document? Early on, you were quite emphatic that Albert Lord, Tom Boomershine, and others were wrong to suggest that the Gospel of Mark is primary orality, composed by dictation. At this point in time, exactly how do you envision Mark's moment of composition?

Kelber: Well, I don't think I can say much more beyond what I've already said. I find it next to impossible to think of a single moment—it's this notion of an epiphanic moment of creation that I feel uncomfortable with. We still have enormous problems in extricating ourselves from what I still perceive to be an approach to Jesus and the gospels deeply embedded in nineteenth- and twentieth-century verbal art.

Thatcher: In *OWG*, you argued that Mark was trying to control—or at least reinterpret—a tradition of prophetic speech. Were there also written sayings collections before Mark wrote his gospel, and if so, to what extent did the technological shift initiated in those documents influence Mark's motives and his way of thinking about Jesus?

Kelber: First, let me go back to what people have called "the Great Divide." I feel that my theory, even as I developed it in *OWG* some time ago now, is more complex than that. I never denied—in fact I have emphasized—the use of writing in pre-Markan tradition. I said that texts *were* used; it cannot be ruled out. I have also said that it is not within the power of a text to stem the tide of oral communication and mute the oral voices. Tradition continues before, during, and after the writing of Mark's text. My understanding of the tradition as a whole is far more complex and nothing that could be reduced simply to a "Great Divide" between oral and written gospel material.

Basically, the tradition as a whole, including Mark's text, can never be reconstructed. When I think of the kind of communal situation that we see glimpses of in the Oxyrhynchus papyri, we begin to get a sense of what happened in these Christian communities. If we imagine tradition as a whole, the living words and the speaking that took place, and then we also observe the multiple textual traditions that co-existed—as unearthed at Oxyrhynchus in particular—we see a tradition that is rich and multiform and that therefore cannot be subsumed under "the Great Divide." It is also a tradition that, in situations like Oxyrhynchus, does not seem to have any concept of a canon, because in this instance what later came to be called "canonical" exists side by side with what later came to be called "noncanonical." There is no canonical boundary line here at all. People should not latch onto this "Great Divide" as if this situation were somehow symptomatic of all early traditions. With Mark in particular, I probably would not use that sort of agonistic language to describe the relationships between the various elements of the tradition anymore.

When I wrote *OWG*, it was necessary to posit a strong thesis because, at that time, scholars tended to blur oral and scribal dynamics to such an extent that there was no real sense of a need to differentiate them, to think that there might be some need to understand a difference in the operations of these two media. And of course, specific communal media situations need to be considered. Mark does not equal Oxyrhynchus, Matthew does not equal Oxyrhynchus, Luke does not equal Oxyrhynchus—each situation is different. But once we begin to narrow our focus to specific situations in which these media dynamics were operative, I still think today that the Markan narrative is so unusual, so unconventional, yes, so radical with respect to its posture toward its own Christian tradition, that I have now come to accept Jan Assmann's term *Traditionsbruch* to describe Mark's situation (Assmann 1992, 218–21). A rupture of tradition is taking place here, where tradition is being reconceptualized and absorbed into a new frame in Mark. I like the term *Traditionsbruch* much better than "Great Divide." In times of crisis—and I see Mark engaged in such a crisis, at least in his own perception and, at the very least of course, in terms of the crisis events of 70 C.E.—a reconfiguration of tradition is necessary in order for the group to survive. This is my answer to those who have accused me of creating a "Great Divide"—I would want to say that a rupture in tradition is taking place at this particular moment, and the text of Mark is one product of that rupture.

Thatcher: So is this part of the reason why you do not wish to attribute the text to Mark's personal genius?

Kelber: There is a communal experience in the background. There has to be a community, for in antiquity all instances of word processing are more complex than the actions of a single individual. I therefore consider a deeper exploration of modes of composing to be one of the most urgent tasks toward getting a better grip on early Christian tradition.

Thatcher: Professor Kelber, let me ask you to comment on the implications of your work for the Two/Four Source Theory of the composition of the canonical gospels. In some respects, your posture on this issue seems ambivalent. For example, in a recent article, you state that the Two Source model is "inadequate at best and seriously misleading at most" because it fails to account for Matthew and Luke's own creative, memorial work in appropriating traditional material. In that same article, you say that gospel parallels "in no way correspond to the oral and chirographic dynamics of the ancient marketplace of communications" (Kelber 2002a, 72). On the other hand, much of your work has focused on the place of Q in early Christian tradition, a text that can be reconstructed only through the assumptions of the Two/Four Source Theory and with the aid of gospel parallel charts, and you also assume that Matthew and Luke are dependent upon Mark. Essentially, you appear to criticize the Two Source model while relying heavily on its conclusions for your understanding of the development of oral tradition, sayings gospels, and narrative gospels. How would you respond to this?

Kelber: I have reflected on this problem. As a general observation, I would say that my approach does not do away with the Two Source Theory altogether, but it does qualify, modify, and soften the implications of that theory. For example, I find it interesting that the Two/Four Source Theory is generally formulated in strictly literary terms, an approach that predetermines the formulation of the problem and its results. Up until very recently, the relationships between the gospels were defined strictly in literary terms, a phenomenon that for me is fascinating to observe. Because we have done this, the "synoptic problem" is, for us, a literary problem; that's the crux of the matter. There are, of course, a few exceptions. At a recent conference in Jerusalem on the gospels and tradition, the oral nature of the tradition was strongly emphasized and also the need to integrate orality into the hypothesis so as to soften the hard image of a purely literary relationship between these texts. But the source theory remains seductive because it can be diagrammed so easily and because most of us have so frequently put it up on the blackboard in front of our students to instill in them an image of literary relationships. We should dismiss this image and try not to think of it anymore.

I must say the same about gospel parallels. To put the Synoptics, sometimes with John or *Thomas*, side by side in columns conveys to our minds a deep-seated image that this is indeed the reality of how the gospels are related. In reality, this whole notion is entirely an abstraction. It's beautiful, you know—it makes everything look so nice and so simple—and we all use it, but still it is deeply deceptive. In reality, the gospels never related to one another like this, text to text on one page. Communal ties, performance ties, memory, tradition—all this is blotted out in the interest of putting them together on a printed page.

In a recent SBL paper, James Dunn has developed a breathtaking theory. I'm not at all sure what to do with it. He says that in cases where Matthew and Luke are close, almost verbatim, especially at the core of a saying or story, while the margins—the intro and the conclusions—vary from one another, that these are actually the symptoms of oral tradition (Dunn 2000). So that even when Matthew and Luke are nearly verbatim, he turns our normal model on its head. Profoundly provocative. I'm not sure he's right—I don't know—but this example at least illustrates the fact that in Anglo-American scholarship the Two Source Theory has been recently challenged much more seriously than in the German tradition, which seems to me to remain deeply committed to literary models of explanation.

So far as my own work is concerned, I see it as a contributing factor toward demonstrating that some of the Two/Four Source Theory's fundamental assumptions are based on very literary understandings of the workings of tradition.

Thatcher: Matthew, Luke, and John obviously appear to be much less reserved toward sayings material than Mark was. Why is this?

Kelber: My argument was and continues to be that there is a *relationship of knowledge* between the Synoptics. I prefer to state it this way rather than to construct any linear diagrams that show linear source relationships. Within these relationships, Mark has to take the brunt—Mark is the one who has to shape the genre. Matthew and Luke don't have to invest their major energies in creating the genre. Once the genre is a given—which was itself created in response to Mark's particular problem with oral speech—once this was done, Matthew and Luke can loosen up and take a more relaxed attitude toward the sayings but now managing them in a genre and medium quite different from their original oral function. John is a different problem. It is not clear to me that we can safely assume that he knows the Synoptics. Like Matthew and Luke, he takes the sayings and uses them in a way quite alternate to Mark's fashion. One can downplay the sayings or take them into the narrative genre to control them. These seem to me to be the two major options from which Mark and John are selecting and preferring: Mark downplaying sayings, John reworking them to serve his own purposes.

Thatcher: Professor Kelber, you have insisted that the attempts to trace the development of Jesus tradition through a variety of stages is misguided. Yet your own work gives an impression of at least five successive phases in the tradition: Jesus; individual oral units; sayings collections (Q, *Thomas*); parabolic written narrative (Mark); gospels combining narratives and sayings (Matthew, Luke, John). How is your model ultimately different from others, and why would it be wrong to trace the development of a pericope through the various stages that you propose?

Kelber: First observation: I would have doubts about the reconstruction of a stratified model of tradition based on any single text, like Mark, Q, John, and so forth. To take a text and derive from it retroactively a developmental model—I have objected to that in the past and I object to it even more so now in view of newer studies on Q and the poetics of narrative gospels. It remains, in my estimation, problematic to comment on the prewritten gospel at all, much less to try to identify distinct stages in its development. Very problematic.

Second observation: I think that if one singles out—if you look at my work and focus on individual sayings and clusters, collections, and narrative gospels, —what I've said about each of these individually, one can indeed get the impression of developmental stages. But this would only be an abstraction from my whole work of certain aspects, without taking the totality.

I continue to have problems with a developmental model if we try to imagine how tradition functions in a variety of communal situations. I find it difficult to conceptualize tradition in any evolutionary sense. Next, to think of the synoptic tradition in the narrow sense as it moves toward canonical gospels in a quasi-Bultmannian sense is now no longer possible for me, if only because we know much more now about the narrative impulse and originality of our gospels. They are not the results solely of the workings of tradition; there are important implications of narrative criticism for our understandings of the gospels and their traditions. I wish narrative critics would reflect more deeply on the implications their research has for the study of gospel traditions. I do not rule out the possibility that single sayings sometimes clustered together. But in terms of the dynamism of the tradition as a whole, I find that model implausible.

Thatcher: Professor Kelber, let me close with a couple of focused questions on Jesus and Paul. From your perspective, what would a media-sensitive study of the historical Jesus look like? What methods would it use, and what results could be expected? What would be, in your view, the reasonable results of a study of the historical Jesus?

Kelber: I couldn't write a life of the historical Jesus. I could not.

Thatcher: Why not?

Kelber: I could not because of what I have called the "equiprimordiality" of his sayings. *Many* sayings, *many* words, *many* stories, primarily parabolic stories. But when we consider that the major impetus of the quest has been for the *one* authentic saying, which to me is orally inauthentic—Jesus speaks many sayings more than once and not the same way every time. Reduce it to the essence? That's not the historical Jesus. As Epp and Parker have revealed, even in the manuscript tradition the presentation of Jesus is variable. This is not because the early Christians didn't take Jesus seriously; it's because they took him *so* seriously that they had to make Jesus speak to their community situations. In this respect, they understood him better than the Questers, who want to take his words back to a core truth. Inasmuch as the oral tradition made him speak to many situations, the early Christians were perhaps more faithful to Jesus' own style and mode of thinking than the eighteenth-, nineteenth-, and twentieth-century Questers have been. Engaging people, encouraging, threatening, advising—that's how he was with the people. I think that those people in the earliest Christian communities understood him very well.

Thatcher: So would it ever be possible to really get back to the historical Jesus, or will we always just be looking at someone's construction of him?

Kelber: Since Schweitzer, that's been the issue. We've known that it's our own face we're looking at, not Jesus (see Schweitzer 1913). But I wanted to raise a different problem: the plurality and multiplicity of speech performances that, if taken seriously, cannot be reduced to one single core message. Jesus' speech situation is historically not reproducible. If he speaks—or maybe we should say, "rhetorically performs"—the parable of

The Mustard Seed six times, never the same way and always to a different audience, to duplicate the historical Jesus we would have to do justice to all six of these speech situations. That's how hard it would be to discuss Jesus from the perspective of oral sensitivities.

Thatcher: Professor Kelber, let's move in an entirely different direction for a moment. You read Paul's comments on the Law as a dissatisfaction with its media status as a written document, as opposed to the living proclamation of the oral gospel. Is it possible that Paul harbored some of these feelings about the Law before he became a Christian?

Kelber: I think that it is under any circumstances difficult to make assumptions about Paul prior to his revelatory experience. For Paul, the experience of Jesus was the single most significant contributing factor. In this respect, Schweitzer's characterization of Paul's "two craters"—his antinomianism and his emphasis on his mystical experience—was quite right (see Schweitzer 1931). Is it anachronistic or non-Jewish to think of the Law as a written authority? I'm not sure it is. It can be maintained historically that in Hellenistic Judaism the written Law was a key element in the synagogue liturgy even though most Jewish people couldn't read it. The book assumed authority as a written authority with symbolic value in Hellenistic Judaism. But with Paul, who has had a revelatory experience of the present Lord, the Law as written authority received a negative connotation. Galatians shows Paul's argument concerning the complexification of the written Law, complicated from the perspective of the contrasting immediacy of revelatory experience.

Two points. First, it is not inconceivable that Jews thought of the Law primarily as a written authority even though they regularly experienced that text as a publicly proclaimed, oral word. Second, Paul's critique of this Law makes sense when viewed in the context of his orally understood and proclaimed gospel.

Thatcher: As a sidenote, why haven't more scholars picked up on your reading of Paul and developed it, or at least discussed it, to the extent that they've discussed your thinking about the gospels?

Kelber: Because it's so unusual. Not many people have looked at Paul from a media perspective. I think also that Pauline scholarship has a diachronic depth, and the disadvantage of scholarship that has a deep history is that one moves in well-established grooves and lines of paradigms. It's not easy to take a fresh approach.

3

ORAL PERFORMANCE AND MARK
Some Implications of *The Oral and the Written Gospel*, Twenty-Five Years Later

Richard A. Horsley

Werner Kelber's *The Oral and the Written Gospel* was a significant breakthrough in biblical studies in general as well as in gospels studies in particular. The book was a major challenge to some of the most fundamental assumptions, approaches, and constructs in the field. Precisely for that reason, few biblical scholars have attempted to come to grips with the implications of Kelber's work. Many of those who are at least minimally aware of his arguments are simply in denial about how they undermine many major subdisciplines in biblical studies, such as text criticism, form criticism, literary criticism, and standard book-by-book, phrase-by-phrase exegesis.

I must confess to having been one of those in denial for over a decade after *OWG*'s publication. But once I "caught on" in the mid-1990s, there was no looking back. The implications of Kelber's work were compelling. I have come to look to Kelber as my principal mentor in the field, mainly for his innovative work on cultural memory as well as the implications of recent studies in orality and literacy for biblical studies in general and the Gospel of Mark in particular. *The Oral and the Written Gospel* has stimulated extensive exploration of orality in, and oral performance of, Mark's gospel. From conversations with Kelber, I am aware that he would like to see fuller exploration of the role of writing in the composition of Mark. I cannot undertake that challenge here, because my own, still-elementary, understanding of the relation between oral cultivation of cultural materials and writing, particularly at the popular level, is not yet up to the task. Instead, I will explore the implications of Kelber's breakthrough book for understanding the composition of the Gospel of Mark, taking into account the further explorations of Kelber's key points in subsequent research both within and outside the field of biblical studies.

Kelber's Breakthrough: Liberating Biblical Studies from Its Captivity to Print Culture

Even in the early days of his career, Werner Kelber was interested in wider humanist learning, far more so than most biblical scholars. He was aware of intellectual currents in fields to which others were oblivious. He thus engaged in biblical interpretation with a far broader interdisciplinary and historical perspective than most do. Perhaps his principal concern in *OWG*, as he stated in the introduction to the 1997 reprint, was the dominant orientation toward print culture in the field of biblical studies (Kelber 1997, xv, xxii). He saw that New Testament studies was conducting its business "largely in the Gutenberg galaxy" (Kelber 1983, 215). So pervasive were the assumptions and procedures of print culture that the form critics, despite having taken many cues from folklore studies, never explored genuinely oral communication (Kelber 1997, xv–xvi). While boldly declaring its "historical-critical" awareness of the difference between the original text and modern cultural assumptions, form criticism had developed little critical reflection on how distinctive, historically, were its own assumptions and procedures.

Kelber discerned and boldly presented the implications for New Testament studies of the pioneering investigations of Milman Parry and Albert Lord on Homeric epics, of Eric Havelock on Plato's attack on poetry, of Walter Ong's groundbreaking theorization of the distinctive media of orality and literacy, and of Ruth Finnegan's reflections on the relation between oral poetry and writing. Kelber understood that it was necessary to state a strong thesis in order "to break theoretical ground and to challenge the chirographic–typographic hegemony that rules biblical scholarship and many of the human sciences" (Kelber 1997, xxii). Accordingly, it seems at many points in *OWG* that what Kelber has in mind in the concept "textuality" is the print mentality of biblical scholarship and its typical concerns with original forms, copies, and textual accuracy (see Kelber 1983, 44, 94, 105). All these are very modern concerns that were evidently of no interest even to the ancient scribes who handled the "biblical" manuscripts.

Against the form critics and other New Testament scholars who had been conceptualizing oral tradition on the assumptions of print culture, Kelber presented ways of understanding oral communication based on recent studies in a range of cognate fields including classics, folkloristics, and anthropology. This, along with the challenge to the print orientation of biblical studies generally, may have been the most influential and significant contribution of *OWG*. Biblical scholars, however, have steadfastly resisted the challenge. And only a small (but growing) number have joined Kelber in further exploration of oral tradition, oral performance, and the relation between orality and literacy. Only a handful of colleagues, moreover, have picked up on one of the most significant aspects of oral tradition: the principle of social identification. "Survival and continuity of spoken words was thus not simply a matter of passive transmission but rather was intimately connected with their social relevancy" (Kelber 1983, 24). The orally cultivated materials in the synoptic gospel tradition that survived were those with which both speakers and hearers alike identified.

In this connection, it may be important to remind ourselves that Kelber gave a great deal of attention to the broader social, even political, context of the early Christian oral materials, particularly those incorporated into the Gospel of Mark. Bultmann and Dibelius, who originally formulated form criticism, considered the social functions of traditions together with their forms. But second- and third-generation form critics tended to forget about the social context and function in their refined reflection on forms. In the last generation or so, biblical scholars have tended to concentrate on one of the cultural or social aspects of ancient Israelite/Jewish and/or early Christian texts and/or groups. Kelber is among the significant few who consistently considered them together.

For example, in contrast to many scholars, Kelber clearly discerned the differences between the social location of Jesus and his followers and that of the priestly scribal Qumran community that produced and/or left the Dead Sea Scrolls. In his view, "conspicuous differences must alert us against projecting the literary proficiency of the Qumran scribal experts upon early synoptic processes of transmission" (Kelber 1983, 16–17). More generally, Kelber has noted explicitly how nonlinguistic features enter into communication, particularly oral discourse. The broader context in which oral communication occurs includes multiple political and economic as well as religious, cultural, and aesthetic factors. Not only does oral communication receive powerful ideological and situational support from the social context in which it is embedded, but "nonlinguistic features have priority over linguistic ones" (Kelber 1983, 75).

Kelber has often been accused of advocating the "Great Divide" between literacy and orality. Despite his presentation of a "strong thesis" to gain traction against the grip of print culture on the field, however, his treatment of Mark as a written text is subtle and nuanced. This is abundantly evident in three interrelated concerns that are central to his analysis of Mark's plotted story and the cultural circumstances of its composition.

First, as a written text, the Gospel of Mark continued to operate in a predominantly oral communication environment. Kelber states repeatedly that Mark and other written texts were meant to be read aloud and heard by an audience (Kelber 1983, 93–94, 217–18). Well into the second century C.E. and beyond, Mark's gospel was heard in a culture that valued the spoken word over the written. For example, as Kelber notes pointedly, the church "fathers" were reticent, even apologetic, about their own writing lest it compromise the (oral) gospel (Kelber 1983, 93). Kelber devoted an entire chapter of *OWG* (chapter 2) to exploration of the oral materials of various forms that comprise most of the written gospel. He observes, although without elaboration of the point, that Mark's narrative was composed "by frequent recourse to orality" (Kelber 1983, 95). Thus Mark, along with the other gospels, has a "performative quality" (Kelber 1997, xxiii).

Second, in dealing with the Markan passion narrative, in which death is closely related to writing, Kelber notes carefully the numerous allusions to and influences of the Hebrew Scriptures. These allusions and influences suggest, however, that "much of Scripture, like much literature in antiquity, was mentally accessible to an oral mode of appropriation" (Kelber 1983, 197). As he had noted earlier, texts used in the composition of other texts "were often assimilated through hearing and 'interior dictation,'" a blurring of the lines often drawn between orality and writing (Kelber 1983, 23). Although he did not have an adequate theoretical model to describe this phenomenon in *OWG,* Kelber soon became conversant with the burgeoning discussion of cultural memory in European academic circles. A text's investment in tradition may not involve a physical intertextuality but rather oral–memorial access to a shared *cultural memory.* What is more, the cultural memory does not simply involve oral–memorial knowledge of written texts. Once he had conceptualized this phenomenon, Kelber could clarify that the composition of Mark involved "plugging into a copious reservoir of memories, retrieving and reshuffling what was accessible memorially" (Kelber 1997, xxiii). In retrospect, Kelber realized that the composition of Mark was unthinkable without cultural memory, which served not primarily to preserve Jesus materials but rather to edify the community or movement and its collective identity. With the breakthrough concept of cultural memory, as with the breakthrough to recognition of the differences and relationship of orality and literacy, Kelber was the pioneer in biblical studies (see Kirk and Thatcher 2005; Horsley, Draper, and Foley 2006).

Third and finally in this connection, Kelber calls attention to the ways that written texts functioned in oral contexts prior to the rise of print culture. Written from dictation, recited orally, and heard aurally, manuscripts were embedded in the dominant oral medium of communication. Texts—of Torah as well as of the *Iliad* or *Beowulf*—were dictated to scribes and recited aloud to audiences. "Most manuscripts were, therefore, meant to be heard and processed in memory" (Kelber 1997, xxii). Kelber's point here is thoroughly documented in discussions by Walter Ong (1982), in studies of the operations of medieval texts (Clanchy 1979; O'Keefe 1990), and more recently in studies of ancient Israelite, Judean, and rabbinic texts (Jaffee 2001; Carr 2005; Horsley 2007).

Kelber developed all of these crucial insights and points in close dialogue with the most recent and well-received scholarship on the principal subjects on which his investigation focused, such as the sayings of Jesus (especially in Q), Jesus' parables, the Gospel of Mark, and Paul's letters. And, with the notable exception of the most fundamental assumptions he was challenging, he couched his investigation in the approaches and concepts of New Testament studies that were standard in the early 1980s, such as form criticism, the development of Christology, the synthetic construct of a monolithic "Judaism," and "the living/exalted Lord" (Kelber 1983, 93, 100, 215–16). It is therefore most impressive, upon rereading *OWG* twenty-five years later, to realize the remarkable extent to which many of the then-accepted scholarly generalizations and standard assumptions, approaches, and concepts are now questionable or simply passé. Meanwhile Kelber's insights and points are steadily gaining attention and being further developed by those he has inspired.

Related Research and Reflection since OWG

Research and investigation into the relations of orality and literacy and of oral performance since *OWG*, both by biblical scholars who have followed Kelber's initiatives and by scholars in other fields, has not only confirmed Kelber's discussion of the oral materials incorporated in Mark's story but has also led to an application of Kelber's insights on pre-Markan materials to the gospel itself. Such research has resulted in a far more precise understanding of society, culture, and political affairs in the Roman Empire and particularly in Judea and Galilee. While Kelber presented his challenges to the field in close conversation with the standard discourse and recent scholarship of New Testament studies, the fuller implications of his challenge can perhaps be more appropriately explored by moving into the ordinary language of history and the human sciences and of the examinations of orality and literacy in other fields less determined by the assumptions and conceptualizations of print culture. Where appropriate, particular assumptions, approaches, and concepts of New Testament studies must be scuttled or seriously qualified.

Research during the twenty-five years since the publication of *OWG* has confirmed and deepened our understanding of just how limited were the spread and the functions of literacies/kinds of writings in antiquity. Kelber simply stated, but did not discuss at length, how limited literacy was in the oral communication environment of Jesus and his followers in Galilee and Judea and in the early Christian communities in the Roman Empire. Book-length studies of kinds of reading and writing in the Roman Empire generally—and books and articles about the extent and functions of literacy in particular areas and sectors of the ancient world—have concluded generally that writing was limited basically to the social and cultural elite (Harris 1989; Beard 1991). One sobering bit of older research had pointed out that the "village scribes" in Roman Egypt, who had been posited as a model on which to imagine lower-level Christian scribes who could have "written" (composed) the "Sayings Collection" Q (see Arnal 2001; Kloppenborg 1992), were not even functionally literate. Inscriptions show, for example, that the village clerk of Ptolemais Hormou, Petaus, could sign his name only by copying a model (Youtie 1971). Not only did literacy correspond to social position, but the wealthy and powerful used writing to exert their power. With most transactions conducted in face-to-face interaction, urban artisans and rural peasants alike had little use for writing.

More recent and extensive studies have uncovered a similar situation in Palestine, where literacy was even more obviously limited to the political and cultural elite (Hezser 2001). These studies have demonstrated that older generalizations about the ubiquity of schools and reading among Jews were based on a wishful misreading of key documents that refer to recitation of texts from memory. At the time of Jesus, reading and writing were confined basically to the Herodian administrators in Jerusalem and the Galilean cities (Greek) and to the retainers of the Jerusalem temple-state, the scribes and Pharisees (Hebrew and Aramaic). A key aspect of the limits of literacy was the limited accessibility of scrolls, which were both extremely expensive and extremely cumbersome. Scrolls of scriptural texts were laid up in the temple as part of their aura of authority. Scribal groups also possessed scrolls of authoritative texts but apparently did not consult them physically on a regular (daily or weekly) basis. Josephus mentions the burning of a scroll of Torah by Roman soldiers in a Judean village (*War* 2.228–31) and someone holding up a scroll of the Laws of Moses in an assembly in Tarichaeae (*Life* 134). But the presence of scrolls in such villages and towns must have been rare. The ordinary people generally could not have read them even if they were available.

Along with these observations on the limited literacy of the general population, the way that written texts were appropriated in the ancient world is illuminating of the predominantly oral communication environment of Jesus and the early Christians. Almost all of what moderns think of as "literature" in ancient Greece, Rome, and Judea involved oral communication: manuscripts were recited or performed, not read silently. We are generally aware that Greek and Latin poetry was chanted or sung and that plays were performed in city theaters in elaborately staged productions. If we think about the dialogue form of ancient philosophy, we can imagine the dialogical oral debate involved. But history and other "literary" forms were also recited orally to groups by their composers. Some of these recitations may have involved a kind of reading. But given the extreme difficulty of physically deciphering ancient manuscript writing, with no breaks between words and paragraphs, "reading" from a manuscript would have required considerable previous familiarity with the text. Written copies of most texts existed, but the existence of written copies did not disrupt the continuity of oral performance. "Literature" was thus experienced orally/aurally in public performances or, for the elite, private banquets. Kelber's observation in *OWG* that ancient manuscripts functioned in a predominantly oral communication environment pointed to a major aspect of the relationship between written texts and their oral/aural appropriation, and his thesis has been confirmed and elaborated with every new study of particular texts in their historical contexts.

Especially pertinent to understandings of the origins of the Gospel of Mark, the synoptic gospel materials from which it was composed, and the process by which it was composed, are the Hebrew Scriptures of the ancient Judean temple-state. Traditional understandings of the social role of these texts offer a prime example of how the field of biblical studies has been captive to modern print culture. But the Scriptures also, as Kelber has suggested, offer a prime example of how such texts can be fruitfully reconceived as components of cultural memory. Those with "eyes to see" and "ears to hear" now stand close to a confluence of heretofore separate strands of research that may soon join together into a new stream of critical awareness of how ancient cultural repertoires functioned. Since some of these strands of research are still in the elementary stages of development, the following sketch may be somewhat tentative at points. Yet the direction of confluence seems clear enough.

Projecting modern assumptions about widespread literacy and the availability of books into antiquity, biblical scholars have imagined the Jews as "a people of the Book," with the spin-off Christian movement quick to develop a collection of its own sacred books. Even after scholars had become aware of the limited literacy in the Roman imperial context of early "Judaism" (and early "Christianity"), they still cited passages from the Flavian Judean apologist Josephus and later rabbinic documents as proof that schools were ubiquitous in Jewish communities and that children were taught to read—especially to read the sacred texts of Torah, which were presumed readily available and readily legible. In fact, these passages indicate rather that those ancient Jewish communities were largely nonliterate and that communication was largely oral. The writings mentioned in these passages, moreover—or perhaps rather, the oral recitation of the texts—were almost magical in their effect: by *hearing* the sacred laws spoken aloud, the laws become "engraved on their [the Jews'] souls . . . and guarded in their memory" (see Josephus, *Antiquities* 4.210; 16.43; *Against Apion* 2.175, 178, 204; cf. Philo, *Embassy to Gaius* 115, 210). Rabbinic fragments once taken to attest people *reading* refer instead to people *reciting* certain well-known psalms and prayers from memory. And rabbinic passages once cited to prove general literacy and the prevalence of schools refer only to the tiny circles of the rabbis and their students (contra Goodman 1983; but see now Goodman 1994). Recent research paints a very different picture of scriptural texts and how they were cultivated by the tiny literate elite of professional intellectuals, the scribes.

Further, the Scriptures of the Judean temple-state were not set or stabilized, meaning that modern scholarly discussion and interpretation of "the Hebrew Bible," "the Torah," or "the Old Testament" is largely anachronistic. Extensive, painstaking, detailed analysis of the manuscripts of the books of the Pentateuch and the books of the Prophets found among the Dead Sea Scrolls has found that 1) there were multiple versions or textual traditions of these texts, and 2) all of these versions/textual traditions were still developing (see Ulrich 1998; 1999). Many of these texts were still undergoing continuing "composition," somewhat as scholars had previously imagined the continuing composition of the book of Isaiah centuries earlier. Part of the explanation for the continuing development and variant versions of these already scriptural texts becomes evident when text critics compare notes with scholars who have been studying the relationship between written texts and the continuing memorization and oral recitation of those texts in scribal circles. On the basis of his illuminating probe of the oral traditions of Jesus' sayings, Kelber challenged the very concept of "original" wording and even of the original structure. It remains for scholars to come to grips with the virtual certainty that the "original text" of a biblical book is a chimera of the modern print-cultural imagination.

As a sidenote, it should be noted that books of Torah very different from the Pentateuchal books of Torah were also found at Qumran. In general, these have been labeled according to the print-cultural concept "rewritten Bible." But in fact, there was no stable "biblical" text to be "rewritten." These were, rather, alternative texts of Torah composed by scribes immersed in Torah idiom and Torah tradition (see Horsley 2007, chapter 6). And texts like these point to the rich reservoir of traditional materials that were available in the Judean cultural memory, which was hardly confined to cumbersome written scrolls.

Several Jewish scholars have pointed out, for example, that texts of Torah were not *read* (a modern mistranslation) but rather *proclaimed* or *recited*. This reality can be seen repeatedly in passages of Deuteronomy and the prophets, as Daniel Boyarin (1993) has shown. For example,

> When all of Israel come to appear before the Lord . . . , *qr'* [recite/proclaim] this torah in the presence of all Israel, in their ears . . . in order that they hear . . . that they learn . . . and perform all of the words of this torah" (Deut 31:11).

The rabbis clearly distinguished between "what is written" (*kethuv*) and "what is recited" (*qere', miqra*). The rabbis viewed the *sefer Torah* as "a holy object, a thing to be venerated . . . with its holy and allegedly unchanged and changeless writing" (see Green 1989, 14–15). The tradition of *qere'* ("what is read"), including the essential vowels, accents, stresses, and pauses, along with euphemisms and the customary melody in which the text was chanted, which were not properties of the script, was different from *ketiv* ("what is written;" *b Berakhot* 62a; *Megillah* 32a). Clearly there was a long tradition of oral recitation that proceeded independently of what lay written on scrolls, and when the rabbis did consult written scrolls, they articulated this difference. But the difference did not appear, to them, to require an explanation, much less an adjustment in the text recited or the manuscript tradition(s).

More extensive recent studies have further clarified how even the literate cultural elite, the scribal circles, cultivated (that is, learned, used, and adapted) texts. As usual in biblical studies, specialists on the Dead Sea Scrolls have typically constructed the scribes and priests of the Qumran community in their own print-cultural image. These scribes are understood to have been engaged in "studying" and "interpreting" the Torah and other texts like modern academics. And, indeed, they did produce written documents of the "interpretation" of Habakkuk and other prophetic texts. But passages that might indicate study and interpretation of the Torah are difficult to find in the scrolls (Horsley 2007). A key passage used to attest such study is in the Community Rule's instructions for the nightly gatherings of ten or more members.

> The congregation shall watch in community for a third of every night of the year, *to read the Book and to study the Law* and to bless together. (1QS 6.6–8, Vermès 1997 translation, emphasis added)

Rabbinics scholar Martin Jaffee has cut through the anachronistic assumptions of this standard translation to discern what was more likely happening in those nightly meetings. A more appropriate (in this case literal) translation would be:

> The congregation shall watch in community for a third of every night of the year, *to recite the book and to search the ruling* and to bless together. (1QS 6.6–8, my translation)

At their nightly meetings, the community members were not "reading" or "studying" the book (*sefer*) but reciting it ritually, parallel to their other oral activities of searching their own community rulings and offering communal blessings. Jaffee's discernment of the ritual recitation of texts of Torah at Qumran is part of a larger study in which he explains that in the circles of the rabbis and their scribal predecessors, the texts of Torah books and other texts were as much or more "inscribed" on their memories as on the scrolls that they may have possessed. In ritual recitations they worked from memory (Jaffee 2001).

The Qumran Community Rule offers other significant indications of the relation between written texts and oral recitations and of what may be called "cultural patterns" operative in Judean cultural memory. The Community Rule itself contains instructions on how the community was to conduct covenant-renewal ceremonies in which new members were inducted into the covenant community. While the first section of the scroll contains a written text of instructions for the performance of a ceremony, it is evident that the community members conducting the ceremony were not physically reading an unwieldy scroll as they pronounced blessings and curses and recited the long historical prologue to the covenant stipulations. Further, it should be noted that the fragmentary copies of the Community Rule found in cave 4 near Qumran contain wording very different from 1QS, another illustration of the difference between "what was written" and "what was recited." A later section of the Community Rule contains the kinds of *mishpatim* that might have been "searched" in the ritual of the nightly meetings mentioned in 1QS 6.6–8.

Both the different sections of the Community Rule and the clearly evident structure of the instructions for the covenant-renewal ceremony show that the traditional pattern of the Mosaic covenant, familiar from Exodus 20 and Joshua 24, was very much alive in late Second Temple times (see Baltzer 1971). But the traditional pattern of the Mosaic covenant was not just written down in the copies of the Community Rule; it was also actively operative in the renewal ceremonies of a community of dissident priests and scribes. The Hymn scroll from Qumran also indicates that new hymns were being composed in Hebrew, patterned after traditional hymns known from the canonical book of Psalms. Again, while 1QHodayot gives us a written collection of these new psalms, these and other psalms were surely being performed from memory in community life at Qumran and perhaps elsewhere as well. The Judean/Israelite cultural memory included many such cultural patterns that, besides being stored on certain written texts, were alive and well and functioning creatively in scribal circles and community life in late Second Temple times.

Other recent studies have fleshed out a fuller picture of scribal practice in ancient Judea against the background of traditional scribal culture in the Ancient Near East more generally. These studies confirm the picture I have sketched so far from bits and pieces of evidence at Qumran and from rabbinic practices. These professional intellectuals—the literate elite who served as administrators and advisers in temple-states and the royal and imperial regimes—were also the professional cultivators of the official cultural repertoire.[1] They learned writing and reading as part of their elementary education and were available to write down letters for delivery in oral presentation to the recipient, to make additional copies of written texts, and to read written texts as necessary. Their more comprehensive learning of the wider repertoire of legal, historical, mythic, mantic, and other texts, however, was by recitation and memorization. With most of the texts of the cultural repertoire "written on the tablets of their hearts" (memory), they could recite them on the appropriate occasions and teach the next generation of scribes (usually their sons). Written copies of texts may well have been available, although in some cases the written texts were laid up in temples or palaces or in storage somewhere (although not like modern archives where documents are readily available for consultation). The fact that these texts existed in written form in such institutions gave them a certain aura and authority. But most scribal learning and knowledge was oral–memorial: texts were stored in memory, were recited orally, and were not usually read physically from manuscripts.

Recent studies also indicate that much of the material in the written and orally recited texts that comprised most of the ancient cultural repertoire had certain discernible forms or patterns. A well-known example would be the book of Deuteronomy, which not only contains material recognizable as covenantal teaching in the tradition of the covenant principles in Exodus 20 and the covenantal laws in Exodus 21–23 but also takes the overall form of the Mosaic covenant. The influence of instructional wisdom, as known from books such as Wisdom of Jesus ben Sirach, may also be discerned. In the book of Sirach itself, contrary to standard generalizations, wisdom does not take the form of individual proverbs, maxims, and admonitions. A better acquaintance with broader scribal practices in Judah/Judea and the Ancient Near East highlights the difference between mere lists or collections of proverbs (such as Proverbs 10–22) and the form taken by instructional wisdom in Sirach and Proverbs 1–9. In addition to the several toward the end and scattered through the book, Sirach consists of many short speeches on different topics, sometimes with three or more speeches on a given topic. These speeches, moreover, were clearly delivered orally, the book of Sirach being a written collection of many of the speeches of the scribe/sage Yeshua ben Sira. In the "late" prophetic books such as Zechariah and in written collections of material such as the book of Daniel and some of the books included in *1 Enoch,* many shorter or longer prophetic visions with interpretation may be found. Also in prophetic books that consist of oracle fragments, one can occasionally discern patterns of (God's) indictments for violation of covenant principles followed by declarations of punishment or a series of woes on those who have done injustices with declaration of punishment. Again, these prophetic materials are oral declarations now written down in our prophetic books. It is important to note that the unit of communication in these books is not an individual statement or saying but an instructional speech of many lines in an argumentative sequence or a more complex prophetic rhetorical form.

From these studies of scribal practice, one may gather some indication of how more-complex texts may have been composed on the basis of the cultural repertoire that scribes had inscribed on their memory from recitation. Scholars of Akkadian and Sumerian texts have discerned that some of these documents are the result of scribes having combined distinguishable earlier texts in alternating blocks of material. This would appear to be the case of the text of Isaiah, where chapters 40–55 are evidently a coherent block, chapters 56–66 have a kind of integrity in themselves, and chapters

26–29 appear to be an inserted block. The comparative material is similarly suggestive for the books of Genesis, where blocks of legends about Abraham, Isaac, Jacob, and Joseph are placed end to end with a red thread of narrative theme; Exodus, where blocks of covenantal legal material are added to historical narrative; and Leviticus, with its different blocks of legal materials. In many cases, there is little reason to believe that the materials combined in these various books existed in writing before their combination in the present texts.[2]

As Kelber recognized, one cannot extrapolate directly from the Qumran community or any other scribal circle or text to the Jesus movements and the synoptic gospel tradition. Jesus and his followers originated and were active in the villages of Galilee, and synoptic gospel material and the earliest discernible texts, Mark and Q, all remained at the popular level. There were no scrolls and no reading and writing in village communities. But nonliteracy does not mean ignorance of cultural tradition. As is known from many crosscultural studies of agrarian societies and from several clues in Josephus and other sources for late Second Temple Judea and Galilee, popular Israelite cultural tradition was alive and well in village communities. Once it is recognized that the cultivation of cultural tradition was largely oral, even in the elite cultural circles of the scribes, it should be easier to understand that peasants could also carry on a rich cultural tradition orally. As anthropologists and historians have explained, in societies where the rulers are of the same ethnic and cultural background as the peasants, the elite tradition and the popular tradition tend to be parallel, variations of one another, each articulating the interest of the people who cultivate it (Scott 1977). In Israelite cultural traditions, for example, the rules about tithes and offerings would have been of considerable concern to the priestly and scribal elite supported by such revenues. Prophetic stories and oracles, on the other hand, articulated the interests of the peasants, although the rulers might attempt to co-opt memories of the prophets by honoring them with monuments, and the scribes might borrow their prestige by adding material favorable to the restoration of temple and priesthood to the prophetic books.

Israelite tradition/culture at the popular level would have included far greater variation than the elite tradition cultivated by small circles of scribes concentrated around the temple. The only contact that villagers would have had with authoritative/scriptural texts would have been by hearing them recited in the temple or recited to them by representatives of the temple, the scribes and Pharisees. Galilean villagers, moreover, were not even subject to the Jerusalem temple-state until about a century before

Jesus' birth, and, further, were not under the Jerusalem high-priesthood's jurisdiction (but rather that of Herod Antipas) during most of the lifetime of Jesus and his followers. Thus, Galileans would have had correspondingly less contact, and less in common, with the elite Judean tradition of Jerusalem (Horsley 1995). It seems unlikely that they would have had much contact at all with any of the still-developing versions of scriptural books. But since Galilean villagers, like Judean villagers, were presumably of Israelite heritage, they cultivated local Galilean variations of Israelite popular tradition. Galilean Israelite tradition, moreover, had many of the same forms as Judean popular and scribal versions of Israelite culture. Galileans were energetic in defending Mosaic covenantal principles, interestingly against elite Judeans compromised by their assimilation to the dominant Hellenistic–Roman culture. Two distinctive patterns may be discerned in Galilean as well as Judean popular traditions: the first in the emergence of popular prophetic movements patterned after the stories of Moses and Joshua; and second in the appearance of popular messianic movements patterned after the anointing of the young David to lead the people against the invading Philistines (Horsley 1984; 1985). It is in the context of this evolving Israelite popular tradition/culture in Galilee that Jesus traditions and their cultivation and development, including both Q and pre-Markan materials, must be understood.

In view of the above considerations, it should be immediately evident that two key aspects of the previous construction of Jesus tradition and its development must be rejected and a more appropriate understanding put in their place. First, the authenticity of Jesus' teaching is typically measured on the basis of how it differs from Israelite cultural materials. A variation of this principle is to find Jesus' teachings to be "countercultural" or "unconventional." All such concepts fail to recognize the differences between the elite tradition, in which most of our textual sources stand, and the popular tradition, for which of course there are virtually no written sources—outside of the gospel materials themselves. As Kelber has stressed, the cultural memory of Jesus' actions and prophetic teaching was rooted in Israelite cultural memory. But the latter was cultivated at the popular level and region by region, alongside the elite scribal level in Jerusalem. Since there are precious few sources for Galilean Israelite popular tradition, one can extrapolate from the elite texts that comprise the majority of our sources only with critically aware historical imagination.

The second key aspect of Jesus scholarship that must be rejected—in fact a fundamental building block of form criticism and subsequent approaches to Jesus materials and their development—is the assumption that "in the beginning" were separate sayings and aphorisms of Jesus. This assumption is questionable simply on the face of things, since no one, including the great revealer Jesus, can communicate in "one-liners" or isolated sayings. But once we recognize how Israelite cultural traditions worked and the shapes and patterns they assumed, as discernible in written textual sources, we can be bolder in recognizing similar forms and patterns in the synoptic gospel materials as well. Thus, just as the instructional wisdom of Ben Sira takes the form of short speeches and the woes in prophetic texts come in a series, so also in Q the prophetic teaching of Jesus takes the form of short speeches and his woes against the Pharisees come in a series of seven. Individual sayings are not the basic units but rather components of the basic units of oral communication, which are speeches on matters of concern to the Q community. Similarly, in the Markan materials, individual sayings are not the basic units but rather controversy/pronouncement stories, of which the individual sayings are key components.

It is possible to go even further. The cultural memory of Jesus' teachings and actions, like those teachings and actions themselves, was rooted and embedded in Israelite popular tradition. Cultural memories do not consist of mere fragments, discrete dates, and names and proverbs, but rather of patterns that inform group identity. As mentioned above, two examples of such cultural patterns in popular Israelite tradition are the Mosaic covenant and memories of prophets such as Moses and Joshua and messiahs such as David. These particular cultural patterns are readily discernible in both the Q speeches and in Markan materials as well as in the revolt against Rome in Galilee in 66–67 C.E. and in contemporary popular movements. The first and longest speech of Jesus in Q (6:20–49) focuses on covenant renewal, and the series of dialogues in Mark 10:2-45 comprise a similar covenant renewal with explicit recitation of covenant principles in two of the dialogues (Horsley and Draper 1999; Horsley 2001). In seeking to identify the cultural patterns by which otherwise seemingly isolated fragments of cultural memory are given coherence, it would be anachronistic to impose modern synthetic scholarly constructs such as "apocalypticism" or theological concepts such as "Christology," which are not attested as operative patterns in contemporary Judean texts (Horsley 2007; see also Horsley and Hanson 1985; Horsley 2000; cf. Collins 1995).

Another significant area of research that has developed since the publication of *OWG* relates to the historical context in which the synoptic gospel tradition developed. Despite the limited sources available, it is remarkable how much more precise our understanding of life in Judea and Galilee has become in the past twenty-five years. This research, moreover, has taken into account the various dimensions of context that Kelber emphasized, including the political and economic as well as the cultural. It is no longer appropriate to use vague synthetic concepts such as "Judaism" and "the Jews," since it is now possible to be more precise about groups and movements, their social and regional location, and their distinctive characteristics. And scholars today are much more aware of the dynamics of the political–economic and cultural conflicts that persisted between the Roman, Herodian, and high-priestly rulers, on the one hand, and the Judean and Galilean peasantry on the other.

To mention just a few examples directly relevant to issues discussed in *OWG*, it is now clear that it is an oversimplification and anachronism to imagine "Jewish" and "Gentile" sides of the Sea of Galilee, such that Jesus' voyages back and forth symbolically mediate between "Jews" and "Gentiles." Jesus' "sea crossings" in Mark, heard in the cultural context of Israelite tradition, would much more likely have resonated with memories of Moses and the Exodus—especially when linked with wilderness feedings (Mark 4:35-41; 6:47-52; cf. 6:30-44; 8:1-9). As a further example, in view of the newer awareness that the Pharisees served as scribal–legal "retainers" representing the Jerusalem temple-state, the controversy/pronouncement stories can be seen implicitly to have serious political implications (Saldarini 1988; Horsley 2001). Being aware now also that there is no evidence outside the gospels that the Pharisees, based in Jerusalem, were active in Galilee during the lifetime of Jesus, the controversy stories appear to be expressions of a more general class and regional conflict between official Jerusalem cultural tradition and Galilean popular tradition. As yet a final example, since the social location and limited use of writing and the regional and political–economic structure and dynamics in Judea and Galilee are now more precisely understood, it is possible to discuss orality and literacy and writing fairly specifically. Scribal oral recitation may well assume acquaintance with manuscripts. Galilean peasant oral cultivation would only be aware of the existence, in the temple or some other distant place, of a sacred writing ("scripture") but would not have any first-hand acquaintance with the written texts.

The allusions and references to Israelite tradition in Mark and/or in pre-Markan material may provide an illuminating illustration of a number of points just discussed, such as the difference between the elite and the popular Israelite tradition and the oral cultivation of Israelite tradition at the popular level. Standard studies of Mark's gospel, embedded as they are in the logic of print culture, talk about Mark's citations of the Bible or the "Old Testament." The Gospel of Mark, however, gives no indication that written texts were involved in its references to Israelite traditions. Some of these references are simply to cultural memories that stand behind and inform Jesus' actions or speech. Jesus' entry into Jerusalem is, as it were, an allusion to the image articulated by the prophet Zechariah of a popular king coming not on a war chariot ("triumphant and victorious") but on an ass, the peasant mode of transportation (Mark 11:2-8; cf. Zech 9:9). In one controversy story, Jesus refers to David and his men eating bread taken from an altar, but the references are not consistent with the written text that has come down to us in 1 Samuel, with the names of priests, for example, being different (Mark 2:23-28; cp. Mark 2:25-26 and 1 Sam 21:1-6; 2 Sam 15:35). The controversy story in Mark must be rooted in popular cultural memory. Similarly, the Markan "passion narrative" has numerous allusions to well-known psalms, especially the one now known as "Psalm 22." But especially in the case of commonly sung psalms and commonly recited prayers, it would be pedestrian to think that these were quotations from written texts. Other references to Israelite tradition are to what characters in the story said and not to written texts (Mark 10:4; 11:9-10; 12:36). Yet other references, such as "honor your father and mother," are the most fundamental and memorable Israelite principles that would have been well known to most Galileans and Judeans (see Mark 7:9-10; 10:19). Even in cases that are presented explicitly as citations of Scripture, the words clearly come from memory and not written texts. Mark 1:2-3, for example, ostensibly cites the prophet Isaiah but begins with a recitation of lines that resemble Exodus 23:20 and Malachi 3:1. This appears to be a composite recitation from popular Israelite memory of prophetic tradition, not a combination resulting from consultation of scrolls.

The lines in Mark introduced by the terms "it is written (in the prophet)" or "Scripture" (γέγραπται and γραφή, respectively) have usually been read as quotations of written texts. But the meanings of these terms may appear quite different in light of the different kinds (and functions) of writing in antiquity as clarified by recent investigation into orality and literacy. In ancient Athens, laws or decrees passed by the assembly were inscribed on public monuments even though Athenians in general mistrusted writing and the courts relied on professional "remembrancers" to know what the laws were. The act of writing the laws on public monuments functioned to enhance the authority of the laws. Something similar was operative in the Judean temple-state when "the laws of the Judeans" or "the Laws of Moses" were inscribed on scrolls (books of the Pentateuch) and laid up in the temple. An early illustration of this can be seen in the account in Nehemiah 9, where Ezra, with great flourish, displays "the document of the covenant/

Laws of Moses" before the people, who worship the numinous scroll, and then recites from the scroll before the assembly. The scrolls of Scripture stored in the temple were symbols of great authority, authority that authorized the temple as the political/economic/religious center of society. If one takes into consideration not only the limited literacy of the general population and the availability of scrolls only to elite circles of priest and scribes but also the functional value of sacred scrolls laid up in the sacred precincts of the temple as symbols of authority, it must be considered whether the formula "it is written" or "the writing" means that Mark was quoting from written texts. And since the words supposedly "quoted" do not accord with what have been judged to be the best early manuscripts of the texts supposedly quoted—texts that often existed in variant versions, anyhow—it seems highly likely that Mark was quoting from memory while also claiming that what he was quoting stood written on a sacred scroll, that is, had authority. The same may be true of other early "Christian" texts and of many contemporary Judean texts.

In the case of Mark's gospel, a close examination of the ostensible "quotations of Scripture" leads us to a previously unrecognized aspect of Jesus' apparent citations of Scripture. In many of the passages where Jesus refers explicitly to "what is written," he is engaged in polemic response to or attack on the official guardians and interpreters of the sacred writings. For example, when he cites "Isaiah" against the scribes and Pharisees (Mark 7:6) and then cites "Jeremiah" and a festival psalm against the rulers of the temple (11:17; 12:10), he is appealing, against the literate elite, to the very authority that they claim as the basis for their power and authority. The same general tactic is evident at several other points in Mark's narrative. In response to the Pharisees' leading question about divorce, Jesus throws back in their face a citation of Moses (Mark 10:3-5). In response to the Sadducees, Jesus appeals to the written text of Moses to refute the high-priestly party that stubbornly accepted only the written "book" of Moses and not other, oral, traditions of Mosaic torah as authoritative (Mark 12:18-27). Only in explaining the events surrounding Jesus' confrontation with the rulers in Jerusalem that may have been difficult to understand—betrayal, arrest, crucifixion, desertion by the disciples—does Mark appeal directly to the general authority of the Scripture (14:21, 27, 49). This is similar to the way that the "creed" that Paul cites in 1 Corinthians 15:3-5 appeals to the general authority of "Scripture" to explain and authorize the death and resurrection of Jesus.

Mark's references to "it is written" and "written" are thus appeals to the authority of Scripture, and when Mark cites lines ostensibly from a particular text, the citation is from memory, evidently at a more popular level. In contrast to the standard view in gospels research, Mark's study was not lined with books. But Mark had access to the popular Israelite cultural memory of what prophets had pronounced, of Mosaic covenantal principles, and of psalms. The Galilean popular tradition may even have known what "texts" the Pharisees would cite as authorization for their interpretation and rulings (for example, Deut 24:1-4 in Mark 10:2-9), just as some of the "traditions of the elders" were known (for example, *korban* in Mark 7:1-13). Not only was Mark citing Scripture from memory, but the citations reveal the ambiguous popular attitude toward "what was written" and the conflict between the popular tradition and its spokespeople and the elite tradition (including Scripture) and its representatives.

Applying Kelber's Insights about Oral Components in Mark to Mark as a Whole

Combining Kelber's breakthrough insights about the oral cultivation of Jesus materials and cultural memory with the implications of recent research on the historical context of Mark and broader units of communication and cultural patterns, there appears to have been much less of a gaping gulf between Jesus' stories and speeches and the later Christian performance of the whole gospel story. The obvious place to start this inquiry, again celebrating the breakthrough made in *OWG*, is by exploring how some of Kelber's observations about the individual oral components of the Gospel of Mark may apply also to Mark as a whole. These observations fall easily into three categories: the stylistic features of oral narrative; the close fit between the theme and plot of Mark's gospel and the historical context that it addressed; and the parabolic plot of Mark's narrative, which incorporates many paradigms of oral performance.

Stylistic Features of Oral Narrative

In *OWG*, Kelber devotes a section of the chapter on "Mark's Oral Legacy" to several key features of oral narration in Mark's gospel (Kelber 1983, 64–70). The many episodes of the gospel are linked together by stereotypical connective devices.[3] Besides the abundant use of paratactic καὶ, not only within episodes but as a connector between episodes (see Mark 9:2; 11:20; 15:42), links such as pleonastic ἄρχεσθαι with infinitive verbs (see 1:45; 2:23; 6:7; 8:31), the adverb (καὶ) εὐθύς (see 1:29; 3:6; 6:54), the iterative (καὶ) πάλιν (see 2:1; 4:1; 7:31; 10:1, 10), and the formulaic καὶ γίνεται/ ἐγένετο (see 1:9; 2:15, 23) are abundant. Some of these connectives may have come from the oral stories that Mark incorporated into the overall narrative, and the overall narrative may have stimulated some of these typical oral connectives. The effect is an exciting, action-packed narrative of "one thing after another."

Among the other features that contribute to Mark's oral feel, Kelber pointed to the folkloristic triads that have deeply penetrated the narrative (Kelber 1983, 66). He had already noted earlier that the healing stories always unfold in three steps and that parables, such as that of The Tenants, feature three messengers. That Peter denies Jesus three times (Mark 14:66-72), and even that Jesus asks the disciples to watch with him three times in the garden (14:32-42), might be explained as features of oral stories that Mark incorporated. In addition, however, Kelber called attention to recurrent appearances of "threes" that cannot be accounted for on the basis of the many oral stories that were combined in the overall gospel. For example, Jesus predicts his arrest, execution, and rising three times (8:31; 9:31; 10:33-34), clearly a structuring element in the middle step of the narrative focusing on Jesus and the disciples. Three disciples are distinguished within the twelve (Peter, James, and John) for special focus, and Jesus enters Jerusalem three times (11:11; 11:15; 11:27). These "threes" are, again, structural features in the overall narrative.

The devices typical of oral storytelling that structure the narrative of the Gospel of Mark suggest that examples of "narrative maneuvering" similar to what Kelber finds in the smaller components of Mark (Kelber 1983, 49) may be found in the larger story as well. In the healing stories and the exorcism stories, for example, Kelber notes that the narrator has flexibility to innovate by inserting several different motifs within the overall structure. While they are not analogous in pattern (not a macrocosm of the microcosm) to the maneuvers in the healing stories, one can detect several narrative maneuvers in the broader Markan narrative. One example is the familiar Markan "sandwich" technique of juxtaposing two stories, with one framed within the other. Mark frames the scribes' charge that Jesus works in the power of Beelzebul with Jesus' family's concern that he is possessed (3:20-35), the healing of the hemorrhaging woman with the raising of the nearly dead young woman (5:21-43), Jesus' prophetic demonstration against the temple with the cursing of the fig tree (11:12-25), and Jesus' trial before the high priesthood with Peter's denial (15:52-72).

A similar but somewhat more complex oral narrative device is the concentric or chiastic structuring of several stories. Most striking, and most carefully studied, is the arrangement of the five episodes in Mark 2:1–3:6 (see J. Dewey 1980). This sequence begins and ends with episodes that have both similar subjects and parallel internal structure:

healing—controversy—healing. The cast of characters is even similar: Jesus, a man paralyzed or with a withered hand, and the scribes/Pharisees. In both, Jesus' direct address to the man sets off the controversy and, in both, Jesus discerns the scribes'/Pharisees' unspoken objection. The reactions are diametrically opposed, but the Pharisees' and Herodians' defensive determination to destroy in the fifth episode corresponds to the people's enthusiastic response to Jesus in the first episode. The second and fourth episodes also display similarities, in subject (eating), parallel structure as controversy stories, and the cast of characters (Jesus, the disciples, and Pharisees). Both stories also conclude with parallel proverbs and parallel "I"/"Son of Man" sayings. The central episode in the sequence of five begins with the opposite of eating (fasting), which leads to the real issue of the whole sequence: something unusual is happening with Jesus! What is fermenting will burst through the old wineskins just as what is happening with Jesus is breaking through the standard, old, officially promulgated social–religious forms that the scribes/Pharisees defend. Interrelated patterns, themes, internal sequences, and overall sequences such as these help both the oral performer and the hearers to remember and create relations of significance between the episodes and to communicate or assimilate the significance of the overall sequence of episodes.

Moreover, the patterning of episodes, with its combination of themes and characters, for oral performance in this sequence displays many connections with the content and themes of the gospel as a whole. Healing (including exorcism) and eating (including the wilderness feedings and covenantal meal at Passover) are two of Jesus' principal activities throughout Mark's narrative. Both actions anticipate but also manifest the coming of the kingdom of God (equals the renewal of Israel), the overall theme of the gospel. This sequence of five episodes also exemplifies how Jesus' actions challenge the dominant order in Jerusalem, as represented here by the scribes and Pharisees, a concern that is also central to the dominant plot of the gospel as a whole. Again, it is typical of oral narrative that particular sequences of episodes/stanzas exemplify in microcosm the overall theme or plot of the narrative/epic poem.

Yet another example of oral "narrative maneuvering," where the composer/performer inserts episodes into a structure or pattern already available in the oral tradition, can be discerned in the second major narrative step of Mark's story, following Jesus' first long speech in and about parables. For some time now, close readings of Mark have discerned two chains of stories with the same order behind the sequence of episodes in Mark 4:35–8:26. The first "chain" consists of a sea crossing, an exorcism, two healings (arranged in one of Mark's "sandwich" formations), and a wilderness feeding (4:35-41; 5:1-20; 5:21-24, 35-43; 5:24-34; 6:30-44). The second has the same sequence up to the last two stories: sea crossing, exorcism, healing, wilderness feeding, healing (6:45-52; 7:24-30; 7:31-37; 8:1-10; 8:22-26). In this second chain, the second healing is placed last in order to frame the next major narrative step (8:22-10:52) with a healing of blind figures at the beginning and end (yet another feature that would aid in oral performance and hearing). Evidently, prior to or parallel to the composition/performance of the Gospel of Mark, sets of stories were told that clearly carried the message of how Jesus was enacting the renewal of Israel as a prophet like Moses and Elijah, the great founder (sea crossing and wilderness feeding) and renewer (healings) of Israel, respectively, in popular Israelite cultural memory.

The broader Markan gospel story incorporates these chains and reinforces and expands the message of the renewal of Israel by inserting additional episodes into the developing narrative. The so-called "rejection" at Nazareth (Mark 6:1-6) indicates that Jesus is far more than a mere local figure. In the mission of the twelve (6:7-13), representative of the twelve tribes, Jesus indicates in no uncertain terms that his program of the kingdom of God is a renewal of Israel. The story of Herod Antipas' arrest and execution of the Baptist (6:16-28) prefigures and exemplifies what happens to prophets engaged in a renewal of Israel and, specifically, what is about to happen to Jesus. In the controversy with the scribes and Pharisees (7:5-13), Jesus appeals to the basic covenantal commandment of God to insist that the people's produce is needed to feed the people, against the temple representatives' attempt, by their "traditions of the elders" (*korban*), to extricate support for the temple. This event both exemplifies and anticipates the escalating conflict between Jesus and the rulers of Israel and their representatives. The theme and narrative line of the gospel as a whole is the same as that of the component "chains" of stories that supply the framework of the Markan narrative but now considerably elaborated by the insertion of additional stories in which Jesus is carrying out a renewal of Israel against the rulers of Israel.

Oral Narrative Engaged with Historical Context

As has become evident in the last few paragraphs above, Mark's overall narrative, like its oral components, directly engages a particular historical context. In contrast with some treatments of oral poetry or narrative in other fields, Kelber's discussion of "Mark's Oral Legacy" discerns that oral communication is embedded in its context. In contrast with many biblical scholars and other humanists, moreover, Kelber recognizes that the context has not only cultural and aesthetic aspects but political and economic ones as well. In fact, "nonlinguistic features have priority over linguistic ones" (Kelber 1983, 75). Oral communication receives powerful ideological and situational support from its context.

At points in his discussion of the various forms of the oral materials incorporated into the Gospel of Mark, Kelber notes how particular stories engage the political conflict inherent in the historical conflict. The storyteller's departure from the standard narrative formula in the account of the Gerasene demoniac (Mark 5:1-20)—not only naming the demon with the code word *legion* but narrating at length the self-destruction of the "battalion" of swine in the sea—"vents anti-Roman sentiments and encourages wishful thinking with regard to the occupying troops" (Kelber 1983, 53). Political or political–economic conflict is evident in other exorcism stories and in many healing stories as well. In many cases, research on the historical context of Roman Palestine (certainly the context of the Markan materials and clearly the background of Mark) since the publication of *OWG*—such as increasing awareness of the division between rulers and peasants and the regional differences between Galilee and Jerusalem/Judea, and the translation of the Dead Sea Scrolls—enables us to see this. Even if the mention of "the scribes (from Jerusalem)" in the Beelzebul controversy comes from the Markan narrator, the story still displays a sharp conflict between Jerusalem rulers and Galilean prophet (3:22-27). Further, as is now apparent from a term used in analogous fashion in the Dead Sea Scrolls, Jesus' "defeat" of the demon in the Capernaum assembly (Mark 1:22-28) alludes clearly to the defeat of an imperial enemy. If one attends to important textual variants in the early manuscript evidence—that Jesus is moved "*to anger*" and not "*by pity*"—then the story of the healing of the "leper" at Mark 1:40-45 clearly represents Jesus in conflict with the temple system and its "scriptural" codes. Other healing stories bring Jesus directly into confrontation with the scribes and Pharisees (2:1-12; 3:1-6). In the oral tradition of stories about Jesus, the striking aspect of conflict is not simply a matter of oral storytelling but is rooted in the conflictual political–economic structures in which both storytellers and the hearers, as well as Jesus, were embedded (cf. Kelber 1983, 54–55)

With the benefit of recent research into several key aspects of the historical context of Mark, it seems clear that political–economic and (inseparably) cultural conflict are also portrayed in the other forms of oral tradition that have been incorporated into Mark: the parables and the controversy/didactic stories. Given the cultural memory of the Song of the Vineyard and the persistent conflict between Judean and especially Galilean peasantry and the temple high priesthood, the parable of The Tenants (Mark 12:1-8) would certainly have alluded to and evoked the fundamental political–economic conflict of rulers and ruled. Recent research makes the most dramatic difference for our ability to recognize the persistent conflict between Jesus and the Jerusalem priestly rulers and their scribal/Pharisaic representatives, and even his conflict with Roman rule, portrayed in the controversy/didactic stories (cf. Kelber 1983, 7–77). The sharpest conflicts are surely Jesus' condemnation of the scribes and Pharisees for attempting to expropriate local food production that was desperately needed by Galilean families for support of the temple (via the device of *korban*, Mark 7:1-13) and Jesus' skillful dodge of the attempted entrapment question of whether tribute to Rome was "lawful" by focusing on "the things of God" (everything) versus "the things of Caesar" (nothing; Mark 12:13-17; see Horsley 1987, 306–17).

Again here, one can go a step further, from the oral components of Mark's gospel to the gospel as a whole. Not only do most of the component oral stories exhibit the conflict inherent in the historical context in which, says Kelber, the oral communication is embedded and upon which it is dependent. The broader narrative of the gospel even more explicitly and fully displays the conflict inherent in the historical context. Almost certainly the gospel narrative is responsible for the explicit mention of "the scribes from Jerusalem" who oppose Jesus (in the framing of the controversies, Mark 3:22; 7:1-2) and probably also for the Pharisees' and Herodians' conspiracy to destroy him (already in 3:6). The gospel narrative must be responsible for Jesus' explanation of the parable of The Sower, which includes "persecution" among the difficulties encountered by the seed/word (4:17). The overall plotting of the gospel is responsible for the insertion of episodes into the two chains of stories (4:35–8:26) that embellish Jesus' renewal of Israel against the rulers of Israel. And the plotting of the gospel as an overall story is responsible for making Jesus' renewal of Israel against the Jerusalem and Roman rulers the main conflict of the Markan narrative. Oral narrative is embedded in a particular context, and Mark's narrative is very closely interrelated with the conflicts inherent in Judea and Galilee under Roman rule in the first century C.E.

Parables and the Parabolic Gospel

One of the highlights of *OWG* is Kelber's discussion of parables as the quintessential form of communication among the oral components incorporated into the Gospel of Mark. Not surprisingly, some aspects of the interpretation of the parables in the early 1980s, on which Kelber's discussion draws, were rooted in the print culture of established biblical studies. Despite his deployment of some of this language, Kelber's own discussion cuts through inappropriate concepts. Perhaps the first step in understanding parables is to recognize that they not only have *no original form* but also have *no meaning* in themselves (Kelber 1983, 62). As a distinctive form of communication, a parable is spoken by a speaker to hearers in a particular context. Indeed, as Kelber himself points out, the very contents of Jesus' parables are "slices of life" drawn from the experiences of Galilean peasants (Kelber 1983, 59). It hardly needs pointing out that, as oral communication to hearers, the voicing of a parable would be accompanied by extra-verbal elements such as tone of voice, gestures, and other aspects of the speaking/hearing context. Parables are mnemonically shaped to facilitate speaking and hearing (Kelber 1983, 58).

The communication conducted in telling a parable is utterly dependent upon both hearers and context (Kelber 1983, 62, 112). Far from having a meaning in itself that the hearer must interpret, a parable metaphorically invites a hearer to recognize a situation and take the appropriate action, one that the story/content of the parable evokes. This also sets up a situation in which some hearers "get it" and others do not, thus creating a potential dichotomy between insiders and outsiders. For example, the parables of The Growing Seed and The Mustard Seed included in Jesus' parables speech (Mark 4:26-29, 30-32) invite hearers to recognize what the kingdom of God is like, to have confidence in its eventual fulfillment, and to join in advancing that fulfillment. More-elaborate parables invite hearers into the story and ask them to identify with what is happening so that they can recognize the relationship between the story and a situation in their own life circumstances (cf. Kelber 1983, 61).

One of Kelber's key insights in *OWG* is that Mark's gospel as a whole is a parable. This observation makes it possible to recognize that, since parables are the quintessential form of oral communication, the gospel as a whole must be oral communication performed to hearers in a particular context. As Kelber notes, "for the Markan Jesus, it seems, the significance of speaking in parables goes beyond those stories technically called parables" (Kelber 1983, 58). The parable of The Tenants (Mark 12:1-12) not only fits well in its immediate narrative context but can be heard as a story analogous to Mark's story as a whole (Kelber 1983, 112–13), a story that stands in continuity with—indeed, presents Jesus' mission as the fulfillment of—the (hi)story of Israel. As is often observed, Jesus' parable of The Tenants of the vineyard is an "updated" version of Isaiah's Song of the Vineyard

(Isaiah 5), which functioned as a prophetic indictment of the monarchic rulers of the people. Moreover, not only do the high priestly rulers of Israel in Mark's story recognize that they are implicated in the parable Jesus just told to them on their own "turf" (the temple), but the hearers of Mark's gospel story are invited to recognize that Jesus, in telling the parable as part of Mark's overall parabolic story, has just pronounced God's condemnation on the rulers of Israel, who not only exploited the people (Israel, traditionally symbolized by the vineyard) but were also about to arrest Jesus to hand him over to be killed by the Romans. Some of the details that now appear in Mark's telling of the parable may have emerged in repeated retellings, because the parable was so readily analogous to the history it invited hearers to recognize.

Kelber also suggests that, just as a speaker tells a parable to move people to action, so Mark's overall story aims to move people to action—in imitation of Jesus. Jesus' discussions with the disciples after his first and third announcements that he must be arrested, killed, and rise (Mark 8:27-38; 10:32-45) have implications for the hearers of the gospel. And if modern, print-oriented readers did not "get it" before, the "open ending" of this parabolic oral narrative (Mark 16:1-8) might well stimulate some leading questions. Mark's ending is not just open but parabolic insofar as the hearer—prepared by earlier indications in the narrative that Jesus will be going back up to "Galilee," the setting of his mission, after his crucifixion—is invited to recognize that not only the disciples but they themselves are to meet him and, presumably, to continue the renewal of Israel. As Kelber notes, like the parables included in the gospel, Mark's overall story of the coming of the kingdom of God points beyond itself to the kingdom of God (Kelber 1983, 123–24).

4

THE GOSPEL OF MARK AS ORAL HERMENEUTIC

JOANNA DEWEY

> If [only] we can wean ourselves from the notion that texts constitute the center of gravity in tradition . . .
> *(Kelber 1995b, 163)*

> [W]e must start with the gospels as narratives and analyze their narrative elements before we think about whatever tradition may have been in existence before them.
> *(Kelber, p. 34 above)*

In 1983, when Werner H. Kelber published his groundbreaking work *The Oral and the Written Gospel* (*OWG*), he argued that the Gospel of Mark was a written as a "counterform to, rather than extension of, oral hermeneutics" (Kelber 1983, 185). "Strictly speaking, therefore, the Gospel arises not from orality *per* se but out of the debris of deconstructed orality" (Kelber 1983, 95). Although Kelber certainly recognized that the written text was recycled into orality, he appeared to imagine that it was read aloud much as one might read aloud today from a printed text. Since then, Kelber has done substantial further work on media differences. He has stressed, first, the great differences between a manuscript and a printed text and, second, the multiple interactions between orality and scribality in the first century, including the variability of early manuscripts (see Kelber 2005b). He has emphasized the importance of understanding the gospel narrative *as* narrative. Furthermore, Kelber has brought cultural memory theory to bear on Christian origins and the Gospel of Mark (see 2002a; 2005). He understands Mark not as "cold memory," which tries to preserve faithfully the traditions of the past, but as "hot memory," which reconstructs the past in order to form and support community identity in the present. Today, Kelber is well aware of the differences between manuscript and print cultures, of the multiple interactions of oral and scribal traditioning, and of the fluidity of both oral performances and manuscript texts. Yet, he still views the written Gospel of Mark as a radical departure from, and reshaping of, the oral tradition.

As I have argued elsewhere, I think that the Gospel of Mark is basically an oral narrative built on oral storytelling, employing an oral style, and plotted according to oral conventions (see J. Dewey 1989; 1994b; 2004). I do not know if it was composed and performed orally and then transcribed or whether it was composed in writing, most likely by dictation, and then performed—a writer familiar with the tradition can write in an oral style. In contrast to Kelber, then, I would argue that the Gospel of Mark as a whole does *not* represent a break with orality but is best understood in light of oral hermeneutics of composition and reception.

In this article, rather than developing my own position, I shall address and challenge Kelber's reasons for viewing Mark's gospel as a sharp break with orality. As I understand it, Kelber's overarching understanding is that early Christian oral tradition focused on Jesus as being present and alive, while the Gospel of Mark focuses on Jesus' death and absence. Kelber offers three major arguments in defense of his claim that Mark was written as a counterform to the oral synthesis: 1) Mark's rejection of those individuals whom Christian communities respected as oral authorities, namely the disciples, the family of Jesus, and prophets/Christs; 2) Mark's silencing of the oral teachings found in the sayings material; and, 3) the gospel's emphasis on death and absence rather than life and presence, which is a major christological shift. I shall address each of these premises in turn.[1] Basically, I will argue that Kelber has not gone far enough in considering the Gospel of Mark as narrative and in recognizing oral narrative possibilities. I look forward to a continuing dialogue about these issues.

Before turning to our differences, however, I wish to affirm both how much I have learned from Kelber and how substantial are our agreements on the significance of media issues for understanding the New Testament. I strongly agree with Kelber that Mark's gospel is not simply a natural evolution of oral tradition—there is no inevitable linear development from Jesus to the gospels. I agree with him also on the importance of cultural memory for the formation of the gospels: memory continually structures and adapts tradition to support community identity and needs in the present. I also agree that the Gospel of Mark was composed around 70 C.E. in part in response to the first Roman–Jewish war and the destruction of the temple in Jerusalem. I agree that the gospel is "hot memory" serving that present situation, not an attempt to preserve some earlier pristine past. I agree that there was some sort of *Traditionsbruch* (break in the tradition) post–70 C.E., due both to the disruption caused by the war and to the passage of time and the death of the first generations (Kelber 2002a, 14; 2005, 244). Finally, I agree that, ultimately, "the books of the New Testament are best understood as attempts to harness and control the forces of orality," as Thatcher states in the introduction to this volume (see p. 2 above).

Despite these many agreements, however, I differ with Kelber on how the written Gospel of Mark fits into the overall media picture. Kelber sees it as the beginning of writing used to control (or at least seriously reconstruct) orality; I see it as still on the oral side of the divide. I turn now to Kelber's reasons for understanding Mark as a written counterform to orality.

Mark's Rejection of Oral Authorities

Kelber's major and continuing argument for Mark as a scribal counterform to orality is his view that the Gospel of Mark rejects all oral authorities, who are represented in the narrative by the disciples, Jesus' family, and prophets/Christs. Here, I shall follow Kelber in treating each of these characters separately. Then I shall raise the question of whether these groups were really viewed as oral authorities who guaranteed the tradition at the time of Mark's composition.

I shall begin with *the disciples* as perhaps the most central to Kelber's argument. For Kelber, the relationship between Jesus and the disciples in the Gospel of Mark is constructed on the oral principle of *mimesis*. The disciples are called to imitate the paradigm of Jesus' life and death. Yet, in Kelber's view, the narrative portrays the disciples' failures and thus "casts a vote of censure against the guarantors of tradition" (Kelber 1983, 97; see also 125–29). I view the disciples' role rather differently. The audience is indeed called to imitate Jesus' life and death but perceives Jesus, not the disciples, as the authority. In the narrative, the disciples provide a means to teach about discipleship and illustrate for the listening audience both successes and failures in following (J. Dewey 1994a).

Mark's gospel does not address the disciples unequivocally. Those who, like Kelber, wish to interpret the gospel as rejecting the disciples wholesale stress that the disciples deny, betray, and abandon Jesus and thus fall under Jesus' saying, "Those who are ashamed of me and of my words in this adulterous and sinful generation, of them the Son of Humanity will also be ashamed when he comes in the glory of his Father with the holy angels"

(Mark 8:38). On the other hand, those who view the Gospel of Mark as expecting the restoration of the disciples stress that the disciples are promised a reward for following (10:29-30), that they do finally understand and accept that following Jesus and the kingdom of God entails persecution by the powers of this age (10:35-40; 14:29-31), and that the repeated pattern of prophecy and fulfillment throughout the narrative suggests the fulfillment of the prophecy that the disciples will see Jesus in Galilee (14:28; 16:7) in spite of the women's silence at the end (16:8). I remain as convinced that the narrative expects the disciples to be restored as Kelber is convinced that their restoration is out of the question.

I suggest, then, that the portrait of the disciples in the Gospel of Mark is ambiguous. Certainly, narrative critics today continue to interpret the disciples both positively and negatively. Here, I believe the practice of performance criticism can help us (see Rhoads 2006a; 2006b). Though scholars have begun to appreciate the significance of the oral/aural first-century media world, mostly we still study the New Testament by analyzing printed texts. If we want to pay attention to the oral dimensions of the extant texts, we need to hear them, performing them ourselves in various ways—in favor of, or rejecting, the disciples. Performance can enhance our understandings and clarify that some interpretations do or do not work orally. Performance criticism may indeed help to show us how truly ambiguous the Markan portrait of the disciples is.

Kelber admits that, when the Gospel of Mark is performed today, there can be sympathetic responses to the disciples (Kelber 1997, xxvi). Yet, he argues that the agonistic (that is, combative) toning and adversarial plotting of the narrative makes that response unlikely in the first century. I have used the same observation of agonistic toning and adversarial plotting to argue the opposite point (J. Dewey 1994b, 150–51). Because ancient audiences were accustomed to agonistic portrayals, they would simply take them less seriously than modern readers do. In fact, in antiquity teaching was often conveyed by examples of how *not* to behave, and audiences may not have interpreted such portrayals as a rejection of the characters in question. As far as audience reception is concerned, the question must be left open, although the acceptance of Mark's gospel into the canon does suggest that it was not generally understood as rejecting the twelve and Peter. The question of the gospel's ending is relevant here. Even the longer endings, although they restore the disciples and present the resurrected Jesus, still leave the gospel with an ambiguous portrait of the disciples.[2]

If the question of audience reception must remain open, can we say anything more certain about composition, about authorial intent in regard to the disciples? Clearly, the subplot of the disciples is used to maintain audience interest. The narrative presents three interacting levels of conflict: cosmic, Jesus and the authorities, Jesus and his followers (see Dewey and Malbon 2009; Rhoads, Dewey, and Michie 1999, 73–97). The cosmic conflict takes place between God and Satan. As Mark tells the story, the audience knows from the beginning that God is the sure victor and that Jesus is God's agent. If the audience rejects this premise, the narrative will be unconvincing. The second, or middle level, is Jesus' conflict with the social, political, and religious authorities, the conflict between the kingdom of God and the kingdom of Rome. These first two plot lines are established early on in the narrative: the gospel of Jesus Christ *is* good news (Mark 1:1, 15), and the authorities reject Jesus, plotting to destroy him (3:6). The narrative is not ambivalent on these conflicts: the authorities will destroy Jesus in this age, but the new age has begun with Jesus and will triumph.

The third, or most embedded, conflict is the conflict between Jesus and the disciples along with the broader group of followers. These conflicts with the disciples occur in private; the conflicts between Jesus and the authorities occur in public, and in those conflicts the disciples stand with Jesus. Thus the disciples are not grouped with the opponents within the narrative. Rather, the narrative uses the disciples to teach the gospel's audience what "following" entails, to emphasize the difficulties of following, and to maintain plot interest as the disciples do and do not succeed in following. The disciples' misunderstandings provide Jesus with opportunities to teach the gospel's hearers the correct understandings. It is only on this third level, the followers' conflict, that the Gospel of Mark is ambiguous. While this observation does not clarify authorial intent, it does suggest that it was not a major aim of this gospel to discredit the disciples and Peter. If Mark's aim was to discredit the disciples, the narrative would be as unambiguous here as it is on the first two levels of conflict, and in that case it would not be possible for hearers or readers to expect the disciples' restoration.

Turning now to *Jesus' family* as representatives of oral authority, Kelber claims that the Gospel of Mark "registers consistent hostility toward Jesus' own family" (Kelber 1983, 102). He cites, first, the two negative instances: Mark 3:20-35, where the family is grouped with the scribes in objecting to Jesus' behavior, and Mark 6:1-6, where Jesus is rejected in Nazareth. Second, he argues (assuming that Mary the mother of James and Joses is also to be understood as the mother of Jesus [15:40, 47; 16:1]) that the family of Jesus (in the person of the mother) is part of the nontransmission of the resurrection message and thus part of Mark's rejection of the oral authorities (Kelber 1983, 102–4). Kelber further asserts that there is evidence that Jesus' family members were understood as oral authorities in Paul, Acts, and elsewhere (Kelber 1983, 102).

Kelber is correct that Mark 3:20-35 and 6:1-6 present a generally negative view of the family of Jesus. Yet the narrative does not group the family of Jesus with the disciples as leaders to be rejected. Rather, to become a disciple requires one to *leave* one's family in order to join the kingdom of God. In the Markan call stories, specific disciples leave their occupations, which in antiquity were typically family businesses—James and John explicitly leave their father as well as his business (Mark 1:16-20; 2:14-15). The disciples (and other followers) who have left families are promised new families, houses, and fields (10:29-30). Finally, Jesus instructs, "If any want to become my followers, let them deny themselves and take up their cross and follow me" (8:34). While Western readers today tend to interpret "denying oneself" in accord with an individualistic self-understanding, in antiquity the kinship unit was central rather than the individual; thus, the kin group is what needs to be renounced to follow Jesus (Malina 1994; J. Dewey 2001). The parallelism of denying kin and taking up one's cross—that is, risking persecution, even execution—suggests that both are understood as costs of discipleship.

Thus, while the family may be understood as leaders, thus oral authorities, in other Christian literature, in the Gospel of Mark they are understood as a unit that must be left in order to become part of the Christian community. In regard to the empty tomb and the ending of the gospel, Mary is no longer portrayed as family but as part of the group of women who follow and minister to Jesus. To lump the family with the disciples as oral authorities to be rejected is a deductive move on the part of a modern reader; it is not part of the ancient experience of hearing the gospel, where the need for the disciples to separate from their kinship group in order to become followers is being stressed. The family is not so much rejected as left for a larger cause. Overall, the negative portrayal of Jesus' family in the narrative is adequately explained by the narrative itself. Any historical inference that Mark is rejecting the family as oral authorities is on shaky ground.

Turning to Kelber's final group of oral authorities, in one instance the Gospel of Mark does warn against *false Christs and false prophets,* rejecting them precisely as leaders of the community (13:21-22). On the basis of 13:5-6, Kelber understands these false prophets specifically as Christian leaders.[3] He understands them as speaking in the name of Jesus, "continuing the present authority of Jesus, the living Lord. It is this oral metaphysics of presence" that Mark is objecting to, in favor of a future return of the Son of Humanity who is now absent (Kelber 1983, 99). I would argue, however, that Mark is simply separating the expectation of the return of the Son of Humanity from the events of the Roman–Jewish war. The future coming of the Son of Humanity was already part of the oral tradition—it is found specifically in Q, the sayings material common to Matthew and Luke (Luke 17:23-37; Matt 24:26-39). One does not need to posit a rejection of oral presence to explain the warning against false Christs.

Furthermore, in Mark's narrative, the false Christs are not grouped with the disciples or with Jesus' family; in fact, it is the inner core of disciples (Kelber's core group of rejected oral authorities) who are instructed to beware of them. Kelber himself has written eloquently and often of the need to understand a narrative as narrative before making theological or historical deductions about the narrative's prehistory. It is also necessary, I would argue, to understand the narrative as narrative before making historical or theological extrapolations from it. In this particular case, an understanding of the narrative prohibits grouping the family of Jesus and the disciples together and, while there is a clear, if isolated, warning against false prophets and Christs, they are precisely distinguished from the core disciples. While disciples, family, and false Christs are each critiqued in various ways in the narrative, they are critiqued for *different* reasons, none specifically to do with oral authority. An understanding of the narrative as narrative mitigates grouping them together as oral authorities to be rejected.

Before closing this section, I wish to raise a historical question: Were these three groups (disciples/family/prophets) clearly perceived as guarantors of the Christian tradition at the time of the composition of the Gospel of Mark? In an argument for resurrection, Paul refers to those who have seen the risen Jesus, including Peter, the twelve, James (family), and finally himself as guarantors that there really was a resurrection (1 Cor 15:5-6). Does this establish these individuals as oral authorities transmitting the whole tradition? Paul certainly feels free to disagree with Peter (Gal 1–2). Our only other pre-Markan source, the hypothetical Q, does not seem concerned with oral authorities at all. Q mentions the twelve only to note that they are given the authority to judge the twelve tribes of Israel in the age to come (Luke 22:29-30; Matt 19:28). It seems to me that it is precisely the *Traditionsbruch* starting some forty years after Easter, when the generations who knew the earthly Jesus were dying out, that led to the need to establish guarantors of the tradition. The Gospel of Mark is a bit too early.

Perhaps it is precisely because Mark was not concerned with oral authorities that he could portray Peter and the other disciples negatively in his plot to teach about discipleship. Matthew and Luke, writing later, were more concerned with establishing authority for the church, and they both softened the negative portrait of Peter. It was Matthew, writing a decade or two after Mark, who specifically established Peter as an authority for the church on earth (16:17-19). The notion of the twelve as eyewitnesses of the earthly Jesus is first found in Acts (1:21-22; see also Luke 1:1-4), which I would date in the second century (see Pervo 2006). As time passed, there was a need to anoint authorities as guarantors of the founding narratives; however, it is only *after* the time of the composition of Mark that this need became acute. Kelber himself notes in his introduction to the 1997 reprint of *The Oral and the Written Gospel* that the notion of eyewitness guarantors of the tradition served the needs of both Christian and Jewish communities beginning in the late first century (Kelber 1997, xxv–xxvi). However, he does not seem to see that this may have implications for the status of Peter, disciples, and family as authorities in the pre-Markan oral tradition.

The Paucity of Sayings Material in Mark

In comparison to the other canonical gospels, the Gospel of Mark contains a smaller proportion of sayings. Kelber asks why this is the case, given that Q existed prior to Mark. Here, he follows Eugene Boring's argument that Mark was leery of the prophets in his community who used the sayings tradition to their own advantage (Kelber 1983, 101). For Kelber, this is part of Mark's rejection of material that suggests the presence of Jesus. By omission of much of the sayings tradition, Mark silences Jesus' direct speaking. Indeed, Kelber argues that even the two discourses of Jesus that the gospel does contain, Mark 4 and 13, "function so as to disallow any oral sense of presence." The parable discourse stresses the mystery of the kingdom, and the eschatological discourse "extricates kingdom hopes from past and present . . . and projects the Son of Man into the future" (Kelber 1983, 101). On the contrary, I would argue that in the very oral performance of these speeches, Jesus is made present to audiences. The hearers of the gospel experience being directly addressed by Jesus; in the parable discourse, they are *both* being given the mystery of the kingdom *and* being admonished to try for greater understanding. Thus, Mark does not reject Jesus as speaker; rather, he allows him to speak and thus to be present to the listening community.

I would like to suggest that the problem of the relative lack of sayings material in Mark is a problem for modern scholars, not for ancient listeners. I am not convinced that ancient hearers would sense any dearth of sayings in Mark's gospel. As is characteristic of oral narrative in general, Mark's gospel embeds teaching in events/episodes, which makes it easier to remember. As Eric Havelock notes, "Information or prescription, which in a later stage of literate culture would be arranged typically and topically, is in the oral tradition preserved only as it is transmuted into an event" (Havelock 1963, 174). For example, unlike Matthew 6 with its general instructions on fasting and prayer, Mark embeds fasting in the controversy over why the disciples do not fast and embeds prayer in the episode of the discovery of the withered fig tree (2:18-20; 11:20-25). The two discourses of Jesus mentioned above, Mark 4 and 13, themselves consist of narrative material: the parables are little stories, and Mark 13 is mostly narrative, albeit of future events.[4] Jesus' exhortation "What I say to you I say to all: Watch" (Mark 13:37) is easily understood in the context of oral performance, for performers often make asides to their audiences in character (Basgöz 1975; Ong 1982, 161). The Gospel of Mark thus conforms to typical oral *narrative* techniques.

Further, I suggest that the major reason for the relative lack of sayings in the Gospel of Mark is not their content or their function in making Jesus present but rather the simple fact that too much direct discourse interrupts narrative flow. Biblical critics apparently feel that the lack of much sayings material in this gospel is in need of explanation. Early source critics sought a textual reason for the omission: Mark did not know Q (the sayings material common to Matthew and Luke and not in Mark). Thinking in terms of the oral/scribal first-century media world, Kelber has sought a theological reason: Mark has silenced the oral teaching with its emphasis on life and presence. The paucity of sayings, however, does not necessarily mean that Mark rejects sayings. I suggest that the omission is due simply to the needs of narrative for oral performance. The Gospel of Mark as a whole works as oral performance in ways that the other gospels do not. It is no accident that Alec McGowan chose Mark's gospel to perform on stage. Long sections of teaching would interrupt the flow of episodes, and the audience (and the performer) would lose track of the plot, the story as a whole.[5] The lack of teaching does not need an external justification; the requirements of effective oral narrative alone suffice.

Life and Presence, Death and Absence

Kelber's third argument for the Gospel of Mark as a written counterform to the oral synthesis is that Mark is concerned with death and absence in contrast to the typical oral emphasis on life and presence. Kelber frequently emphasizes that oral communication binds together speaker, words, and listeners into a whole, while scribality separates them, creating distance (see, for example, Kelber 1983, 19). He argues that the distance and separation from an audience that writing provides is necessary for dealing with death (Kelber 1983, 19, 91–92, 193).Throughout *OWG,* Kelber stresses the connection between life and orality, "the oral equation of the earthly Jesus with the living Lord," which he sees present in Q and elsewhere (Kelber 1983, 199, 201–3). Further, he stresses the association of writing with death, citing Walter Ong's dictum that "the association of writing with death is not total, but it is manifold and inescapable" (Kelber 1983, 184; see also 197–99).

In what follows, I hope to demonstrate that, although orality does reinforce life and although scribality may indeed encourage distance and facilitate a focus on death, scribality and orality *both* deal with life and *both* deal with death. First, I shall argue that the way Mark deals with Jesus' death and subsequent absence is possible orally—that is, that the gospel's content is compatible with oral composition. Here, I am countering Kelber's specific arguments for viewing the passion narrative as a scribal composition. Second, I shall argue that the very performance of Mark's gospel, whether it was composed orally or in writing, makes Jesus and the kingdom of God alive and present to listening audiences.

In *OWG,* Kelber describes Mark's passion narrative as a story of three deaths: Jesus' death, the temple's destruction, and the disciples' failure (Kelber 1983, 185–86).[6] I have discussed the disciples earlier and noted above that I concur that Mark is reshaping the tradition to deal with the Roman–Jewish war and the destruction of the temple. I turn now to a consideration of Jesus' death and absence in the Gospel of Mark. First, orality, even within the Christian tradition, can and often does deal with death, as Kelber himself seems to acknowledge. For Kelber, Q is an example of oral hermeneutics, and in *OWG* Kelber wrote that Q does not refer to Jesus' suffering and death (Kelber 1983, 201–3). More recently, however, he has noted that Q "keyed Jesus' own death to the fate of prophetic personalities in Jewish history" (Kelber 2005, 246; see Luke 11:49-51). I would add that Q also intimates the death of the disciples: Jesus' followers will be brought before the synagogues and rulers, and whoever does not carry the cross cannot be Jesus' disciple (Luke 12:11-12; 14:26-27). Persecution, even execution, is understood as part of discipleship. Finally, the theme of Jesus' absence is also present in Q: the Son of Humanity will return in the future (Luke17:[22]23-30). Thus, death and absence are to be found in the oral hermeneutics of Q.

The Gospel of Mark expands the Q tradition of rejection of the prophets, applying it to John the Baptist as well as to Jesus and the disciples.[7] All three are (or will be) "handed over" (παραδίδωμι; John the Baptist, 1:14;

Jesus, 9:31, 10:33, 14:21, 14:41, 15:1, 15:10; followers, 13:9, 13:11). The allegory of the wicked tenants clearly portrays the son (Jesus) as the culmination of the persecution of the prophets (12:1-10). The view of death in Mark is aligned with the view in Q; it is not a sharp break with it.

Mark's gospel, however, goes considerably further than Q by *narrating* the deaths of John the Baptist and Jesus. For the Baptist, Mark includes the story of Herod Antipas' promise to the dancing girl, resulting in John's severed head on a platter (Mark 6:14-28). For Jesus, Mark's narrative leads up to the crucifixion and includes eighteen verses on the crucifixion itself (15:21-39). Kelber argues that the written medium, which permitted greater distance, was necessary to bring crucifixion to narration. "The stunning realism of the passion narrative is most likely the result of artistic distanciation by written words that empty events of their immediacy. Close proximity to the event and the oral metaphysics of presence are a persistent obstacle to bringing death to language" (Kelber 1983, 198). I question this claim for the following reasons.

The difference in genre between Mark and Q remains relevant. Q consists of short discourses, it does not contain much narrative, and it certainly is not a connected narrative; the Gospel of Mark is a carefully constructed (oral) narrative. I suggest that the presence of the two death narratives in Mark is not an indication that the gospel was composed in writing. It is, rather, due to the difference in genre. *Narratives* about violent death *are* part of oral literature. To take one very notable example from the ancient world, the opening of the *Iliad* tells the audience its narrative will be about many violent deaths.

> The wrath sing, goddess, of Peleus' son Achilles, the accursed wrath which brought down countless sorrows upon the Achaeans, and sent down to Hades many valiant souls of warriors, and made the men themselves to be the spoil for dogs and birds of every kind; and thus the will of Zeus was brought to fulfillment. Of this sing from the time when first there parted in strife Atreus' son, lord of men, and noble Achilles. (1.1–9)

It is even possible that the narration of Jesus' crucifixion may have fit better in oral narrative than in writing, since, as Kelber himself points out, in Mark's day crucifixions tended not to be described in writing (Kelber 1983, 193).

Kelber is correct that the passion narrative seems less oral in character than Mark 1–13. As he notes, oral forms are not so much in evidence in the passion narrative (Kelber 1983, 186–87). Yet, it might perhaps be more accurate to say that the passion narrative consists of the repeated use of a single oral form, the biographical apophthegm—that is, a little story about a particular event. The passion narrative consists of a concatenation of short biographical apophthegms. The narrative remains episodic—it does not flow the way Luke's narrative does. Its episodic character is certainly possible orally.

A second argument for scribality is that Mark's passion narrative is filled with allusions to the psalms. From our print perspective, the inclusion of the psalm allusions suggests scribal activity. Yet their inclusion could also be oral. These psalms dealing with the suffering of the righteous could well have been part of the oral or little tradition and thus available to an oral performer (see Horsley and Draper 1999, 98–104). In the ancient media world, the Gospel of Mark was likely to have been oral, written, recycled into orality, rewritten, and so on (Parker 1997, 19, 179). So, another possibility is that scribes, in the process of transmission, have clarified and extended allusions to the psalms. Neither the narrative style of Mark 14–16 nor the allusions to the psalms require writing. The passion narrative is within the realm of oral composition.

Kelber argues that the passion narrative needs the distance of writing in order to understand Jesus' death as salvific. He sees a real shift in Christology from the oral tradition to the Gospel of Mark. In the oral tradition, "Jesus is a wholly unambiguous figure who cures diseases and conquers evil spirits. The terrifyingly ambiguous notion that the protagonist must first be crushed himself for evil to be conquered lies outside the mental horizon of this oral Christology of heroism and polarization" (Kelber 1983, 55). I question the claim that the Gospel of Mark actually presents Jesus' death as the conquering of evil: Jesus overcomes Satan (evil) in the wilderness and forgives sins during his life (Mark 1:12-13; 2:1-12). Mark's emphasis in the narrative is simply that Jesus' death is according to the will of God. In addition to Mark's placement of the crucifixion in the tradition of the persecution of prophets and the death of innocent righteous ones, the signs of darkness and the rending of the temple curtain, the phrasing of the passion–resurrection traditions, and the allusion to Scripture ("For the Son of Humanity goes as is written of him") all affirm that Jesus' death is God's will (15:33, 38; 8:31; 9:31; 10:33;14:21). Given first-century understandings of the role of gods in human affairs, if the death of Jesus were not according to God's will, it would be some other god or goddess' will, and the gospel would not be good news. The Gospel of Mark shows Jesus' death as consistent with God's will. The gospel is *not* concerned to interpret *how* it is God's will. It simply places Jesus' death in the longstanding tradition of the persecution of the prophets and the suffering of righteous ones.

In fact, the Gospel of Mark does not include much reflection on the significance of Jesus' death in particular. A full discussion of the two passages where modern critics read a saving death into Mark's gospel is beyond the scope of this article. Briefly, the combination of body and blood at the Last Supper suggests martyrdom (which fits in with the persecution of the prophets), not sacrifice (Mark 14:22-25; see Mack 1988, 118). The saying "For the Son of Humanity came not to be served but to serve and to give his life as a ransom for many" (Mark 10:45) has come to be understood as atonement in later theological interpretation. In its own narrative context, however, it is a continuation of Jesus' life of service: Jesus' entire life and death are a model of service (Dowd and Malbon 2006). Theological reflection on the meaning of Jesus' death might well be facilitated by the distance that writing provides, as Kelber argues. But Mark generally eschews such theological interpretation in favor of repeated assurances that Jesus' death is according to God's will. This seems to me well within the possibilities of oral narrative.

In order to understand Mark's treatment of Jesus' death and Mark's Christology, it is important to hear his story through the *both/and* hermeneutic characteristic of oral narrative rather than reading it according to print standards of linear construction. The gospel fits oral narrative style: it is additive and aggregative, episode piled upon episode (Ong 1982, 36–41, 158; J. Dewey 1989). As Kelber himself notes, oral plots are cumulative and additive so that "knowledge is gathered and multiplied more than critically developed" (Kelber 1983, 80). This applies well to the Gospel of Mark, composed with oral compositional methods and heard orally. But if we read Mark's narrative according to norms of modern print, then we use an either/or rather than a both/and hermeneutic. Within this framework, the emphasis on persecution and death in the second half of the gospel appears to call into question the hermeneutic of life in the healings, sea crossings, and feedings found in the first half. Heard with oral hermeneutics, persecution—suffering and death—is *added to* the good news of the kingdom; it does not replace it. In Mark's narrative, most normal human suffering is in fact overcome with the healings, feedings, forgiveness, and the new community of God's kingdom. What is added, however, is that those who join the kingdom on earth will not only experience the blessings of the kingdom now but will also be persecuted by the powers of this age as long as this age continues. The oral/aural logic is thus both/and: *both* miracles, which are to be prayed for confidently, *and* persecution, which is to be expected (Mark 11:22-25, 13:9-11; see J. Dewey 1994b, 149–50).

Because of its episodic character, oral narrative can tolerate greater inconsistency than linear print narrative; it can sustain both/and. Thus, contra Kelber, in Mark the heroic Christology of the miracles can co-exist comfortably alongside the emphases on Jesus' death and the coming persecution of the disciples. Indeed, I suggest that for early Christian community formation, cultural memory even prior to the composition of Mark would require both the heroic Jesus and some understanding of Jesus' execution. No matter how much Christians emphasized that Jesus is alive, they simply could not ignore his crucifixion. Mark's portrayal of Jesus' death does not, in my opinion, require scribality nor does it make the written gospel a counterform to the living oral tradition.

Kelber also stresses Jesus' *absence* at the end of Mark in contrast to Jesus' continuing presence. In the gospel, Jesus was present in his earthly life and will be present again when the Son of Humanity returns. Thus, Jesus is a figure of the past and the future but not of the present. Logically, Kelber is correct here. While Jesus is not left dead in the tomb—the gospel clearly affirms resurrection (see Kelber 2002a, 77)—he is also not immediately present to the hearer. But I wonder if this absence would seem more than momentary for those first-century audiences who heard the story. The expectation is that Jesus will return soon: "Truly I tell you, there are some standing here who will not taste death until they see that the kingdom of God has come with power" (Mark 9:1; see also 13:30). Jesus also instructs the audience to keep alert because no one knows the day or hour (13:32, 33, 37). The disciples, the women, *and* listening audiences are told to go to Galilee where they will see Jesus (14:28; 16:7).[8] They/we are told to return to the place of the in-breaking of the kingdom of God, the place of the miracles, the healings and feedings. The end is at hand; persecution and death are not the end of the story; the good news of God's kingdom, including the presence of Jesus, will continue in Galilee.

Kelber interprets the Gospel of Mark's lack of resurrection stories as a deliberate stress on Jesus' absence (Kelber 1983, 100–101; 2002a, 77). Once again, I suggest (as have others) that there are good narrative reasons for omitting resurrection appearances (see J. Dewey 1994a). The narrative is encouraging the audience throughout to be faithful followers. The abrupt ending of the gospel implicitly exhorts the audience to continue following Jesus. As the women have replaced the disciples as followers in the narrative itself, so now the listening audience replaces the women. Any resurrection appearance would dilute the appeal to the audience. This ending would be particularly effective in performance, where the performer is interacting directly with a live audience. In a written narrative, particularly one that is read silently and not heard, there is greater distance between the text and the reader, and an ending that brings closure to the narrative becomes more desirable, as the longer endings found in the manuscript history of the Gospel of Mark indicate (J. Dewey 1994b, 156–57). For listening audiences, narrative reasons seem fully adequate to explain the lack of resurrection appearances.

Kelber is correct that, in the Gospel of Mark, Jesus is a figure of the narrator's and audience's past and projected future and not of their present. In the first century or two after its composition, however, the gospel was performed orally. This would be true whether the gospel was originally composed orally or in writing. All ancient literature was designed for oral performance and would be composed with a listening audience in mind. The Gospel of Mark, with its oral style, is easy to remember and perform orally. In fact, I have argued that Mark's gospel survived to become part of the four-gospel canon precisely because it was a good story and widely performed orally (J. Dewey 2004). If early Christian communities had relied primarily on writings for transmission of the tradition, and not oral communication, then the Gospel of Matthew would likely have completely replaced the Gospel of Mark. There would have been little reason to recopy Mark, and it likely would have been lost as Q was lost. In fact, Augustine considered the Gospel of Mark merely an abbreviation of Matthew, and his view prevailed for centuries.

In oral performance, however, the gospel and Jesus come alive. Kelber himself stresses that "the challenge for the storyteller is not to contemplate Jesus with theological acumen, nor to restore his historical actuality, but rather to make him live in the imagination of the audience" (Kelber 1983, 55). Kelber wrote this about the exorcism stories, but his comment applies to the Gospel of Mark as a whole. Jesus comes alive in oral performance in the immediacy of the narrative. Jesus is present in the telling to the community. A prophet speaks in the name of Jesus; a narrative provides a different way of making Jesus present, a way that makes audiences feel as if they were there at the very events. The experience of listening to the Gospel of Mark is not an experience of Jesus' absence but of Jesus alive and present. As John Miles Foley has said:

> When you voice a text, wherever and whenever you do, you cause it to live and to mean by being present; when you perform within a community, you bind the community together in a shared experience that far supersedes the authority of any artifact. That is the inimitable power of voice—to give presence, literally to "em-body." (Foley 2006b, 139)

The Effects of Writing

Whether composed in performance, by dictation, or in writing, the Gospel of Mark was composed in an oral style and performed orally. The gospel remains fundamentally on the oral side of the oral/written divide. It is best understood using oral hermeneutics. In performance, the gospel is not perceived as discrediting oral authorities, as lacking sayings, or as replacing the heroic Jesus with a suffering and dying savior. Rather, it is heard and experienced as making Jesus alive and present, both the Jesus of the miracles and the Jesus who is persecuted and executed. The gospel, however, was surely written down relatively quickly. And then retold. And then rewritten. And so forth. This was characteristic of the oral and written media mix of the first centuries. The Gospel of Mark was likely adapted to audiences in each oral performance and modified in each rewriting. Kelber (1995b) has argued persuasively that we should not speak of "original" Jesus sayings; perhaps we should not speak of the "original" Gospel of Mark, either.

What difference, then, does the existence of manuscripts make? Over time, over decades or centuries, the written forms gradually exert control over oral versions. This can be observed in the sixteenth-century English ballad tradition, where oral versions deviated more and more from the printed text and then returned to the printed versions as broadsheets were reissued (Finnegan 1977, 162–63). The same trend can be observed in the northern European fairy tale tradition. The first written (printed) versions of the northern European fairy tales were a counterform to the oral stories, taming the active and often magical roles of women and girls to make them more passive, obedient figures (Lurie 1990; J. Dewey 1996). For these materials, we can compare the first printed versions of Perrault in 1667 and the Grimm brothers in 1812 with oral versions of the stories collected from women storytellers in the early twentieth century. These oral versions have not yet been affected by the printed texts. The women and girls remain active agents, often with magical powers. However, with the growth of mass literacy and cheap books, it is now the printed versions that mothers tell their children today. The counterform eventually has triumphed.

The manuscript and printed gospels, which made Jesus primarily a figure of the past and an indefinite future, have indeed largely triumphed over the living, speaking Jesus—the New Testament writings have ultimately silenced and largely controlled him. Here, I am in fundamental agreement with Kelber. But this was a process of centuries, not of the initial composition of New Testament texts like Mark. The Gospel of Mark was composed and performed in an oral style to bring Jesus and the kingdom of God alive for listening audiences. The gospel was *not* a radical written counterform to oral memory. It was not trying to silence and control the oral tradition. But over time, as the manuscript and then print media triumphed and the New Testament became a sacred book, Jesus became a figure of the past whose death was redemptive. The written texts have in due course triumphed over the living tradition.

5

STORYTELLING IN ORAL AND WRITTEN MEDIA CONTEXTS OF THE ANCIENT MEDITERRANEAN WORLD

HOLLY E. HEARON

In his many writings, beginning with *The Oral and the Written Gospel* (1983), Werner Kelber has challenged students of the Bible to reflect on the media contexts that gave shape to the form and content of these texts and, in turn, on the interplay between these media contexts and the social dynamics that both supported and were supported by them. He further presses us to consider the implications of diverse media contexts for our understanding of the fundamental nature of these texts and, consequently, for interpretation. The implications of Kelber's work are far reaching and have prompted studies on tradition history, performance and performance criticism, the relationship between oral and written texts, the role of cultural memory in communication and the formation of identity, dynamics of orality, and book culture in early Christianity. At the twenty-fifth anniversary of the publication of *The Oral and the Written Gospel*, it is appropriate to pause and consider the impact of Kelber's work as well as avenues that his work has opened that are only beginning to be explored.

In this essay, I wish to examine the oral and the written where they intersect at the point designated "storytelling" in the ancient Mediterranean world. Kelber states that "there is little justification for limiting the transmission of traditions to the twelve apostles. . . . In addition to disciples, apostles, teachers, and prophets, the 'common folk' cannot be ruled out from the telling of stories. Those who were healed or exorcised, impressed or offended by Jesus became the potential carriers of tradition" (Kelber 1983, 21). While emphasizing the oral dimension of the transmission of tradition, Kelber also allows for the possibility of notes and other textual aids (Kelber 1983, 23). Thus Kelber's study invites a closer examination of the evidence for storytelling in oral and written media contexts as revealed in primary source materials from the first centuries B.C.E. and C.E. It is here that I will pick up the thread. Working with primary source materials, I will explore ancient oral and written storytelling, the functions it served, the interaction between oral and written media contexts, the social dynamics involved in each context, and the implications of all these issues for our understanding of storytelling in relation to the emergence of early Christian traditions.

I wish to acknowledge at the outset that this essay will not draw a distinction between storytelling and the transmission of tradition. My goal is to describe the ancient communication practices surrounding storytelling, broadly conceived. This description, in turn, could provide a context for a reexamination of the nature of the "transmission" of tradition in relation to ancient media contexts in future studies. Further, space will not permit me to enter into extended dialogue with secondary studies on the topic, a growing number of which have appeared in recent years (see, for example, Bauckham 2006; Byrskog 2002; Hearon 2004; Horsley and Draper 1999; Wire 2002). In view of the scope and emphasis of the current volume, I will focus on the work of Werner Kelber as a conversation partner for the implications of the primary source materials.

For this study, I have sought to take what might be called a "core sample" by drawing from a limited number of written texts that represent a variety of genres, authors, and social perspectives, most dating from 100 B.C.E. to 200 C.E. These include the philosophical discourses of Plato and Aristotle; the *Progymnasmata* of Theon; historical writings such as those of Dio Cassius, Strabo, and Josephus; popular novels such as *Daphnis and Chloe*; the letters of Pliny; the writings of the church father Clement of Alexandria, among others; and the New Testament. Some of these texts discuss story and storytelling explicitly, while others simply provide examples of storytelling in oral- and written-media contexts. This "core sample" is in no way comprehensive, yet it covers a cross-section of interests and goals and includes texts addressed to a variety of audiences. The sample has been further delimited by focusing on the language of μύθος, with attention to where its usage overlaps with the terms ἱστορία and λόγος.[1] This article may be considered, therefore, an exploratory effort to describe some of the features of the terrain while leaving other areas open for future studies.

The Language of Storytelling

The most common word employed for "story" in the writings under consideration is μῦθος, defined by Danker as "tale, story, legend, myth" (2000, 660). An additional note observes that μῦθος was used earlier of "narrative" or "story" "without distinction of fact or fiction, then of fictional narrative (as opposed to *logos,* the truth of history)" (Danker 2000, 660). Danker's definition echoes Theon, who defines fable (μῦθος) as "a fictitious story giving an image of truth" (Theon, *Progymnasmata* 72).[2] It is this understanding of μῦθος that is most often employed in Plato (see *Republic.* 377A.3).

Some ancient writers make a clear distinction between μῦθος and λόγος. In Longus' *Daphnis and Chloe*, the title characters "thought they heard a tale (μῦθον), not a true discourse (λόγον)" (2.7.1.1).[3] Plutarch, similarly, describes a μῦθος as a "false tale" (μῦθος λόγος ψευδὴς; *On the Fame of the Athenians* 348a). Yet Theon goes on to observe that "some of the ancient poets called fables *ainoi,* some *mythoi.* Prose writers most often call them *logoi* rather than *mythoi* and thus refer to Aesop as a *logopoios,* and Plato, in a dialogue on the soul, sometimes uses the word *mythos* elsewhere *logos*" (Theon, *Progymnasmata* 73; see Plato, *Phaedo* 60c–d).[4] Thus, the distinction between μῦθος and λόγος does not always hold fast. In *Leucippe and Clitophon*, the character Sostratus, recounting all that has happened, says, "My part of the story (τοῦ λόγου) . . . is very simple. . . . As for the rest, do you, my boy Clitophon, relate whatever the story (μῦθος) is and do not be shy about it" (Achilles Tatius 8.4.3.4; see also 8.4.2.4). Here, the two words are used interchangeably: since what is related is the story of their adventures (personal experience), it is understood to be a true account. A particularly striking example of the fluid nature of these terms is found in Clement of Alexandria, who writes, "hear a story (μῦθον) that is no mere story (μῦθον), but a true account (ὄντα λόγον) of John the apostle that has been handed down (παραδεδομένον) and preserved in memory" (μνήμῃ; *Salvation of the Rich Man* 42.1.2). This last example is important because it identifies this story (μῦθον) as a tradition that has been transmitted over time, providing evidence that stories may be counted among early Christian traditions.

Μῦθος also overlaps with the term ἱστορία. Dio Chrysostum speaks of walking through the Hippodrome and spotting various entertainers, one "telling some story (ἱστορία) or myth (μῦθος)" (Dio Chrysostum,

Discourses 21.10; cf. Aristotle, *Poetics* 23.1). It is possible that "myth" is here understood to refer to a story about the gods, yet, as was seen above, it can refer to other kinds of stories as well. Regardless, Dio recognizes both the ἱστορίαν and the μῦθον as entertainment, drawing no distinction between them. Strabo ascribes greater weight to ἱστορία as "that which is trustworthy," whereas μῦθοι (here referring to stories about Odysseus, Menelaus, or Jason) are entertaining but do not contribute to "practical wisdom" (Strabo, *Geography* 1.1.19; 1.2.8). Papias uses ἱστορία to describe various stories he has heard, including those he received from the daughters of Philip (cited by Eusebius, *Ecclesiastical History* 12:2; see also 3.39), as well as another "recorded by the Gospel of the Hebrews, about a woman who was accused of many sins in the Lord's presence" (Eusebius, *Ecclesiastical History* 3.17). Here, ἱστορία appears to be used in a way similar to μῦθος and λόγος in the quote from Clement cited above. From the perspective of Papias, these ἱστορίαι are both trustworthy and useful.[5] Writing about the novel in antiquity, Thomas Hägg observes that the Greeks did not distinguish between "an epic like the *Odyssey* and what a historian like Herodotus may narrate. The demand for 'truth' in the broad outlines and the freedom to embroider the details in one's own way apply to both" (Hägg 1983, 112). Thus the terms μῦθος, λόγος, and ἱστορία overlap in ways that make it difficult to make clear, unequivocal distinctions between them. An argument may be made for defining each term within the context of the source employing it; yet, as has been seen, even a single source may not be uniformly consistent in its usage of the terms. It is also difficult to assign a single genre to these terms. As will be shown below, these terms encompass a wide range of narrative subjects.

The language of storytelling is relatively rare in the New Testament. Λόγος, in the sense of "story," occurs in only a very few instances. Nonetheless, these instances are instructive because they describe storytelling practices among followers of Jesus. In Mark 1:45, for example, a leper approaches Jesus for healing. It is probable that the leper has heard stories about Jesus' ability to heal, as has the woman with the flow of blood (Mark 5:27). After being healed, the leper spreads the λόγος ("story"; NRSV "word"; cf. Luke 5:15; 7:17). These references point to stories that have arisen both from personal encounters *with* Jesus and from reports *about* Jesus' activities.[6] As described, these stories are circulating in a free-flowing way, with no effort to control the content, who tells the story, or the context in which the stories are told. While this theme serves Mark's purposes by describing how Jesus' power and authority comes to be widely recognized (if not understood), it also must describe the reader's experience of how stories about Jesus were told and heard. If this description violated known practices, both narrator and narrative would lose credibility.

Λόγος also appears in Matthew 28:15 in reference to the "story" that the disciples stole the body of Jesus from the tomb. This example is particularly interesting since, from the narrator's perspective, this story is clearly false (cf. Apuleius, *Golden Ass* 1.4.4). Matthew's choice of λόγος over μῦθος demonstrates the difficulty in ascribing "fact" to the former and "fiction" to the latter. A similar challenge is presented in the use of λόγος as "story" in John 21:23. The NRSV translation, "rumor," points to the porous boundaries between words and concepts. What distinguishes rumor from story? Is the report heard by the leper in the Gospel of Mark a rumor, while the λόγος Mark tells is a story? No clear distinction is made in the gospel texts (see Vansina 1965, 10). Thus, the same ambiguity that was noted in the language of storytelling in Greek texts is found also in the gospel narratives. In any case, these references demonstrate that storytelling was regarded as a familiar Christian activity and as one that was central to making Jesus known (see Hearon 2004, 19–42).

Outside the gospels, μῦθος appears in the New Testament only in the Pastoral Epistles (1, 2 Timothy and Titus) and 2 Peter. In each case, the context is polemical. These letters describe the μῦθοι of opponents as profane (1 Tim 4:7) or cleverly devised (2 Pet 1:16) and associate them with old wives' tales (1 Tim 4:7; cf. 5:13) and genealogies that promote speculation (1 Tim 1:4). Although drawing on inferential evidence, MacDonald has made a persuasive case that the reference to "old wives' tales" may allude to the story of Thecla (MacDonald 1983, 54–77). Titus 1:14 gives some suggestion of content, referring to "Jewish" stories or myths, possibly such as those found in Second Temple literature or the Mishnah (see Wire 2002 for examples); 2 Peter 1:16 more specifically refers to stories regarding the future coming of Christ (cf. 2 Thess 2:1-3). In each case, μῦθος conjures the image of something fictional or even fabulous. The various μῦθοι referred to in these letters are contrasted with faith (1 Tim 1:4), the truth (1 Tim 4:7; 2 Tim 4:4), and sound doctrine (Titus 2:1), language similar to the polemical uses described in Greek and Roman texts. In 2 Peter "cleverly devised myths" are contrasted with eyewitness testimony (ἐπόπται).[7] Yet, it is not just the "eyewitness testimony" itself that trumps the "cleverly devised myths" but the credibility of the witness (ostensibly Peter) versus the incredibility of the stories (see Barrett 1957, 347). Therefore, 2 Peter cannot be read as an absolute contrast between story and eyewitness accounts; a true story might equally trump an unreliable witness.

The use of the language of story in the New Testament reflects the usage found in the other Greek sources.[8] In particular, the overlap between μῦθος and λόγος cautions against making clear distinctions between these terms, although such distinctions may be drawn by some ancient writers for the purposes of polemic. Regardless, the language of story was clearly known to the early Christian movement and used by its members to describe traditions circulating among themselves.

Stories and Storytelling

The ubiquity of storytelling in the ancient Mediterranean world is signaled by the many kinds of stories that have been preserved in written sources. These include stories about animals and plants; stories about the origins of places and geographical features; stories describing personal adventures; stories about heroes, legendary figures, and historic events; stories about people (some of which border on gossip); love stories; ghost stories; stories of marvelous happenings and healings; stories describing the origin of customs and festivals; and stories about the gods (see Wire 2002). Sometimes the stories are identified with geographic regions or ethnic groups. For example, Theon notes that fables are often called Libyan, Sybaritic, Phrygian, or Cilician (*Progymnasmata* 73); Apuleius tells a Milesian tale (*Golden Ass* 1.1); and Josephus refers to stories about the Jews (*Against Apion* 1.229). There are also children's stories (παίδων ... μῦθον; Plato, *Timaeus* 23.b.5), old stories (μυθεύμασιν τοῖς παλαιοῖς; Ignatius, *Magnesians* 8.1.1), traditional stories (παραδεδομένων μύθων; Aristotle, *Poetics* ix.8; xiv.10), theological stories (θεολογουμένοις μύθοις; Clement of Alexandria, *Miscellanies* 5.4.21.1), unauthenticated stories (ἀδεσπότους μύθους; Josephus, *Against Apion* 1.287), and, of course, old wives tales (μῦθος ... γραός; Plato, *Gorgias* 52.a.5; 1 Tim 4:7; cf. *anilibusque fabulis* in Apuleius, *Golden Ass* 4.27). The wide range of stories encompassed in this list points to the difficulty of assigning to "story" and "storytelling" a single form, content, context, or purpose.[9]

The stories recorded traverse oral and written media contexts. In some cases, the kind of story told is determined by literary genre or narrative function. For example, Ovid sets out to tell the stories of classical mythology and in many instances uses personal narrative as the literary device for the telling of particular stories. A similar technique is employed in *Leucippe and Clitophon* and *Daphnis and Chloe*, where the characters relate stories of their personal adventures as a means of moving the plot forward. Although employed as a literary device, the telling of personal stories likely reflects oral media contexts where personal stories would be among the most common stories told, particularly as they became part of a cultural repertoire of stories that could be drawn upon as occasion warranted (see Stahl 1989, 12–28). In the gospels, the stories told all revolve around the primary character, Jesus, and show him performing marvelous deeds or besting his opponents in debate. Although these Jesus stories serve the purposes of continuous written narratives, stories of different lengths could be expected to be told about individuals, heroes, and gods in oral media contexts (see Hearon 2004, 19–42, 97–100, 199–220; Wire 2002). In other cases, the stories told in written media contexts seem to more nearly imitate oral media contexts. This is particularly true in those texts that do not set out to tell stories. It is here that the greatest variety of stories is found, entering into the written text as asides, examples, or simply part of the conversation. In this way, for example, Pliny tells stories about notable figures in Roman life, but also personal stories, ghost stories (Pliny, *Letters* 7.27), and a true story *(materiam veram)* that he says "sounds very like a fable" *(simillimam fictae*; *Letters* 9.33.1). Clement of Alexandria tells the stories of two minstrels who were legendary for their skill (*Exhortation to the Greeks* 1.1), a story about John the apostle (*Salvation of the Rich Man* 42.1.2), stories about Celtic women (*Christ the Educator* 3.4.27.2), and, ironically, a number of stories about the pagan gods that serve his arguments. Thus there is interplay between oral and written media contexts both in terms of the kind of stories told and the way in which the stories are told.

In the written sources, love of stories (φιλομυθεῖ) is ascribed to the illiterate and uneducated, who are said to be like children, and to the half-educated, whose reasoning faculty is not yet fully developed (Strabo, *Geography* 1.2.8). Reflecting this perspective, Plato's "stranger" tells "young Socrates" to "please pay careful attention to my story (μύθος), just as if you were a child; and anyway you are not much too old for children's tales" (Plato, *The Statesman* 268.E.4). Women, also, are described as being especially fond of stories (φιλόμυθον; Achilles Tatius, *Leucippe and Clitophon* 5.5.1.1), although Longinus remarks, "Homer shows that, as genius ebbs, it is the love of romance (φιλόμυθον) that characterizes old age" (Longinus, *On the Sublime* 9.11). Certainly, popular novels such as *Chaereas and Callirhoe* appear to be aimed at mass appeal, being filled with rustic characters, adventure, scandal, and romance. Yet these texts were read not by the masses (who could not read) but rather by the literate elite and their friends, who were also responsible for recording the stories.[10] Further, primary sources reveal that Augustus would call for a storyteller when he could not sleep (Suetonius, *Augustus* 78.2), that Pliny recommended a story he heard over supper about a quite ordinary boy to a friend as a subject fit for a poem (Pliny, *Letters* 9.33), and that Ovid viewed storytelling as a frequent activity among elite men and women. Thus, despite popular stereotypes, class is not an obvious indicator in the telling, content, or enjoyment of stories. It is an activity found throughout the ancient Mediterranean world, crossing both social and media boundaries.

Social Functions of Ancient Storytelling

While the ancient stories serve the written media contexts in which they now appear, the written texts themselves often identify other functions of storytelling. Among the most common is entertainment. Dio Chrysostum's encounter with storytellers entertaining the crowds as he strolls through the Hippodrome has already been noted above (Dio Chrysostum, *Discourses* 21.20; see also Pliny, *Letters* 2.20.1). Storytellers also could be employed for entertainment in private settings. Suetonius reports that Augustus invited not only musicians and actors to perform at dinner parties, but "especially storytellers" (*frequentius aretalogos*; Suetonius, *Augustus* 74.1). In addition, stories served as entertainment in informal storytelling contexts. In *The Golden Ass,* a story told by Aristomenes is said to have "shortened this long and weariful journey" (Apuleius, *Golden Ass* 1.20), while Ovid describes how "the daughters of Minyas while spinning wool at home tell stories to one another to pass the time" (Ovid, *Metamorphoses* 4.32). In Xenophon's *An Ephesian Tale,* an old woman at an inn offers a story to a drinking party of men (3.9; see also Longus, *Daphnis and Chloe* 2.32). In all of these examples, an oral storytelling context is assumed. However, Apuleius can also describe his written story of the golden ass as an effort to "delight your kindly ears" (Apuleius, *Golden Ass* 1.1), perhaps in anticipation of the story being read aloud to a listening audience.

Stories also could be told for purposes of education. Theon notes that μῦθοι (stories) are also called αἶνοι (stories with a moral) because they provide παραίνεσις (advice): "The whole point is useful instruction" (Theon, *Progymnasmata* 73). Plato encourages the use of stories for instilling values in young boys, because they "charm them into belief" (Plato, *Laws* 840.C.1; see also *Republic* 378.E.1). The result is that they will "honor the gods and their fathers and mothers, and not . . . hold their friendship with one another in light esteem" (Plato, *Republic* 386.B.9; cf. 377.A.3). Here, the entertaining quality of stories is viewed as a means to facilitate learning; they are, Plato observes, more pleasing than argumentation or discourse (Plato, *Protagoras* 320.C.3). Strabo, in a similar vein, comments, "It is fondness for tales, then, that induces children to give their attention to narratives and more and more to take part in them" (Strabo, *Geography*

1.2.8; so also Kelber 1983, 163). Perhaps for this very reason, ancient writers caution against a careless use of stories. Plato states that children should be protected from hearing "chance stories (μῦθοι πλασθέντας) fashioned by chance teachers and so to take into their minds opinions for the most part contrary to those that we shall think it desirable for them to hold when they are grown up" (Plato, *Republic* 377.B.6; 391.E.12; cf. Strabo, *Geography* 1.2.8). This is why, says Plato, storymakers (μυθοποιοῖς) should be censored (Plato, *Republic* 377.C.1; 392.A.9). Plutarch likewise remarks, "For just as seals leave their impression in soft wax, so are lessons impressed upon the minds of children when they are young"; therefore stories (μύθους) must be chosen with care (Plutarch, *The Education of Children* 5). Plato's use of the term μυθοποιοί (storymakers) suggests that these didactic stories were generated in oral media contexts such as the classroom, home, or nursery.

The comments of these writers reveal their awareness of the capacity of stories to shape identity. Strabo in particular points to the way in which stories invite the hearer to enter into the narrative, shaping identity through identification with the story. It is precisely this effect that is described in *Leucippe and Clitophon* when Clitophon recalls the story (μῦθος) of Niobe and recognizes in her grief his own sense of despair (3.15.6.2). It is a story, in Kelber's words, that has found an echo in the heart and mind (Kelber 1983, 24). The story of The Good Samaritan in the Gospel of Luke (10:25-37) is narrated precisely for the purposes of inviting identification ("Go and do likewise"; v. 37). Stories can also be used to establish a sense of shared identity between storyteller and audience. In *Leucippe and Clitophon*, two characters form a bond when, after exchanging stories about their reasons for traveling, they realize that they are both in exile (2.33–34). These stories shared become a means of creating a sense of common identity or community. This common identity also can be evoked by the telling of stories for the purposes of offering comfort. In *The Golden Ass*, an old woman tells a young woman who has been kidnapped by a band of thieves "a pleasant old wives' tale (*anilibusque fabulis*) to put away all thy sorrow and to revive thy spirits" (4.27). Similarly, mothers are said to tell stories (μῦθοι) in order to comfort and encourage their children (Plutarch, *Theseus* 23.3). In these instances, the storyteller identifies with the audience and establishes a shared identity through the act of storytelling.

Stories can be used in a variety of contexts as the basis for drawing morals (Plato, *Gorgias* 524.A.9). Pliny offers such an example in a letter to Junius Avitus, where he tells a story about dining with a man who served the best dishes to himself, reserving the cheaper food for his company. "The point of this story," Pliny writes, "is to prevent a promising young man like yourself from being taken in by this extravagance under the guise of economy" (Pliny, *Letters* 2.6.6). Another example may be found in Ovid's *Metamorphoses*. When someone mocks a story about the gods, Lelex, a man "ripe in mind and years," counters with a story of how an old man and woman welcomed gods in disguise into their home (8.612). A less-exalted example may be found in Apuleius' *The Golden Ass*, where an "old bawd" tells the baker's wife a story about a clever lover in order to point out the defects of the woman's own "fearful lover" (9.16). These stories are exchanged in social contexts but are told for the purpose of offering instruction. So, as Strabo observes, stories can be used both to promote good behavior and to inspire fear (Strabo, *Geography* 1.2.8; see also Plato, *Laws* 865.D.5; *Republic* 330.D.7).[11]

The functions of edification, identification, comfort, and exhortation come together in storytelling associated with religious instruction. Plato and Plutarch, for example, observe (negatively) that adults are drawn to worship of the gods because they first hear the stories of these gods when they are children from mothers and nurses (Plato, *Laws* 10.887D; Plutarch, *Theseus* 23.3). Stories were also told at festivals in celebration of the gods (Plutarch, *Theseus* 23.3) or could be performed as dramas (Clement of Alexandria, *Exhortation to the Greeks* 1.2) or dances (Longus, *Daphnis and Chloe* 2.37.1.3). Hymns were another way in which stories were communicated (Clement, *Exhortation to the Greeks* 1.2; Achilles Tatius, *Leucippe and Clitophon* 2.2.1). Plato, speaking for Socrates, describes how he composed a hymn to a god whose festival was being celebrated. He goes on to suggest that, as a poet, he was also expected to produce stories or myths (μύθοι), but since he had no talent in that area he drew on the fables of Aesop (Plato, *Phaedo* 61.B.4.1). Clement of Alexandria mentions reliefs in which Egyptians portrayed the myths (μύθοι) of the gods, pointing to the importance of visual imagery as a means of relating story (Clement of Alexandria, *Miscellanies* 5.21.1; cf. Achilles Tatius, *Leucippe and Clitophon* 5.4.1.4). These examples point to the variety of ways in which storytelling occurred not only in oral media contexts, but visual contexts as well. Religious stories also are found in written texts that were read aloud. The narratives of the New Testament portray scenes in which the Hebrew Scriptures are read aloud in the context of the synagogue (see Luke 4:16-20) and also personal study (see Acts 8:26-34). The gospels provide additional examples of religious stories that were written; however, it is not wholly clear whether these texts were read aloud in the context of worship, performed as dramas, or employed as memory devices in the period of roughly 60–150 C.E. (see J. Dewey 1995b, 52). The examples from Papias and Clement of Alexandria indicate that, in any case, these written texts did not replace unwritten story or the practice of storytelling (see Kelber 1983, 93).

A final function to be identified within the limits of this essay is the use of storytelling for persuasion. Strabo remarks, "For in dealing with a crowd of women, at least, or with any promiscuous mob, a philosopher cannot influence them by reason or exhort them to reverence, piety and faith . . . this cannot be aroused without myths (μύθοποίας) and marvels" (Strabo, *Geography* 1.2.8; cf. Plato, *Phaedrus* 243.A.4). This principle is illustrated by a story recorded in Dio Cassius' *Roman History*. Dio relates how a mob of debtors took possession of a hill; in an effort to defuse the situation, Agrippa addressed the mob with a story (μύθος) about the mutual dependence of the various parts of the body on one another in order to illustrate how the abundance of the rich also supports the poor (Dio Cassius, *Roman History* 4.1.10.9). The story had the desired effect and the mob dispersed. However, stories could also produce the opposite effect, pitting the claims of one person or group against those of another (as in Titus 1:4; 2 Peter 1:16). In *Against Apion*, Josephus critiques Manetho because he, "under the pretext of recording fables (γράψειν τὰ μυθευόμενα) and current reports (λεγόμενα) about the Jews . . . took the liberty of introducing some incredible tales (λόγους ἀπιθάνους)" (1.229). Clement of Alexandria might be accused of the same thing when he critiques the stories told by the Greeks: "For surely, after believing in the poetic legend (μύθῳ . . . ποιητικῷ) which records that Minos the Cretan was 'a familiar friend of Zeus,' you will not disbelieve that we, who have becomes disciples of God, have entered into the really true wisdom" (Clement of Alexandria, *Exhortation to the Greeks* 11.112.2.1; cf. *Miscellanies* 1.11.52.2; Ignatius, *Magnesians* 8.1). Competition among storytellers did not always reach the heights of polemic. In *Leucippe and Clitophon*, two characters exchange stories in a kind of friendly contest: one warns the other not to underestimate the ability of a gnat to torment an elephant; the other retorts with a story about the gnat becoming caught in a spider web (2.21.5.4). A similar exchange is suggested in Longus' *Daphnis and Chloe* when old men "a little whittled with wine" compare stories from their youth: "Here one bragged that he had killed a wolf, here another that he had been second to Pan alone in the skill and art of piping" (2.32). The examples here show that stories could serve persuasive purposes in both written and oral media contexts.

Storytelling in Oral and Written Media Contexts

There is good evidence that the ancient authors of written texts conceived of their works as just that: written texts. The narrator in *Daphnis and*

Chloe speaks of having "a mighty instigation to write something" (Longus, *Daphnis and Chloe*, Proem 2). Pliny speaks in his letters of laboring over written compositions (Pliny, *Letters* 1.8). Apuleius begs that the reader "not scorn to look upon this Egyptian paper written with a ready pen of Nile reeds" (Apuleius, *Golden Ass* 1.1). Two of the canonical gospels self-consciously describe their narratives as written texts (Luke 1:3; John 20:30-31). Kelber is thus correct to claim that "in Mark textuality asserts itself in its own right, decisively shaping the oral legacy according to the imperative of the written medium" (Kelber 1983, 91). Yet there is also good evidence of the close relationship between spoken word and written text. Pliny, for example, offers a story he has heard to a friend so that he might turn it into a poem (Pliny, *Letters* 9.33). The first-person narrator of *The Golden Ass*, having been turned into a donkey, regrets that he lacks materials to write down the story of Cupid and Psyche: "but I, poor ass, not standing far off was not a little sorry in that I lacked pen and book to write so worthy a tale (*fabulum*)" (4.25; see Sedgwick 1947, 290). Papias is said to have set forth "other matters that came to him from the unwritten tradition (παραδόσεως ἀγράφου)" (Eusebius, *Ecclesiastical History* 3.39). This use of oral stories as the basis of written texts draws attention to the borderland that exists between the two media contexts, that broad place where the one overlaps the other.

Letters also belong to this borderland to the degree that letters stand in for absent presence. Kelber observes that letters provide a forum by which personal authority can be extended into written verbalization (Kelber 1983, 140). In this respect, letters can effect a kind of face-to-face exchange, building on and furthering established social relationships in particular times and places. This is evident from the tone and content of Pliny's letters, where he offers advice, makes inquiries into personal affairs, and evokes shared memories. His letters also can serve as an occasion for storytelling: "Have your copper ready and hear a first-rate story (*fabulum*), or rather stories (*fabulas*), for the new one has reminded me of others. . . . Are two stories (*fabulae*) enough, or do you want another according to the rule of three?" (Pliny, *Letters* 2.20.1). Employing the street cry of an itinerant storyteller, Pliny evokes an oral storytelling context. This context is, within a written letter, a literary fiction, and the social parameters that describe an oral storytelling context are absent. Nonetheless, Pliny, as storyteller, is not a fiction but a presence activated by the letter for the friend to whom the letter is addressed. Thus the boundary between oral and written story in letters is somewhat porous. Novels may strive for a similar effect. Apuleius, for example, writes in order to "delight your kindly ears with a pleasant history" (Apuleius, *Golden Ass* 1.1). In this case, however, the literary fiction is more evident: Apuleius writes for an anonymous audience, where no established relationship between author and audience is assumed. In this case, the text is the all.

Written texts read aloud may also be said to overlap with oral story. Theon asks, "Who would not take pleasure in *akroasis* (hearing a work read aloud)?" (Theon, *Progymnasmata* 61). Pliny, similarly, remarks to a friend, "You may say that you have authors as eloquent whose works can be read at home; but the fact is that you can read them any time. . . . Besides, we are always being told that the spoken word is much more effective" (Pliny, *Letters* 2.3.9). Both of these comments underscore the impact of face-to-face interaction, where delivery, expression, appearance, and gesture work in concert with the spoken word to move an audience (so Kelber 1983, 75). Readers provided entertainment at dinner parties (Pliny, *Letters* I.xv.2; Suetonius, *Augustus* 78.2), and the Emperor Augustus was said to call in a reader (*lectoribus*) or storyteller (*fabulatoribus*) when he could not sleep (Suetonius, *Augustus* 78.2). This passing comment in Suetonius suggests that an oral reading could serve a purpose similar to that of storytelling (in this case entertainment); less clear is whether these two activities were perceived and experienced in the same way. A reader, for example, would be restricted by the number of texts in hand; a storyteller by the stories available at recall. While both might be judged by their delivery, expression, appearance, and gesture, the storyteller could, in addition, adapt the story to the interests and taste of the audience; a reader would be expected to present the text as written.

Writers could, and did, rely on the response of an audience to a public reading for the purposes of revision. Pliny read his writings in public, because "the reader is made more keenly critical of his own work" and "receives suggestions from different members [of the audience], and failing this, he can infer their various opinions from their expressions, glances, nods, applause, murmurs, and silence, signs which make clear the distinction between their critical judgment and polite assent" (Pliny, *Letters* 5.3.7). Yet Pliny's ultimate aim is the publication of a well-written text; embedded in this is a clear sense of authorship. Pliny chides a friend for withholding from publication works that have been read aloud, noting, "Some of your verses have broken free in spite of you and have become more widely known; unless you recall them to be incorporated in the whole, like runaway slaves they will find someone else to claim them" (Pliny, *Letters* 2.10.1). Pliny's comment reveals how a written text, when read aloud, can take on new life in an oral context, where it circulates freely. In this case, the consequence is unintended; Pliny is eager to recapture the verses and restore them to rightful ownership. In contrast, the daughters of Minyas share no such concern as they exchange stories, nor does Pliny when he shares a story about a boy and a dolphin with his friend. These stories are in the public domain, as it were, passed on by word of mouth and from one generation to another (Ovid, *Metamorphoses* 12.540; Euripides, *frag.* 488). Similarly, no sense of individual authorship is attached to the "unwritten traditions" recorded by Papias; these traditions are represented as the collective possession of the community. Thus, while written texts read aloud share with oral stories the spoken word and the effects created by delivery, a distinction exists between written texts to which individual authorship could be ascribed and texts that circulated by word of mouth, where ownership is held, in effect, by the community.[12]

Much has been made of public reading as a means of access to written texts by a largely illiterate public (see Shiner 2003, 39–40; Gamble 1995, 205). Yet, it is uncertain whether large numbers of people had access to many such hearings. When Pliny, for example, holds or attends a reading, it is clearly for a limited and elite audience (Pliny, *Letters* 1.13.5; 2.19; 3.18; see Harris 1989, 226). Some readings go on for as long as three days (Pliny, *Letters* 4.27.1), a period few workers could afford to take off for the sake of such enjoyment. Pliny also complains that those who attended the readings sat about "gossiping and wasting time when they could be giving their attention" (Pliny, *Letters* 1.13.2). Even a literate audience, with time on their hands, could view public readings as occasions for socializing rather than opportunities to hear a good story or speech.

At least some public reading took place within first-century Christian communities. Gamble asserts that most Christian communities had access to someone who could read (Gamble 1995, 9); certainly, Paul expected his letters to be read aloud (1 Thess 5:27), although this may have been done by the one who delivered the letter (a person who was not necessarily a member of the community). The writing of the gospels also presupposes that they were read aloud, although no evidence remains to specify in what contexts.[13] Nonetheless, it is difficult to know how great a role reading aloud played within these early Christian communities. The sheer presence of written texts argues for little. Carr states that "copies of texts served as solidified reference points for recitation and memorization of the tradition. . . . But they were not for the uninitiated. Few of the literate would have progressed to the point where they would be able or motivated to use such texts to access traditions they did not already know" (Carr 2005, 6;

see also Kelber 1983, 17). This suggests that whatever stories, traditions, or teachings were found in Paul's letters and the gospels were known through aural reception and oral circulation and were not wholly dependent upon the written text.

However broad the borderland between oral and written media contexts, there is a point at which distinctions between them begin to emerge. These distinctions can be described by three changes that occur when oral story becomes written text. The first of these changes is illustrated by the example from Pliny mentioned earlier (*Letters* 9.33). Pliny writes to Caninius Rufus that he has "come across a true story (*materiam veram*) which sounds very like a fable (*simillimam fictae*)" and proposes that it would be a suitable subject for poetry. Pliny says that he heard the story over dinner "when various marvelous tales (*varia miracula*) were being circulated" (Pliny, *Letters* 9.33.1) The story is of a young boy who, while swimming with his playmates, was lifted up on the back of a dolphin, carried out to sea, and later returned safely to land. Pliny reports that "the tale spread through the town; everyone ran up to stare at the boy as a prodigy, ask to hear his story and repeat it" (Pliny, *Letters* 9.33.1, 5). As spoken word, this story had a wide circulation, being repeated by those who witnessed the event, the boy himself, "the town," Pliny's acquaintances, and Pliny himself.[14] Yet its oral existence is fragile and fleeting. Thus Plato can observe in the course of discussion how an argument defeated vanishes and is "lost, like a tale (μύθος) that is told" (Plato, *Philebus* 14.A.4). Story spoken is always on the verge of extinction; without human agency to give it voice, it cannot continue to exist. Once written, however, the story will continue to exist as long as the pages do not crumble. This new material reality represents the first major change in the shift from oral story to written text: the written text is not bound by time.

The timeless quality of written text points to a second change that occurs when oral story becomes written text. Stories unspoken may exist through time only so long as they are preserved in memory. The story told by Pliny continues to exist because it is told again and again, passed from memory to memory. Clement of Alexandria, quoted earlier, makes mention of a story about John the apostle that, he says, was preserved in this way (Clement of Alexandria, *Salvation of the Rich Man* 4.1.2). Once it has been written, however, an unspoken story is no longer dependent upon memory for preservation or on the social referents necessary to sustain its memory over time. Translated into written text, the story takes on an existence not only outside of time but also beyond the control exercised by social memory. Thus, while spoken story is controlled by the persons and contexts necessary to preserve its memory and shape its narrative, the absence of hearers "permits the writer to effectively control both the text and its readers" (Kelber 1983, 115).

This distinction becomes clearer when references to memory in relation to oral and written story are examined. Oral storytellers, both professional and informal, held collections of stories at their recall. In Ovid's *Metamorphoses*, for example, one of the daughters of Minyas muses "which she should tell of many tales, for very many she knew" (4.42), while Eusebius says that Papias inherited stories that belonged to "unwritten tradition" or memory (Eusebius, *Ecclesiastical History* 3.39).[15] Similarly, Pliny writes that a new story about Regulus reminds him of other stories at his recall (Pliny, *Letters* 2.20.1). In this case, the stories are more nearly gossip, yet they clearly belong to a repertoire of stories enumerating examples of Regulus' outrageous behavior. The *rhētōr*, too, could be expected to have stories held in memory. Theon advises learning fables of the ancients by heart so that the *rhētōr* might develop a simple and natural style for the telling of tales. He indicates that fables can be expanded "by lengthening the remarks of the characters and by describing a river or something of that sort" and that they can likewise be condensed. Several conclusions also may be applied to any single fable (Theon, *Progymnasmata* 74–75).[16] These fables, then, seem to serve as a template while the telling of the story is a creative process, not necessarily a recitation of words fixed on a page.[17] Yet Theon urges students to engage in daily writing in order to improve their style (Theon, *Progymnasmata* 61)—these stories, then, are not preserved by the exigencies of social contexts but by the exigencies of style and discourse. Thus a distinction begins to appear between oral and written media contexts. This distinction becomes clearer when Quintilian urges that "our reading must be almost as thorough as if we were actually transcribing what we read" (Quintilian, *Orations* 10.1.20). Indeed, he says, the virtue of the written text is that "we can reread a passage again and again if we are in doubt about it or wish to fix it in the memory" (Quintilian, *Orations* 10.1.19). Memory, in this case, is dependent not upon social referents, but upon the written text. A similar example is described by Pliny, who writes that Iaseus had "an amazing memory, so that he [could] repeat his extempore speeches word for word without a single mistake" (Pliny, *Letters* 2.3.2; 3.5.11).[18] Although Iaseus is reproducing a speech without aid of a manuscript (an oral text reproduced orally), his feat of memory resembles more nearly Quintilian than Theon. It is the text that provides the foundation for memory.

This distinction between spoken and written story holds when one considers the reverse side of memory: forgetting.[19] In *Leucippe and Clitophon,* Clitophon reports, "When I came to the part of the story in which Melite was concerned, I gave such a turn to the sequence of events that I made them appear greatly to the advantage of my continence, yet without any departure from the truth. . . . Only one thing I omitted in all my adventures, and that was the somewhat delicate matter of my connection with Melite after the events just mentioned" (8.5.2–3). Here Clitophon finds it convenient to omit a part of his story for purposes of preserving social harmony. The omission remains undetected and his relationship with those present is preserved. An act of forgetting in Ovid's *Metamorphoses* produces a different result. Telepolemus challenges Nestor for having forgotten to speak in praise of Hercules, to which Nestor replies, "Why do you force me to remember wrongs?" (12.536). Clearly the omission of Hercules from the narrative has been deliberate on the part of Nestor; yet in a clash of social worlds, he gives offense to Telepolemus, for whom Hercules remains a hero. These two examples demonstrate how acts of forgetting in the context of spoken word have a direct and immediate social impact. If these examples are translated into an encounter between a reader and a written text, the effect is different. In the case of the first illustration, the omission will similarly be undetected, but any social impact will be secondary;[20] assuming there is a social and geographic distance between author and reader, there is no social contract to be violated. In the case of the second illustration, the omission will be noted, but there is no person to engage; only a text, which may be thrown onto the fire. Thus, while acts of memory and forgetting may be ascribed both to spoken words and written texts, the function of memory and the effect created by forgetting draw attention to the differences rather than the similarities between these two media contexts.

This separation of the written text from the frameworks of memory points to the third change that occurs in the transition from orality to writing. The stories cited in this essay are accessible today because someone has written them down, not because someone has told them to us. Stories written no longer depend on social exchange in order to be brought from memory into existence. Oral story, by contrast, exists *only* in the context of face-to-face exchange. As Ong observes, "Spoken words are always modifications of a total situation which is more than verbal. They never occur alone, in a context simply of words" (Ong 1982, 101). Thus, for example, modern readers cannot separate Pliny's hearing of the story from the context in which he heard it or those people from whom he heard it (Kelber 1983, 92). In contrast, writes Kelber, "An author . . . writes for readers who are normally absent at the time and place of writing" (Kelber 1983, 15). As readers, the "other" from whom we hear the story is a written page; the inflection of voice given to the text is our own. The text, for all the imaginative qualities it inspires, does not look us in the eye or lean close to emphasize a point. It requires of us no social niceties of etiquette; it does not know our secrets; it will not tell to others how we responded to its tale (see Kelber 1983, 75).

These distinctions between storytelling in oral and written media contexts invite consideration of storytelling in contexts where no written word was immediately accessible and the effect of the written word was experienced only indirectly, if at all. These may be described as "informal" as opposed to "formal" (or professional) storytelling events. Our evidence for these storytelling events is, ironically, embedded in written texts, but the contexts described are clearly oral: "Come, then, just as if we were telling stories or fables (μύθῳ μυθολογοῦντες) and had ample leisure" (Plato, *Republic* 376.D.9). These written remains reveal both men and women telling stories that tend to revolve around personal experiences, the experiences of others, or the gods (see Hearon 2004, 199–213). In this respect, the stories are localized and closely tied to day-to-day experience or the religious worldview that frames that experience. A frequent setting for the telling of stories is meals, during "the time when wine is going around" (Achilles Tatius, *Leucippe and Clitophon* 8.4; see also Apuleius, *Golden Ass* 2.19–31; Longus, *Daphnis and Chloe* 3.9), or other times of leisure such as traveling on a journey (Longus, *Daphnis and Chloe* 3.22.4.4; Ovid, *Metamorphoses* 14.158–441). The home is another common setting for the telling of stories: over housework (Ovid, *Metamorphoses* 4.32), while strolling in the garden (Achilles Tatius, *Leucippe and Clitophon* 1.17.3.2), or watching over children (Plato, *Laws* 887.D.2). The storytelling is often described as reciprocal, that is, with first one and then another individual telling a story (Achilles Tatius, *Leucippe and Clitophon* 8.15; Longus, *Daphnis and Chloe* 2.32, 3.9; Xenophon, *An Ephesian Tale* 5.1) and, occasionally, may involve one storyteller trying to outdo the other (*Daphnis and Chloe* 2.32; *Leucippe and Clitophon* 2.20–21). This evidence points to the existence, at certain times and places, of a distinctly oral media context in which stories are told and retold for the purposes of entertainment, comfort, encouragement, edification, and the shaping of identity.

While stories told were recorded and preserved in written texts, evidence suggests that stories could circulate in oral media contexts without reference to written media. A good example is found in the first chapter of the Gospel of John (1:40-46). Here, Andrew has been introduced to Jesus by John the Baptist. Andrew, in turn, goes and tells his brother Simon. The next day, Jesus encounters Philip, who is from the same village as Simon and Andrew (one wonders whether Philip has heard about Jesus from them). Philip then goes and finds Nathaniel (also, perhaps, from the same village) and introduces him to Jesus. This passage is illuminating because it suggests the social web along which a story might travel: first from relative to relative, then to someone from the same region or town, who tells it to a relative or acquaintance or even a tradesman from yet another town. Ancient stories also were passed down from parent to child: Telepolemus has heard stories about Hercules from his father (Ovid, *Metamorphoses* 12.536), while Melanippe was taught a story by her mother (Euripides, *frag.* 488). They might also be learned from friends (Pliny, *Letters* 9.33). A remarkable account is reported by Josephus of a woman named Mary who, in the midst of the first Jewish revolt in Jerusalem, slaughters her own child, crying out, "Come, be thou food for me, to the rebels an avenging fury, and to the world a tale (μύθος) such as alone is wanting to the calamities of the Jews" (Josephus, *Jewish War* 6.207). The latter is a stunning example of how certain events could be expected to give rise to memory and to story.

Storytelling and the Emergence of Traditions in Early Christian Communities

Kelber writes, "the challenge posed by orality–literacy studies is to reimagine the life of tradition, constituted by both chirographs and speech, and its appropriation by the gospel chirograph" (Kelber 1997, xxii). The ubiquity of storytelling in the ancient world points to the importance of story for any study of tradition. The question, however, must be reframed: How does an understanding of story and storytelling in oral and written media contexts of the ancient Mediterranean world challenge us to reimagine the life of tradition and its appropriation by the gospel chirograph?

The emergence of stories about Jesus must surely have begun with a spoken word; indeed, stories may well represent the earliest incipient Jesus traditions. Pliny's encounter with the story of the boy and the dolphin supports passing references in the gospels to how stories about Jesus could have gained wide and rapid circulation (see Mark 1:45; Matt 4:24). Quite possibly a repertoire of "Jesus stories" emerged, associated with Jews in urban and rural areas of Galilee and Judea. To understand the transmission of these stories, one must consider established social networks. The evidence cited earlier points to transmission within extended kinship groups: from sibling to sibling, neighbor to neighbor, friend to friend. However, stories also would have been overheard by slaves and strangers, thus transporting the stories to new circles of acquaintance. Sometimes they would be passed from stranger to stranger as people were drawn together in shared social circumstances.

Kelber writes that "the concept of *social identification* allows characteristic speech forms . . . to serve as focus of identification for more than one social group. The question is thereby raised about the form-critical thesis of *setting in life,* the notion that forms of speech are tied to specific social settings" (Kelber 1983, 25–26). The settings for storytelling identified earlier are notable precisely for their lack of specificity. They are, above all, settings in which people find themselves able to enjoy a moment of leisure or in need of entertainment when there is work to be done. Setting, therefore, is less about *place* than it is about *group:* Who is present, what kind of story is called for by the particular group that is present, and what social need(s) is the story being called to serve? "What is summoned for transmission is . . . selected for immediate relevancy, not primarily for historical reasons" (Kelber 1983, 71, 147).

The now oft-cited example of Pliny is suggestive of at least one way that oral story becomes written text: a story told, then captured in writing; a written story read aloud, then retold. At what point the writing began is impossible to determine. The storytelling described *within* the gospels consistently occurs in oral media contexts; in contrast, the gospels represent a self-conscious decision to embrace written media contexts (so, especially, Luke 1:1-4 and John 20:30-31; 21:24-25). However, the evidence presented here suggests that, like other written texts, the gospels may have been read aloud and revised in response to nods or applause along with other signs of approbation or approval.[21] Such a possibility is suggested by textual remains with their "variant" readings. Thus written stories, at whatever point they emerged, are not wholly removed from oral media contexts nor, as has been shown, does their emergence put an end to the circulation of "unwritten tradition." Oral and written exist both side by side and in the borderland between them.

If oral and written story co-exist in a complex relationship, how is the one to be viewed in relation the other? The evidence from this short study suggests that both oral and written story also must be understood in relation to group. For Pliny and his peers, written story is a sign of status, a form of expression, and a means of engaging one another. For others, written story is something to be heard, through a reader who mediates the text. Yet the written text may echo that which the audience already knows as oral story (Carr 2005, 6). Thus the authority ascribed to the written text may have less to do with the text itself than with the correspondence of the text to that which is already known. Less clear is whether authority would be ascribed to the text simply on the basis of its chirographic nature. If that authority is viewed as representative of an oppressive regime (as, for example, an imperial decree) the written text may be received with derision. A similar pattern may describe response to oral story. For some, it may represent a form of expression and a means of engaging others. For others, it may be eschewed as an activity associated with children or those who lack maturity.

The emergence of story as written tradition, then, is far more complex than simply movement from one medium to another. The writing down of stories about Jesus reflects a blending of media contexts as well as a blending of social worlds. It also may represent a divide in social worlds. Written stories, which reach audiences across geographical boundaries, mark movement away from local communities. One effect of such a move is to challenge the authority embedded in individuals in local communities: prophets, teachers, elders, storytellers—many of whom were women (so Kelber 1983, 98–99, 147; see Hearon and Maloney 2004). Although writing does not silence these voices, it does represent the potential for a shift of authority away from the local community to someone or something outside that community. This would have an impact most directly on those whose access to written texts must be mediated through another person.

A second effect of the emergence of written stories about Jesus revolves around remembering and forgetting. When story begins to transcend geographical boundaries, whose stories are remembered and whose are forgotten? In the telling of those stories recorded, whose interests are remembered and whose are forgotten? Written texts have no less interest in what is remembered or forgotten than an individual or community, yet it is not as easy to challenge the memory of a written text. Unknown to us, but worth considering, is whether the gospels, or other early written texts, were subjected to a process of revision through community applause or approbation. This introduces another layer of complexity to the process of remembering and forgetting.

A third effect of the emergence of written stories about Jesus is movement toward a reconceptualization of the self in relation to community. With written story, the possibility exists for the authority that governs the community to no longer necessarily be rooted in individuals who reside locally, but in a text that transcends geographical boundaries and that is subject to multiple interpretations. On the one hand, this allows individuals in diverse geographical locations to assume more nearly a common identity to which they can appeal on the basis of this written text. Something similar can be achieved through the effective use of visual images—a technique of which the Romans were well aware. On the other hand, precisely because written texts are subject to multiple interpretations, people in diverse geographical locations may begin to find themselves identifying not with those who live nearest to them but with those who reside five-hundred miles away. The emergence of written story, then, has the potential to reorganize social relations to the degree that it transcends the authority of individuals embedded in local communities.

It is easy to underestimate the complexity of the diverse media contexts present in the ancient Mediterranean world. This brief overview of story and storytelling has attempted to reveal some of the distinctive features of, specifically, oral and written media contexts and to call attention to the broad expanse of borderland where they came into points of contact, interplay, and exchange. It has also endeavored to emphasize the complex web of social relationships that govern the use of these media and that influenced how they were received. It is as we gain further insight into not only these media and the ways in which they interacted, but their use in the construction of identity, community, and power, that we will begin to understand, also, the complex path leading to the emergence of early Christian traditions.

6

VICE CATALOGUES AS ORAL-MNEMONIC CUES
A Comparative Study of the Two-Ways Tradition in the *Didache* and Parallels from the Perspective of Oral Tradition

Jonathan A. Draper

In their well-researched and important book, *The Didache: Its Jewish Sources and Its Place in Early Judaism and Christianity* (2002), Huub van de Sandt and the late David Flusser conclude that a written Greek source, which they designate the "Greek Two Ways," lies behind all the various sources of the Two-Ways tradition. This "pristine pre-*Didache* form" was a Jewish text that was subsequently edited by the addition of the Jesus tradition in 1:3b–2:1 and various elements in 6:2–16 to define the Christian community over against Judaism (van de Sandt and Flusser 2002, 34). Van de Sandt and Flusser argue that the *Syntagma Doctrinae* and the *Fides Nicanae* (variants of the same text, ca. 350 C.E.), and the Two Ways in the *Vita Shenoudi* (ca. 450 C.E.)[1] are all independent and earlier variants of the same (textual) tradition represented by the *Doctrina apostolorum* and *Didache* (final form ca. 80–100 C.E.). In the text as presented by the last two witnesses, *Doctrina* represents the earlier form, though as a Latin edition rather than a strict translation. The *Epistle of Barnabas*, on the other hand, represents a later reworked form of the source found in *Doctrina* and the *Didache*. This reconstructed Greek Two Ways Jewish source can then be identified and compared with the Hebrew Two Ways in the *Manual of Discipline* from Qumran (dated approximately between first century B.C.E. and first century C.E.) and the *Derek Erets* in the Rabbinic tradition. The *Manual of Discipline* is a reworking of an earlier text represented by the *Derek Erets* in order to formulate the teaching of the sect over against the dominant tradition. On the basis of this comparison, Flusser and van de Sandt argue that the teaching of Jesus in the Sermon on the Mount also appears to reflect this underlying textual tradition of the putative first-century B.C.E. archetype of the *Derek Erets*. According to this hypothesis, then, the Two Ways can be traced back behind the time of Jesus and must be ranked as one of the most important texts now available that connects the Jewish and the Christian ethical traditions.

In this paper, I wish to question the underlying model of textual transmission on which van de Sandt and Flusser's hypothesis is based. Certainly, this broad Two-Ways tradition is very widespread and ancient. But does it represent an identifiable textual chain, or should it rather be seen as an oral tradition anchored in the deep cultural reservoirs of first-century C.E. Israelite tradition? Reverence for oral tradition over written text was a strong and demonstrable feature of first-century culture, which can be traced from Plato to Irenaeus and the Rabbis. The face-to-face encounter takes precedence over the written text, which is treated with suspicion. This is still the case, for instance, with the Desert Fathers of Egyptian monasticism (Burton-Christie 1997), among whom the Two-Ways tradition was a living tradition in the third and fourth centuries (witness the *Syntagma Doctrina,* the *Fides Nicanae,* and the *Vita Shenoudi*). Our own cultural facility and dependence on the easily available printed text blinds us to the technical limitations of the first century, where texts were scarce and expensive and where few could read and even fewer could write (probably between eight and ten percent of the total population; see Harris 1989). In addition to these issues, the genre of the Two-Ways tradition, namely catechesis, must be considered, whether instruction of the ignorant "people of the land" (*'am haarets*) or of converts from the Gentiles. Such catechesis would have been delivered orally by a teacher over a lengthy period, during which the teaching would have been committed to memory. The text would never have been read in a silent or even in a public recital in the form that is found either in the Jerusalem Manuscript of the *Didache* (H54) or in the reconstruction of the Two Ways provided by van de Sandt and Flusser. The text is simply a skeleton, an *aide de mémoire* for the oral instructor.

In view of these considerations, it would seem that a different approach to the material, based on modern anthropological studies of the relationship between orality and literacy, may be more fruitful than the model adopted by van de Sandt and Flusser, without detracting from the value of their research. For instance, oral tradition is, by its nature, constantly changing and developing in performance, often without the knowledge of the performer. There may be, indeed, no "original version at all," as Jan Vansina has indicated with regard to stories in oral tradition.

> We cannot think of an archetype, and we cannot claim for certain that the parts common to all versions existed in a supposed original. . . . With oral tradition these questions [of authenticity, antiquity, and authorship] receive very different answers. All we have are performances. As we have seen, original compositions do not exist in several genres of oral tradition. It follows that the question of authenticity is posed very differently. We can only ask whether a given performance that claimed to be part of a tradition is indeed part of a tradition or not. (Vansina 1985, 54)

The oral performer claims to be rendering the tradition exactly "as s/he her/himself received it." As Ruth Finnegan points out, the categories and perspectives that would inform understandings of written texts cannot be used when dealing with oral tradition.

> The truth of the matter is that our concept of "the original", or "the song", simply makes no sense in oral tradition. . . . There is no correct text, no idea that one version is more "authentic" than another: each performance is a unique and original creation with its own validity. This is so even when the poet claims to be singing "the same" poem as one he had heard, or to be repeating a poem in exactly the same form as he sang it before. (Finnegan 1977, 65)

From an oral point of view, if the written (or printed) text differs from the orally performed "text," then the written text is not reliable. Indeed, the written text was all too often used to subvert the oral text for political ends, as the rich and diverse studies edited by Craig Cooper, *Politics of Orality* (2007), show only too well. The authenticity of the oral text, on the other hand, was held to be guaranteed by the authenticity of the performer. After all, "s/he received it from so and so." Even what is written down, then, is liable to change with each writing down, under the authority of a respected oral performer.

Since the first publication of *The Oral and the Written Gospel* in 1983, Werner Kelber has highlighted the continuing interplay of orality and textuality in the formation of the gospel tradition. Already in this groundbreaking work, which has influenced a new generation of research on the gospel tradition, he insisted that the search for an "original form" was an illusion reflecting a textual bias, since "each oral performance is an irreducibly unique creation. . . . The concepts of *original form* and variants have no validity in oral life, nor does the one of *ipsissima vox*, if by that one means the authentic version over against the secondary ones" (Kelber 1983, 30). Kelber has questioned the search for a core group of "authentic sayings" in the continuing search for the Jesus of history, since ancient texts did not function independently of oral performance but in constant interaction with it (see Kelber 1995b; 1999). The boundaries between these media were not at all watertight in the first-century Mediterranean world, and there were no "original texts" but only multiple performances (Kelber 1995b, 146). Kelber's argument has been taken up forcefully and convincingly with respect to the continuing fluidity of the text of the New Testament by David Parker in *The Living Text of the Gospels*. "What is the original text? This question obscures the truth, and we need instead to find a new way of thinking about the different printed texts and the process which they represent. There is no *original* text. There are just different texts from different stages of production" (Parker 1997, 4).

In this respect, the instruction in *Didache* 4:13—"Do not depart from a commandment of the Lord, but you shall keep what you have received, neither adding nor subtracting"—does not necessarily protect the text when the oral tradition changes. Oral reception stands in contrast to the insistence of the scribe, Matthew, that "not one jot nor tittle shall pass away from the Law" (5:18). The problem is neatly posed in the curse on adding to or subtracting from the book of Revelation, which is addressed to "everyone who *hears* the words of the prophecy of this book" (22:18). If what is *heard* determines what is authoritative, then we are in the pliable world of oral tradition despite the protestations of the author of Revelation.

Oral Tradition and Textual Transmission

Central to oral performance is the problem of memory, another major concern in Werner Kelber's work on the gospel tradition (see, e.g., Kelber 2002b). It is extremely unlikely that the performer in the ancient world would have read directly from a book, although that may sometimes have been the case in certain contexts. If it is used at all, the book organizes memory ahead of time. Memory in a successful oral performance depends, in turn, on the interaction of a number of elements, which have been set out economically by John Miles Foley (1995) and which may be briefly summarized here.

First, the *context of performance* is itself a necessary aid to memory. The context evokes and creates the performance. The context creates expectations in both the performer and the hearer/observer and is a necessary component of any understanding of the oral tradition.

> To play down the social context and mode of performance of oral literature is to give a very truncated picture of its nature and essence. Even with written literature, to ignore the social background and public to which it

is addressed gives a misleading view of its significance. And with oral literature, the import of a particular piece can scarcely be discovered from the textual content alone, without some attention to the occasion, audience, local meaning, individual touches by the performer at the moment of delivery, and so on. (Finnegan 1977, 42)

As has often been demonstrated, "We hear what we expect to hear," and the context cues the performer and the hearers to the right mode for remembering and reception. In the case of the Two Ways material of the *Didache*, the communication context is described in the text itself.

> My child, remember the one who speaks the word of God to you night and day, and you shall honor her/him as the Lord. For when the things of the Lord are spoken, the Lord is there. And you shall seek out daily the presence of the saints, in order that you may rest in their words. You shall not make division, but you shall reconcile those who are fighting. You shall judge rightly; you shall not take sides in reproving transgressions. You shall not be in two minds whether it shall be or not. (4:1–4)

The overall context of the *Didache*'s performance, as indicated earlier, is that of catechesis, where the "ritual elder," to use Turner's language (1967a, 100–101; cf. 1969), is honored as a fictive parent. Attendance is to be very regular during the period of initiation ("seek out daily"), and the material is the subject of continual meditation ("night and day"). The words are held to mediate the divine presence and power when they are spoken. Instruction is received in a group ("the presence of the saints"), presumably other catechumens and members of the community. Argument and dissension about the teaching given, in the manner of Greek philosophy, is forbidden ("not make division"). Instruction is accompanied by critical public examination of the lifestyle and progress of the catechumens ("reproving transgressions"). Unequivocal allegiance and acceptance of the teaching without reservation is required ("you shall not be in two minds"). It is also likely that the catechumens were required to contribute financially to their teacher and to the support of other members of the group (*Didache* 4:5–8). Clearly, such an intensive and extensive initiation process involved more than reading the text of the *Didache* aloud! Such a reading would take only a few minutes and would hardly be memorable. The current text is simply the frame around which the discourse would be constructed.

Second, a successful oral performance depends on the use of the appropriate *register*, the system of signs and signifiers designated for the context. There is no direct correspondence between the signs and signifiers and their referents. It is the more-or-less arbitrary social convention of the context that prescribes them, though usually there is an internal logic to the system that does have reference to the world of the senses. Victor Turner views such symbols as having a bipolar reference to sensory appeal and ideological reference (1967b, 19–47). The oral register consists of *field* (what is taking place and where), *tenor* (who is speaking to whom), and *mode* (the outward form and structure of the communication).

As noted earlier, in the context of the *Didache,* the *field* is the catechetical instruction of those wishing to join the community, while the *tenor* is the quasi-parental relationship of the teacher to prospective new members. The *mode* provided by the Two Ways is that of the presentation of binary oppositions leading to irrevocable choice: life or death, light or darkness, good or evil. Choose now and do not be in two minds, for that is "the snare of death" (*Didache* 2:4). The oral mode also uses structural techniques to aid the process of remembering, such as formula, parallelism, couplets, triplets, ring composition, chiasmus, and so on.

Third, a successful oral performance depends on what Foley calls "communicative economy" (1995, 54). According to this understanding, single words or phrases have a *metonymic reference* and stand for whole concepts.

> In fact each metonymic integer functions as an index–point or node in a grand, untextualizable network of traditional associations. Activation of any single node brings into play an enormous wellspring of meaning that can be tapped in no other way, no matter how talented or assiduous the performer may be; everything depends upon engaging the cognitive fields linked by institutionalized association to the phrase, scene, paralinguistic gesture, archaism, or whatever signal the performer deploys to key audience reception. Once those signals are deployed, once the nodes are activated the work issues forth with surpassing communicative economy, as the way of speaking becomes a way of meaning. (Foley 1995, 54)

Words and phrases can have a metonymic reference even where the meaning of the words has become archaic or lost—perhaps particularly when this has occurred, because then such words have a "dedicated meaning." Think, for instance, of the metonymic reference of "hallowed be thy Name" in English-speaking cultures today, where the word "to hallow" is no longer used in common parlance and now has a "dedicated register" associated solely with its ritual use in the Lord's Prayer. In the same way, when the terms in the vice lists in the *Didache* are named, they evoke a world of meaning beyond themselves and would, no doubt, have been elaborated and expanded in the actual performance.

The problems inherent in analyzing a written text for oral traits and mode are obvious. If it is written, it is no longer an oral performance. In addition, with an ancient text, the clues that set up the context of performance have been lost. Modern readers do not belong to that context and cannot feel the *field*, *tenor,* and *mode* as these would have impacted audiences in the first century C.E. In any case, as indicated earlier, questions must be asked about the way the text functioned. It cannot be that the text was simply read aloud without elaboration, and the performance cannot have been simply the pronouncement of the words now printed in our modern texts. These are simply cues to the performance. The written text served as a mnemonic framework and memory prompt for a longer oral performance elaborating on the meaning of its contents in a ritual context. The mnemonic framework would, in turn, have served as the basis for memorization and recall of the material by catechumens for whom the performance was designed. In terms of the present study, *Didache* and other ancient texts would have functioned as guidelines for multiple oral performances of their content in the appropriate "field."

A striking example of the way this kind of mnemonic structure functions can be found in the initiation rites of the Luba people of the Congo, as pointed out by Mary ("Polly") Nooter Roberts and Allen Roberts in a presentation at the colloquium on Orality, Literacy, and Memory at Rice University organized by Werner Kelber (10–12 October 2003). Roberts and Roberts use the model of Francis Bellezza (1981), which divides mnemotechniques into "peg types" and "chain types." The peg type is related to the ancient use of *loci,* where information is organized by visualizing a walk through a set of rooms in a public building. Series of "peg words" are memorized as static lists signifying data placed next to other data to "provide the learner with a cognitive cuing structure that is permanently stored in memory and can be used when needed for both associating information to it and later recalling that information by a process of self-cuing. This cuing structure, such as a series of loci or a series of peg words, is usually first memorized before the mnemonic system is put to use." The "chain-type" mnemonic requires one "to form a visual image associating the first and second word of the list, then form a completely different visual image connecting the second and third word, then the third and fourth word, and so on. The overlapping series of images associating the sequence of pairs of items in the list act like interlocking links in a chain" (Bellezza 1981, 225).

Luba "peg types" include the incisions made on the body of adepts in the initiation cult, while "chain types" include necklaces.[2] However, the key mnemonic artifact in Luba culture is the *lukasa* or memory board, which consists of a small wooden board with multiple pegs and patterns, such as that pictured below.³

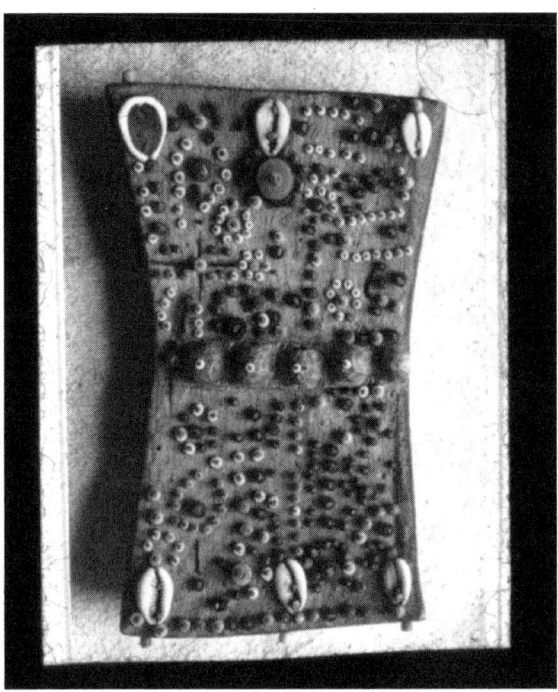

A Luba Memory Board

Each peg on the memory board has significance both in itself and in relation to the other pegs. The board is divided into two halves by a band representing the "veil" or threshold that the initiates must pass through, so that the memory board serves to differentiate insiders and outsiders, initiated and uninitiated. The pegs and shells differ in size, nature, and relation to one another. They are each allocated a precise significance and serve to recall particular aspects of the history of the Luba, its kings, and its sacred significance. Each *lukasa* board is different, according to local customs and local conditions, and yet each represents the same worldview and the same initiation process. Pegs represent places that can be imagined and that can evoke and house memory. They can be added or removed; they can be read in almost any direction. However, they can also be constructed in hierarchical chains of knowledge and association, analogously to a Luba necklace "in an ensemble that produces knowledge and communicates power and order" (Nkindi and de Plaen 1996, 97).

I would like to examine the virtue and vice lists of the Two-Ways tradition as a kind of memory board in which a series of verbal pegs of varying size is presented, each positioned in relation to the others purposively and yet capable of being read as chains in several directions. Major pegs retain their static nature as *loci,* but lesser pegs are liable to movement or elaboration according to circumstances. These "memory boards" would enable the teacher to perform the catechetical material of his/her community. They are cues rather than content. They have a certain consistency and definition and yet can evolve and vary from place to place as circumstances change. When we compare the *Didache, Epistle of Barnabas, Doctrina apostolorum, Canones Ecclesiasticae,* and *Constitutiones Apostolicae,* we are not really comparing texts so much as variant memory boards.

Memory Buttons and the Vice Catalogues in Didache *2, 3, and 5*

The image of a list of vices as "buttons" on a memory board has heuristic potential for examining the parallel lists in *Didache* 2, 3, and 5. It will be seen that the major buttons remain present and retain their basic relation to each other even as they shift their focus, and new buttons and chains emerge to displace their status in the hierarchy of meaning. In the Two-Ways tradition, one sees a process at work in which two series are interacting with one another and tending to displace one another. The first represents the second half of the Decalogue (murder, adultery, theft, covetousness, and false witness), while the second might be termed the Noachic laws (idolatry, *porneia,* and blood). One can observe, for instance, the way in which a version of the "Apostolic Decree" has found its way into the *Syntagma/Fides Nicanae* performance of the Two Ways and also precedes the Ethiopic text of the *Didache,* just as a form of the "Apostolic Decree" follows the Two Ways in *Didache* 6 and precedes the "liturgical material" in 7–14. This pattern of static "pegs" and dynamic "chains" emerges clearly when the two lists are set side by side.

As Table 1 indicates, each of the lists clusters around the second table of the Ten Commandments: you shall not murder, you shall not commit adultery, you shall not steal, you shall not covet the things of your neighbor, you shall not bear false witness. These are memorized at a fundamental level and repeated across the range of Jewish and Christian rituals and writings. Bellezza argues for the effectiveness of a memory schema and mnemonic system that taps into an existing memory structure: "If information

TABLE 1

Didache 2	Didache 3	Didache 5
οὐ φονεύσεις	μὴ γίνου ὀργίλος	φόνοι
οὐ μοιχεύσεις	φόνος	μοιχεῖαι
οὐ παιδοφθορήσεις	ζηλωτής	ἐπιθυμίαι
οὐ πορνεύσεις	ἐριστικός	πορνεῖαι
οὐ κλέψεις	θυμικός	κλοπαί
οὐ μαγεύσεις	φόνοι	εἰδωλολατρίαι
οὐ φαρμακεύσεις		μαγεῖαι
οὐ φονεύς.τέκν.ἐν φθι	μὴ γίνου ἐπιθυμητής	φαρμακίαι
οὐδὲ γεννηθὲν ἀποκτ.	πορνεία	ἁρπαγαί
οὐκ ἐπιθυμησεις.τ.τ.πλησίον	αἰσχρολόγος	ψευδομαρτυρίαι
οὐκ επιορκήσεις	ὑψηλόφθαλμος	ὑποκρίσεις
οὐ ψευδομαρτυρήσεις	μοιχεῖαι	διπλοκαρδία
οὐ κακολογήσεις		δόλος
οὐ μνησικακήσεις	μὴ γίνου οἰωνοσκόπος	ὑπερηφανία
οὐκ ἔσῃ διγνώμων	εἰδωλολατρία	κακία
οὐδὲ δίγλωσσος	ἐπαοιδός	αὐθάδεια
παγὶς γὰρ θανάτου ἡ	μαθηματικός	πλεονεξία
διγλωσσία	περικαθαίρων	αἰσχρολογία
οὐκ ἔσται ὁ λόγος σου	μηδὲ θέλε βλέπε	ζηλοτυπία
ψευδής οὐ κενός ἀλλὰ	μηδὲ ἀκούειν	θρασύτης
μεμεστωμένος πράξει	εἰδολολατρία	ὕψος
οὐκ ἔσῃ πλεονέκτης		ἀλαζονεία
οὐδὲ ἅρπαξ	μὴ γίνου ψεύστης	ἀφοβία
οὐδὲ ὑποκριτὴς	κλοπή	φονεῖς τέκνων
οὐδὲ κακοήθης	φιλάργυρος	φθορεῖς πλάσμα θεοῦ
οὐδὲ ὑπερήφανος	κενόδοξος	
οὐ λήψῃ βουλὴν πονηρὰν	κλοπαί	
κατὰ τοῦ πλησίον σου		
οὐ μισήσεις πάντα ἄνθρω.	μὴ γίνου γόγγυσος	
ἀλλὰ οὓς μὲν ἐλέγξεις	βλασφημία	
περὶ ὧν δὲ προσεύξῃ	αὐθάδης	
οὓς δὲ ἀγαπήσεις	πονηρόφρων	
ὑπὲρ τὴν ψυχήν σου.	βλασφημίαι	

is presented whose underlying conceptual structure reflects the structure of some memory schema possessed by the learner, then the information may automatically activate the appropriate schema, which in turn assimilates the new information.... This involves learning by comprehension....

However, a schema facilitates learning only if it fits the material and only if it already exists in the memory of the learner" (Bellezza 1981, 253). The third commandment of the Decalogue, "you shall not take the Name of the Lord your God in vain by swearing falsely," also occasionally appears in the form of the prohibition against blasphemy and is connected with the prohibition against bearing false witness, since the Lord's Name might be used in making vows. However, a second memory schema exists deriving from the so-called Noachide commandments, which are set out in the "Apostolic Decree" of Acts 15. Overt traces of its influence are found in *Didache* 6, the beginning of the Ethiopic text of the *Didache,* and the *Syntagma* (1:6)/*Fides* (III.5) recension. Two items from the list of Noachide commandments (πορνεία and εἰδωλολατρία) have intruded, most clearly in the second list in *Didache* 3, where πορνεία has replaced μοιχεία as the bold key on the memory board (although it remains highlighted in the second statement of the key) and has also subsumed and subordinated ἐπιθυμητής. Presumably, covetousness is now understood in terms of coveting the neighbor's wife and hence as formally equivalent to adultery and fornication. In its place as a major button comes εἰδωλολατρία. Interestingly, εἰδωλολατρία appears in chapter 5, and the contents of the list occurring under this key appear in chapter 2 as well (οὐ μαγεύσεις; οὐ φαρμακεύσεις), though without the memory button itself.

Another notable feature of the lists in *Didache* is that the order of the five commandments varies. This problem derives from the different order of the five prohibitions in the Hebrew (murder, adultery, theft, false witness, covetousness) and Greek (adultery, theft, murder, false witness, covetousness) texts of the Decalogue in Exodus 20:13-17. The first and last memory buttons remain constant, but the buttons in between tend to float a little within the same tradition. The way the three lists operate is somewhat different: chapters 2 and 5 operate in a static way as "peg types," whereas chapter 3 operates dynamically in a "chain type" of patterning. Nevertheless, the material in the three lists is really the same, suggesting a case of variants rather than new tradition. Redundancy serves the purpose of reinforcing memory. The intermediate list in chapter 3, which does not appear in the other forms of the Christian Two Ways, serves a bit like a buffer between the ways of life and death. Here it is not just a matter of characterizing the Two Ways but of providing advice concerning the best way to avoid falling foul of the major prohibitions—keeping the minor ones.

What strikes me here is the similarity with the *lukasa*, where the beginning and ending pegs of the board (cowries shells) are arranged in parallel with a dividing line in the middle. The first series of vices is in the negative, to characterize the way of life. The final series of vices is in the positive, to characterize the way of death. But it is essentially the same series viewed from different angles, those of the outsider and the insider. This marks the transition of the neophyte from outsider to insider but essentially reinforces the same pattern of behavior by repetition and elaboration. The smaller pegs can be clustered differently but still in relation to the larger pegs, just as in the *Didache*. In addition, the minor vices, the smaller memory buttons, are often recited in pairs or triplets even when the order of the list changes. The vices are carefully arranged in a pattern of sound and association in which the major memory buttons from the Decalogue usually stand alone. The pairs are linked by repetition of either initial, medial, or final consonants, vowels, and syllables, which could be reconstructed as a "sound map" (cf. Scott and Dean 1993). Initial vowels and symphonies carry over from couplets into the next series, creating a chain effect, as indicated below. This is a particularly effective method of constructing memory chains from the smaller pegs.

> Οὐ φον**εύσεις**
> Οὐ μοιχ**εύσεις**
> οὐ παιδοφθορ**ήσεις**/οὐ πορν**εύσεις**
> Οὐ κλ**έψεις**
> οὐ **μαγεύσεις**/οὐ **φαρμακεύσεις**
> οὐ **φονεύσεις** τέκνον ἐν **φθορᾷ**/οὐδὲ γεννηθὲν ἀπ**οκτενεῖς**
> Οὐκ **ἐπιθυμήσεις** τὰ τοῦ πλησίον/οὐκ **ἐπιορκήσεις**
> Οὐ ψευδομαρτυρ**ήσεις**
> οὐ **κακολογήσεις**/οὐ μνησικακ**ήσεις**
> οὐκ ἔσῃ **διγνώμων**/οὐδὲ **δίγλωσσος**/παγὶς γὰρ θανάτου ἡ **διγλωσσία**
> οὐκ ἔσται ὁ λόγος σου ψευδής οὐ κενός [ἀλλὰ μεμεστωμένος πράξει]
> οὐκ ἔσῃ πλεονέκτης/οὐδὲ ἅρπαξ/οὐδὲ **ὑποκριτὴς** /
> οὐδὲ **κακοήθης**/οὐδὲ **ὑπερήφανος**
> οὐ λήψῃ βουλὴν πονηρὰν κατὰ τοῦ πλησίον σου
> οὐ μισήσεις πάντα ἄνθρωπον
>   ἀλλὰ **οὓς** μὲν ἐλέγξεις / περὶ ὧν δὲ προσεύξῃ /
>   οὓς δὲ ἀγαπήσεις ὑπὲρ τὴν ψυχήν σου.

In *Didache* 5, as in chapter 2, there is a preference for doublets.

> μαγεῖαι/φαρμακίαι
> διπλοκαρδία/δόλος
> ἀλαζονεία/ἀφοβία
> φονεῖς τέκνων/**φθ**ορεῖς πλάσμα θεοῦ

Vice Catalogues as Oral-Mnemonic Cues

In chapter 3, on the other hand, it is a matter of triplets held together by sense rather than sound.

ὀργίλος/ζηλοτής/θυμικός
ἐπιθυμητής/αἰσχρολόγος/ὑψηλόφθαλμος
οἰωνοσκόπος/ἐπαοιδός/μαθηματικός
περικαθαίρων/θέλε αὐτὰ βλέπειν/μηδὲ ἀκούειν

This double and triple patterning is designed for memory in oral recital. As will be seen, this holds true across the other versions of the Two Ways as well, so that these memory buttons are working independently of specific textual traditions.

A Comparison of Witnesses to the Two Ways-Tradition in Didache 2

When parallels to the material found in the vice list in *Didache* 2 are set out, it becomes clear that the same kind of doublets and triplets carry over between the different witnesses to the tradition in a way that shows oral transmission rather than textual transmission, at least between *Didache/Doctrina apostolorum* and *Barnabas*. These tendencies can be seen in Table 2 on the following pages.

TABLE 2

Didache	Doctrina apos.	Barnabas	Canones Eccl.	Epitome
2. οὐ φονεύσεις οὐ μοιχεύσεις οὐ παιδοφθορήσεις οὐ πορνεύσεις οὐ κλέψεις οὐ μαγεύσεις οὐ φαρμακεύσεις οὐ φονεύσεις τέκνον ἐν φθορᾷ οὐδὲ γεννηθέντα ἀποκτενεῖς οὐκ ἐπιθυμήσεις τὰ τοῦ πλησίον.	2. Non moechaberis, non homicidium facies non falsum testimonium dices non puerum uiolabis non fornicaberis non magica facies non medicamenta mala facies non occides filium in abortum nec natum succides non concupisces quicquam de re proximi tui.	4. οὐ φονεύσεις οὐ μοιχεύσεις οὐ παιδοφθορήσεις, Οὐ μή σου ὁ λόγος τοῦ θεοῦ ἐξέλθῃ ἐν ἀκαθαρσίᾳ τινῶν. Οὐ λήμψῃ πρόσωπον ἐλέγξαι τινὰ ἐπὶ παραπτώματι. Ἔσῃ πραΰς, ἔσῃ ἡσύχιος ἔσῃ τρέμων τοὺς λόγους οὓς ἤκουσας. Οὐ μὴ μνησικακήσεις τῷ ἀδελφῷ σου. 5. Οὐ μὴ διψυχήσῃς πότερον ἔσται ἢ οὔ. Οὐ μὴ λάβῃς ἐπὶ ματαίῳ τὸ ὄνομα κυρίου. Ἀγαπήσεις τὸν πλησίον σου ὑπὲρ τὴν ψυχήν σου. οὐ φονεύσεις τέκνον ἐν φθορᾷ, οὐδὲ πάλιν γεννηθὲν ἀνελεῖς. Οὐ μὴ ἄρῃς τὴν χεῖρά σου ἀπὸ τοῦ υἱοῦ σου ἢ ἀπὸ τῆς θυγατρὸς σου, ἀλλὰ ἀπὸ νεότητος διδάξεις φόβον κυρίου. 6. Οὐ μὴ γένῃ ἐπιθυμῶν τὰ τοῦ πλησίον σου. Οὐ μὴ γένῃ πλεονέκτης, οὐδὲ κολληθήσῃ ἐκ ψυχῇ σου μετὰ ὑψηλῶν ἀλλὰ μετὰ δικαίων καὶ ταπεινῶν ἀναστραφήσῃ. Τὰ συμβαίνοντά σοι ἐνεργήματα ὡς ἀγαθὰ προσδέξῃ, εἰδὼς ὅτι ἄνευ θεοῦ οὐδὲν γίνεται.	6. Πέτρος εἶπεν· οὐ φονεύσεις οὐ μοιχεύσεις οὐ πορνεύσεις οὐ παιδοφθορήσεις οὐ κλέψεις οὐ μαγεύσεις οὐ φαρμακεύσεις οὐ φονεύσεις τέκνον ἐν φθορᾷ οὐδὲ γεννηθὲν ἀποκτενεῖς οὐκ ἐπιθυμήσεις τὰ τοῦ πλησίον	3. οὐκ Πέτρος εἶπεν οὐ φονεύσεις οὐ ποιήσεις ἁμαρτίαν τινὰ τῇ σαρκί σου οὐ κλέψεις οὐ μαγεύσεις οὐ φαρμακεύσεις οὐ ἐπιθυμήσεις τὰ τοῦ πλησίον σου

Vice Catalogues as Oral-Mnemonic Cues 125

Didache	Doctrina apos.	Barnabas	Canones Eccl.	Epitome
3. οὐκ ἐπιορκήσεις οὐ ψευδομαρτυρήσεις οὐ κακολογήσεις οὐ μνησικακήσεις. 4. οὐκ ἔσῃ διγνώμων οὐδὲ δίγλωσσος· παγὶς γὰρ θανάτου ἡ διγλωσσία. 5. οὐκ ἔσται ὁ λόγος σου ψευδὴς οὐ κενός ἀλλὰ μεμεστωμένος πράξει. 6. οὐκ ἔσῃ πλεονέκτης οὐδὲ ἅρπαξ οὐδὲ ὑποκριτής οὐδὲ κακοήθης οὐδὲ ὑπερήφανος οὐ λήψῃ βουλὴν πονηρὰν κατὰ τοῦ πλησίον σου. 7. οὐ μισήσεις πάντα ἄνθρωπον ἀλλὰ οὓς μὲν ἐλέγξεις περὶ δὲ ὧν προσεύξῃ οὓς δὲ ἀγαπήσεις ὑπὲρ τὴν ψυχήν σου.	3. Non periurabis non male loqueris non eris memor malorum factorum. 4. Nec eris duplex in consilium dandum neque bilinguis tendiculum enim mortis est lingua. 5. Non erit uerbum tuum uacuum nec mendax. 6. Non eris cupidus nec auarus nec rapax nec adulator nec contentiosus nec malemoris. Non accipies consilium malum aduersus proximum tuum. 7. Neminem hominum oderis quosdam amabis super animam tuam.	7. Οὐκ ἔσῃ δίγνωμος οὐδὲ δίγλωσσος· παγὶς γὰρ θανάτου ἐστὶν ἡ διγλωσσία.	οὐκ ἐπιορκήσεις οὐ ψευδομαρτυρήσεις οὐ κακολογήσεις οὐδὲ μνησικακήσεις οὐκ ἔσῃ δίγνωμος οὐδὲ δίγλωσσος παγὶς γὰρ θανάντου ἐστὶν ἡ διγλωσσία οὐκ ἔσται ὁ λόγος σου κενός οὐδὲ ψευδής οὐκ ἔσῃ πλεονέκτης οὐδὲ ἅρπαξ οὐδὲ ὑποκριτής οὐδὲ κακοήθης οὐδὲ ὑπερήφανος οὐ λήψῃ βουλὴν πονηρὰν κατὰ τοῦ πλησίον σου οὐ μισήσεις πάντα ἄνθρωπον ἀλλ' οὓς μὲν ἐλέησεις οὓς δὲ ἐλεήσεις περὶ ὧν δὲ προσεύξῃ οὓς δὲ ἀγαπήσεις ὑπὲρ τὴν ψυχήν σου.	οὐκ ἐπιορκήσεις οὐ ψευδομαρτυρήσεις οὐ κακολογήσεις οὐδὲ μνησικακήσεις οὐκ ἔσῃ δίγνωμος οὐδὲ δίγλωσσος οὐκ ἔσται σοι λόφος κενός οὐχ ἅρπαξ οὐδὲ ὑποκριτής οὐκ ἔσῃ κακοήθης οὐς ὑπερήφανος οὐ λήψῃ βουλὴν πονηρὰν κατὰ τὸν πλησίον σου οὐ μισήσεις πάντα ἄνθρωπον ἀλλ' οὓς μὲν ἐλέγξεις περὶ ὧν δὲ καὶ προσεύξῃ οὓς δὲ ἀγαπήσεις ὑπὲρ τὴν ψυχήν σου

Even though the material in *Barnabas* 19:2c–7, which has added elements that belong elsewhere in the Two Ways, is very disordered, it nevertheless preserves elements of the mnemonic patterning. Some of the material beginning the list in *Barnabas* comes at the end of the list in *Didache* and *Doctrina* (οὐ λήμψῃ βουλὴν κατὰ τοῦ πλησίον σου and the teaching about hating, which echoes—but in some ways inverts—the teaching in the other two). Thus, although the word order is different, many of the elements confirm that the memory buttons are still in place. Theft (κλέψεις) has dropped out of the list in both *Doctrina* and *Barnabas*. Murder (φονεύσεις) has dropped out in *Barnabas*, but here the list begins with material concerning taking evil counsel against the neighbor (οὐ λήψῃ βουλὴν πονηρὰν κατὰ τοῦ πλησίον σου), which may indicate a memory of murder being in this position. *Barnabas* also has lost a direct reference to false witness (ψευδομαρτυρήσις) but prefaces the material relating to this after οὐ μὴ λάβῃς ἐπὶ ματαιῷ τὸ ὄνομα κυρίου, which is functionally equivalent to false witness. A similar shift in *Didache* 3 has already been noted, where ψευδομαρτυρήσεις is replaced by βλασφημία. The triplet in *Barnabas* οὐ πορνεύσεις/οὐ μοιχεύσεις/οὐ παιδοφθορήσεις and *Canones Ecclesiasticae* 3:6 οὐ μοιχεύσεις/οὐ πορνεύσεις/οὐ παιδοφθορήσεις remains the same in content but different in ordering in comparison with *Didache's* οὐ μοιχεύσεις/οὐ παιδοφθορήσεις/οὐ πορνεύσεις, whereas *Doctrina* has displaced *non moechaberis* before *homicidia* to the beginning of the list, following the traditional order of the Decalogue in the Septuagint version of Deuteronomy 5:17-21 as opposed to the Masoretic text. Then *non puerum uiolabis/non fornicaberis* form a couplet. The *Epitome* replaces the triplet with a single periphrastic: οὐ ποιήσεις ἁμαρτίαν τινὰ τῇ σαρκί σου. In addition, *falsa testimonium dices* joins the first two vices from the second table of the Decalogue at the beginning, which comes fifth in the order of the *Didache*. In addition, couplets and triplets, which are displaced in *Barnabas*, remain as couplets or triplets in their new position:

οὐ φονεύσεις τέκνον ἐν φθορᾷ/οὐδὲ πάλιν γεννηθὲν
οὐκ ἔσῃ διγνώμων/οὐδὲ δίγλωσσος/παγίς γὰρ θανάτου ἐστὶν
ἡ διγλωσσία

Apart from this, where *Didache* has a larger button (οὐκ ἔσῃ πλεονέκτης) followed by two couplets (οὐδὲ ἅρπαξ/οὐδὲ ὑποκριτής and οὐδὲ κακοήθης/

οὐδὲ ὑπερήφανος), *Doctrina* has added *nec auarus* after *non eris cupidus* to make two balanced triplets, one relating to greed and one relating to wrong thinking.

It does not seem possible that the author of *Barnabas* has taken material from a written source; rather, he has taken it from the memory of oral performances. Like all members of the church, Barnabas would, of necessity, have learned the material during catechesis, but the control of the tradition is poor. On the other hand, the *Doctrina* differs from *Didache* in only a few details of order but still could represent material written from memory of performance.

More revealing, in some respects, is the way the tradition is rendered in three larger incorporations or "performances" of the tradition in *Constitutiones Apostolicae* VII.2.8–5.3, *Syntagma Doctrina/Fides Nicanae* and *Vita Shenoudi*, where the vice list follows the sequence of *Didache* closely but the items are interspersed with commentary and Scripture references. Although these are written texts, they seems to reflect the way an oral performance of the Two Ways as catechesis would have gone, with continual elaborations and additions reflecting the particular interests of each performance. Indeed, the Two Ways in the *Vita Shenoudi* is set in the narrative as an oral performance by Mar Visa of what his predecessor Abba Shenoudi used to perform.

> Listen attentively to me all of you when I begin to speak of the wonders and the miracles which God has worked by the hand of our pure father, the desired Abba Shenudi, which I have seen with my own eyes, I, Visa, his son and his disciple, signs which my holy father has told me, that he has given to me through his pure mouth, without deception or trickery. And what I tell you is only a little. And surely he always used to teach and say that, "The way is easy and the path twofold, one of life and the other of death." (my translation)

The skill and interests of the teacher would be seen in the way the oral framework provided by the text was elaborated in performance, as can be seen in the following table.

TABLE 3

Syntagma/Fides[4]	Const. Apostolicae	Vita Shenoudi
οὐ φονεύσεις οὐ μοιχεύσεις οὐ πορνεύσεις οὐ παιδοφθορήσεις οὐ κλέψεις	οὐ φονεύσεις That is, you shall not destroy a human being like yourself: for you would be breaking apart what was well made. It is not as if all killing were wicked, but only that of the innocent: but just capital punishment is reserved to the magistrates alone. οὐ μοιχεύσεις For you are dividing one flesh into two. For, He says, "The two shall be one flesh": for the husband and wife are one in nature, in consent, in union, in disposition, in life, in conduct; but they are separate in form and number. οὐδὲ παιδοφθορήσεις For this evil is contrary to nature, and grew from Sodom, which was entirely consumed by fire sent from God. "Let such a person be accursed: and all the people shall say, Amen." Οὐ πορνεύσεις For, He says, "There shall not be a fornicator among the children of Israel." οὐ κλέψεις For Achan, when he had stolen in Israel at Jericho, was stoned to death; and Gehazi, who stole, and told a lie, inherited the leprosy of Naaman; and Judas, who stole the money for the poor, betrayed the Lord of glory to the Jews, and repented, and hanged himself, and burst asunder in the midst, and all his bowels gushed out; and Ananias and Sapphira his wife, who stole their own goods, and "tempted the Spirit of the Lord", were immediately, at the sentence of Peter our fellow apostle, struck dead.	οὐ φονεύσεις οὐ πορνεύσεις οὐ παιδοφθορήσεις οὐ κακήσεις[5] οὐ κλέψεις
οὐ φαρμακεύσεις οὐ διχοστατήσεις	οὐ μαγεύσεις οὐ φαρμακεύσεις	οὐ μαγεύσεις οὐ φαρμακεύσεις
Keep from what is strangled	For, He says, "You shall not allow a witch to live."	

Vice Catalogues as Oral-Mnemonic Cues

and from food offered to idols and from blood. And these things indeed are the obvious sins but the lesser revealed commandments, for which we shall also give account, are these: And so then those living both as monks and encratites must withdraw from women and not come into contact with them if possible and they should contrive not to see them so that no punishment should come upon them if the heart should commit adultery through the vision of the eyes. φυλάττεσθαι τε μὴ εἶναι **δίγλωσσον μὴ δίγνωμον** or a liar or a slanderer or untimely distracted or shameless or a gadabout or lacking perception or self-willed or bringing forth an evil word	οὐ φονεύσεις **τέκνον ἐν φθορᾷ οὐδὲ γεννηθέντα ἀποκτενεῖς** For, "Everything that is created in His image, and receives a soul from God, if it is killed, shall be avenged, as having been destroyed unjustly." **οὐκ ἐπιθυμήσεις τὰ τοῦ πλησίον.** Such as his wife, or his servant, or his ox, or his field. **οὐκ ἐπιορκήσεις** For it is said, "You shall not swear at all." But if that cannot be avoided, you shall swear truly; for "everyone that swears by him shall be commended." **οὐ ψευδομαρτυρήσεις** For, "He that falsely accuses the needy provokes to anger him that made him." **οὐ κακολογήσεις** For says he, "Love not to speak evil, lest thou beest taken away." **οὐ μνησικακήσεις** For, "the ways of those that remember injuries are unto death." **Οὐκ ἔσῃ δίγνωμος οὐδὲ δίγλωσσος**	οὐ φονεύσεις **τέκνον ἐν φθορᾷ οὐδὲ γεννηθέντα ἀποκτενεῖς** οὐκ ἐπιθυμήσεις τὰ τοῦ ἑταίρου ἢ τοῦ πλησίον. **οὐκ ἐπιορκήσεις** οὐ ψευδομαρτυρήσεις οὐ κακολογήσεις τινα lest the Lord be angry with you. **οὐκ ἔσῃ διπλοκαρδία**
[F]rom the lips or making oaths at all to fall into sin but yes, yes, no, no and if	παγὶς γάρ "[For] a strong [snare] to him are a man's lips." And, "A talkative person shall not be prospered upon earth."	ἐν πράξεσιν πᾶσιν σου **οὐκ ἔσται ὁ λόγος σου ψευδής**

TABLE 3 (cont.)

Syntagma/Fides	Const. Apostolicae	Vita Shenoudi
necessary to say publicly, "Know that I speak the truth and do not lie." And do not take the sacred name in oath or any other vow as the gospel says. For all these false steps are improper and inappropriate to do but they will also cast out from the church those who do not guard against them and some of them may even kill.	5. οὐκ ἔσται ὁ λόγος κενός For, "you will have to give an account for every careless word you utter." οὐ ψεύσῃ For, He says, "You shall destroy those who speak lies." οὐ ἔσῃ πλεονέκτης οὐδὲ ἅρπαξ For, He says, "Woe to the one who is covetous toward the neighbor with an evil covetousness." οὐκ ἔσῃ ὑποκριτής Lest, "His share shall be placed with the hypocrite." οὐκ ἔσῃ κακοήθης οὐδὲ ὑπερήφανος For, "God opposes the proud." οὐ λήψῃ [You shall not show] favoritism toward a person in judgment, "For judgment is the Lord's." οὐ μισήσεις πάντα ἄνθρωπον Ἐλέγμῷ ἐλέγξεις "[You shall surely reprove] your neighbor, and you shall not incur guilt yourself."	οὐ κενός You shall not deduct anything from the salary of the hireling for fear that he may not cry to the Lord and he should not listen, for the Lord Jesus the Messiah is not far from us. τέκνον μου οὐκ ἔσῃ πλεονέκτης οὐδὲ ἅρπαξ οὐδὲ ὑποκριτής τέκνον μου οὐκ ἔσῃ ὑπερήφανος for pride is detested by God; οὐ λήψη βουλὴν πονηρὰν κατὰ τοῦ πλησίον σου or your parent, or your adversary, for, if you do it, God loves him more than you. τέκνον μου οὐ μισήσεις πάντα ἄνθρωπον for (man) is in the image and likeness of God; but if anyone slips, transgresses and falls into a fault, ἀλλὰ ἐλέγξεις αὐτὸν in private as as happened to others. οὓς δὲ ἀγαπήσεις ὡς σεαυτὸν

This is not to say that the *content* of the *Constitutiones Apostolicae* and the other later versions is necessarily to be credited with an antiquity beyond its fourth-century origin. Rather, these texts constitute the local geographical and ideolectical variants of the various authors of the particular performance—and it should be called a "performance" even though that performance is rhetorically coded in a written text (see Foley 1995, 60–98)—each of whom drew on the understanding current in the environment and his own particular spin on the material. So, for instance, the *Syntagma* has retained only the first six vices in the list followed by the teaching on double-mindedness, which is coupled with a variant form of the "Apostolic Decree" found in Acts 15. This acts as the cue for teaching on monasticism. The vice list constitutes only the obvious sins, which introduce the advanced teaching of the life of an encratite: "And these things indeed are the obvious sins but the lesser revealed commandments, for which we shall also give account, are these. . . ." The material designated originally for the catechesis of all converts to the Christian way is put to use in the initiation of novices in the monastic life. It is viewed as "advanced *gnosis*" already in *Barnabas* (see Draper 1995) and continues to develop in this way in the monastic rules of the church (see Rordorf 1996).

A Comparison of the Witnesses to the Two-Ways in Didache 5

A similar picture emerges upon examination of the witnesses to the Two-Ways tradition in *Didache* 5 (see Table 4 on p. 132). Again, the elements of the tradition are remarkably constant, and even where material is displaced, it maintains the couplets and triplets in their new position.

TABLE 4

Doctrina 5	Didache 5	Barnabas
moechationes	φόνοι	εἰδωλολατρία
homicidia	μοιχεῖαι	θρασύτης
falsa testimonia	ἐπιθυμίαι	ὕψος δυνάμεως
fornicationes	πορνεῖαι	ὑποκρίσις
desideria mala	κλοπαί	διπλοκαρδία
magicae	εἰδωλολατρίαι	μοιχεία
medicamenta iniqua	μαγεῖαι	φόνος
furta	φαρμακίαι	ἁρπαγή
uanae superstitiones	ἁρπαγαί	ὑπερηφανία
rapinae	ψευδομαρτυρίαι	παράβασις
affectationes	ὑποκρίσεις	δόλος
fastidia	διπλοκαρδία	κακία
malitia	δόλος	αὐθηδεία
petulantia	ὑπερηφανία	φαρμακεία
cupiditas	κακία	μαγεία
impudica loquela	αὐθάδεια	πλεονεξία
zelus	πλεονεξία	ἀφοβία θεοῦ
audacia	αἰσχρολογία	φονεῖς τέκνων
superbia	ζηλοτυπία	φθορεῖς πλάσματος θεοῦ
altitudo	θρασύτης	
uanitas	ὕψος	
non timentes	ἀλαζονεία	
abortuantes	ἀφοβία θεοῦ	
auertentes se a bonis	φονεῖς τέκνων	
operibus	φθορεῖς πλάσματος θεοῦ	

The list is given in the plural in the *Didache* and *Doctrina* and in the singular in *Barnabas,* but it is clearly the same list. The schema arising from the Noachide commandments, applicable to all human beings and not just Israelites, has again interrupted the major mnemonic buttons drawn from the second table of the Decalogue—in particular, the concern with εἰδωλολατρίαι in all three and πορνεῖαι in *Didache* and *Doctrina*. However, again, the arrangement of vices into couplets, which stay together even when the order changes, is noticeable.

θρασύτης/ὕψος
φόνοι/μοιχεῖαι

κακία/αὐθάδεια
μαγεῖαι/φαρμακίαι
ὑποκρίσεις/διπλοκαρδία

On the other hand, πλεονεξία retains its position alongside these couplets as does the triplet that concludes the vice list: ἀφοβία θεου/φονεῖς τέκνων/ φθορεῖς πλάσματα θεοῦ.

There is a remarkable overlap between the content of this list and the commonplace vices cited by Paul, no less than thirteen (see Wibbing 1959, 86–88): φόνοι; μοιχεῖαι; ἐπιθυμίαι; πορνεῖαι; εἰδωλολατρίαι; φαρμακίαι; ἁρπαγαί; δόλος; ὑπερηφανία; πλεονεξία; αἰσχρολογία; ἀλαζονεία. Clearly, it is not the content that is particularly unique to the Two-Ways tradition, but the order in which the material is arranged.

This article has been a very short and preliminary foray into the question of the oral nature and roots of the vice and virtue lists in the Christian Two-Ways tradition. Perhaps it has raised more questions than answers. There is a need to work in the same way with the material in the *Derek Erets* and the *Manual of Discipline*. My intention was to try to view the material in a different way, one in which the actual oral performance of the material determines the way we look at it rather than the usual way of viewing it in terms of text and redaction.

7

HUMAN MEMORY AND THE SAYINGS OF JESUS
Contemporary Experimental Exercises in the Transmission of Jesus Traditions

April D. DeConick[1]

For years, as a pedagogical exercise in parables as metaphor, I have asked my students to listen to my own parable, the "Parable of the Lottery Ticket." I use this exemplar in class because its internal references are contemporary, allowing the meaning of the parable to easily emerge as metaphor rather than allegory. I recite the parable exactly the same each time I perform it, as follows:

> The kingdom is like a young woman who found a lottery ticket in the street. The next day, when the numbers were posted, she won twenty-four million dollars.

What the students do not know is that I have another pedagogical objective when I ask them to listen carefully to this parable: I want to make concrete for them the role of real-life memory and its effect on the transmission of Jesus' sayings. So, at the beginning of the subsequent class period, I ask my students to take out a blank piece of paper and reproduce in writing the parable of The Lottery Ticket as accurately as they can. Of course, students offer the normal objections, several typically pointing out that I did not tell them that they needed to "memorize" the parable, before they settle down to the task. In only a few minutes, they are finished. Without another word, I collect their papers.

The next class period, I show them a chart that reproduces their versions of the parable side-by-side with the original. The entire class period is filled with howls of laughter at the twenty-five versions that are displayed. Not a single student in any of my courses has ever replicated the parable exactly, although most students have faithfully reproduced the "gist" of it. This has never been a big surprise to me, since all the classic studies in orality have demonstrated again and again that the reproduction (equals *R* throughout this essay) of a story will maintain the overall meaning of the narration while sacrificing the verbiage and details (see Parry 1971; Lord 2000; Havelock 1963; 1976; Ong 1967; 1971; 1982; Foley 1991; 1995).

What I have experienced in my classroom is summarized well by Kenneth Bailey, who writes about his own experience within the oral culture of the Middle East (Bailey 1991). Bailey describes three types of transmitted materials, the most inflexible being proverbs and poems, which are often remembered verbatim, and the most flexible being jokes and casual news, which "float" and "die" in a state of "total instability" (Bailey 1991, 44). He says that the transmission of the remaining materials—including parables and historical narratives—was accomplished with "continuity and flexibility," not "continuity and change." This continuity with flexibility works to "control" the transmission of the material. Bailey could be writing about my classroom exercise when he writes about his own experience in the Middle East as follows.

> Continuity and change could mean that the storyteller could change 15% of the story—any 15%. Thus after seven transmissions of the story, theoretically *all* of the story could be changed. But *continuity* and *flexibility* mean that the main lines of the story *cannot* be changed *at all*. The story can endure one different transmission through a chain of a hundred and one different people and the inner core of the story remains intact. Within the structure, the storyteller has flexibility within limits to "tell his own way." But the basic story line remains the same. By telling and retelling, the story does not evolve from A to B to C. Rather the original structure of the story remains the same but it can be colored green or red or blue. (Bailey 1991, 45)

The Role of Memory in Orality and Scribality

This relatively simple classroom exercise has gradually eroded my confidence in traditional approaches to and explanations of the similarities and variations among the early sources for Jesus. The fact that traditional methods and models are highly problematic is not a new insight. Werner Kelber's *The Oral and the Written Gospel* (1983) was bold and pioneering for many reasons, among them his criticism of the traditional model of literary dependence and the traditional methods of biblical studies that created it. Kelber's book pushed scholars to start remapping the oral/scribal culture and consciousness that dominated the ancient world and to work out its implications for the transmission of traditional material, including the words of Jesus. My classroom parable experiment, however, highlights an enormous facet of orality and scribality that has yet to be taken seriously by biblical scholarship: the role that human memory plays in the process of transmission in rhetorical cultures dominated by orality. In other words, *how* did human memory affect both the transmission and preservation of stories about Jesus and sayings attributed to him?

When I began prodding the research literature for answers to this question, I was disappointed to find that psychological models have not been incorporated into biblical studies to the same extent as anthropological, sociological, and literary models. Further, I found only one article, published by Robert McIver and Marie Carroll (2002; 2004), in which biblical scholars report the results of psychological experiments that they themselves have conducted to elucidate the traditions of Jesus. McIver and Carroll asked student subjects to reproduce, orally and in writing, various secular narratives, jokes, and aphorisms that were presented to them. The researchers concluded that direct literary dependence or copying is likely in the biblical sources in cases where eighteen or more words are found in exact sequence, with the exception of aphorisms, poetry, or lyrics, which tended to be remembered and repeated with very little variation.[2] Orally transmitted narratives evidence a high percentage of common vocabulary, but words found in the exact same sequence generally appear only in short phrases. McIver and Carroll observed shifts in the tenses and mood of verbs; often synonyms were substituted. When applied to the synoptic problem, McIver and Carroll found eighteen parallel passages in which there are eighteen or more words in exactly the same sequence and grammatical form.

Objections to McIver and Carroll's research have been raised.[3] The biggest question surrounding their work is whether such an experiment can produce valid conclusions about ancient documents given our vast distance from the ancient people. This is the objection of anachronism, since only modern people can be the subjects of such memory experiments. But though the problem of anachronism should be kept in mind, it should not rule out further experimentation. Nor should it be used to justify the marginalization of information on memory generated by psychologists who use contemporary people as their subjects. In particular, the appeal to anachronism should not be used by biblical scholars as an excuse to continue theorizing without also conducting their own field research. We will not know the results of our experimentation until we conduct our own experiments—whether it will reveal striking similarities or differences when compared to our ancient sources. If the results of such experiments are compatible with the evidence from the ancient literature, then the long distance between modern subjects and ancient people may not be as insurmountable as might first appear.

To say the least, it is lamentable that biblical scholars have not readily embraced psychological theories or methods, especially given the fact that Jesus traditions were fixed in human memory long before a single word of Jesus was scribed down. Again and again, the available sources clearly state that the composition of ancient Christian documents involved "remembering" the words and deeds of Jesus.[4] Even after their initial scribing, these traditions continued to be performed and transmitted without the aid of texts. Thus, the written texts were affected by human memory, since their scribing may have been based on the memory of a performance or a remembered version of another text rather than on direct copying from a written manuscript. This being the case, a successful understanding of the ways in which Jesus traditions were transmitted will require a firm grasp of how the human memory operates.

Studies in the field of cognitive psychology have demonstrated that human memory has a double nature, like the two sides of a coin. One facet of memory is its *instability*, its tendency to distort and forget. The other is memory's tendency toward *stability*, its ability to preserve and to reconstruct with accuracy. Memory's dual nature must be faced if one is to explain the multiformity of the Jesus traditions.

The Instability and Stability of Memory

The subject of memory distortion is its own field within cognitive psychology. The literature is vast, written mostly after 1970, and much of it has focused on "false" memories (see Roediger and McDermott 2000, 158–60; Loftus, Feldman, and Dashiell 1995; Ceci 1995; Loftus 1998). Since 1980, a large amount of research on memory distortion has explored the interface between neuroscience, neuropsychology, and cognitive psychology (Schacter 1995, 14). Studies on errors of commission generally try to explain *why* memory distorts rather than *how* memory distorts (see especially Roediger and McDermott 2000; Schacter 1995). Researchers have found that many factors combine to distort memory, including the "relatedness effect." If people experience something that strongly relates to something they have already experienced, their memories of these two experiences will affect one another. "Interference effect" is similar. It has been demonstrated that events immediately before and after an experience will affect the recall of that experience. "Imagination" plays a strong suggestive role, affecting recall to the point that people sometimes "remember" imagined events as if they were physically experienced events. Psychologists have also explored memory effects in terms of guessing, social factors, and differences between individual subjects (Roediger and McDermott 2000).

Since this article is focused on *how* memory distorts information rather than *why*—that is, how Jesus traditions were shaped rather than why the early Christians remembered the way they did—most of the psychological research is of limited value for the present study. One psychological study, however, stands out from the rest, because it was conducted in conditions as natural as possible using complete narratives rather than laboratory lists, strings, or patterns. I refer here to the classic series of experiments conducted by Sir Frederic C. Bartlett and published in 1932. Bartlett wanted to determine how memory affects the reproduction of a presented narrative (Bartlett 1932, 63). In order to explore this thesis, he asked a series of students to read twice a short North American folktale and then reproduce it. Bartlett noticed that the folktale became significantly shorter, until it condensed to a bare skeletal outline. After only a few *R*s, the story began to develop a fairly fixed form—concise, concrete, and undecorated. Original details vanished, and new details replaced them, details that were more meaningful to contemporary culture and society. Synonyms were substituted so that more familiar words replaced the less familiar.

Bartlett observed that his subjects remembered a general scheme, form, order, and arrangement of material, even the general impression of the story. But the actual style and verbiage of the original was rapidly transformed. The farther away in time from the original presentation, the more the subjects elaborated and invented new material. Hermeneutical insertions and moralizing tendencies that brought the story into the subject's own experiences and sensibilities were quite common. Other than general impression and structure, the repeated *R*s retained the setting of the story and a few outstanding details, particularly words or phrases that were prominent. The accuracy of a *R* in terms of precise construction of words was a rare exception, not the rule. Further, although the tendency is for the unusual to be denuded or erased, there are two sets of conditions in which Bartlett found it more likely to be maintained: when the novel feature is the single unusual element of a bland story or when the novel feature is repeated several times in the story. Occasionally, Bartlett noticed a transposition in the order of elements: things the person identified with emotionally would move to the front of the sequence. For the most part, however, the order and number of events remained constant.

From these and other experiments, Bartlett surmised that human memory is (re)construction and that this (re)construction is a social act.

This being the case, one must discard the view that memory recall is a matter of "fixed and changeless traces." Recall, in fact, includes more than what we actually perceived. Humans remember by filling in the gaps with experiences from other similar situations or with what they believe suits the occasion. So, recall is in part imagining, with the details being drawn from many sources. Memory does not correspond to simple experience not only because memories are constantly mingled with constructions but also because they are, in fact, "constructive in character" (Bartlett 1932, 128). Bartlett concluded that memories are imaginative reconstructions of the past, largely influenced by preexisting knowledge structures ("schemas").

Referring to Bartlett and other cognitive psychologists (cf. Allport and Postman 1947), David Rubin laments in *Memory in Oral Traditions* that our knowledge of memory has come from experiments in which memory performance was not impressive (Rubin 1995, ix). When Rubin began reading in the field of oral traditions, he found that oral traditioning was "a case where memory worked extraordinarily well" (Rubin 1995, ix). As an experimental cognitive psychologist, Rubin became fascinated with studies in orality and has attempted to explain the stability of oral traditions after generations of transmission by word of mouth.

When Rubin talks about the "stability of oral traditions," he does not necessarily mean that oral transmission preserves exact verbatim recall. Although verbatim recall can occur in orally transmitted material, it is usually tied to genres like lyrics and rhymes, which include embedded memory aids (rhythm, counting, music). But even these genres are subject to variation, as Rubin demonstrates with the common English rhyme *Eenie Meenie*, eighty-two versions of which are known. Although Rubin understands oral tradition to be remarkably stable and conservative, he does not understand this stability in terms of long strings of words reproduced verbatim. He points to the work of Hunter, who has shown that there are no documented cases of oral *R*s where over fifty words are recalled verbatim, except where a written record is available to the performer. Rubin therefore concludes that long verbatim recall requires a record other than human memory (Rubin 1995, 6; cf. Hunter 1984, 425–40; 1985, 207–35). Rubin thinks this flexibility of the tradition aids in its long-term stability and retention, because the variability allows each performer to develop an easier-to-recall variant adapted to the performer's taste and to the audience or culture. This increases the likelihood that the material will be preserved by the new generation rather than forgotten (Rubin 1995, 6–7).

Rubin concludes that a specific "variant" of a unit is not being transmitted. Rather, the oral performer transmits "the theme of the song, its imagery, its poetics, and some specific details" (Rubin 1995, 7). Oral traditions survive because they develop certain strategies and forms of organization, including meaning structures and patterns of sound, that work to stabilize human memory and decrease the types of changes that naturally occur when material is transmitted more casually.

This development of material into an oral tradition is particularly important to the present study, which is focused on the initial decades of the transmission of Jesus traditions—traditions that had not yet become stable oral performances with a long history of intergenerational transmission or stable scribed copies. Although oral traditions tend to stabilize eventually, their origin and first years of transmission are not stable. Until the early Jesus traditions began to be scribed down, they were fixed only by the accuracy of human memory. Even a casual analysis of the variants of Jesus' sayings found in the early Christian literature demonstrates that, until the Jesus traditions began to be perceived as Scripture and canonized, their oral and scribal transmission was susceptible to exactly the types of alterations demonstrated in Bartlett's lab and my classroom.

So how does oral material come into a stable form that can be passed from one generation to the next with only slight variation? The answer to this question lies at the intersection of Bartlett's and Rubin's theories. The formulation of the material as it is initially reproduced would mold the story into a concrete, formulaic, and conventional script, a form acceptable to the social group transmitting the material. Once this is done, the material would take on a shape that is easily recalled orally across generations (see Rubin 1995, 130–32). It is important to recognize, however, that the oral recollection and transmission of the conventional material would continue alongside its scribing and that the reshaping of the conventional material would have continued within the scribal context until the text took on scriptural status and was canonized.

Two Pilot Experiments

In order to begin to address the problem of the operation of human memory in the transmission of Jesus traditions, I conducted a series of real-life memory exercises in consultation with Professor Jean Pretz, a cognitive psychologist at Illinois Wesleyan University (Bloomington). Although the experiments were controlled, the results were based on the responses of only forty-four subjects. My goal was modest: to conduct two short pilot experiments and then determine if my results warranted further experimentation on enough subjects to generate more-significant statistical data.

Four specific questions informed my experiment. First, are there characteristic memory distortions (instabilities) and verbal agreements (stabilities) that occur in real-life recall that likely affected the process of passing on traditions about Jesus? Second, what are the variations and verbal agreements that arise in different media environments: oral to oral (OO); oral to written (OW); written to oral (WO); written to written (WW); written sources retained (WSR)? Third, do certain memory distortions and patterns of verbal agreement occur in certain of these modes of transmission? Fourth, what might these memory distortions and patterns of verbal agreement mean for our understanding of source dependence and composition in the ancient world?

My subjects consisted of student volunteers between the ages of eighteen and twenty-two. All were studying at Illinois Wesleyan University and chose to participate in the experiment as an optional class assignment. They were randomly assigned to one of the four media environment groups described above. Their membership within their assigned groups remained constant throughout the course of the experiment. The subjects were asked to complete a questionnaire for control purposes and to read and sign an informed consent. Twenty-four were female, twenty male. Their degree concentrations varied widely: Art (2); Biology (1); Business (6); Chemistry (1); Computer Science (1); Economics (1); Elementary Education (3); English (3); Greco-Roman Studies (1); History (3); Math (2); Music (3); Music Education (2); Music Theatre (2); Nursing (1); Philosophy (1); Political Science (3); Psychology (3); Religion (7); Theatre (1); Undecided (3). All students had taken at least one religion course previously.

The first experiment was explained to the subjects in these terms: "You will be asked to listen and/or read some proverbs, parables, and short narratives. Then you will be asked to speak into a tape recorder and/or write as accurately as possible what you have heard or read."

- *Group 1: Oral to Oral.* Subjects listened to an unfamiliar, tape-recorded male voice that instructed them: "Listen attentively to this saying. I will repeat it three times." After listening to the recorded saying three times, the subjects were instructed to immediately take a tape recorder into a private room and "repeat as accurately as possible the saying you just heard."
- *Group 2: Oral to Written.* Subjects listened to the same tape recording with the same instructions: "Listen attentively to this saying. I will repeat it three times." After listening, the subjects were instructed to immediately "write down as accurately as possible the saying you just heard."

- *Group 3: Written to Oral.* A written version of the recorded saying presented to Groups 1 and 2 was distributed to the subjects. They were asked to read the saying three times. The written versions were then collected, and the subjects were asked to immediately proceed into a private room and "repeat as accurately as possible the saying you just read" into a tape recorder.
- *Group 4: Written to Written.* A written version of the recorded saying presented to Groups 1 and 2 was distributed to the subjects. They were asked to read the saying three times. The written versions were then collected, and the subjects were asked to immediately "write down as accurately as possible the saying you just read."

Once the subjects finished their initial tasks, they were asked to complete the same task with a parable and a miracle story. The reproductions generated from these tasks represent short-term memory (STM) recall. The text for the saying, the parable, and the miracle story were derived from unfamiliar extracanonical sources and were modified so that responses from previous memory would be impossible. The subjects were presented with novel material, yet within the genre of traditional words of Jesus and stories about him found in ancient sources.

- *The Test Saying* (cf. *Gospel of Thomas* 75): "Many people are standing at the door, but those who are virgins are the people who will enter the bridal chamber."
- *The Test Parable* (cf. *Gospel of Thomas* 97): "The kingdom is like a woman carrying a jar filled with meal. While she was walking on the road still a long way from home, the handle of the jar broke. Behind her, the meal leaked out onto the road. She did not realize it. She had not noticed a problem. When she arrived at her house, she put the jar down and found it empty."
- *The Test Miracle Story* (*Infancy Gospel of Thomas* 10.1–2): A young man was chopping wood and the axe fell and split open the sole of his foot. He bled so much that he was about to die. When Jesus heard the crowd calling out for help, he ran over to the man, forcing his way through the crowd. He took hold of the injured foot, and it was healed immediately. And he said to the young man, "Arise now, cleave the wood and remember me."

Because I wished to know how the transmission of this type of material is handled in real-life memory beyond STM recall, I did not tell the subjects that they would have to do anything further. But one week later, to test long-term memory (LTM) recall, I called upon the subjects to take up their pencils or their tape recorders once again and reproduce "as accurately as possible the saying that they had heard or read." Similarly, *R*s were requested for the parable and the miracle story.

For the second experiment, twenty-seven subjects were given a handout that read:

> Read the selected sayings and stories of Jesus. Compose in your own words a short narrative about Jesus with reference to the text you have read. You will retain the text during composition. You can also use your own remembrances of Jesus' words and actions in order to present what you want to say about Jesus. You are limited to no more than two pages.
>
> - "Many people are standing at the door, but those who are virgins are the people who will enter the bridal chamber."
> - "The kingdom is like a woman carrying a jar filled with meal. While she was walking on the road still a long way from home, the handle of the jar broke. Behind her, the meal leaked out onto the road. She did not realize it. She had not noticed a problem. When she arrived at her house, she put the jar down and found it empty."
> - A young man was chopping wood and the axe fell and split open the sole of his foot. He bled so much that he was about to die. When Jesus heard the crowd calling out for help, he ran over to the man, forcing his way through the crowd. He took hold of the injured foot, and it was healed immediately. And he said to the young man, "Arise now, cleave the wood and remember me."

Students were told to complete the task within twenty minutes. Their written *R*s were then collected.

My two pilot experiments have generated data that warrants further investigation. Although my subject sample is too small to be statistically meaningful, the data supports the outcomes of other experimenters as well as theoretical studies of folklore, orality, scribality, and rhetoric. Here again, I will first describe observable patterns of stability in memory and then notable patterns of instability.

Results and Analysis: Patterns of Stability

Notable patterns of stability were evident in sequenced verbal agreement, the openings and closings of the *R*s, and the repetition of major images and themes. Each of these patterns will be discussed briefly below, along with the relevant tabulated data.

On the topic of *sequenced verbal agreement,* the number of words reproduced in exact sequence appears to be significantly different between media modes that were entirely dependent upon memory and those where written sources were retained. This trend is indicated in Tables 1–4 below. For these tables, averages were calculated since there was no significant difference between the average and the mean.

As Table 5 below indicates, when written sources were retained, the longest string of verbatim words in sequence is significantly higher than any of the reproductions relying on memory (cp. Tables 1–4). The degree of difference was substantially higher when the statistics for WSR *R*s are compared to LTM *R*s within any of the memory-dependent environments. For WSR *R*s of the Virgin Proverb, on average the longest string of exactly sequenced words reproduced was 18–19 (86% of the proverb). For WSR *R*s of the Jar Parable, on average 22–23 words (33% of parable) were preserved. For WSR *R*s of the Foot Miracle story, on average 9–10 words (12% of story) were copied verbatim.

The LTM *R*s of the presented material did not produce long verbatim strings: Virgin Proverb (maximum 8, 1 *R*; average 3 words); Jar Parable (maximum 11, 1 *R*; average 6 words); Foot Miracle (maximum 15, 1 *R*; average 7 words). When the written source was retained, the *R*s had very different numbers. The longest verbatim strings reached 20–21 for the Virgin Proverb in 13 *R*s; 3 *R*s of the Jar Parable reproduced 26, 44, and 76 words in order; 2 *R*s of the Foot Miracle story managed 20 and 26. The only other occasions where verbatim sequences surpassed 15 words were in immediate STM reproductions. The only time that exact reproduction of the presented material occurred was in STM *R*s of the Virgin Proverb and WSR *R*s of the Virgin Proverb and the Jar Parable (see Tables 1–4).

These results do not come as a surprise. In fact, they reflect what psychologists have concluded about the phonological or articulatory loop, one of the components of human memory (see Baddeley 1995). In the short term, presented words can be stored in this articulatory loop in verbatim form. But the loop has a limited capacity. This means that the words in the loop are quickly replaced by subsequent words, and verbatim recall of the presented material decays substantially with as little as twenty intervening syllables (Sachs 1974, 99). Thus, even when there is a desire to do so, it is extremely difficult to recall lengthy exact sequences of words without access to written texts (see Hunter 1985; Goody 1998).

Since it is highly unlikely that the Jesus traditions were transmitted via immediate STM recall, I conclude from this experiment that exact reproduction of sequences of sixteen or more words in length is suggestive of copying from a written source, confirming what McIver and Carroll found in an earlier study.[5] It also appears from the results of this pilot experiment

TABLE 1
VERBAL AGREEMENT PER REPRODUCTION OF VIRGIN PROVERB

Media environment	Average longest string of verbatim words in exact sequence (out of 21 words)	Average longest string of verbatim words in exact sequence (% of proverb)	% of reproductions with exact strings of words above 17	% of reproductions that were exact reproductions of the proverb	% of subjects who did not attempt to reproduce the proverb
OO: STM Memory	14.75	70	25	25	0
OO: LTM Memory	2.14	10	0	0	13
OW: STM Memory	13	62	11	11	0
OW: LTM Memory	3	14	0	0	44
WO: STM Memory	12.28	58	21	21	0
WO: LTM Memory	3.62	17	0	0	50
WW: STM Memory	17.38	83	46	40	13
WW: LTM Memory	3.66	17	0	0	47

TABLE 2
VERBAL AGREEMENT PER REPRODUCTION OF JAR PARABLE

Media environment	Average longest string of verbatim words in exact sequence (out of 66 words)	Average longest string of verbatim words in exact sequence (% of parable)	% of reproductions with exact strings of words above 17	% of reproductions that were exact reproductions of the parable	% of subjects who did not attempt to reproduce the parable
OO: STM Memory	13.56	21	22	0	11
OO: LTM Memory	7.67	12	0	0	11
OW: STM Memory	10.57	16	33	0	0
OW: LTM Memory	4.63	7	0	0	38
WO: STM Memory	14.11	21	7	0	0
WO: LTM Memory	4.4	7	0	0	46
WW: STM Memory	15.57	24	28	0	46
WW: LTM Memory	6.75	10	0	0	38

TABLE 3
VERBAL AGREEMENT PER REPRODUCTION OF FOOT MIRACLE STORY

Media environment	Average longest string of verbatim words in exact sequence (out of 76 words)	Average longest string of verbatim words in exact sequence (% of story)	% of reproductions with exact strings of words above 17	% of reproductions that were exact reproductions of the story	% of subjects who did not attempt to reproduce the story
OO: STM Memory	18.11	24	33	0	10
OO: LTM Memory	5.22	7	0	0	10
OW: STM Memory	12.22	16	22	0	0
OW: LTM Memory	6.50	9	0	0	56
WO: STM Memory	16.07	21	36	0	0
WO: LTM Memory	7.13	9	0	0	36
WW: STM Memory	18.08	24	31	0	7
WW: LTM Memory	7.13	9	0	0	43

TABLE 4
VERBAL AGREEMENT WHEN WRITTEN SOURCES RETAINED

Presented material	Average longest string of verbatim words in exact sequence (when not paraphrased)	Average longest string of verbatim words in exact sequence (% of story when not paraphrased)	% of reproductions with exact strings of words above 17 (when not paraphrased)	Exact reproduction of presented material (when not paraphrased)	Paraphrase reproduction of presented material	% of subjects who did not attempt to reproduce the material
Virgin Proverb (out of 21 words)	18.93	90	81	80	38	11
Jar Parable (out of 66 words)	22.89	35	33	11	63	11
Foot Miracle Story (out of 76 words)	9.75	13	25	0	67	11

TABLE 5
Average Number of Words Occurring in Exact Sequence in LTM Rs and WSR Rs

	OO: LTM	OW: LTM	WO: LTM	WW: LTM	WSR
Virgin Proverb	2–3 words (10%)	3 words (14%)	3–4 words (17%)	3–4 words (17%)	18–19 (86%)
Jar Parable	7–8 words (12%)	4–5 words (7%)	4–5 words (7%)	6–7 words (10%)	22–23 (33%)
Foot Miracle Story	5–6 words (7%)	6–7 words (9%)	7–8 words (9%)	7–8 words (9%)	9–10 (12%)

that there is an enormous difference in the accuracy of reproductions of the three genres presented. This conclusion also complies with McIver and Carroll's earlier experimental findings and with Rubin's interdisciplinary treatment of various genres found in oral tradition. Rubin found that certain genres have multiple constraints, making (near) verbatim recall easier. These constraints are imagery, rhythm, and rhyme (Rubin 1995, 300). In line with this observation, Walter Ong has noted that the one genre that *can* reproduce verbatim words at length is song lyrics. Based on the fieldwork of other scholars, Ong notes that poetry in oral cultures has a 60 percent accuracy rate when it comes to verbatim reproduction (1982, 61–63).

Analysis of my own experimental data suggests that the proverb was more accurately transmitted in all media environments, including WSR, although it was *only reproduced exactly* in STM *R*s (24%) and WSR *R*s (80%; Tables 1 and 4). This may be because of the proverb's shorter length, pithier imagery, and parallel structure. The parable held the middle ground with 11 percent verbatim reproduction when the written source was retained. It was never duplicated exactly in any of the memory-dependent environments (Table 2). The miracle story (which was only ten words longer than the parable) appears to be the most pliable and least accurately transmitted of the three genres studied. No subject reproduced it exactly in any of the media environments, including WSR (Tables 3 and 4). It is worth noting that any advantage that the WSR mode had in terms of verbatim reproduction of the proverb and the parable collapsed in reproductions of the miracle story. In LTM *R*s, the longest string of words reproduced verbatim was between 5 and 7; for WSR *R*s, 9–10.

The *openings and closings* (the first 8–9 words and the last 3–4 words in the test texts) were the most stable elements in the sample reproductions. This was the case across the board in all media environments, although in the WSR *R*s it was often the case that the presented material was framed out with substantial editorial, sometimes moralizing, material immediately preceding or following the saying or story. This was usually attached to the stable opening or closing of the presented saying or story.

Examples of WSR editorial openings:

- "*While Jesus was walking*, a young man . . ."
- "*One such was* a young man . . ."
- "*Also Jesus would tell stories or parables such as that of* the woman . . ."
- "*Turn down in your mind all other images and prepare to know him; he calls us to void ourselves of every evil and sin, for it is said*, many people are standing . . ."

- *"Jesus was walking with his disciples on the way to Capernaum. As he passed a certain town, a few villagers approached him and begged that he come to where a young man lay dying. He had been chopping wood..."*
- *"Now Jesus' disciples sat about him and asked him questions such as 'What is the kingdom like and which of us will enter?' And Jesus said to them,* "Many people are standing..."
- *"Some people in the crowd accused Jesus of using demonic powers to heal the man. Jesus said, 'Can a Kingdom divided against itself stand? Many people are standing..."*

Examples of WSR editorial closings:

- "... will enter the Bridal Chamber. *Virginity is a sign of purity, and the bridal chamber represents the kingdom of heaven. Jesus is teaching us that we must be pure in soul in order to become one with God.*"
- "... 'remember me.' *He wanted people to know how having faith can save a person.*"
- "... 'remember me.' *Keeping one's mind focused on higher things is of utmost importance.*"

This type of editorial adjustment was not noted with the memory-dependent modes since the subjects' task was recall, not recontextualization. There was a tendency, however, in the memory-dependent modes to reproduce typical formulaic introductions to folklore narratives. Quite frequently, subjects began the saying or story with "there are/was/were," "one day," "one time," or "there once was." This occurred more consistently in introductions to the miracle story than in either of the other genres. On three occasions, a short pithy interpretation was tacked onto the ending: "This is what the kingdom of heaven is like"; "she was confused"; "she is confused."

The final notable pattern of stability in my test samples relates to major *images and themes*. Within each genre, there were several words that were very stable and consistently remembered in both STM *R*s and LTM *R*s. Since LTM *R*s were more distorted, they show the minimal images recalled. As for the proverb, the words that were retained consistently were "virgin(s)," "enter," and "brid(al) chamber." In *R*s of the parable, the words that were reproduced consistently were "the kingdom is like a woman," "jar," "meal," "walking," "the jar broke," and "empty." For *R*s of the miracle story, the stable words included "man chopping wood," "axe," "his foot," "crowd," "foot," "healed," "said," and "remember me." It appears that these images represent the core of the presented material. The rest of the saying or story was then reconstructed from memory to connect these fragmented images into a coherent whole with a meaning quite close to the original material. The gist was what mattered, not the exact words or details.

This finding is consistent with research on how remembered "texts" are performed orally as well as how human recall functions. A theory called "fuzzy trace" has developed from studies on verbatim memory and gist memory. It has been found that as children mature beyond middle childhood, there is a shift to dependency on gist memory from verbatim. This means that, for the adult, what makes it into long-term memory is not exact verbiage but the meaning or gist of the presented material (Miller 1998). The basic premise of the material is remembered, along with vivid themes or images. So the premise helps the subject recreate the "text" by reconnecting the themes or images into a rational whole. This results in reproductions that have shifts in details but stability in meaning and short phrases.

The WSR *R*s did not have this same pattern. What was reproduced was fairly accurate, especially within the proverbial material (Virgin Proverb and Cleave the Wood saying). This is not to say that substantial material was not deleted or moved into paraphrase in WSR *R*s. But the subject of WSR reproductions appeared to be selective in what was remembered very accurately and in what was modified. The results of these experiments suggest that the WSR subjects were more likely to be conservative in their reproductions of the words of Jesus than they were in their reproductions of stories about him. Although they did take minor liberties, adjusting parts of the proverb and parable to fit their larger narrative, these adjustments were far less severe than the ones made to the miracle story, which was pared *substantially*. Thus, the Cleave the Wood saying at the end of the miracle story (Table 6 below) was reproduced far more accurately than any of the other aspects of the miracle story in the WSR *R*s: 63 percent copied exactly the words "cleave the wood," while taking much greater liberties with the other portions of the story. Contrast this with the fact that none of LTM *R*s were able to reproduce the Cleave the Wood saying exactly (or the Virgin Proverb).

This data suggests that the subjects who retained the written source were less willing to alter Jesus' words than to change drastically narrative material about him. Thus, if we have two copies of a narrative that contains words of Jesus, and in those two copies the words of Jesus are exact duplicates while the narrative is similar but not verbatim, it is highly probable that a copyist has reflected on a written source.

TABLE 6
Verbal Agreement per Reproduction of Cleave the Wood Saying

Media Environment	Exact Reproduction	Sample Alternate Reproductions of Cleave the Wood Saying
OO: STM	78%	Arise now and remember. Rise and cleave your wood.
OO: LTM	0%	Cleave to the wood and be healed. Remember me and continue to chop the wood. Go forth and remember me. Arise. Go cleave your wood and remember me.
OW: STM	22%	Rise now. Cleave the wood and remember me. Go now. Cleave wood and remember me. Cleave the wood and remember me. Get up. Cleave the wood and remember me Now go. Cleave wood and remember me.
OW: LTM	0%	Be healed and remember me. Get up and walk. Believe in me. Arise. Cleave the wood and remember me.
WO: STM	14%	Cleave the wood and remember me. Now go, cleave the wood and remember me. Arise. Cleave the wood and remember me. Continue to cleave the wood and remember me. Arise now. Cleave the wood and you are healed. Continue cleaving wood and remember me. Go now. Cleave the wood and remember me. Arise. Cleave to the wood and remember me. Arise. Cleave your wood and remember me. Arise now and cleave the wood and remember me.
WO: LTM	0%	Continue to cleave the wood and remember me. Believe in me. Go forth and remember me. Rise. Go cleave the wood and remember me. Rise and follow me and go.
WW: STM	15%	Be healed and remember me. Get up and walk. Believe in me. Arise. Cleave the wood and remember me. Arise now. Cleave wood and remember me. Arise and cleave this wood and remember me. Cleave wood and remember me. Arise. Cleave wood and remember me. Arise now and cleave the wood and remember me. Arise. Arise now. Cleave the wood and follow me.

Human Memory and the Sayings of Jesus 155

WW: LTM	0%	Rise and cleave the wood and remember me. Arise. Chop wood and remember me. Get up. Go on and remember me always. Go and remember me. Go. Cleave wood and remember me. Go and cleave this wood and remember me.
WSR	63%	Go finish your work. Jesus told the man to continue his love and remember Jesus. Arise now and remember me. Arise now. Cleave wood and remember me.

Furthermore, because I doubt that the transmission of Jesus' sayings relied on STM reproductions, and because none of the LTM *R*s in my experiment were able to reproduce either proverb verbatim while the WSR *R*s readily and consistently did so, when two sources offer identical reproductions of a saying of Jesus, copying is most likely involved in that transmission (compare McIver and Carroll 2004, 1263–64).[6] This does not mean that it is impossible for a proverb to have been transmitted verbatim within an oral environment, especially if it were very short. Kenneth Bailey, in fact, points out a publication by Isa Atallah of Middle Eastern proverbs whose contemporary use is "in a totally fixed form" (Bailey 1995, 365). But this type of fixed form requires a lengthy intergenerational traditioning process that had not yet occurred when the early Christian sources were first scribed. This suggests that verbatim oral transmission of sayings of Jesus would have required from the orator a determined effort to memorize the sayings and a 100 percent accuracy rate in that recall. Since verbatim reproduction does not appear to have been the goal of even trained ancient rhetoricians, I find it much more plausible to concede literary dependence even for Jesus' proverbs when we see verbatim reproductions in our sources and when the material is not liturgical or conventional. More experimentation will be needed to confirm or repudiate this finding.

Results and Analysis: Patterns of Instability

The presented material was modified by my subjects in several consistent ways. All STM *R*s showed that the majority of the presented material could be recalled very accurately, while LTM *R*s demonstrated a great loss or decay in the retention of the material after only a week's interference. This seemed to work on a sliding scale, with the least loss in reproductions of the proverb and the most loss in reproductions of the miracle story. The same was true for the WSR *R*s *although to a much lesser extent*: the distortion of the material was minimal in the proverb *R*s and greatest in the miracle story *R*s. Notable patterns of instability included deletions, additions, substitution of synonyms, and paraphrases.

The most substantial modification to the presented material was in terms of *deleted words* (see Tables 7–9 below). The number of deletions appeared to be dependent upon the genre, with the proverb least affected and the miracle story most affected. In all memory modes, words unimportant or unnecessary to the meaning of the presented material were deleted. Particularly vulnerable were prepositional phrases and relative clauses. Details extraneous to the meaning, disliked by the subject, or unfamiliar to the subject vanished.

The deletions in the reproductions of the proverb (Table 7), although relatively high in the LTM modes (9–10 words per *R*), were stable and persistent across many of the *R*s in all memory modes (Table 10 below). The subjects did not recall words extraneous to the meaning of the proverb. Particularly vulnerable were the relative clause constructions: "those who are"; "are the people who will." The proverb was severely and consistently condensed in terms of words but not of meaning. Frequently in LTM *R*s, the first clause of the proverb was eliminated so that the saying condensed to its last clause: "Only those who are virgins will enter the bridal chamber"; "Only a virgin will enter the kingdom of heaven"; "Only virgins may enter the door"; "The virgins are many but the bridegrooms are few." These cases show the connection of the presented material with already existing schema familiar to the subjects. In the last example above, the proverb has been fitted into the memory of a well-known Jesus saying about the few who find the gate (cf. Matt 7:14) or enter through the door (cf. Luke 13:23-25). Comparatively, the number of words deleted was insignificant in STM *R*s (1–2) and WSR *R*s (>1).

In the Jar Parable, the words that were not reproduced from the presented parable were quite consistent in the LTM *R*s (Table 11). This amounted to a shortening of the parable by half the words in LTM *R*s (average 30–31 words per *R*; Table 8). The beginning and ending of the parable were relatively stable when compared to the middle, where most of the deletions occurred. The cases in which a high number of *R*s deleted exactly the same words are "woman," "filled with meal," "on the road," "still a long way," "while," "behind her," "carrying," "onto the road," "(she) had not noticed a problem," and "at her house." These are all details that are not necessary to the central meaning of the parable. The result is LTM *R*s condensed and focused on only the central pithy features, its thematic bones. As one *R* has it, "The kingdom of heaven is like a woman with a jar of meal. At the beginning of her walk the jar was full, but there was a hole in it that she did not notice. When she arrived, she went to get the meal only to notice the jar was empty." The deletions were half as many in STM *R*s (14–15) and WSR *R*s (17–18; Table 8).

The most pliable of the genres was the miracle story, although stability is observed even in LTM *R*s in the opening of the story ("a young man was chopping wood and the axe fell") and in the end, which contained the Cleaving saying (Table 12 below). In STM *R*s, the entire saying was faithfully recounted, "Arise now! Cleave the wood and remember me," but in LTM *R*s it often was shortened to some variation of "Arise and remember me." Deletions were massive. In STM *R*s, an average of 13–14 words per *R* were not recalled; in LTM *R*s, this doubled to 37–38 words lost per reproduction on average. In WSR *R*s, deleted words averaged 32–33 per *R* (Table 9). The lost details occurred mostly in the middle of the story: the man split open "the sole" of his foot; he bled "so much that he was about to die"; "Jesus heard the crowd calling out for help"; "forcing his way" through the crowd; he "took hold of the injured" foot; Jesus said "to the young man"; "cleave the wood." The result is versions of the story stripped of details, condensed to the bones, as noted in this LTM *R*: "A man was chopping wood. The axe slipped and cut his ankle. The crowd began to shout and Jesus heard and came over. He grabbed the man's foot and immediately healed it. The man looked up and Jesus said to him, 'Remember me, and continue to chop the wood.'"

A second notable pattern of instability in the *R*s related to *additions* of material. Contrast the deletions with the number of words added, and it quickly becomes clear that even moderate expansion of the presented material is not the norm in any of the memory environments. This is particularly the case for reproductions of the proverb, with more flexibility demonstrated for parable and miracle story reproductions. In the LTM *R*s of the proverb, additional words per *R* averaged between 2 and 3 (Table 7). Very little was added in STM *R*s (>1 word). What was added most consistently in these LTM *R*s was the concept that "only" the virgins will enter. A few LTM *R*s began the proverb with a more traditional opening: "There are. . . ." Also added was the notion that the virgins were "allowed" to enter. The WSR *R*s showed on average that less than 1 word was added per reproduction. What this means, practically, is that 5 *R*s added 1–2 words to the proverb: "(waiting) outside"; "only (virgins)"; "(but) only"; "the (virgins)"; "only (ones)"; "allowed to (enter)."

The unique additions in the LTM *R*s appear to result from the tendency of human memory to connect new material to similar material or

TABLE 7
AVERAGE NO. OF WORDS DISTORTED PER REPRODUCTION OF VIRGIN PROVERB

Media Environment	Number Change	Tense Change	Synonym Substitute	Words Added	Words Deleted	Pronoun Change	Transposition
OO: STM Memory	.13	0	.33	1.0	2.71	.33	0
OO: LTM Memory	.44	.33	1.22	2.78	9.33	.11	0
OW: STM Memory	0	.13	.22	.13	2.56	.22	0
OW: LTM Memory	0	.60	1.2	1.2	11.40	.20	.20
WO: STM Memory	0	.07	0	.21	.79	.14	.21
WO: LTM Memory	.25	.50	.29	1.14	9.71	0	0
WW: STM Memory	0	.07	.15	.15	1.23	.15	0
WW: LTM Memory	.44	.33	.50	5.75	8.75	.11	.11
WSR	0	.07	.26	.27	1.07	.07	0

TABLE 8
AVERAGE NO. OF WORDS DISTORTED PER REPRODUCTION OF JAR PARABLE

Media Environment	Number Change	Tense Change	Synonym Substitute	Words Added	Words Deleted	Pronoun Change	Trans-position
OO: STM Memory	0	1.33	4.44	6.11	8.22	.33	.56
OO: LTM Memory	0	2.33	4.56	11.11	30.66	.89	.78
OW: STM Memory	0	1.11	5.67	3.66	16.22	.56	1.4
OW: LTM Memory	0	1.8	3.8	13.00	33.00	.40	1.0
WO: STM Memory	0	1.14	3.93	3.00	20.86	.14	0
WO: LTM Memory	0	1.88	6.86	8.29	29.57	0	.25
WW: STM Memory	0	1.33	5.14	3.57	11.71	.22	.66
WW: LTM Memory	0	.71	7.25	6.25	28.88	.57	1.00
WSR	0	.67	3.33	7.22	17.44	.33	.11

TABLE 9
AVERAGE NO. OF WORDS DISTORTED PER REPRODUCTION OF MIRACLE STORY

Media Environment	Number Change	Tense Change	Synonym Substitute	Words Added	Words Deleted	Pronoun Change	Transposition
OO: STM Memory	.33	.89	4.66	2.89	14.89	1.44	.44
OO: LTM Memory	0	1.22	4.38	15.63	40.38	.88	1.25
OW: STM Memory	.22	1.22	6.25	4.88	16.89	1.11	.56
OW: LTM Memory	0	.75	5.5	11.75	39.25	1.25	1.25
WO: STM Memory	.29	.86	5.21	5.29	13.36	2.21	.57
WO: LTM Memory	0	1.25	8.00	7.63	37.50	1.38	.50
WW: STM Memory	.15	.85	4.46	2.31	10.69	2.61	.46
WW: LTM Memory	0	1.38	6.00	9.38	31.75	2.13	1.25
WSR	0	1.4	3	17.8	32.5	0	.9

to confuse related items (Table 13). For instance, one *R* added "Truly I tell you" at the beginning of the saying, thus bringing the saying in line with other sayings of Jesus familiar to the subject. Another subject put the saying into the context of the parable of The Maidens and the Lamps (Matt 25:1-13), a connection that appears to have been triggered by shared bridal imagery (although that imagery was not reproduced by the subject!): "The kingdom of heaven is like a virgin with a jar of oil." Another subject confused the saying with the parable of The Wedding Banquet (Matt 22:1-10): "The kingdom of heaven is like a wedding banquet." Two other subjects remembered two keywords: "virgin" and "door." One of these subjects remembered the words but not their exact relationship and so recalled, "A virgin is like a door." The other subject appears to have had the same difficulty and reproduced, "A virgin on a doorstep." This tendency of memory was not found in any of the WSR *R*s, where unique additions were not noted, nor in STM *R*s.

The number of words added to LTM *R*s of the Jar Parable was substantially higher than in the LTM *R*s of the Virgin Proverb: 9–10 (Table 9). Quite consistent was the addition of the phrase "of Heaven" or "of God" to "kingdom" in LTM *R*s, while no such addition occurred in the STM *R*s. Preexisting schema appear to have impacted these cases. The other common addition was verbal adjustment: "start to" or "begin to" was added to "leak onto the road." STM *R*s added 3–4 words on average. These were relatively minor distortions: "one day"; "there was"; "(broke) off"; "all the way." WSR *R*s held the middle ground with 7–8 new words added per *R*. These additions were more substantive than those found in the STM *R*s: "coming home with the jar"; "broke unbeknown to her"; "leaking out of a hole in the container, it trickled out little by little."

Most unique additions (Table 14) were embellishments of preexisting elements of the story like "the woman filled the jar and placed it on her back, not noticing that the jar was broken," or "the jar was full but there was a hole in it." There was also a tendency to rationalize or explain the parable. Two STM *R*s added a note at the end that "she was confused," while a LTM *R* added, "she figured out something was wrong." The tendency to explain the parable was most prominent in the unique LTM addition, "She did not realize it was empty until she was at her house. *This is what the kingdom of heaven is like.*" These interpretive additions are very simple when compared with the constant push to reflect and moralize in the WSR *R*s. As noted earlier, the WSR subjects tended to append significant interpretive matter to the closings of the presented material.

TABLE 10
PERCENTAGE OF SAME ALTERATIONS IN REPRODUCTIONS OF VIRGIN PROVERB

Alteration	OO: STM	OO: LTM	OW: STM	OW: LTM	WO: STM	WO: LTM	WW: STM	WW: LTM	WSR	Total %
+ There are				40	29					8
– many people are	13	57		40	7	75		38		19
– people	13			60	14	83		63		32
– many people are standing at the door		63		40		40		38		20
stand < wait/knock/come	38	25		40	50	17	7		6	15
– standing		57		40		67		50		29
– the door		57		60		50		38	6	23

Human Memory and the Sayings of Jesus

door < gate	25						13		4
− those who are	71		60	7	67	7	75	12	33
+ only	43	11	40	21	50	7	88	20	31
those < people/ones	13		20				13		6
− the people who will		55	80	36	100	29	100	12	46
people < ones/those	38	22		14		14		6	10
+ allow (to enter)							25	6	3
− bridal chamber	13	37	40		33			6	14
bridal chamber < Kingdom of Heaven/door/ Bed Chamber/Bridal Suite/Bridal Party/Bride Chambers/Bride Groom Chamber	37		20		17		38		12

TABLE 11
PERCENTAGE OF SAME ALTERATIONS IN REPRODUCTIONS OF JAR PARABLE

Alteration	OO:STM	OO:LTM	OW:STM	OW:LTM	WO:STM	WO:LTM	WW:STM	WW:LTM	WSR	Total %
– The Kingdom is like		33		20	7	20		40	11	15
Kingdom < Kingdom of Heaven		44		80	14	80	14	60	11	34
– woman		44		20	14	20				11
– carrying		67		20	21	20		80		24
– filled			57	60	36	30		60	33	31
filled with < full of			22	20	36	20	57	40	22	24
– filled with (meal)		100		20	7	20		40	33	24
meal < mead/water/grain/sand/seed/wine	11			40	14	40		20	22	15
while < as/when			33		21			20		9
– while		78		100	43	100	14	60	33	48
she < woman	22		22		7	20	14	20	11	9
– she	11	44	22	80	28	80	43	40	33	42
– walking	22	22	22	60	57	60	29	60	22	39
on < down/along	11	33	11		14		29	80	11	21
– on the road	44	44	44	100	43	100	29	100	78	65
– still a long way (from home)	22	100	33	80	50	80		20	67	50
long way < far (away)	11		11				14	40	11	10
– handle	22	33	22	60	14	60		40	22	30
– of the jar	78	44	22	80	43	100	14	60	22	51

− behind her	89	78	11	30	86	40	57	80	67	60
behind her (transposed)	22	33	56	40	14	60	43	20	11	33
− leak		22	11	40	29	20		40	11	19
leak < spill/pour/fall		56	33	60	29	40	43	60	33	39
+ start/begin to	67	11	22		14	20	29		11	19
− onto the road	67	66	66	80	79	80	29	80	44	66
− she did not realize it	22	33	11	20	29	40	14	20	44	26
realize < notice/know	11	11	44	60	29	60	43	60		35
− it	44	44	33	20	64	100	57	20	56	49
− (she) had not noticed a problem	33	67	44	60	43	80	14	60	67	36
notice < realize/know/see	22	22	11	40		7	29	20		17
a problem < there is a problem		11	22	20	29		43		22	16
arrive < get		67	87	40	86	60	86	40		52
arrive < reach/return			11	20	7	20		20		9
− at her house	89			80	100	100	100	80	11	62
at her house < home	89	56	100	80	100	100	100	80	57	85
− the jar down		33	22		38	60				17
down (transposed)	33			20	21	40	14	20		16
− put down	56	44	22	80	29	60	28	80	57	51
put < set/place	11	11	22		36			20		9
− found	11	44	22	60	43	60	14	60	22	37
find < notice/realize/discover	64	22	33	20	21	20	14	20	11	25
empty < almost gone/gone	33		11			20				7
empty < is/was empty	33	67	33	80	71	60	57	80	22	56
+ she is confused							14	20		4

As for the miracle story (Table 9), additions to STM *R*s were relatively minor (average 3–4 per *R*). The added words shifted the verbiage slightly: "was (bleeding)"; "began to (shout)." But in LTM *R*s, this average tripled (11–12 per *R*) and resulted in many more unique and elaborate additions (Table 15 below). LTM additions included new "starts" for the story: "Jesus was teaching and a man . . ."; "While Jesus was preaching, a man with a broken foot . . ."; "One day a man . . ."; "Using an axe while trying to chop the wood . . ."; "One day while . . ."; "One time, Jesus was walking. . .". Story embellishments were observed: "a man cleaved his foot using an axe while trying to chop wood"; "the axe fell and hit his foot and broke it open and there was a crowd around"; "and he heard a man scream"; "cutting down a tree." End additions served to interpret the miracle story, to explain it more fully: "Jesus says, 'Your faith has saved you'"; "and this displayed his power."

In WSR *R*s, 17–18 words on average were added to each reproduction of the miracle story (Table 9). This suggests that the miracle story is the most pliable genre studied even when the written source was retained. Elaboration of some details was observed: "nearby accidentally"; "a man lay dying"; "who had cut his foot badly"; "was losing so much blood"; "the people begged Jesus to heal the man"; "without hesitation"; "the foot was healed the instant Jesus touched it." As noted earlier, additions to the openings and closings of the miracle story were also noted, lengthy and reflective appendices that serve to contextualize and moralize the story.

The presented material, especially in the memory-media environments, underwent a vast shift in verbiage, particularly the *substitution of synonyms*. Words were not simply deleted and added but rather were shifted to completely different synonymous terms. Sometimes the new word was more suitable for modern conversation or represented a particular shift for schematic reasons.

The proverb experienced the lowest number of synonym shifts: practically 0 in STM *R*s (average >1); 1–2 in LTM *R*s; >1 in WSR *R*s (Table 7). The types of STM substitutions were common words: "waiting" < "standing"; "those" < "people." In WSR *R*s, one subject shifted "standing" < "waiting" and another subject shifted "people" < "only ones." In the LTM *R*s, the subjects appear to have adjusted the proverb more heavily, fitting it into preexisting schema: instead of standing at the door, the people "knock," a word choice likely connected to a familiar Jesus saying about knocking (cf. Matt 7:7-8; Luke 11:9-10; Luke 13:25; *Gos. Thom.* 94). The "door" became the "gate," a shift that may have been influenced by prior knowledge of Matthew 7:13-14. Since the bridal chamber is not a very familiar image

TABLE 12
PERCENTAGE OF SAME ALTERATIONS IN REPRODUCTIONS OF MIRACLE STORY

Alteration	OO:STM	OO:LTM	OW:STM	OW:LTM	WO:STM	WO:LTM	WW:STM	WW:LTM	WSR	Total %
– young	11	75	11	75	47	88		63	26	44
man < boy		25			7	13			38	4
– was chopping wood		25		25	47	26	38	13	26	15
and < when/as/but	22	13	33	25	7	50	8	26	63	31
– and	56	38	44	75		38		50	63	42
– fell	11	13	11	50	21	13		26	63	23
fall < slip/drop		25	11			26		26	13	11
split < cut/cleave/injure/slice/land	11	88	56	50	21	38	23	38	63	43
– split		13		25	29	26	8	26	13	16
– open	56	88	56	100	79	75	31	100	75	73
– the sole of (his)	11	75		50	14	63		38	38	31
so much < profusely/heavily/a lot/bad/bled and bled/losing so much blood	11	13	11		29	38		13	26	16
– he bled so much	22	63	11	50	7	50		50	38	32
– that he was about to die	22	63	11	50	7	38		63	38	32

TABLE 12 (cont.)
PERCENTAGE OF SAME ALTERATIONS IN REPRODUCTIONS OF MIRACLE STORY

Alteration	OO:STM	OO:LTM	OW:STM	OW:LTM	WO:STM	WO:LTM	WW:STM	WW:LTM	Retain Sources	Total %
about to die < almost died/to point of death/near death/nearly died/to death/could have died/would soon die	33	25	33	25	14	38	31	13	26	26
– when Jesus heard	11	88		50		63	16	50	75	39
– when	22	88	44	100	7	63	31	50	75	53
– heard	11			50		63	8	50	75	29
– crowd	11	38		50	14	13		50	63	27
crowd < people/townspeople	11	13	11	25		50				12
crowd < man/him			11		7		8	26		4
call out < cry/shout/yell/cheer	22	25	44	25	21	63	38	50	13	33
– calling out for help	22	75	44	75	36	63	23	63	50	46
– for help	44	75	56	100	43	50	23	63	50	56
– run		38	44	25	21	38	16	50	38	30
run < make his way/rush/go/come	33	25	33	50	43	38	16			26

Human Memory and the Sayings of Jesus

– over	67	87	44	75	71	50	62	100	100	73
– to the man	44	87	67	50	50	50	31	88	38	56
– forcing his way	33	38	22	50	21	88		38	38	36
force < push/work/make	11	50	11	50	21	13	46	38	26	30
– through the crowd		50	22	50	21	75	8		38	29
take hold of < hold/grab/touch/clasp/lift/ place/heal	33	63	57	50	50	38		38	50	42
– (took) hold of		38	57	25	50	63	69	88	88	53
– injured	56	100	78	100	86	100	77	100	88	87
– to the young man	22	63	44	75	14	88	23	38	38	45
– young	78	63	100	100	64	100	85	75	75	82
– arise	11	75	22	25	29	50	8	26	26	30
arise < rise/go/get up and walk/continue	11		33	50	21	50	16	63	13	29
– now	22	100	33	100	57	100	54	100	38	67
– cleave the wood	11	75		75		75	8	50	50	38
– and remember me	11	38		25	7	38	8	26	13	18
remember me < believe in me/follow me/you are healed			25	25	7	26	8		13	9

TABLE 13
UNIQUE ADDITIONS TO VIRGIN PROVERB

Media Environment	Additions
OO: STM	None
OO: LTM	Truly I tell you The virgins are many, the bridegrooms are few Only a virgin will enter the Kingdom of Heaven
OW: STM	None
OW: LTM	A virgin on a doorstep A virgin is like a door
WO: STM	None
WO: LTM	The door to heaven
WW: STM	None
WW: LTM	The Kingdom of Heaven is like a virgin with a jar of oil Purity is like faith The Kingdom of Heaven is like a wedding banquet
WSR	None

in the traditional words of Jesus, "bridal chamber" became "kingdom of heaven." Because the subject was unfamiliar with this image, the reproduction often shifted to compatible bridal images: "bed chamber"; "bridal suite"; "bridal party"; "bridegroom chamber."

For the Jar Parable, the synonym shifts were not as disparate in the STM *R*s and LTM *R*s: 4–5 words per STM *R*; 5–6 per LTM *R* (Table 8). The synonym shift was lowest in WSR *R*s: 3–4 words per *R*. The important observation here is that the subjects shifted several of the same words in the same ways consistently (Table 11). The shift from "kingdom" to "kingdom of heaven" was quite popular, especially in LTM *R*s where as many as 80 percent of subjects in a particular memory mode made this shift. This shift is the result of preexisting schema, which developed out of knowledge of the gospel tradition. Some substitutions appear to represent popular American dialect:"Filled with" < "full of"; "long way" < "far (away)"; "leak" < "spill/pour/fall"; "arrive" < "get"; "at her house" < "home"; "find" < "notice/realize/discover"; "empty" < "is/was empty/almost gone." Also shifted was the word "meal," to "mead/water/grain/sand/seed/wine." The subjects transmitting by memory appear to have known that the jar was full and became empty (the point of the parable) but showed some difficulty reproducing exactly what was in the jar (a detail). This suggests that the subjects recalled the point of the parable but not nonessential details, and that these details shifted without conscious effort. "Meal" became "water" and "wine" without any intention on the part of the subject to redact the meaning. Two WSR *R*s shifted "meal" to "grain." This shift does not appear to involve the kind of memory distortion just noted but rather a copyist moving arcane language into common American vernacular.

I also observed that subjects in all modes *except WSR* confused certain elements within the parable. The first mention of "she did not realize it" was mixed up with the later reference, "she had not noticed a problem." Because of the close association of these phrases, in all memory-dependent modes the verb "notice" often replaced "realize," and the verb "realize" frequently became "notice," trading places in the phrases.

The *R*s of the miracle story show a roughly equal number of synonyms substituted in STM and LTM *R*s (5–6 per *R*), but only 3 per WSR *R* (Table 9). The substitutions in all modes were consistent: "split" became "cut"; "call out" became "cry/scream/shout/yell." The subjects appear to have consistently avoided reproducing the word "forced" in reference to Jesus making his way through the crowd: this term was either eliminated or shifted to alternatives like "pushed," "rushed," "went," or "came." This replacement

TABLE 14
UNIQUE ADDITIONS TO JAR PARABLE

Media Environment	Additions
OO: STM	None
OO: LTM	She did not realize it was empty until she was at her house. This is what the kingdom of heaven is like.
OW: STM	None
OW: LTM	Carrying a jug of water back from the well The woman filled the jar and placed it on her back not noticing that the jar was broken The jar was full but there was a hole in it
WO: STM	None
WO: LTM	A jug of meal balanced on her head
WW: STM	She is confused She was confused
WW: LTM	When it got a hole She figured out something was wrong
WSR	The meal was leaking out of a hole in the container. It trickled out little by little. All of the meal spilled out

TABLE 15
UNIQUE ADDITIONS TO FOOT MIRACLE STORY

Media Environment	Additions
OO: STM	None
OO: LTM	Jesus was teaching and a man cleaved his foot While Jesus was preaching, a man with a broken foot One day a man Using an axe while trying to chop the wood He pushes his way through the crowd and approached Jesus Jesus says, "Your faith has saved you." And he touched the man's foot and it is healed. And this displayed his power
OW: STM	None
OW: LTM	One time, Jesus was walking and he heard a man scream. "Be healed and remember me." And the man was healed.

TABLE 15 (cont.)

Media Environment	Additions
WO: STM	By accident chopped into the sole "Cleave the wood and you are healed."
WO: LTM	One day while Cutting down a tree Accidentally slipped "Believe in me" "Follow me and go"
WW: STM	As fast as he could "Cleave the wood and follow me."
WW: LTM	Drops the axe Was dying from blood loss "Remember me always"

may be the result of a contemporary theological apology on the part of the subjects, whose schema may not know of a Jesus who would "force" anything. "Took hold of" was shifted frequently to alternatives such as "touched," "put his hand on," or "grabbed." Several of the LTM synonym shifts appear to have been affected by other related words in the miracle story. Some subjects replaced "split open" the foot in the beginning of the story with "cleave" while at the same time eliminating "cleave the wood" from the final saying. Another shift was to replace "cleave" in the final saying with "chop" from the beginning of the story. This type of confusion of internal elements, which never occurred in the WSR *R*s, appears to be a signal of transmission involving memory rather than copying.

A fourth notable pattern of instability in the *R*s was *paraphrase*. One of the most surprising findings of these experiments related to the WSR *R*s. There were a few general responses to the WSR exercise.

- Some subjects chose to ignore altogether the direct discourse of Jesus' sayings and developed instead an interpretive homiletic paraphrase of them (Virgin Saying: 9/27; Jar Parable: 15/27).
- Some subjects ignored the written source completely and did not reproduce or paraphrase the presented material (Virgin Saying: 3/27; Jar Parable: 3/27).
- Some subjects reproduced the written versions of the sayings practically verbatim (Virgin Saying: 15/27; Jar Parable: 9/27) while liberally modifying the narrative material, especially in the miracle story.

The subjects who opted for homiletic paraphrase often integrated materials they knew from previous exposure to biblical materials. From their responses, it appears that they struggled to give contemporary meaning to archaic and unfamiliar words of Jesus. It seems that some chose paraphrase so that they could more easily modify and explain material that was for them uncomfortable or unknown. The following instances of homiletic paraphrase may serve as representative examples.

- Christians are those in the kingdom often falling away from Jesus like the meal from the jar. . . . Jesus does not want people to sin. He wants them to retain virginity to go to heaven; but he also forgives sinners, like he did with Judas.
- The virgins in the first story are those who have put the physical world behind them in order to be part of something greater. The woman with the jar lost her "reward" because she wasn't paying attention to what was important, but other less significant things. And the young

- man who was healed is told to go back about his business, but always to "remember me." Keeping one's mind focused on higher things is of utmost importance.
- Jesus' second coming marks the end of the world. It will come unexpectedly. As followers we must always be ready and waiting. We cannot be like the woman with the jar full of meal. If we don't watch, by the time we realize, it will be too late. Jesus will come like a thief in the night.
- God was witnessing his kingdom being ruined and destroyed, much like the jar of meal the woman was carrying. God sent Jesus to refill the jar so that his kingdom could be great again. Jesus showed us ways to live our lives so that we may remain in God's kingdom. Rules such as abstinence until marriage were established.
- Jesus wanted to help us, to save us from going down paths that didn't lead to the kingdom. His mission was to get us on track, and "heal our split feet."

These data may suggest that paraphrase is the form of reproduction most consistent with copying or consulting a written text. This appears to be particularly true if the paraphrase involves reflective abstract thinking, commenting at some length on the transmitted material and its meaning or life application. In media environments that rely *solely* on human memory, this type of abstraction and reflection on the presented material does not appear to be primary. What is primary in these instances is the reproduction of the "gist" of the tradition with occasional pithy and concrete interpretive clauses or familiar formulaic phrases to introduce or conclude the material. What I observed in the WSR paraphrases was the move to be analytical, evaluative, and abstract with the transmission of the retained written material rather than concrete and situational.

Having said this, it should be kept in mind that ancient rhetorical training involved teaching young men how to transform a traditional story or aphorism into paraphrase and to point out the moral character of the conventional material. This being the case, it is also true that in these classroom situations, the consultation, memorization, and composition of written speech texts were preparatory to the delivery of the speech. So it remains to be demonstrated that paraphrastic reproduction is *solely* derivative of reliance on written sources, although it surely is a tendency of writers who have in their hands a written source that they are consulting and reflecting upon.

What Does All This Mean?

As I reflect on these experiments and the data they have generated, I am reminded how different experimentation is from theorizing alone. With theory, any reasonable scenario is possible. With experimentation, only scenarios that are supported by the data are possible. In this case, the data says that Rudolf Bultmann's form-critical theory about orality was incorrect because his assumptions were wrong (Bultmann 1962, 1). Although he knew that when narratives pass from mouth to mouth the main point is retained while the details change, Bultmann also believed that there was an original "pure form" of the narrative (Bultmann 1963, 4–5). The oral traditioning process resulted in the transmission of material from original simplicity and purity to versions of increasing complexity and length. In Bultmann's view, it is possible to recover the pure form by removing the later "Hellenistic" layers that had overlaid the primary "Palestinian" original (Bultmann 1958, 12–13).

In the oral traditioning process, however, Jesus traditions (including proverbs) were not expanded, except for an occasional new detail or brief interpretive clause tacked onto the end of the teaching. Instead, the traditions in the oral environment suffered drastic condensation and remodeling until a) they became fixed oral traditions that could easily be passed on intergenerationally with little variation, or b) they entered liturgy, or c) they were copied as sacred texts. Although it might be possible to detect some secondary features in the scribed Jesus traditions—since received material, upon each oral or written performance, is remodeled for a new time and place and purpose (see DeConick 2005; 2006)—any hope of recovering a pure originating oral form (if there ever was one) is dashed.

The idea that the verbatim words of Jesus, or any other "originating" oral source, can be recovered must be tossed out. There is no experimental data that can support this search for "the original," unless we envision a situation where the presented material was passed on immediately upon hearing from one person to the next, or where Jesus' words were scribed down as he spoke and then memorized. Further, in both cases we would have to imagine that the transmitted material was remembered with 100 percent accuracy on the part of the traditioners. Neither of these scenarios seems historically plausible or even possible.

My experimental data did not show any defining characteristics of different media environments where human memory was involved except that STM *R*s in the same media environment (OO and WW) were more accurate than mixed environments (OW and WO). This accuracy degraded completely in LTM *R*s. All media environments that depended on human memory consistently showed that deletion of the presented material was highest in terms of the amount of distortion per *R*. The number of added words and synonym substitution held middle ground. Transpositions of words and phrases and changes in number, tense, and pronouns were minimal. The important point for any discussion of source derivation and dependence is that these memory distortions were consistent throughout the presented material. One of the distinguishing characteristics of literary material that has been derived through a media environment that is dependent upon human memory (OW and WW) is that these sorts of distortions should be consistent throughout the parallel in question. In addition, not only were these memory distortions consistent internally—that is, in any given *R*—but also across *R*s. This means that the same alterations across texts may have absolutely nothing to do with the conscious editorial policy of a redactor or reliance upon the same source.

The data also suggests that when the text in question shows a tendency to preserve the words of Jesus more accurately than the surrounding narrative, the author likely had consulted a written source. This manner of reproduction is not unique to Christian authors. It appears that the words of heroes were retained (near) verbatim in similar but variable literary contexts, too. The recitation composition found in three versions of Plutarch's recounting of Lysander's use of his sword is demonstrative of this principle (see Robbins 1991, 149–51).

Other signs of literary dependence include verbatim strings of sixteen or more words and exact reproductions of sayings and narratives. I did not observe WSR *R*s confusing similar elements within the presented material as was constantly done in LTM *R*s dependent on memory ("noticed" < "realized"; "realized" < "noticed"; "chopped" < "cleaved"; "cleaved" < "chopped"). Authors who were able to consult a written document exercised the choice to paraphrase and also tended to move the presented material into larger interpretive contexts, dialogues, and homilies. These tendencies were not observed in the memory-dependent *R*s, which appeared content to recall the gist of the presented material. Deep reflections on the presented material and abstractions were not observed in the memory-dependent environments. Whether such reflections and paraphrastic constructions are also common in memory-dependent environments should be tested in the future.

These conclusions also suggest that several of the synoptic sequences considered "ambiguous" by McIver and Carroll should be understood as further evidence that the synoptic problem is mainly a problem of literary dependence. To their seven certain instances of "copying" in the Synoptics,[7] we can add at the very least Mark 1:24-25//Luke 4:34-35, Matthew 8:20//Luke 9:58, Mark 12:38-40//Luke 20:45-47, Matthew 8:9//Luke 7:8, and Mark 10:13-16//Luke 18:15-17. All these cases are examples of parallels where there are lengthy verbatim strings of words, and all reflect a tendency to reproduce Jesus' words accurately while dramatically modifying the surrounding narrative.

What remains ambiguous are those texts that show variance—especially deletions, additions, and synonym shifts—since this sort of distortion also can be the result of memory distortions or modifications of a written source that has been consulted. This is particularly the case for narrative materials and even parables. However, when a written source is being consulted and the proverbial words of the hero reproduced (rather than paraphrased or moved into indirect discourse), the Rs do not show the same quantity, quality, and consistency of distortions that occur when the tradent is relying on long-term memory.

Even though these findings should be tested further, the results of these pilot experiments are in line with the results of other experimental data that have been produced by psychologists who study human memory. This fact has broad implications for any theory proposing to establish the historical accuracy, authenticity, or reliability of the gospels as eyewitness testimony. To trust the eyewitnesses because testimony asks to be trusted is nonsense. Whatever memories are preserved in the gospels, they are reconstructed and highly interpreted memories. It is distressing to see a renowned scholar like Richard Bauckham so easily dismiss the work of Bartlett and misappropriate the vast literature on false memories by concluding that "the eyewitnesses behind the gospel accounts surely told what was prominent in their memories and did not need to attempt the laborious processes of retrieval and reconstruction that make for false memories" (Bauckham 2006, 356).

More specific applications of the results of my experiments may help us think more deeply about the synoptic problem and may shed new light on discussions of the *Gospel of Thomas* as a text *literarily* dependent upon the Synoptics. It is my firm opinion that the time has come for the theory of *Thomas*'s literary dependence to be put to bed. More suitable solutions and explanations emerge when we do not ignore experimentation as a means to inform our research, solutions that take seriously the centrality of human memory by recognizing the enormous footprint it has left behind in the early Christian literature.

8

THE GOSPEL OF TRAJAN

Arthur J. Dewey

Footfalls echo in the memory
Down the passage which we did not take
Towards the door we never opened
Into the rose-garden.

                      T. S. Eliot, "Burnt Norton" 1.11–14 (1943)

New Testament scholarship has been recently enhanced through pioneering investigations in social memory. We have begun to see with renewed eyes the necessity of understanding the social cues and defaults of the ancient world. Memory is not a simple action of an individual; rather, it is a social art and habit carved in the words, walls, and woodwork of a world. We have begun to revisit how the ancients tried to communicate. We listen intently to detect echoes we have long overlooked. Werner Kelber has long since led the advance of scholarship in regard to how New Testament writers attempted to communicate. His sensitivity to the means of communication has led him from his original investigations of orality and writing to the consideration of social memory. Kelber has shown a remarkable touch when it comes to the texture of ancient media. He has discerned how orality and writing both play off and against one another in the ancient world. More recently, he has continued his explorations into the ancient means of communication by investigating the deeper and broader aspect of the Greco–Roman echo chamber: its collective memory. This essay has been written not simply to honor Werner Kelber but to contribute to the critical discussion that he continues to engender in the academy. I shall attempt to throw light on one area of this ancient "surround system" by considering how the word "gospel" (εὐαγγέλιον) can be heard within the imperial atmosphere of the Roman Principate. What happens when this word and its associated images are heard within the propaganda world of Rome?

The term *gospel* (εὐαγγέλιον) has often been taken for granted, confined within the New Testament text. Of course, a distinction between the use of εὐαγγέλιον by Paul and its sense in the gospels has often been made. But this is still an internal affair. The primary difficulty with so understanding the term εὐαγγέλιον is that, even when comparisons are made with contemporary nonbiblical usage, investigators are still deaf to the probable echo chamber of the ancient world. In fact, the term was already part and parcel of the Roman propaganda machine that helped establish and maintain the Principate. This essay will sketch out how the "gospel" of Rome developed and then was transformed specifically under the influence of Trajan (ruled 98–117 C.E.). This investigation will not only clarify the historical currents of the imperial sweep but will also throw Paul's use of the term into relief, suggest a possible explanation for the construction of 2 Corinthians (as it stands in the canon today), and cast some light on the subsequent appearance of the narrative gospels.

The Augustan Project

Εὐαγγέλιον takes its primary meaning from the propagandistic activity of the Roman Empire. In a decree of the Provincial Assembly of Asia, dated 9 B.C.E., the Priene inscription presents the benefits of Roman peace as the reason for the worship of the emperor. This inscription illustrates the default usage of εὐαγγέλιον. Implicit in this inscription is the assumption of how the Roman world was composed and worked, and the text underlines that sense of reality.

> Whereas the Providence (*Pronoia*) which has regulated our whole existence, and which has shown such care and liberality, has brought our life to the climax of perfection in giving to us Augustus, whom it filled with virtue for the welfare of men, and who, being sent to us and our descendents as a Savior (*soter*), has put an end to war and has set all things in order; and having become manifest (*phaneis*), Caesar has fulfilled all the hopes of earlier times . . . not only in surpassing all the benefactors (*euergetai*) who preceded him but also in leaving to his successors no hope of surpassing him; and whereas, finally the birthday of the god has been for the whole world the beginning of good news (*euaggelion*) concerning him [therefore, let a new era begin with his birth, and let his birthday mark the beginning of the new year]. (Grant 1957, 174)

Helmut Koester has pointed out that this usage of the term εὐαγγέλιον is new in the Greco-Roman world, in that "it elevates this term and equips it with a particular dignity." He notes that "most likely... early Christian missionaries were influenced by the imperial propaganda in their employment of the word" (Koester 1990, 4). Despite this insight, Koester moves quickly through the Pauline evidence to his real concern, the early Christian collections of sayings and narrative material. For this investigation, however, it is crucial not to leave the scene of the evidence too soon. The term εὐαγγέλιον cannot be read in isolation. The Priene inscription was part of a complex propaganda project. The language in the inscription not only reinforced the accomplishments of the Emperor Augustus (ruled 31 B.C.E.–14 C.E.) but placed him in the mythic realm of Alexander the Great, who also had been sent to deliver the order and harmony of a civilized world. A genuine revolution (of the ages) had begun. The golden age of Virgil's *Aeneid* (book 6) and the Fourth Eclogue was underway. Furthermore, it must be remembered that this inscription, which reflected the revelry and proclamation of the celebrants at Priene, was not originally mute. The term εὐαγγέλιον, then, was part of a larger cultural complex of action and imagination, song and ritual, which enacted devotion to the emperor, thereby sustaining a definite vision of the world.

Further instances of the spectacle of Roman propaganda can be found among the imperial artifacts. Inscriptions under statues, the restrained Ara Pacis, the Gemma Augustea, and the *Res Gestae* of Augustus sustained and attempted to seal the imperial momentum. The Myra inscription found at Myra in Lycia and dated to the early first century C.E., for example, reiterated what was proclaimed at Priene:

> The god Augustus, Son of God, Caesar, Autocrat of land and sea, the Benefactor and Savior of the whole cosmos, the people of Myra [have set up this statue]. (Grant 1957, 175).

Similarly, the Ara Pacis rehearsed the Pax Romana, specifically celebrating Augustus' conquest and pacification of regions in Spain and Gaul. The Roman Senate commissioned the construction of this altar in 13 B.C.E. Its consecration in 9 B.C.E. embodied the vision of Roman religion and life sustained by imperial domination. The marble screens around the altar portray a dedicatory scene in which the piety of Augustus is demonstrated. Engaged in the sacrificial procession, Augustus recapitulates the figure of the legendary Aeneas, portrayed on the adjoining side as veiled in the act of sacrifice. This extensive configuring of *pietas,* of course, reinforced what

Virgil had already published in the new propaganda confabulation for Roman youth: the *Aeneid*.

The Gemma Augustea, a small onyx cameo produced between 10 and 20 C.E., succinctly demonstrates the gospel of the imperial world. In this cameo, Augustus sits enthroned as Son of God, with Jupiter's eagle at his feet and Jupiter's spear in his left hand. He is being crowned by the goddess of Peace, Irene, while captives of the Alpine and Danube areas await their fate below. As the Roman soldiers in the lower left erect a trophy, the message is clear: order is maintained by violent control. On the upper left, dressed in a triumphal robe, Tiberius descends from his chariot. Behind him is the figure of Victory, and the young man in military dress between him and Roma, the goddess of Rome, is his nephew Germanicus, son of his brother Drusus. Nevertheless, the triumphs belong to Augustus, upon whom Roma gazes with admiration.

Perhaps the greatest example of the efforts of Augustus to spread his message comes with the *Res Gestae*. This is Augustus' own summary of his lifetime accomplishments that was originally erected in Rome (14 C.E.). In many respects, it is dependent upon the form of aretalogy prevalent throughout the ancient world. However, this is not simply a litany of the wondrous deeds of Augustus. It is a genuine propaganda product. Although the original no longer exists (probably inscribed on great bronze pillars outside his mausoleum) the inscription found in Ancyra provides us with the text. Evidently copies of the original were set up throughout the empire. Even beyond death, Augustus attempted to maintain control of the way in which his story was to be told.

Res Gestae reiterates through every portion of the text the success story of Augustus. After a brief introduction, enjoining that the text be set up on tablets in Rome, the inscription can be divided into four sections. The first (paragraphs 1–14) deals with the political career of Augustus, detailing his public offices and honors. Next follows a section (15–24) indicating the benefits Augustus provided through donations (money, land, grain), public works projects, and spectacles. The third section (25–33) focuses on his military exploits and alliances. The final section (34–35) points out his influential position in Roman history, his extraordinary virtue, and the recognition of being called "father of the country." There follows some more postmortem notes by someone other than Augustus. It is important to see that Augustus makes it very clear that he has written this in his old age ("When I wrote this I was seventy-six years old"; par. 35). While he had consciously adopted a diffident attitude to acknowledgements of his power and influence throughout his life, he did not shy away from writing and ordering the construction of this final testimonium.

In effect, *Res Gestae* sums up all the propaganda moves that preceded it. The image of a pious and responsible Roman, linked to the mythic figure of Aeneas, modest in respect to the display of power, comes under the influence of this catalogue format. The sheer repetition of offices and honors, donations and benefits, victories and alliances, carry an effective rhetorical weight. The recitation of such a scroll would have a considerable effect, reinforcing all that had been kept in play by the Augustan Principate. The public recitation of the massive rebuilding and new construction projects, the enormity of funds expended for the benefit of Rome and its people, and the longstanding story of success in war and in the maintenance of peace would deliver an overwhelming impression. The mere retelling of these deeds would evoke nothing less than awe.

Trajan's Gospel

We do not have a *Res Gestae* of the Emperor Trajan, but we do have his column. I would contend, in fact, that Trajan's Column represents a significant turn in the advancement of the gospel of Rome. The archeological, architectural, rhetorical, and political elements of this artifact present a case for a monumental development of the εὐαγγέλιον of Rome.

Trajan's Column arose out of urban demands. Despite the enormous construction projects of Augustus, the Rome of Trajan was experiencing serious space problems. Continued population growth and the fact that the other fora were too small for imperial and urban business necessitated new projects. The construction of Trajan's Column was actually part of a solution to this problem, involving a larger building complex. The complex replaced an ancient hill and atrium from the Republican period. At the same time, the booty from the Dacian campaigns gave Trajan the wherewithal to initiate construction. The completed complex would serve as a triumphal reminder of these campaigns.

The column itself was located between two libraries and behind the Basilica Ulpia, which bordered the new Forum Traiani. In the middle of the Forum Traiani stood the Equus Traiani. Although an ancient hill of Rome was actually leveled for the construction of the column, the column's height restored and even added to the lost elevation of the hill. Indeed, one could ascend a spiral staircase within the column and look out upon the new reconstructions of the city (see Figure 1 below). With skylight pouring in from the few windows, the climber would experience a turning, dizzying ascent, punctuated by rectangles of light. On reaching the top, one would emerge into the full light of day on the platform to enjoy a dominating view of the new and old fora.

The construction of this complex was an act of public memory. As Mary Carruthers has pointed out, memory is implicitly social, embedded in the discourse of the day (Carruthers 1998, 9, 11). The act of memory starts with rhetorical *inventio*. This means that memory is not a reiteration or a re-presentation. Instead, it is a crafting of images as well as a construction of a place for the images to inhabit. *Inventio* means both the construction of something new (the memory store) and the storage of what is remembered. *Memoria* is, therefore, a locational memory. Further, *the shape or foundation of a composition must be thought of as a place where one invents.* Thinking is like constructing a building or a column. The act of memory is the work of invention. The person who would tell a story first invents, that is, creates a structure and provides thereby a place for the inventory of images and things about which he would talk.

Trajan's Column provided the space for an unwinding scroll of stone, which wraps around the column and contains an enormous number of running scenes. The stone scroll provides the space for remembering. It wants to be memorized. It presents a public location and structure for viewers to take these scenes to heart and to keep the momentum going until they reach the imperial figure on top. It is not only Trajan's success story; it becomes a memory locus, a place where others can begin to learn to remember and thus retell the story. As the story spirals higher and higher, one climbs with it. The machine of memory lifts the images. The apotheosis of Trajan "authorizes" (in the root sense of the word "to create") the reader to come along for this transcendent experience of victory and honor (*imitatio Traiani*). In effect, the column invites the viewer to enter the momentum of the narrative. It provides the viewer with the means whereby one can continue to tell this story. Every viewer can "author" his or her own version of Trajan's victory story through the workings of memory. It further gives the viewer the mechanism for repeating and revising this and other stories.

It has often been pointed out that, given the location of the column, there was no true opportunity for the viewer to walk around the column and see every scene in order. Although one could have seen portions of the column from the flanking libraries, it does not seem that, until the modern age, the column could be viewed in its entirety. But attempts to gain a "literal" reading of the column may well miss the intended rhetorical

The Gospel of Trajan

Figure 1: Trajan's Column. Note the upward spiral of the images, forming something of a vertical scroll, and the viewing platform just below the statue at the pinnacle.[1]

effect. Viewers would have been impressed with the unrolling campaigns. The column would have "authorized" the viewers' own recollection of the recent events. In sum, the initial impression would invite the viewer to become caught up in the momentum of victory.

Indeed, both the publication of the *Res Gestae* and the erection of Trajan's Column were propaganda pieces intended to be noticed and "read" by the public. Usually one would like to compare like with like, text with text. Yet, as a matter of fact, Trajan's Column was designed as an unfolding scroll with a succession of narrative scenes. Thus, it is possible to compare these pieces of propaganda in order to discover some significant "literary" differences. The thirty-five paragraphs of the *Res Gestae* represent a display of Augustus' deeds and benefits throughout the Roman world. Yet, there is no connected narrative—except for the voice of the aged Octavian. Rather, it is a litany of remarkable performances, an aretalogy of monumental enumeration, displayed to achieve propagandistic effect. The column, on the other hand, presents a running narrative of scenes from the two Dacian campaigns. In contrast, in the *Res Gestae,* Augustus spends only half a paragraph describing his Danube adventures in rather broad strokes (Augustus, *Res Gestae* 30). For Trajan, on the other hand, the Dacian campaigns are the column. Whereas the *Res Gestae* has a universal reach through a piling up of accomplishments, honors, and benefits that would be published in a variety of locations, the column, centered in the capital, draws attention to itself as it focuses on a concentrated narrative about an extraordinary individual. In contrast to that specific narrative, and despite his enormous listing of accomplishments, Augustus still practiced restraint, submerging his extraordinary life within the overall flow of benefits that came from the divine during his regime.

As mentioned above, Augustus attempted to recapitulate the figure of Aeneas. This was done not only within the *Aeneid* (e.g., book 6) but also in the iconography of his principate. Thus, an echo effect was achieved from the image of Aeneas to that of Augustus, which even the coinage indicates. For Trajan, however, the typological becomes transmuted. While the scenes within the column deliver the typical scenes of conquest, the realism of the early second century pushes the portrayal of Trajan away from the earlier iconic imperial pattern of succession. On the Ara Pacis, for example, the sacrificial scene in which Augustus participated becomes a slow motion illustration of what ancient piety means and how it can be imitated; on the column, by contrast, sacrificial scenes are regularly placed within the postures and preparations for war. They are enwrapped in the ongoing narrative scroll. Thus, two different typifications are at work in these two eras. The *Res Gestae* exploits the universal aspects and echoes of the *tupos*, while Trajan's Column offers a slice of an extraordinary *bios*.

Many scholars would simply write off Trajan's Column as an exercise in mythmaking. But that would miss a wonderful clue to the ancient art of memory. Like much of Roman art, ancient memory is locational. It is about invention and inventory, about finding a place to put things. But it is not about repetition or re-presentation. Instead, it is essentially a craft of construction. The teller of stories discovers those structures, which can accommodate what she has to say. The writer (here, architect) devises those patterns, which can provide a superstructure.

In this light, forgetting becomes essentially a displacement. Within the oral competition of the ancient world, there was a struggle for space. This included memory space, especially the location of public memories. Forgetting comes about through displacement or translation: a better pattern has been invented to locate and order the images. Indeed, Trajan's removal of a Roman hill along with republican buildings represented a massive effort in public displacement or forgetting. The column and the Trajanic complex would not only offset the loss but would displace what had been there.

Certainly Trajan could have been honored with something less monumental. A number of scenes around an altar might have pleased Augustus' taste. But the intention was different with Trajan's Column. The very structure delivered a lasting message that was located within the unfolding of the column scroll. The dizzying spiral helped place the reader on the royal road to the star—Trajan! At the same time, one identified with each advance of the legions over the Dacians. The story literally unrolled in front of the viewer. As the viewer moved around, one's memory was exercised. Carruthers put it nicely: "remembering is a task of finding and of getting from one place to another" (Carruthers 1998, 23). Thus, readers find themselves in one scene and then move on to the next, with the overall scroll providing the superstructure or memory location.

As mentioned above, the column was placed between two libraries. It has been speculated that these libraries would have contained the *Commentarii Traiani*. In effect, the column (and the entire complex) delivers the commentaries of Trajan in a different way. The column artistically presents a religious and political coup. While Trajan's commentaries replay the literary achievement of Julius Caesar (in first-person plural), the column delivers a rhetorical *tour de force*. It goes beyond the structure and

Figure 2: Trajan's Column. Trajan addresses his troops as they prepare to embark on a campaign.

intention of a commentary; it has turned the commentary into the monumental. The very placement of the column between the two libraries suggests that Trajan is *vir fortis sapiensque*. He embodies what Alexander, Caesar, and Augustus enfigured: the courageous and wise individual. Pious Aeneas has been brought forward in distinctive second-century features. Wisdom and power meet in this *theios kai mousikos aner*. This is also suggested in the early coins depicting the column with the goddess Minerva atop (later to be replaced by Trajan's statue).

Trajan's Column presents the typography of conquest. The glimpse into a world maintained by violent power offered by Gemma Augustea is now carried forward scene after scene. The order of such disparate military campaigns is organized in a routine, bureaucratic, efficient fashion. Mayhem has been redacted as method; the ordinary preparations for battle become monumental. The scenes flow one into another as graphic reiterations of Roman organization and power.

The column is also a funereal locus. The base of the column would serve as the repository of Trajan's ashes, while the statue atop would announce

Figure 3: Trajan's Column. The vanquished Dacians plead for mercy at the emperor's feet.

his apotheosis in advance. At the same time that Trajan anticipates his death, he looks forward to his divinization. After Trajan dies, the tomb will be filled with his urn; the heavens await the Son of God, and the statue atop the column echoes his heavenly enthronement. This exalted status was later ratified by Hadrian's construction of a temple dedicated to Trajan.

The εὐαγγέλιον of Rome has thus become the personal gospel of Trajan. His military success embodies the good news of the empire. The imperial narrative becomes highly individual (matching the development in Roman art and literature, such as the works of Suetonius, Tacitus, and Plutarch). News has become narrative.

New Testament Correlations: Paul

Dieter Georgi pointed out that the closest historical parallel to Paul's notion of εὐαγγέλιον was found in the Priene inscription. Romans 1:16 indicates that Paul saw his message as a dynamic communication (οὐ γὰρ ἐπαισχύνομαι τὸ εὐαγγέλιον δύναμις γὰρ θεοῦ ἐστιν εἰς σωτηρίαν παντὶ τῷ πιστεύοντι Ἰουδαίῳ τε πρῶτον καὶ Ἕλληνι) that was set very much in competition with the imperial sense of a universal message (cf. Rom 1:1-4; Georgi 1991, 83–90). Yet it is not the case that Paul saw himself as an extraordinary figure in the service of this divine vision; on the contrary, he cast a very human, even comic figure (cf. 2 Cor 4:7ff.; 11). It is the reconstruction of the image of Paul in the second century that has led to this romantic reading of the apostle. The second-century Acts of the Apostles has turned Paul the human actor into a domesticated character, while the Pastorals (1, 2 Timothy and Titus) employ Paul's name and lingering authority to effect a domination stance over the inclusive communities in Asia Minor in that later period. Thus, much of Paul's rhetorical intent with the word εὐαγγέλιον is missed when institutional and compositional developments that occurred after his death are read into it. Εὐαγγέλιον has a much broader echo chamber for Paul than for the later church. For him, it was a dynamic message that was set off against the versatile Roman propaganda machine. His missionary activity, including his letters, represents a concerted effort to announce a new foundation for the world (Gal 6:15; 2 Cor 5:16-21).

While the letters of Paul were collected and edited by the end of the first century, 2 Corinthians was not cited during that period. Apparently for some reason, 2 Corinthians was lost for about fifty years. Neither 1 Clement nor Ignatius of Antioch make any mention of this letter. Marcion is the first to use it (140 C.E.). As the earliest "text critic" of the Christian tradition,

Marcion was the first person to combine a collection of Pauline letters with a gospel (Luke). With his "new testament" in codex form, Marcion had a literary basis for renewal in a church he thought had greatly compromised the original inspiration of the apostles. He wanted to purify the church from the meddling effects of the God of Israel, who was not the Father of Jesus but a violent demiurge. Marcion also wanted to make sure that the church realized that it was in a radically new situation brought to light through the appearance of Jesus. He wanted to move away from old appearances to the revolutionary reality of God's Anointed. There is a further element to this mystery. It has been often noted that 2 Corinthians is filled with discrepancies—literary, rhetorical, and logical. In light of such observations, the question of the unity of 2 Corinthians has arisen as a consistent problem for Pauline critics: 2 Corinthians can be divided into six different fragments: 2:14–6:13 and 7:2-4; 10-13; 1:1–2:13; 8; 9; 6:14–7:1 (the last non-Pauline; see A. Dewey 2002, 149–51).

There are several possible reasons why Marcion or a follower "unearthed" 2 Corinthians: the themes of the "new covenant versus the "old covenant" (chapter 3); darkness opposed to light (chapter 4); a new creation in God's Anointed (5:17); the linkage of the old covenant with slavery (chapter 3); Moses' God seems to be like the Platonic demiurge; the apparent docetic remarks (5:16) and anthropological dualism (4:16) utilized by Marcion; the condemning of false emissaries (11:13-15). In brief, this material gave Marcion considerable justification for his argument. The present canonical version of 2 Corinthians may well be a Marcionite reconfiguration of Pauline fragments. In other words, under the Marcionite view, the earlier Pauline fragments were recombined. It fits in with the extravagant time that was the first third of the second century. Some scholars have called it an age of triumphalism. The emphasis upon the extraordinary individual had reached its zenith. Trajan's Column was only one instance of the apotheosis of the individual. At the same time, the empire was undergoing significant centralization. It was also a period of canonization (note, for example, the Rabbinic canon) as well as an anti-Judean period (Bar Kokhba revolt). There were shifts in eschatological thought and increased religious activity with competing movements and mystery religions.

From the point of view of the present reader of 2 Corinthians, this "unified" text greatly resembles the flow of Trajan's Column, displaying a great individual (Paul) endowed with power and spirit. The canonical 2 Corinthians very much bears the imprint of the second century. This "apotheosis on a scroll" might be summarized as follows:

Thanks to God for Paul, who is truthful and reconciling, triumphant in adversity; who recognizes the old is replaced by the new; who bears up in dire straits for personal glory; who is leading a triumphant procession across the world, making a collection which is a token of the universal movement; who warns all to be aware of false prophets; who might encourage a return to the ways of the Old Covenant; who blesses all in the spirit.

I would contend that those today who would argue for the rhetorical unity of 2 Corinthians not only have too quickly dismissed the serious discrepancies in the text but also have been tacitly persuaded by the restructured enhancement of the figure of Paul. Such a reading plays into the Roman triumphalism of the early second century. Coupled with a romantic image of Paul as a theological genius or maverick Jew, such a monumental reading of Paul becomes an unspoken template for subsequent discussion.

New Testament Correlations: Gospels

Finally, let me consider the implications of this discussion for understanding the composition of the gospels. In a previous article, I have explored the development of the passion narrative within the understanding of constructive social memory (A. Dewey 2005). Given the transition from the propaganda patterns of Augustus to the Column of Trajan, is there any cultural connection to the composition and development of the gospel tradition? In other words, can scholars take a wider look around? What comes into view when one asks if the development of the gospels emerged within the cultural, historical, political, and imaginative fronts of the empire?

I have already noted that the term εὐαγγέλιον comes out of this competitive ἀγών. It is time to consider a further phase in the "gospel traditions." Can the transition from the Jesus sayings traditions to written materials be understood within the larger cultural developments? Source and redaction critics have determined that these sayings collections and narrative texts have come out of particular communities with specific agendas. Nevertheless, the question can be asked: Why was there a shift from collections of sayings (such as Q) to the paratactic narrative of Mark? There has been much discussion over the notion of *bios* as the underlying structure for the gospel narratives. In other words, various sayings collections were reconfigured along the lines of a particular life. Yet, there is more in the development of the gospels than a simple shift in genre. I would contend that we have already seen in the Roman material a major change in the focus and intensity of propaganda. With Trajan's Column

The Gospel of Trajan

Figure 4: Trajan's Column. The goddess Nike (Victory) surveys the spoils of Trajan's conquest.

comes the evidence of a sustained focus upon an extraordinary individual. The differences between the column and the *Res Gestae* noted above argue for a dramatic change in perspective. The shift from a sayings format to that of a narrative in early Christianity may well be symptomatic of the larger cultural shifts occurring in the late first and early second centuries. And with this shift came a reimagining and thus a restructuring of how the Jesus traditions were remembered and communicated.

A rereading of the Gospel of Mark after closely examining Trajan's Column bears interesting results. The column unwinds in paratactic scenes. One can even note Trajan speaking to his followers from a boat. An angelic Nike stands by trophies at an empty tomb. But the individual scenes, however suggestive, should not divert the reader from the larger picture, namely, that the column provides the location for the Dacian campaign narratives. Similarly, the structure of the Gospel of Mark provides the frame not only for the earlier passion citations but also for sayings and healing traditions. Moreover, this gospel is distinctly untriumphal. As such, it stands in opposition to what is found both in the Augustan and Trajanic material. Indeed, the triumphal flourish of the Roman material has been dramatically turned upside down. This last point has been made before in terms of Mark reversing a messianic or Jewish triumphalism. However, a critical reading places the Gospel of Mark within the larger imperial echo chamber. A discordant sound comes from such a reconstruction.

In what may well appear as an impressionistic sketch of ancient imperial culture, I have tried to open up the reading of New Testament material to the echo chamber of the empire. Of course, all the remaining evidence stands mute. Yet, even from those silent figures, from the debris of monuments and cities, come some exciting interpretive possibilities. To extract some inkling of ancient social memories demands work among the ruins and engagement with these materials in a controlled and disciplined imaginative dialogue. The material of the New Testament cannot receive a fair and adequate hearing without taking into account these imperial sound waves caught forever in stone.

9

THE SCAR OF THE CROSS
The Violence Ratio and the Earliest Christian Memories of Jesus

Chris Keith and Tom Thatcher

[W]hat we celebrate under the title of founding events are, essentially, acts of violence legitimated after the fact by a precarious state of right. What was glory for some was humiliation for others. To celebration on one side corresponds execration on the other. In this way, symbolic wounds calling for healing are stored in the archives of the collective memory.

—*Ricoeur 2004, 79*

For well over a century now, form critics, historical Jesus scholars, and, more recently, orality/literacy specialists have been attempting to uncover the earliest Christian memories of Jesus. A key point of debate relates to the formation and role of passion narratives—stories about Jesus' suffering and death—in early Christian tradition. Many scholars today continue to support the theory that the Gospels of Mark, John, and possibly *Peter* absorbed and adapted pre-formed oral stories about Jesus' death. Resisting this trend, Werner Kelber has consistently argued, on the basis of extensive interdisciplinary research on orality/literacy transitions in traditional cultures, that oral passion stories did not exist. According to Kelber, the gospel writers developed passion narratives after substantial reflection on Jesus' death and with a view to silencing prophetic preachers who blurred the boundary between the historical Jesus and the risen Lord. In Kelber's model, Mark essentially invented the genre of the passion narrative by including in his gospel a connected account of the events surrounding Jesus' death (Mark 14–16). Obviously, this issue raises significant implications for understandings of the historical Jesus, early Christian tradition, the gospels, and the history of Christian origins.

The present article will argue that Kelber is *correct* to assert that there was no single, monolithic passion narrative that was transmitted from one Christian to the next until its inevitable inclusion in the Gospel of Mark but *incorrect* to assert that Mark essentially created the genre of the passion story. Recent research on social memory, and specifically on the impact of traumatic violence on group memory, suggests that Jesus' followers must have developed coherent stories of his death at a very early date and that Mark's strategy for managing the memory of that event was likely typical of prior oral performances.

Social memory theorists show particular interest in the impact of trauma on personal and group recollection. Groups depend heavily on images of the past to establish and maintain a sense of heritage and identity. For this reason, traumatic events, including experiences of extreme violence, present a serious challenge to group cohesion. Not only have some members of the memory circle disappeared, the past now includes a significant moment that cannot be forgotten but also cannot easily be worked into the group's worldview. Notable recent examples include the Holocaust, the genocides in Rwanda and Bosnia, and the 9/11 terrorist attack. Events of this type must be explained and somehow incorporated into group consciousness in a way that allows survivors to feel connected to the past and hopeful for the future. Groups normally attempt to cope with such traumatic experiences by "keying" them to other events and themes in their established heritage stories, creating new narratives on the basis of cherished values. The sudden and violent death of Jesus presented such a memory crisis to the earliest disciples, who must have quickly responded by keying the events surrounding the cross to well-known Jewish themes. If they had not been able to do this almost immediately, the Jesus movement would have dissolved long before people like Mark and John could write gospels.

Kelber on the Genesis of the Passion

Kelber's thesis that Mark essentially created the genre of the connected passion narrative is a reflex of his larger understanding of early Christian media culture and, in many respects, a rebellion against earlier form-critical models. It will be convenient here to summarize the older form-critical understanding of the origins of the passion narrative before discussing the reasons why Kelber's oral hermeneutic led him to reject this approach. The discussion below will focus on one of the most prominent early proponents of a pre-Markan passion narrative, Martin Dibelius.

Martin Dibelius' monumental *From Tradition to Gospel* (first edition 1919) laid the theoretical groundwork for much subsequent discussion of early Christian tradition. Dibelius' model of form development in many respects anticipated Kelber's work by emphasizing the social dimension of oral communication. Specifically, Dibelius argued that the set "forms" of primitive Jesus tradition that are observable in the gospels today—paradigms, tales, legends, and so forth—were natural byproducts of typical situations in the life of the church, arising as early Christians shaped their collective memories of Jesus to meet the needs of preaching and teaching. In Dibelius' view, three categories of individuals were particularly influential in the development of gospel materials: "evangelists," "teachers," and "preachers." "Evangelists" appropriated Jesus tradition in their attempts to persuade Jews and Gentiles to accept Christ; "teachers" offered moral and doctrinal instruction to new converts; "preachers" exhorted established Christians to remain faithful, normally in contexts of worship. The unique social dynamics of each rhetorical situation caused aspects of the tradition to become "fixed" in their "outer and inner structure," creating distinct forms appropriate to these various speech contexts (Dibelius 1971, 10). For Dibelius, then, any discussion of the development and transmission of early Christian tradition is essentially a discussion of the situations in which early Christians exchanged words about Jesus.

Following the logic that form follows function, Dibelius argued that a relatively stable passion narrative must have arisen early in the church's life. Indeed, the passion narrative was likely the first fixed unit of Christian tradition simply because its content was relevant to all three of the rhetorical situations outlined above. Evangelists needed a passion story to rationalize the scandalous events of Jesus' crucifixion and explain his connection to prophecy; teachers would draw from this account to discuss the theological significance of Jesus' death; preachers would cite the passion narrative to remind worshippers of Christ's example of self-sacrifice and to prepare them for the observance of the Eucharist. In view of these typical applications, the primitive passion story emphasized three themes: Jesus was sent to the cross by his own people; Jesus died in accordance with Scripture and in fulfillment of divine purpose; Jesus rose from the dead and appeared to many of his disciples. These themes must have characterized the passion story from an early date, as evident from the outlines of the evangelistic speeches in Acts and Paul's primitive summary of the gospel message at 1 Corinthians 15:1-8 (Dibelius 1971, 15–23).

Dibelius' approach to the development of early Christian tradition, including his theory on the early emergence of a fixed passion narrative, informed his understanding of Mark's place in the history of Christian origins. In one respect, Mark's attempt to integrate traditional sayings and stories into a larger narrative that culminates in Jesus' death was revolutionary, "a development of greatest consequence" (Dibelius 1971, 261). Yet Mark was a redactor, not an author: in Dibelius' view, Mark simply collated pre-formed units of oral tradition. As a result, the Gospel of Mark is not so much an original literary work as a "handing down, grouping, and working over" of earlier material (Dibelius 1971, 3). Traditional narratives and sayings, and sometimes primitive sequences of events, were cited intact. In organizing these materials, Mark composed narrative bridges and adjusted the introductions and conclusions of the smaller units to create smooth transitions, but this work was so minimal that the contours of the tradition are immediately evident behind his light editing (Dibelius 1971, 44–45, 224–25, 237). Following this logic, Dibelius argued that Mark's passion story was drawn directly from primitive Christian tradition—Mark 14–16 would closely resemble any sermon on Jesus' death that one might have heard in a Pauline church in the mid-50s C.E. Mark's only original contribution lay in the juxtaposition of the passion with other traditional stories and sayings, a move that connected "the life and sufferings of Jesus with the faith and hopes of Christians" by orienting Christ's earthly activity toward a death that the church already understood to be soteriological (Dibelius 1971, 226).

While Dibelius' model conveniently explains the emergence of the passion narrative in early Christianity and Mark's appropriation of that story into his book about Jesus, Kelber rejects this approach for two reasons. First, in Kelber's view, every early oral performance of Jesus material was equiprimordial, a discrete and independent utterance with no textual relationship to other performances. This being the case, Kelber cannot accept the notion that an "original" story of Jesus' death gradually evolved through oral transmission until its inevitable assimilation into Mark's gospel. Second, in Kelber's view, there is no real evidence that early Christians felt compelled to tell connected narratives about Jesus, particularly the type of complex sequence that appears in Mark 14–16. In the oral period, episodes from Jesus' life were generally discussed in isolation, sometimes strung together paratactically to emphasize a theme but never really organized into cause–effect plots. This being the case, Kelber can find no motive for the development of a narrative about Jesus' death in the oral milieu of early Christianity. The logic of both of these arguments, particularly as developed in *The Oral and the Written Gospel* (1983), will be briefly reviewed here.

Kelber's model of early Christian tradition is predicated on the notion that oral words are absolutely occasional and, therefore, utterly discrete. "Spoken words have no life apart from speakers and hearers," and utterances take the situations in which they are exchanged as the intertexts that give them meaning (Kelber 1983, 23). This understanding of the dynamics of oral speech forces Kelber to reject conventional models of "tradition." Specifically, since all acts of speech are independent and, indeed, "equiprimordial," early Christian tradition should not be viewed as the transmission of a specific content from one speaker to another but rather as "a plurality of forms and directions" (Kelber 2002a, 64; 1983, 33). The term "Jesus tradition" rightly refers *not* to a specific set of words or a narrative content handed down from one preacher to another but rather to the total number of instances in which all early Christians everywhere told stories about Jesus or repeated his sayings. Indeed, "in orality, *tradition is almost always composition in transmission*" (Kelber 1983, 30, emphasis original). Following this logic, Kelber can scarcely accept Dibelius' premise that an early passion story was repeated and handed down, gradually becoming more and more complex on its way into Mark's gospel. As a corollary, any attempt to work backward through the traditioning process and uncover an "original" version of the story of Jesus' death is futile. "We are not concerned with questing after the *original form*, for no such thing ever existed in oral speech" (Kelber 1983, 45–46, emphasis original).

Kelber's view of oral speech and his understanding of early Christian tradition force him to reject any attempt to reconstruct the evolution of Mark's passion story or to locate the primitive "original version" of Jesus' death. But even if Mark was not copying a fixed account, could one argue that he was building on the precedent of a series of prior oral performances? If Dibelius was wrong to suggest that a relatively fixed passion narrative had evolved several decades before Mark composed his gospel, could it still be that Mark was simply following a typical Christian practice of telling connected stories about Jesus' death? In Kelber's view, the emergence of the passion narrative is only one instance of a more general problem in Christian origins: "The issue raised is whether there exists in orality the impulse to collect material into an *oral gospel* of the nature and scope of the written gospel" (Kelber 1983, 77, emphasis original). In other words, before discussing the passion narrative specifically, one must ask whether early Christians were interested in connected narratives about Jesus' life *at all*. A number of factors force Kelber to answer this question in the negative and to conclude that Mark was, in fact, the first Christian to produce a passion narrative. Because Kelber's arguments for this conclusion are central to the concerns of the present essay, three of his more notable points will be briefly reviewed here.

First, in Kelber's view, Dibelius' notion of a fixed, primitive passion narrative is inconsistent with oral psychology. Mark and Q, two texts heavily dependent upon oral tradition, illustrate the fact that orality organizes information in a paratactic, rather than a programmatic, fashion. "The oral mind collects and clusters similar materials by virtue of analogical or associative thinking. . . . [K]nowledge is gathered and multiplied more than critically developed." Hence, when early Christian preachers told several stories about Jesus in sequence, they were not attempting to string the episodes together into an overarching plot but were rather simply presenting multiple examples of the same point for emphasis (Kelber 1983, 80). This disinterest in continuity and uniformity explains, for Kelber, the remarkable diversity of forms and genres evident in Mark's gospel. "Given this [observable] heterogeneity, there exists [in early Christian culture] no imperative need for the telling of a single, comprehensive story about Jesus"—in live performance, even occasional conflicts in detail would be overlooked because the oral mindset "can subscribe to multiple truths and identities without any apparent concern for an encompassing logical arrangement" (Kelber 1983, 79). Simply put, the evidence does not suggest that oral cultures generally, and early Christian oral culture specifically, would feel any need to combine a number of discrete scenes into a logically coherent story of Jesus' death.[1]

Second, Kelber rejects the theory of a pre-Markan passion narrative on the grounds that this notion is inconsistent with the ideological history of Christian origins. In Kelber's view, Dibelius' arguments for a fixed oral passion story were implicitly driven by "theological presuppositions," specifically by the belief that early Christian preaching must have focused on Jesus' sacrificial death. This line of thinking is undermined, however, by the absence of a passion account in Q, a source at least as old as Mark. "The very theology of the sayings source casts doubt on the assumed existence of an early passion narrative" or at least proves that not all early Christians were especially interested in the crucifixion (Kelber 1983, 191–92). Further, the oral materials that Mark has incorporated into his gospel, when removed from their current narrative framework, betray a Christology that is inimical to meditation on the cross. "The heroic [healing] and polarization [exorcism] stories display an oral Christology decidedly antithetical to passion Christology"—in other words, healings and exorcisms emphasize Jesus' power and authority, a theme that would be undermined by an account of his gruesome death. Nor do the didactic stories promote reflection on Jesus' demise, focused as they are on morality and community problems. Perhaps one could discuss the mystery and paradox of the cross through parables, but Kelber notes that Mark generally does not talk about Jesus' death in parabolic sayings, and the few exceptions to this rule certainly do not suggest that conditions were ripe for the development of a pre-Markan, parabolic passion story. In summary, "one must conclude that the bulk of the synoptic tradition . . . shows little interest in the suffering and death of Jesus . . . [and] reflects a hermeneutical climate that is anything but favorable to the composition of a passion narrative" (Kelber 1983, 192–93).

Third and finally, Kelber contends that Dibelius' arguments for a fixed, oral passion story are burdened by an essential misinterpretation of Mark's posture toward prior Christian tradition. As noted above, in Dibelius' model, Mark played a passive role, collecting and preserving the creative work of others with little reflection on the content or theology of these oral materials. Kelber, however, concludes that "the very genre of the written gospel may be linked with the intent to provide a radical alternative to a preceding tradition" (Kelber 1997, xvii). The evidence from Paul's letters and Q suggests that "speech in the early [Christian] period thrived in a social world in which . . . prophets, unbounded by place or commissioned by a local community, and authorized by the Spirit, prompted a rapid if irregular dissemination of words" (Kelber 1983, 31). These charismatic prophets and teachers claimed that their utterances were inspired by God's Holy Spirit; speaking from this platform, they could evoke "the present authority of Jesus," an authority that would be enhanced whenever they recited traditional sayings (Kelber 1983, 201). This rhetorical posture would, however, necessarily decontextualize Jesus' words and blur the boundary between his historical ministry and his ongoing spiritual presence in the church— past, present, and future all run together in the moment that the living Lord's words are spoken (Kelber 1983, 203). In Kelber's view, Mark wrote a narrative gospel specifically to combat such oral performances of Jesus tradition and to counter the Christology that they promoted. Exploiting the potentials of both narrative and writing, Mark contextualized Jesus' mighty words and deeds in an overarching story that climaxes in his death—a graphic reminder that Christ said and did these things in the past, not in the present. "Mark writes primarily not for the sake of continuing the sayings genre, and not at all to duplicate oral Christology, but rather to overcome what are perceived to be problems caused by oral speech and its authoritative carriers" (Kelber 1983, 208). Mark's passion story was, then, a key aspect of his overall strategy to undo the hermeneutics of orality, a genre he invented to combat both those people who based their authority on oral proclamation and the immanence Christology that they promoted. This being the case, one can scarcely suggest that Mark was a passive redactor who simply preserved an oral passion account; one must, rather, view "the written gospel as a counterform to, rather than an extension of, oral hermeneutics" (Kelber 1983, 185).

While the above review dramatically simplifies a complex set of arguments, it has hopefully indicated the main contours of Kelber's position on the emergence of the passion narrative. Kelber's understanding of oral cultures generally, and early Christian culture specifically, forces him to conclude that Mark was the first person to compose a connected account of the events surrounding Jesus' death. Further, because Kelber dates the composition of the Gospel of Mark shortly after the events of 70 C.E. (Kelber 1983, 210–11; 1997, xxiii; 2002a, 80), his theory suggests that passion narratives first emerged some forty years after the crucifixion.

Social approaches to memory, and to tradition as a form of collective memory, would suggest that Kelber's theory on the genesis of the passion is both accurate and inaccurate. Kelber is *correct* to argue that there was no single, monolithic passion narrative transmitted from one Christian to another and inevitably moving toward Mark's presentation. At the same time, however, Kelber is *incorrect* to suggest that Mark essentially invented the passion narrative as a genre. Violent events, like Jesus' crucifixion, traumatize group memory to such an extent that memorialization is necessary almost immediately, and the development of commemorative narratives is a typical mnemonic strategy for the maintenance of group identity. Simply put, the followers of Jesus could not continue as a coherent group without a strategy for moderating and rationalizing the trauma of his death, and it seems that the development of a passion narrative keyed to major themes from Jewish Scripture and tradition would be a likely means of accomplishing that goal.

The remainder of this essay will take the form of a loose dialogue with two further points of Kelber's argument against the early development of a passion narrative. First, in discussing whether the early oral Christians would feel compelled to create a connected account of Jesus' gruesome demise, Kelber notes that ancient writers generally say very little about crucifixion and seem particularly hesitant to relate specific details of the practice. This fact, alongside the general oral disinterest in Jesus' death noted above, leads Kelber to ask, "[I]s it plausible that the first recollection early Christians committed to writing would become one of the most realistic of all passion narratives in antiquity?" Kelber does not answer this question directly but suggests an obvious solution by noting that Jesus' death was extremely traumatic for his disciples and that "*distance from the trauma* [is] an essential psychocultural prerequisite for most mediations of death." In Kelber's view, at least as expressed in *The Oral and the Written Gospel*, one must "assume geographical, chronological, and psychological distance" from the cross before any passion narrative could develop, a theorem that obviously weighs against the existence of a fixed, pre-Markan account (all quotes Kelber 1983, 193–94, emphasis original). As will be seen, the impact of violence and trauma are, indeed, key issues in group commemorations of the past, but contemporary approaches to memory do not support Kelber's specific application of this principle to the genesis of the passion narrative.

Second, having dismissed the notion that Mark passively appropriated a pre-formed passion story, Kelber proceeds to offer an alternate view of Mark's compositional technique. Mark's "passion narrative is largely built on [Old Testament] texts and texts recycled into the oral medium, that is, secondary orality." Indeed, as is often observed, Mark 15 would essentially be reduced to nil if all allusions to Psalm 22 were removed from the account. Kelber concludes from this that, for Mark, the notion that Jesus' death was a fulfillment of Scripture is "not merely a theological principle, but a compositional one as well" (Kelber 1983, 196–97). One may say, then, that Mark wished for his readers to experience the death of Jesus through the medium of a connected narrative that is closely keyed to passages from the Hebrew Bible. As will be seen, this procedure is a typical cross-cultural method of memorializing and managing experiences of traumatic violence.

Scarred Memory

Kelber's more recent writings, influenced by the emergence of social approaches to memory, call for a substantial reconsideration of the nature of early Christian tradition (see especially Kelber 2002a; 2005). Until recently (and often still today), biblical scholarship has been driven by the Aristotelian notion that "memory" is essentially a biomechanical capacity of individual human brains. Following this model, individuals store images of empirical experiences in their bodies like imprints on a wax tablet; one "remembers" by mentally perusing these catalogued images at some later time; the accuracy of any individual's memory is a function of the quality of her neurological organs (Aristotle, *On Memory* 450a25–31). Applied to Christian origins, this approach to memory would suggest that Jesus' associates recorded sensory impressions of things he said and did in their brains; at some later time, they pulled out these recollections "like checked baggage from storage" and shared them, more or less accurately, with other people; these second-generation Christians subsequently shared their own recollections of the stories they had heard; the total transmitted content of these various memories represents "the Jesus tradition" (first quote Lowenthal 1985, 252).

This model of tradition and transmission informed Dibelius' understanding of the development of the passion narrative, as described above. Some of Jesus' followers observed the events of his death; later on, these individuals shared recollections of this experience with other people; these second-generation Christians recalled this information and reshaped it to fit the needs of their own preaching and teaching, variously adding, subtracting, and revising information; ultimately, Mark wrote his account of the cross on the basis of his own recollections of such sermons and lessons. Viewed in this light, the passion narrative was essentially a fixed content that was handed down from one individual to another like a family heirloom, fading over time through the gathering of dust and occasionally renovated for new contexts of display.

As Kelber has noted, this approach to tradition fails to account for the situational nature of all oral language and incorrectly understands "memory" as a purely individual, biological experience of storage and recall. Recent approaches to group memories—such as the memories of Jesus shared among early Christians—are less concerned with the specific content of memory than with the social circumstances under which statements about the past are produced and communicated. The concept of "memory frameworks," first developed by French sociologist Maurice Halbwachs, has become foundational to social memory theory (Halbwachs 1992). Whereas popular conceptions portray "memory" as a recall of individual experience, social approaches see "memory" as a representation of the past in service of present realities and needs. The "frameworks of memory" are the social and physical contexts in which discourse about the past is produced and communicated (see Thatcher 2006, 54–60). A social approach to early Christian memory would be less interested in the transmission and mutation of a specific body of content about Jesus than in the reasons why different Christians at different times and in different locations thought about him in different ways.

In terms of the present study, a social memory approach would ask *why* any early Christian, like Mark, would feel compelled to tell stories about Jesus' death and *how* such narratives would help Christian communities establish their own collective identities as followers of Christ. Specifically here: *Why would early Christians invent passion narratives, and at what stage of the church's history would they have been most likely to do so?*

A preliminary answer to the first part of the above question—Why would early Christians invent passion narratives?—may be derived from Michael Schudson's observation that certain events cannot be ignored in a group's collective memory of the past. "Not only must Americans confront slavery, not only must Germans face the Holocaust, but they must do so repeatedly, obsessively, necessarily, whether they like it or not" (Schudson 1989, 110). As Schudson's examples suggest, collective memory rarely overlooks instances of unusual violence, as evident from the emphasis on wars and battles in many history textbooks. Violent events are remembered for two reasons. First, violent events demand controlled commemoration simply because they bend the social frameworks of memory by disrupting the normal flow of life and suddenly changing the structure and membership of the group. If one member of a family is killed in an automobile accident, the remaining members cannot overlook this event simply because the death of their loved one necessarily reconfigures the structure of their primary social unit. For the same reason, Germans must remember the Holocaust simply because that event suddenly and dramatically eliminated a large portion of their national population. Second, and much more substantially here, violent events are remembered because they inherently threaten a group's sense of order and identity. Arthur Neal has noted that violence not only mars the bodies of individuals but also creates "an injury, a wound, or an assault on social life as it is known and understood" (Neal 1998, 4). Violent events may force the members of a memory group to recognize the vulnerability of their sense of identity, way of life, and perception of reality, as evident from American reactions to the 9/11 attack. In such cases, the group must develop commemorative strategies that rationalize the experience of violence by casting it in familiar forms. Social memory cannot tolerate meaningless violence.

Obviously, a group does not commemorate every violent event that in some way impacts some of its members, and sometimes groups forget events that are much more violent than others that are remembered. A great many Americans are murdered each year, yet the social impact of the total number of these violent deaths is inconsequential when compared to the social impact of John F. Kennedy's assassination, an event many

Americans still recall vividly more than four decades later. In his book *National Trauma and Collective Memory*, Arthur Neal explains this phenomenon by noting that "the [defining] test for a national trauma is that of the disruptive effect of an extraordinary event on the institutional underpinnings of social order" (Neal 1998, xi). Schudson refers to events of this type as "scars" (Schudson 1992, 218–19). Violent events become traumatic scars on a group's memory when they not only suddenly eliminate members of the group but also threaten the group's sense of continuity and identity. The litmus test for a traumatic violent event, then, is not necessarily its degree of violence or the scope of its effect but rather its perceived impact on the social order. The assassination of John F. Kennedy remains significant in American national memory simply because that event appeared to threaten "the integrity of the social fabric." "Under conditions of national trauma, the borders between the sacred and the profane, between good and evil, between life and death become fragile. People individually and collectively see themselves as moving into uncharted territory. The central hopes and aspirations of individual lives are temporarily put on hold and replaced by the darkest of fears and anxieties" (Neal 1998, 7). Thus, the atomic bombing of Hiroshima continues to play a key role in the collective memory of the human race despite the fact that this event caused only a tiny percentage—indeed, a statistically insignificant percentage—of the total number of casualties of World War II.

As Alan Kirk has noted, mnemonic scars typically evoke "the exertion of strenuous effort to restore moral coherence and social continuity by working out the *meaning* of the violence suffered" (Kirk 2005, 193, emphasis original; see also Keith 2006). Faced with the loss of significant members, groups scramble to tie traumatic experiences to a meaningful past in order to maintain a sense of continuity. In cases of extreme trauma, these commemorative strategies are set in motion almost immediately. Liisa Malkki's study of the genocide of the Hutu nation in Africa illustrates this phenomenon particularly well. In 1972, members of the minority Tutsi nation began to randomly murder Hutu living in Burundi in an ethnic-cleansing campaign, causing many Hutu to flee to refugee camps in Tanzania. These events obviously challenged the Hutus' sense of identity and disrupted connections to their former way of life, forcing them to manage the trauma through commemorative activities that could provide some level of continuity between past and present. Malkki notes that "the arrival of tens of thousands of Hutu into exile in Tanzania was seen as the period when a collective, overarching understanding of the apocalypse began to be formed" (Malkki 1995, 101). Indeed, "accounts of these key events [of the genocide] very quickly circulated among the refugees, and, *often in a matter of days*, acquired what came to be characterized as 'standard versions' in the telling and retelling" (Malkki 1995, 106, emphasis added). The speed with which these standardized accounts were produced is evidence of the Hutus' perceived need for identity repair and recovery following this traumatic experience.

Malkki's study suggests that the urgency of a group's need to commemorate violent events and, consequently, the lapse of time between those events and the group's attempts to heal its mnemonic scars are directly related to the degree of trauma that the events cause. This relationship between trauma, commemorative urgency, and time may be referred to as "the violence ratio." As used here, the "violence ratio" theorem suggests that when groups experience sudden and violent change, the urgency of their need to reestablish links with the past will increase in direct proportion to the degree of disruption caused by the traumatic experience. As a corollary to this principle, events that are more traumatic will require commemorative management more quickly simply because the group cannot continue to function in a coherent fashion until these experiences are rationalized in a way that provides a sense of continuity between past, present, and future. In instances where this commemorative activity fails or is delayed, the group will dissolve due to lack of a unifying identity.

To return to the above example, Malkki notes that the Hutu refugees could not wait until the end of the conflict (which is still ongoing) or a return to their homeland to discuss the significance of their shared experiences. "Instead of losing their collective identity, this [the Tanzanian refugee camp] is where and how they made it" (Malkki 1995, 4). In this instance, the speed with which the traumatic experience came to be memorialized in standardized ways reflected the high degree of trauma caused by the genocide. Similarly, American newscasters had already begun to analyze the attack of 9/11 even before the second tower of the World Trade Center was struck by an airplane on live television. Although the events of 9/11 directly impacted only a small percentage of the total American population, the high trauma of these events, which in many respects challenged fundamental beliefs, called for the immediate deployment of collective mnemonic strategies.

A final observation on memory and trauma is particularly relevant to the present study. Many of the violent events that impact a group's collective memory are neutral in and of themselves, lacking inherent value. For example, Hurricane Katrina, which destroyed New Orleans and much of the surrounding region in 2005, deeply impacted the lives and memory frameworks of local communities and the U.S. population at large, but the storm itself was a random accident of nature. Similarly, the murder of John F. Kennedy deeply impacted Western consciousness, but this impact was not directly related to the weapons used—the fact that Kennedy was shot rather than poisoned did not substantially contribute to the commemorative urgency of his assassination. Some acts of violence, however, are explicitly and intentionally charged with implications that transcend the damage done to physical bodies, giving them a precise rhetorical value. In these cases, a group's memorial strategies will often seek to counter the implied rhetoric of the traumatic experience.

Malkki's study is again illustrative. In many instances, Hutu victims were killed by impalement on bamboo poles, obviously not the quickest or most efficient method of genocide. Aside from the fact that this form of death is particularly painful, the Hutu survivors saw "the penetration of the head through the anus . . . as decapitation of the intellect, and on a more general level, as an effort to render the Hutu people powerless, politically impotent." Similarly, the disemboweling of pregnant women was interpreted as a symbolic gesture, an attempt to destroy the future of the Hutu nation—"in several accounts [from survivors], the unborn child or embryo was referred to, simply, as 'the future'" (Malkki 1995, 92). Traumatic events of this type are embedded with "nuclear scripts" that attach specific value to the violence suffered, and these scripts are normally calculated to further disrupt the identity of the victimized group (Bonanno 1990, 179–82; see Kirk 2005, 192–93). The violence ratio theorem would be particularly applicable to traumatic events of this type, which are explicitly formulated to destroy not only the lives of individuals but also the very existence of social groups. In such cases, a group must quickly counter the nuclear script embedded in a violent act in order to survive the attempt to annihilate identity.

Stories as Keys to the Past

How do individuals and groups cope with mnemonic scars that threaten their sense of reality and identity? A number of theorists, including most notably Barry Schwartz, have demonstrated that groups normalize such experiences through "keying," a memory strategy that connects events from the recent past with images from more-distant times. Schwartz stresses that "'keying' is more than a new word for analogical thinking, more than a way individuals mentally organize their social experience. . . . Keying transforms memory into a cultural system because it matches publicly accessible . . . models of the past to the experiences of the present" (Schwartz 2000,

226). Keying filters current social realities through the group's established heritage; in the process, the past is reinterpreted by present circumstances, and present circumstances are made meaningful and socially manageable by connection to the familiar past (see Schwartz 1991, 226–28).

The commemorative technique of keying is graphically illustrated in Yael Zerubavel's *Recovered Roots*, which explores the construction of contemporary Israeli national identity. To take but one notable example from her study: during World War II, Zionists living in Palestine began to associate their current political situation with that of the Zealots who died at Masada during the Jewish revolt of 68–74 C.E. Faced with swift German movement across North Africa and the possibility that hostile Arab nations might ally with the Axis powers, the Zionists began to view Masada as "a dignified alternative to the European Jews' [passive] response to the Nazi persecution." Suicide as a free person, or death in a hopeless fight rather than surrender, were seen as heroic and dignified options; the submission of the Holocaust victims was seen as weak and cowardly (Zerubavel 1995, 71–74). In this instance, present political realities were keyed to a heroic past (Masada) to solidify Zionist identity and encourage resistance. A similar mnemonic move, with very different political intentions, is evident in recent attempts to key the American/British war against Iraq to events of the Vietnam conflict or, in some Arab contexts, to the Crusades. Here again, analogy with a known past interprets an uncertain present and suggests appropriate responses to current events.

Keying is a convenient strategy for managing trauma because it uses the known (past) to organize, and fix the value of, the unknown (present). This is especially the case when current experience can be keyed to what Zerubavel calls "master commemorative narratives." In Zerubavel's view, every act of commemoration—every way in which a group preserves the past in some standardized form, whether textual, ritual, or monumental— "reproduces a *commemorative narrative,* a story about a particular past that accounts for this ritualized remembrance and provides a moral message for the group members" (Zerubavel 1995, 6, emphasis original). To take an obvious example, the Eucharist is a ritual that does not explicitly take the form of a narrative, yet participants in that rite are at every moment aware that it recalls a series of events surrounding Christ's passion and death. The sum total of the commemorative narratives operative in any group at a given moment forms a "master commemorative narrative," the overarching story arc that informs group members' thoughts about the past (Zerubavel 1995, 6). Master commemorative narratives "function as *myth plot structures*" in the sense that they organize past events in a way that reflects the group's values and sense of identity (Zerubavel 1995, 216, emphasis original). In times of violent trauma, groups can readily manage sudden change and create continuity with their past heritage by using these established narrative frameworks to organize present experience. As Yerushalmi notes, "even the most terrible events are somehow less terrifying when viewed within old patterns rather than in their bewildering specificity" (Yerushalmi 1989, 36).

Memory Can't Wait That Long: The Cradle of the Passion

The above considerations shed significant light on the central question of the present essay: *Why would early Christians invent passion narratives, and at what stage of the church's history would they have been most likely to do so?* Social approaches to memory—and, particularly, to the impact of violent trauma on group memory and identity—would suggest that Jesus' followers told passion stories in order to key the traumatic experience of his death to familiar themes from Jewish tradition in a way that would preserve the identity and continuity of their group. Further, the violence ratio theorem would suggest that this process must have begun very quickly, certainly long before Mark wrote his book about Jesus. Finally, while Mark was not the first Christian to produce a connected narrative of the events surrounding Jesus' death, his method of managing that traumatic event likely utilized strategies typical of the earliest Christian memories of Jesus. These conclusions engage Kelber's theory at several points.

First, while Kelber is likely correct to suggest that there was no single, fixed passion story, his contention that "*distance from the trauma* [is] an essential psychocultural prerequisite for most mediations of death" seems inconsistent with the fact that social memory cannot tolerate meaningless violence (Kelber 1983, 193–94, emphasis original). Obviously, Jesus was a/ the central figure among the earliest group of his followers; "for the social life of the group identified with him, the death of Jesus . . . would have constituted a massive rupture" with the past (Kirk 2005, 205). For the first disciples, Jesus' death was not only unusually violent but also "traumatic" in the sense that it threatened to dissolve the social frameworks of the new kingdom movement. The sudden disappearance of a central figure requires immediate commemoration so that members of a group can explain the loss of this individual and rationalize its implications in a way that creates continuity between past and present experience. Jesus' death would certainly be no exception to the rule.

While it would be impossible to date the first oral accounts of Jesus' passion with any level of precision, it is relevant to note that the mode of Jesus' demise would ignite an unusually high commemorative urgency among his circle of followers. Alan Kirk has observed that "torturous deaths—such as crucifixion was—can be highly symbolized forms of violence, with the disfiguring, distending, dismembering, smashing, and perforation of the human body routinized and choreographed to display and enact publicly the socially degraded status of the victim" (Kirk 2005, 192). From a Roman perspective, scourging and crucifixion were calculated to graphically illustrate the inevitable end of any story that begins with resistance to imperial rule; from a Jewish perspective, crucifixion ("hanging on a tree") was evidence of God's curse (see Deut 21:23; Gal 3:13; 4Q169, frags. 3–4, col. 1; 11Q19–20, col. 64, lines 7–13). Nailed to these two embedded narratives, enemies of the state and rejected by God, Jewish crucifixion victims were dehumanized and erased. The violent act that led to Jesus' death, then, was directed not only against his body but also against his memory and against the foundational frameworks of his movement. Whether Jesus' original followers thought of him as a messiah, a Rabbi, an exorcist and magician, or some combination of these, no aspect of their thinking about him—or about themselves as his followers—was compatible with the nuclear scripts embedded in a Roman cross. In order to continue as a coherent group, the disciples were faced with the daunting task of replacing the cross script with alternate ways of remembering Jesus and his untimely demise. The violence ratio theorem would suggest that this commemorative work must have begun almost immediately.

Second, while Kelber is doubtless correct to suggest that no fixed, monolithic passion narrative existed in early Christian tradition, it seems likely that Mark's strategy of moderating Jesus' death through a commemorative narrative keyed to the Jewish Scriptures was not untypical of early Christian rhetoric. As noted above, groups often attempt to manage trauma by distributing current experience across the spectrum of mythical plot structures that provide a sense of continuity and familiarity. For Jesus' Jewish disciples, these plot structures would most likely be derived from folk traditions and religious concepts based on the authoritative texts of the Hebrew Bible. By redistributing the events of the crucifixion along the framework of sacred stories and oracles, the disciples could counter and neutralize the nuclear scripts embedded in the violence of the cross. If the earliest disciples had been unable to do this, the primitive Christian movement could not have survived as a coherent group up to the consensus view of the date of Mark's composition (65–80 C.E.). Of course, it is now impossible to determine the extent to which Mark's particular strategy of narrating Jesus' death on the framework of Psalm 22 resembled earlier performances of the passion story.

In summary, while Kelber was right to resist the notion of a monolithic, evolving passion narrative, Dibelius was likely correct to suggest that passion narratives were the original genre of Christian memory. Passion stories were doubtless discrete, plural, and equiprimordial, but they must have existed decades before Mark wrote his gospel. Luke is not unreasonable to suggest that followers of Jesus had begun to tell stories of his death keyed to texts from the Hebrew Bible within fifty days of the cross (Acts 2:1-36).

10

MANUSCRIPT TRADITION AS A *TERTIUM QUID*
Orality and Memory in Scribal Practices

Alan Kirk

Orality invaded writing, oralizing and destabilizing written words.
—*Doane 1991, 82*

We are dealing with the literature of an age . . . when language was fluid.
—*Chaytor 1945, 1*

Ζῶν γὰρ ὁ λόγος τοῦ θεοῦ καὶ ἐνεργής.
—*Hebrews 4:12*

Scholarship on the gospel tradition frequently approaches its major research problems in terms of the cognitive habits of print culture. This is a point that Werner Kelber has often made in the course of clarifying the distinctiveness of oral vis-à-vis written communications media and the ramifications of this distinctiveness for the study of the history of the tradition. This essay will take its cue, however, from the increasing emphasis Kelber has given to the active *interface* of orality, writing, and memory. It will argue that this interface entails a distinctive phenomenology for manuscript tradition. From this sharpened analytical perspective, it will identify key respects in which work by Vernon Robbins, David Parker, and Bart Ehrman on the written gospel tradition and its manuscript transmission continues to show the effects of print conceptions.

Orality and Writing at the Interface

Oral tradition comes to tangible expression in live utterance, or "performance," that taps into the oral-traditional register, the body of tradition carried by a community "inter-mnemonically" and that is constitutive of its cultural identity (Parks 1991, 57; also Foley 1999, 26–31). The contemporary social and historical realities of the tradent community contribute to the reconstitution of the tradition in these face-to-face enactments, a dynamic W. F. Hanks describes as "internalizing reception into the production process itself" (Hanks 1989, 112). Performance is thus critical to transmission, which is a matter of effectively actualizing normative tradition within a community's ever-shifting present frameworks. This entails, moreover, that variability, or better, *multiformity* will be an index feature of oral tradition, each multiform being to a significant extent a response to the exigencies of specific enactment contexts (Doane 1991, 103; Finnegan 1988, 69). In other words, in oral tradition interpretation occurs "*textintern*" ("internal to the text"; Assmann 1992, 295).[1] By the same token, multiformity is the mark of the tradition's authority.

As stated above, Kelber's work is notable for its attention to the effects of media properties upon the dynamics of tradition. Shifting a tradition into writing—its externalization as chirographic tradition—stabilizes it dramatically. In Jan Assmann's words, the *Verschriftlichung* (inscribing) of tradition amounts to its *Verfestigung* (hardening) (Assmann 1992, 165). This operation moves tradition from its primary expression in oral-mnemonic utterance in contingent enactment settings into self-contained complexes of literarily realized, ordered textual arrangements existing externally in fixed material artifacts. Martti Nissinen says of the inscription of neo-Assyrian prophecies that they "no longer belong to concrete contexts in time and space; instead they have become part of textual contexts created by the craftsmen of the literary works and inscriptions" (Nissinen 2000, 268; see also Kelber 1983, 111; Olson 1994, 121–22; Parks 1991, 58). Suspended in spatial extension in the materiality of the written medium, tradition takes on a "thicker consistency" (Casey 1987, 273; see also Foley 1995, 57). It receives a more durable representation as a visually perceptible script that thereby becomes an increasingly normative reference point for the tradition's enactment and hence its transmission (Doane 1991, 78; Foley 1995, 157; Jaffee 2001, 6; Kelber 1983, 31–34, 105; 1997, xxiv; Parks 1987, 512–13; Vanstiphout 1995a, 2181–82; Zumthor 1990, 196).

Notwithstanding their distinctive properties, however, the boundary between orality and writing in the ancient world was both indistinct and highly active. These media stood, in other words, in a charged *interfacial* relationship. "[S]cholarship over the past twenty years," Foley states, "has taught us to distrust the false dichotomy of 'oral versus written' and to expect complex inventories and interactions of oral and literate in the same culture and even in the very same individual" (Foley 1999, 3; see also Alexander 1998, 95; Finnegan 1988, 62; 1992, 178–79; Kelber 1997, xxiv; Morgan 1998, 11–12). In antiquity and the medieval world, writing was positioned within pervasively oral and aural communications environments. Accordingly, oral phenomenology was in crucial respects determinative of utilization practices with respect to written artifacts. A written work was published and diffused through oral recitation, depending for its reception and transmission on its constant reentry into the oral and aural register (Chaytor 1945, 10–11; Crosby 1936, 88–89; Fantham 1999, 222; Sedgwick 1990, 90). The primary concern of the Greco-Roman literate sensibility was for effective oral utterance. Medieval literature, Crosby points out, "is filled with expressions which indicate the author's intention that his work shall be read aloud, shall be heard" (Crosby 1936, 98), and the same may be said of the major genres in the classical *polis* (Thomas 2003, 162–63; see also van der Toorn 2007, 11–12). Written texts found their actualization, their *telos,* in conversion into oral enactment. The medieval scholar Richard de Fournival viewed his *escrit* as visible depiction (*painture*) signifying and enabling reconstitution of what was primarily auditory (*parole;* see Clanchy 1993, 284).

The sensory register tuned to the reception and cognition of the manuscript work, therefore, was not so much the visual as the aural, and reading itself was likewise "primarily oral rather than visual" (Clanchy 1993, 267; see also Carr 2005, 72–83, 160; Jaffee 2001, 17–18; Kelber 1997, xxii; Stock 1983, 14–15; Sweeny 1987, 7–8). The "instinctive question" of a medieval person "when deciphering a text, was not whether he had seen, but whether he had heard this or that word before; he brought not a visual but an auditory memory to his task" (Chaytor 1945, 14). This is to say that the reification of the written word distinct from its embodiment in speech, "the separation of the visual and aural aspects of the text that enable us to treat print and speech differently" (Small 1997, 20), was not established in antiquity (also Corbier 1991, 113; Cribiore 2001, 174; Olson 1994, 196). In sum, written artifacts "enjoyed an essentially oral cultural life" (Jaffee 2001, 125). In utilization and transmission, they existed as "performative tradition," open to some extent to the transformations and multiformity characteristic of oral tradition (Jaffee 2001, 25–27; see also Doane 1991, 82; van der Toorn 2000, 233–34).

Nevertheless, it would be an error to simply dissolve ancient writing back into oral dynamics. As Kelber has stressed, the respective media properties remain wholly pertinent. Though not able to fix tradition, the written—or, to speak more precisely, the chirographic—medium gave words a level of stabilization impossible in orality as well as a corollary material and visual existence that was distinct from and inassimilable into any act of performance (Kelber 1997, xxiv). In fact, Assmann argues that the programmatic inscription of tradition marked a strategic shift in transmission, a cultural memory project to secure a community's normative tradition in response to breakdowns in the social frameworks for its oral cultivation (Assmann 1992, 159–65, 218–221; 2000, 29–37, 53–54, 87–88). Written artifacts of this sort inherently possessed an "erhöhte Normativität" ("heightened normativity"), and in their function as scripts they exerted strong effects upon the ambient oral tradition (Assmann 1999, 27). Foley uses the term "inertia" to characterize the effect of "manuscript text" upon the oral performance tradition of Homer (1990, 27). The crucial issue for analysis, therefore, is the *interaction* along the oral and written axes that is definitive of what Armin Sweeny terms "oral manuscript culture" (Sweeny 1987, 73).

Scribal Memory

It is on the issue of interaction that the factor of memory becomes highly pertinent. In contrast to its complete inconsequence in print culture, in the literate practices of antiquity memory played the major operational role. Memory was "*the* classical means of cognitively organizing and, most significantly, retrieving words" (Small 1997, 71, emphasis original; see van der Toorn 2007, 21–22). Oral manuscript culture was a memory culture "to the same profound degree that modern culture in the West is documentary" (Carruthers 1990, 8). Committal of core texts to memory was a principal element of ancient scribal and literate-rhetorical education, a memorative competence gained and expressed, moreover, through oral recitation (Carr 2005, 29–30; Cribiore 2001, 213–26; Fraade 1999, 45; Williams 1972, 219). In ancient and medieval pedagogy, reading and memorizing were viewed as undifferentiated activities (Carruthers 1990, 156). Memory ingestion of this sort pertained primarily to the repertoire of *cultural texts,* namely the narrative and instructional works whose cultivation and transmission in scribal memory was crucial to the reproduction of a community's identity "from one generation to the next" (Assmann 2006, 81; see also Bruner and Feldman 1996, 295; Carr 2005, 19, 29–30, 75; Cribiore 2001, 193–94; Rainey 1969, 131; Vanstiphout 1995a, 2189).[2]

Memorative control of a written artifact was requisite for its practical utilization, given the problems of visual access presented by the cumbersome scroll format and unbroken scripts that rendered not just reading but also search and location operations extraordinarily difficult (Derrenbacker 2005, 116; Pelling 1979, 92–93; Reynolds and Wilson 1991, 2–5; Small

1997, 219–20). But memory competence was a good deal more than just a practical matter. It lay at the core of the scribal ethos, according to which a text was not truly learned unless it had been internalized by thorough assimilation to memory (Carr 2005, 209; Carruthers 1990, 10, 156–63; Cribiore 2001, 178–79; Fraade 1999, 45). Memorial internalization, moreover, was essential to the scribal project of *moral* transformation that Carr describes as "the cognitive internalization of 'wisdom' . . . on the heart of the student" (Carr 2005, 210; also Assmann 2000, 136; Carruthers 1990, 164–73). Memory, in other words, was the principal faculty for intellectual and moral formation. The effect, at least ideally, was that the scribe educated in this manner came to be the living, orally proficient embodiment of the community's tradition.

Correspondingly, the work itself existed most pristinely and authentically in its memory version and its corollary oral and aural expression. The written manuscript was, as Jaffee puts it, "an almost accidental existent, a material object whose most authentic being resided as a spiritual possession in the memory of its student" (Jaffee 1999, 9; also Assmann 2006, 81; Kelber 1997, xxii). As an unformatted, undifferentiated stream of letters, the manuscript text had only a weak representational correspondence to the composition that it recorded. David Olson points out that "as long as knowledge was thought of as in the mind . . . writing could only be seen as reminder not representation" (Olson 1994, 196). The manuscript was ancillary; it was the visual, material support—an external "reference point" (Carr 2005, 160)—for the primary existence and transmission of the text in the medium of memory. Likewise, it was not in minute textual dissection but in oral enactment out of memory that the text's meaning was actualized (Bäuml 1984, 38–39; Gerhardsson 1961, 81; Jaffee 1994, 145–46; Olson 1994, 180–82; Snyder 2000, 1).

In effect, scribal memory was the interfacial zone where writing and oral-traditional practices converged and interacted. The text was restored to oral utterance primarily out of memory, just as through its conversion to aural and oral utterance in ruminative reading or recitation it came to be inscribed upon memory. Hence it was in memory that manuscript tradition was opened up to oral phenomenology in its utilization and transmission and accordingly led its cultural existence as an "oral-performative tradition" (Jaffee 2001, 141; see also Kelber 1997, xxii; Mandel 2000, 77). More to our point, the oral enactment of memory-based works very much colored scribal conceptions of textual transmission. Conversely, the existence of texts as chirographic traditions injected into their memorative cultivation the countervailing, stabilizing effects of the written medium, with their assimilation to memory frequently described in terms of graphic inscription upon material surfaces (Carr 2005, 160; Carruthers 1990, 16; Elman 1975, 20; Jaffee 1994, 144; Small 1997, 99–100).

Scribes as Tradents

It is clear that construing scribes narrowly as "copyists"—that is, as better or worse transcriptional functionaries—gives them short shrift. To be sure, transcription was central to the vocation, and it is also important to distinguish among the various sorts of tasks and functions scribes might perform. Moreover, there were many scribes capable of only routine clerical operations. Overall, the term is imprecise and obscures wide educational disparities. It is nevertheless the case that scribes with more extensive grounding in literacy might act as full-fledged tradents, exercising in the chirographic transmission of their community's tradition a performative competence that significantly resembled that of the oral-traditional performer (Doane 1991, 81; 1994, 421–31; see also Beit-Arié 2000, 238; Jaffee 2001, 18–19; van der Toorn 2007, 109–10). Doubtless a very great many manuscript variants arose from carelessness or ineptitude, as well as from the susceptibility of transcriptional operations to particular sorts of errors. Likewise, scribes might differ significantly in their approaches to transcribing a particular text (see Colwell 1969, 117). The point here is not to flat-iron scribal practice but to grasp a core phenomenon of oral manuscript culture that is likely to be missed or misconstrued from a print culture perspective.

In transcription, a scribe converted a portion of manuscript text through vocalization into the aural and oral register and simultaneously into a memory trace; the trace was, in its turn, reconverted to manuscript copy, likewise through low-voice dictation. In other words, the scribe grasped the manuscript text not just as a visual but as an auditory entity, even preponderantly so (Chaytor 1945, 19; Clanchy 1993, 267; Junack 1981, 281–82; Sweeny 1987, 7–8). In Sweeny's words, "the transmission of the text from one manuscript to another—from an 'original' to a 'copy'—is oral rather than visual" (Sweeny 1987, 90). By the same token the scribe apprehended the written work cognitively "not as a string of written signs" as in print culture but in its reconstitution as oral utterance (Dagenais 1994, 145; also Corbier 1991, 109; Gamble 2004, 31; Junack 1981, 282–83).[3] The effect of engaging the manuscript text in this manner, moreover, would be to cue and activate the memory version of the work. To return to Chaytor's point, the scribe "brought not a visual but an auditory memory to his task. . . . [H]e had learnt to rely on the memory of spoken sounds, not upon the interpretation of written signs" (Chaytor 1945, 14). These statements on the oral and auditory nature of scribal transcription should be tempered, however, by the facts that transcriptional errors sometimes arose from visual misapprehension of the text and that scribes often faithfully transcribed solecistic and defective readings (Metzger and Ehrman 2005, 251–54, 271; van der Toorn 2007, 126). Nevertheless, it is clear that transcription had some of the qualities of oral enactment of the tradition.[4]

A more precise account can be given of the forces at work upon the manuscript tradition as, restored to oral/aural form, it traversed the interfacial zone of scribal memory to its transcriptional destination. In turning from exemplar to copy, the scribe must carry shorter or longer textual sequences in short-term memory. Short-term memory traces are quite unstable, and if the peripheral role that memory plays in print culture is the point of reference, this instability would seem to give a plausible account of the effects of memory on manuscript transmission. There can be little doubt that variants arose for this reason. However, in manuscript culture, where the text existed primarily as a memory artifact, the fleeting quality of short-term memory would not have been a significant factor. Instead a wider range of memory and oral/aural dynamics may be considered. Phenomena such as transpositions in the grammatically flexible Greek word order, as well as phonetic substitutions, indicate that scribes worked with the text as an oral and auditory entity (see Colwell 1969, 110; Royse 1979, 152). The migration of vocabulary and syntactic constructions from nearby contexts, as well as familiarized phraseology from elsewhere in the work, into the transcription of a phrase is likewise intelligible in light of the operational role of memory. Colwell labels these phenomena "harmonization to the immediate context" (Colwell 1969, 113). More specifically, they are cases of what researchers on the cognitive aspects of memory refer to as "proactive interference"—that is, of one memory upon another (Baddeley 1999, 126). The reciprocally active openness of the transcriptional unit to the ambient field of scribal memory that it traverses as an auditory memory trace also helps to account for substitutions of synonyms and synonymous expressions as well as for the displacement of words and phrases by more familiar or naturalized expressions from other well-known texts. Greenstein, in his discussion of 4QPs[b] and other Qumran texts, characterizes these phenomena as "memory contamination" (Greenstein 1993, 77; see Carr 2005, 42–43; Himbaza 2002, 411–28; Yamagata 2005, 117–18).

The effects of memory on manuscript traditions were, however, even more far-reaching than these perhaps often involuntary changes. Trained scribal memory was an active competence in the wider community repertoire of both oral and written tradition, memorially ingested, constituting what Dagenais refers to as a scribe's "oral-memorial register" (Dagenais 1994, 145; also Haines-Eitzen 2000, 106–7) and corresponding in important respects to Foley's "traditional register" (Foley 1999, 26–31, 89–90). As the manuscript text was activated in scribal memory in recitation and transcription, it had the potential to intersect and react with this traditional repertoire at many points. "The performing scribe produced the text in an act of writing that evoked the tradition by a combination of eye and ear, script and memory" (Dagenais 1994, 436). In consequence, the text might undergo characteristic sorts of transformations—conflations with or substitutions of similar traditions, harmonizations, integration of different materials, in some cases hybridizations with other works—even to a point where the transmission of the text might be taken up into the project of composing a new work (Dagenais 1994, 137–46; Doane 1994, 432–33; Carr 2005, 35–40, 148–62; Kelber 1997, xxiii; see also Fishbane 1985, 430–31; Gerhardsson 1961, 80; Schäfer 1986).

Certainly, scribes made bona fide memory mistakes, but memory-based transformations such as those described above were integral to the more thoroughgoing performance competence that capable scribes might exercise with respect to their manuscript tradition. "Der Sänger und der Schreiber," observes Assmann, "sind zunächst beide nichts anderes als Tradenten, Träger der Überlieferung, lebendige Verkörperungen der zerdehnten Situation. Beide haben die Aufgabe, den kommunikativen Prozeß in Gang zu halten" (Assmann 2000, 136–37; Author's translation: "Both the singer and the scribe are in fact tradents, bearers of tradition, living embodiments of the 'extended communication situation.' Both have the task of sustaining the communicative course [of tradition]." The written work existed not as a typographic fixation but as a cultural tradition memorially and orally embodied in the persons of scribes who were themselves socially embodied in live community contexts and whose acts of transcription were extensions of their oral-recitational tradent role in the community. The activities of scribes were driven by the exigency of any enactment of tradition—namely, to render in this case the *chirographic* tradition responsive to the realities and crises of the tradent community. Thereby they sustained the critical continuity between the historically situated community and its foundational tradition (Fishbane 1985, 412–13; Kelber 2006, 21).

This tradent competence operated through the course of scribal activities, from the fashioning of recognizably new works out of the repertoire of memorially ingested oral and written traditions to the transmission of the manuscript tradition of established works. The author of Chronicles, for example, has "taken over older historical traditions and reformulated them in the light of contemporary emphases.... In this way ... the post-exilic generation, not only retrieve their past but also reorient themselves toward the future" (Fishbane 1985, 413). Similarly, van der Toorn notes that "[t]he expansion of the Masoretic text of Jeremiah 33 [vv. 14-26] is an instance of a teacher explaining the meaning of received oracles for his own time" (van der Toorn 2007, 132). In the course of the manuscript transmission of the Babylonian version of *Lamentations Rabbati,* the conventional sequence of nations that ruled over Israel, namely the Babylonians (*Bavel*), Persians (*Paras*), Greeks (*Yavan*), and Romans (*Edom*), is extended by the addition of *Ishmael* to incorporate the Muslim domination that was the contemporary historical framework of the tradent community (Mandel 2000, 95). The dynamism in the manuscript tradition of the Hebrew Bible during the Second Temple period is a striking case of performative competence in scribal transmission of cultural texts. Similarly, "in light of the evidence provided by the larger collection of biblical scrolls from Qumran," writes Eugene Ulrich, "it can be recognized that small additions, omissions, and rearrangements are *characteristic* of the biblical text throughout its history up to the second century C.E." (Ulrich 1998, 88, emphasis original; see also Vanstiphout 1995b, 8). Ulrich's construal of this phenomenon as "*repeating it* [the tradition] *faithfully* but *reshaping it creatively* in the light of the exigencies of their current cultural situation" neatly identifies the major vectors at work in scribal cultivation of manuscript tradition (Ulrich 1999, 74, emphasis original; see also Sanders 1999, 11).

As with oral-traditional performance, scribal operations of the sort observed, for example, by Vanstiphout for Mesopotamian texts and Fishbane and Ulrich for the history of the texts of the Hebrew Bible amounted to internal transformations of the tradition itself. In other words, the *traditum* and its scribal *traditio* were co-constitutive, though with the *traditum* "dominat[ing] the *traditio* and condition[ing] its operations" (Fishbane 1985, 86–87). This entails that no hard-and-fast distinction existed between the ostensible "author" of a work and its scribal tradents. The redaction of a work and its transmission were on a continuum (Fishbane 1985, 85; Schäfer 1989, 90). Scribes, positioned as they were at the interface of orality and writing, were instrumental in shifting normative tradition into the written medium. In other words, many cultural texts originated as mostly anonymous scribal compositions that, like their constituent traditions, existed from the outset as the collective possession of the community. Correspondingly, as its embodiments and tradents, scribes exercised a shared authority with respect to the written tradition—a collective authorship, as it were. Their operations upon it in the course of its chirographic transmission effectively amounted to the continuation of the tradent dynamics that had brought the work into existence (Fishbane 1985, 86–87; see also Carruthers 1990, 191; Chaytor 1945, 128; Eisenstein 1979, 122; Zumthor 1990, 203–4). Even in the case of the prophetic books or the named sages of the Talmud, the voices of anonymous scribal tradents merged with the tradition in the course of its transmission (Carr 2005, 148–49; Segal 2004, 83). Such authority was grounded in an ethos that, as noted above, rendered scribes living embodiments of the normative tradition, and it found expression in tropes that construed interpretive scribal activity in terms of revelatory inspiration (Fishbane 1989, 66–69; Floyd 2000, 141–42).

On this point, it is important to note salient distinctions between the respective compositional *Sitze* of scribal tradents of cultural texts and aristocratic Greco-Roman authors (the latter sometimes adduced as the relevant comparison for the authorship of the gospels). In elite Greco-Roman literary circles, authorial and transcriptional functions were typically separated; scribes were of low status and marginal to the compositional process (Alexander 1998, 81–86; Haines-Eitzen 2000, 7; McDonnell 1996, 477–83; Starr 1987, 214–15). Correspondingly, an overt authorial ethos controlled these works, only some of which might subsequently enter into the cultural tradition. This contrasts not just with the primacy but also with the anonymity of scribes in the production and cultivation of cultural texts. The identity of the scribal composers, that is, receded behind works that were formulated from the outset to secure the deposit of tradition that already constituted and sustained a community's identity. The distinctions should not be pressed too far. Elite Greco-Roman authors possessed compositional competence comparable to that of educated scribes in other cultural contexts. Likewise, scribes who labored in low-status Greco-Roman occupational settings may not infrequently have possessed some literary competence. It is likely that some of the tradents of early Christian texts were to be found among scribes such as these, in which case they were users of those texts and hence vitally situated within communities where those texts operated as normative tradition (Gamble 1995, 78; Haines-Eitzen 2000, 16–17).

It is important emphasize again that the picture of the scribal tradent just outlined is a type: these competencies would have been unevenly distributed and realized in actual scribes. The earlier warning against dissolving scribal operations into oral dynamics likewise bears repeating. Scribes were copyists and composers bound to and defined by the written medium. The visual materiality of the chirographic tradition exerted strong inertial effects upon its oral-traditional utilization. Emanuel Tov points out, for example, that "the rigid form of the manuscript" rendered scribal glosses visible (Tov 1998, 424), and Fishbane notes that "the written form of the *traditum* and its textual context impose certain inevitable restraints upon the *traditio* which copies it" (Fishbane 1985, 88). Similarly, the tradition, inscribed upon memory as upon the page, was transmitted as a *work*, that is, "in a very definite formulation" (Fishbane 1985, 87), although, as will be seen below, not a fixed one.

Manuscript Mouvance

It emerges that dynamism was a core feature of ancient manuscript tradition, in contrast to the stasis, the motionlessness, of print. John Dagenais has in fact applied the concept of *mouvance,* Paul Zumthor's term for the emblematic indeterminacy of the oral text, to manuscript tradition to capture this, its most striking property (Dagenais 1994, 130; see Zumthor 1990, 207–8). The text, "apparently fixed on the manuscript page, is actually in constant flux, changing its shape, order, texture to suit the needs of the reader, who also inhabits a soul, body, and world in constant flux" (Dagenais 1994, 58). Analysis grounded in print assumptions typically attempts to line up the *mouvance* observable in the history of the manuscript tradition of a text into a succession of fixed "editorial stages" (though to be sure, transmission might be punctuated by the appearance of new editions) or, alternatively, to construe a manuscript tradition in terms of "variants" on a fixed original. But the prolific multiformity of manuscript traditions simply eludes these sorts of print-inspired reductions (Schäfer 1986, 147–51; also Dagenais 1994, 19; Eisenstein 1979, 11).

Many factors contribute to manuscript *mouvance,* but in many cases it may be analyzed in terms of the operation of oral-traditional dynamics in the manuscript medium, not as an "invasion" (as our superscripted citation from Doane dramatizes it) but as one of its constitutive vectors—hence Dagenais' characterization of *mouvance* as the essential indeterminacy of manuscript tradition (Dagenais 1994, 17). Peter Schäfer argues that rabbinic literature is best understood "as an open continuum in which the process of emergence is not to be separated or distinguished without further ado from that of transmission" (Schäfer 1989, 89). The scribal practices discussed above, in other words, are reflected back in the very nature of the manuscript medium. In chirographic transmission, the person of the scribe was kinetically, cognitively, and existentially bound up in the re-creation of the text in a way that is incomprehensible in our era of mechanically mass-produced documents. Transcription was a socially embodied *reading* that effaced any absolute distinction between reader and manuscript. "[T]he medieval text transcends the letter and escapes into a unique and personal ethical realm" (Dagenais 1994, 16).

The principle of *mouvance* means that manuscript texts would come to bear in their receptive materiality the marks of the social and cultural contexts that they traversed in the course of transmission. In the traces of the transmission of the Mishnah, for example, may be found harmonizations with current halakhic and commentary traditions as well as divergences reflective of Palestinian and Babylonian cultural environments (Strack and Stemberger 1996, 139–40). Similarly, the medieval text of the Latin Vulgate absorbed elements from its contemporizing usage in missionary homiletics as well as from the authoritative tradition of patristic exegesis (Loewe 1969, 109–10, 131, 141–42). No sharp distinction existed between the text and its mediating glosses (Dagenais 1994, 21–27; Jaffee 2001, 18–19). The boundaries of the manuscript work, moreover, might be open to enlargement with other materials or to rearrangements of order. Accordingly, a text might proliferate in different versions or undergo significant development in its contours along the course of its transmission, as with the Isaiah scroll (Assmann 2006, 79; Dagenais 1994, 19; Reynolds and Wilson 1991, 235–36). It is difficult, however, to generalize. Variables like genre, whether a text originated with a named authorial personality or in tradition, and context-specific contingencies might affect the ground rules for the utilization and transmission of given texts and hence the nature and extent of such transformations.

Phenomena like those of the examples surveyed above are alien to a print sensitivity habituated to the typographically fixed original exactly replicated in mechanically produced copies. Far from indicating its weak prescriptiveness, however, variability in manuscript transmission may in many cases be understood as the means by which a normative base tradition, the *traditum*, reacted with the historical realities of a tradent community. "[I]n the mixed vocal/writing medium of manuscripts ... a particular message continues to be authorized by its status as a performance.... [V]ariability would have been seen as a positive value, as a kind of authorizing afflatus in itself. From this point of view, the scribe-as-performer would see the rewriting as enhancing the traditional text by giving it life in the present" (Doane 1994, 433; see also Carruthers 1990, 91). As with oral tradition, therefore, the most pertinent expression of a chirographically transmitted work would have been its contemporizing enactment in recitation and transcription. "Manuscript culture put the emphasis in any text on its current presentation rather than its archaeological correctness"

(Clanchy 1993, 265; see also Carr 2005, 46; Jaffee 2000, 28; 2001, 18; Mandel 2000, 76; Schäfer 1986, 151).

Given the multiformity of manuscript tradition, the question put trenchantly by Peter Schäfer is whether it makes sense to continue to speak of the existence of the "work" as though of an integral entity. So great are the variations between the Vatican and London manuscripts of *Bereshit Rabba*, for example, "that the redactional unity of the work is debatable. . . . What then constitutes the identity of the work of 'Bereshit Rabba'?" (Schäfer 1986, 146). Schäfer proposes for rabbinic literature an "open text–continuum" model instead, one that approaches a text as "a dynamic *process* that has entered into various and changing configurations and fixations" (Schäfer 1986, 146, emphasis original). Nevertheless—and somewhat paradoxically—it is difficult to dispense with the notion of the work as in some respects a traceable constant whose realization in the materiality of the chirographic medium accounts for a capacity to persist in transmission. *Lamentations Rabbati* is a case in point. Paul Mandel points out that the Babylonian and Palestinian versions of this text diverge so much that their parallel units have the appearance of oral variants. Nevertheless, "a comparison between the two manuscript traditions demonstrates that they constitute exactly the same work. Almost all the passages found in one recension are found in the other, in *similar* language, and in *approximately* the same order" (Mandel 2000, 80, emphasis original; see also Ulrich 1999, 109). Preferable, therefore, is Dagenais' further characterization of the *mouvance* of manuscript tradition as "the peculiar way in which handwritten texts 'move' about each other *and a presumed originary center*" (Dagenais 1994, 130, emphasis added).[5]

What seems difficult to square with what has been argued so far about memory competence and manuscript *mouvance*, however, is the manifest scribal concern for fidelity in copying operations. Close visual contact with exemplars, transcription of even defective readings, collation of copies, counting lines, and appending colophons that certified accuracy and sometimes warned against altering the text were characteristic scribal practices. Scribes were alive to the concept of textual corruptions and hence to the normativity of the work; they were "well aware of the 'mistakes' in their texts and often took great pains to 'correct' these and prevent further mistakes" (Haines-Eitzen 2000, 106; see also Metzger and Ehrman 2005, 198–202).[6] Van der Toorn accounts for this curious duality in scribal practices by distinguishing "copying" from "editing," modes that would have been respectively pertinent to different sorts of textual projects (van der Toorn 2007, 126–27). However, at a deeper level, this duality was likely reflective of the reality that scribes *embodied* the interface of oral and written competencies. Thus it was grounded in the scribal ethos itself, where the obligation to preserve and pass on written tradition was conjoined with the didactic obligation to render the tradition responsive to present community contexts (Fishbane 1985, 538).[7]

A few examples will clarify how the differential interaction of these two vectors is constitutive of manuscript tradition. Beit-Arié discusses the case of Joseph ben Eliezer of Spain, "who copied, in 1375, a supercommentary to Ibn Ezra's commentary on the Pentateuch. . . . He tells us that he copied the text from an extremely erroneous exemplar and was able to emend part of the mistakes. . . . In addition, there were many cases where the author's explanations seemed to him unreasonable, and there he integrated [glossed] his own opinion into the text" (Beit-Arié 2000, 235). At Qumran, fluid biblical text histories and memorative trafficking with texts coexisted with visual copying practices (Carr 2005, 232–33). It was noted that, in the course of its transmission, the medieval text of the Vulgate not only absorbed contemporizing usages from monastic preaching but was also subjected to scholastic attempts to align its wording with patristic exegesis. But there were also countervailing attempts at its restoration, such as Alcuin's, to a normative standard defined by correct Latinity, or that of post-Carolingian Irish scholarship, which even restored to it some Old Latin readings (Loewe 1969, 132–39).[8] Finally, Colwell's comparison of the biblical manuscripts P^{45}, P^{66}, and P^{75} shows that concerns for textual replication vis-à-vis transformation might vary greatly from scribe to scribe (Colwell 1969, 117).

Given its *mouvance* properties, therefore, the manuscript medium *per se* was characterized by only a relative stability (relative to other variables). Accordingly, the trend of manuscript tradition toward transmission in an increasingly stabilized form may in important respects be accounted for in terms of the continuing effects of cultural memory forces. More precisely, it amounted to a strategic securing of long-term cultural identity in response to significant changes in the historical and social frameworks that had defined the boundaries for the more dynamic cultivation of chirographic tradition, changes particularly of the sort that heightened the historically situated community's sense of discontinuity with its salient past. The most pertinent aspect of this shift in transmission was the rendering of the act of interpretation increasingly extrinsic to the tradition, rather than immanent in its scribal performances (Assmann 1992, 165, 218–21; 2000, 29–30, 53–54, 87–88; 2006, 80–81).[9]

The greater stabilization of Hebrew Bible texts after the destruction of Second Temple society is a case in point (see Ulrich 1998, 83), as is the standardization of Homer against local textual traditions in the wake of the collapse of the society centered on the classical *polis* (Assmann 1992, 274–78; see also Foley 1990, 28–29) and perhaps also the stabilization of the transmission of the Babylonian Talmud after the loss of continuity "with past modes of learning" with the closing of the geonic yeshivas in the eleventh century (Mandel 2000, 100; see also Ephrat and Elman 2000, 114).[10] The curious fact that most transformations in the gospel manuscript tradition occurred "in the earliest period of text transmission (that is, the second and third centuries)" while "later manuscripts are remarkably more stable" (Haines-Eitzen 2000, 113) may also be accounted for in terms of this dynamic. Seen in comparison with the synoptic tradition, the early manuscript tradition in fact already registers a major abatement in variation. Absolute fixation, however, the cessation of *mouvance,* is inconceivable for manuscript culture.

Scribal Tradition in Early Christianity

Dagenais observes that, despite "the chasm that separates medieval scriptum and modern textuality," the "author/print paradigm" continues to affect scholarly approaches to manuscript tradition (Dagenais 1994, 28). Print replaced the transmission of manuscript tradition by scribal tradents with the mechanical replication of typographically fixed works. Moreover, with the wide mechanical dissemination of texts in the visual clarity and uniformity of type, memory shifted from being central to literate activities to completely peripheral (Eisenstein 1979, 66, 125). Correspondingly, in place of its embodied existence in memory and oral/aural utterance, "the work" came to be identified primarily with the external written artifact, optically processed and autonomous with respect to its user. In a reversal of function, in other words, the book became less a reminder of the work and more its full representation (Olson 1994, 110, 196). Textual variants were uniformly *errata,* deviations from the norm of typographically exact copies of the original. Mechanical rather than human replication effectively uncoupled the composition of a work from its transmission and, as a result, intentional alterations came to be viewed as vitiations of the authorial original (Chaytor 1945, 34; Eisenstein 1979, 80–83, 122–26).

As Dagenais points out, modern scholarship has tended to internalize print norms and generalize them unreflectingly to manuscript textuality, superimposing modern conceptions of the authorial text, construing scribes narrowly as copyists, and measuring transcription solely against the standard of exact replication, while the scribal tradent function hardly registers. Inevitably scribes are viewed "as inept defilers of the sacred authorial text," and "transmission" is conceived as the cumulative scribal corruption of a fixed original (Dagenais 1994, 113; also Doane 1994, 432). The greatly diminished role of memory in print culture is similarly projected upon ancient literary practices. Memory is adduced only rarely in biblical source criticism and then mostly in reference to the instability of short-term memory as an *ad hoc* expedient to account for certain textual variations.

As noted earlier, intentional scribal transformations have in fact been recognized as emblematic of the early manuscript tradition. Colwell identified many such changes as "editorial" and "doctrinal," while suggesting that these scribal operations might actually be indicators of the canonical authority of the tradition (Colwell 1969, 118; 1952, 51–55). Epp recognizes that the biblical manuscript tradition bears the marks of its social contextualizations and also that the "original" text and hence textual authority are essentially multiform (Epp 1999, 257–63, 278; 2004, 10). Nevertheless, gospels text critics have struggled to develop explanations that do not at least in part revert to print assumptions, and perhaps it is no coincidence that their accounts conspicuously lack engagement with research on the dynamics of tradition. One suspects that the artificial disciplinary boundaries that separate the history of the synoptic tradition and the history of the manuscript tradition into different academic subfields (though see Karnetzki 1956) prevent text critics from recognizing the pertinence of oral-traditional phenomenology to their research problems. Some reflections on the work of Robbins on the synoptic tradition and of Parker and Ehrman on the manuscript tradition will illustrate these problems and, it is hoped, sharpen the insights of their analyses.

Robbins has long recognized the significance of "the dynamic relation between oral speech and written literature" in antiquity, which he prefers to characterize as the "rhetorical" quality of ancient composition, for the study of the origins of the gospels (Robbins 1991, 147–48; 1993). His correlation of rhetorical composition techniques to key features of the synoptic tradition has cast a great deal of light upon the latter's formation and history. However, Robbins misconstrues the specific practices of elite Greco–Roman literary-rhetorical circles, a particular cultural permutation of the oral/written dynamic, as its definitive expression. In other words, he does not place his observations of this particular setting into the wider framework of tradition, orality, and writing in antiquity. This leads him to distinguish "scribal culture" categorically from "oral culture" on the one hand and from "rhetorical culture" on the other and, accordingly, to describe scribal culture largely as rote copying and minor editorial operations (Robbins 1991, 145, 148). His model and its rubrics, that is to say, reflect the low status and adjunct role of scribes in Greco–Roman literary circles, who copied works they had no hand in composing and who likewise exercised no true tradent function in the circulation of those texts within elite friendship networks (McDonnell 1996, 477–84; Starr 1987, 214–15). A similar criticism may be leveled at Robbins' attempt at a cross-correlation of this typology of "cultures" to the graduated steps of the Greco–Roman educational curriculum. In the resulting schema, "scribal culture" putatively corresponds to mastery of basic reading and copying skills and "rhetorical culture" to the progymnastic rhetorical composition taught at the very highest level of education (Robbins 1991, 145–46). Viewed in the whole framework of Robbins' model, this amounts to a correlation of low social status with low skill levels. In reality, however, scribes were to be found at all gradations on the educational scale, from those capable of only simple clerical tasks to skilled literary tradents, and scribes laboring as low-status, transcriptional functionaries for Greco–Roman elites might in fact possess advanced literary training.

In appealing to these practices, Robbins is seeking for a viable alternative to the tendency of gospels scholarship to interpret synoptic patterns of variation and agreement implausibly in terms of the direct copying and editing of exemplars. However, in taking such as emblematic of "scribal culture" and associating it with manuscript transcription while distinguishing it categorically from the literary competencies of "recitational" and "rhetorical composition," Robbins runs the risk of reproducing print-culture caricatures of scribal function and manuscript transmission. A more satisfactory solution may be found in approaching synoptic patterns of variation as the manifestation of scribal tradent activities, more precisely, of oral-traditional utilization practices vis-à-vis written sources like Mark and Q.

In his book *The Living Text of the Gospels*, distinguished text critic David Parker demonstrates through a comparison of manuscript witnesses of parallel passages in the gospels that intentional scribal changes were profusely *characteristic* of the early manuscript tradition. His survey of the over twenty variations of the four synoptic passages on divorce and remarriage, for example, brings to light the remarkable range of interpretation and application of Jesus' aphoristic pronouncement (Parker 1997, 80–90). Nevertheless, though aware of the historical contingency of print-culture perspectives, Parker does not frame this phenomenon adequately in terms of the dynamics of tradition in an oral manuscript culture. Accordingly, he gravitates toward interpreting it along the lines of the print norm that fixation is indexical of textual authority. "For it is of the essence of a manuscript tradition that every copy is different," he writes. "It follows that while early Christianity may have come to make lists of authoritative books, there were no authoritative copies of them" (Parker 1997, 188). Similarly, the question of the authority of variant dominical sayings "in establishing authoritative moral teaching is very sharply posed. . . . [T]here is no dominical prescript on which church discipline can call as its authority" (Parker 1997, 183). Pursuing this line of analysis, Parker argues that the imputation of canonical textual authority coincides with the appearance of the printed book (Parker 1997, 188–89, 206–207). Research on the dynamics of tradition, however, identifies multiformity as in fact consistent with a tradition's authority, its prescriptiveness for the life and identity of its tradent community (Kelber 2006, 20; see Haines-Eitzen 2000, 124).

Bart Ehrman is also an accomplished text critic who has written extensively on the phenomenon of intentional scribal changes in the New Testament manuscript tradition. However, his analysis, like Parker's, remains significantly affected by print conceptions, perhaps even more so. Ehrman is quite cognizant of important aspects of the ancient media environment. He recognizes that the transmission of early Christian manuscript traditions was socially contextualized in a way that would be impossible for print, and he also recognizes the affects of ambient oral tradition upon scribal transmission. He is aware that the low literacy rates, and hence oral communications environment, of antiquity would have been marked features of the early Christian communities (Ehrman 1993, 3–4, 277; 1995, 362; 2005, 37–39, 97–98). However, his enumeration of these realities does not lead to a rethinking of the standard approaches to manuscript tradition. The programmatic print distinction between authentic originals and variant copies still structures his analysis (Ehrman 2005, 55–69). Moreover, though he stipulates that his use of the term "corruption" is ironic (intentional alterations being what scribes took to be implicit in the tradition), Ehrman's evaluative terminology of intentional scribal changes is likewise expressive of print norms. In his view, changes of this sort occur with a frequency that is "alarming"; they amount to "misquoting," to "tampering with the text" (Ehrman 1993, xii, 31, 59, 275). We have to "admit," he says, that scribes were "changing Scripture" (Ehrman 2005, 210), a sentiment echoed by his student Wayne Kannaday, who speaks of "catching scribes in the act of altering the Scriptures" (Kannaday 2004, 23).[11]

As noted earlier in this essay, ancient scribes certainly had an ingrained sense of obligation to the integrity of the written work. They were capable of contesting written tradition and the reliability of its transmission and they were practiced in applying the evaluative categories of textual corruption and transcriptional malfeasance. Ehrman, however, tends to comprehend most manuscript variation under these rubrics. Though acknowledging Haines-Eitzen's point that early Christian scribes, unlike many of their working counterparts, were users of the literature they transcribed, Ehrman views scribes largely as copyists. In other words, Ehrman appears to have virtually no conception of scribes as tradents or of written artifacts (manuscripts) as comprising and hence behaving like a genuine *tradition*. Instead, he distinguishes the transmission of the written tradition categorically from the acts of transforming it and hence finds it anomalous, an "acute irony," that second- and third-century Christian scribes (or, for that matter, even Matthew and Luke) should do so to authoritative texts (Ehrman 2005, 69; see also 1993, 14; 2005, 50, 210–15).

The irony here perhaps lies in the fact that Ehrman's assessment of scribal activity is predicated on the very print assumptions that underlie the view of scriptural authority (God's Word fixed in originals) that he has come to reject and now makes the chief butt of his criticism. The inadequacies of this analytical framework are particularly evident in the tensions in Ehrman's account of why most variations arose in the early rather than the later manuscript tradition. Ehrman suggests that early Christian scribes were amateurs whose replacement, after Constantine's conversion, by a cadre of professional scribes better at exact copying resulted in a more stable transmission. However, he simultaneously characterizes these early scribes as theologically and politically sophisticated, capable of shaping the manuscript tradition in a manner responsive to the second- and third-century christological conflicts (Ehrman 2005, 51–52, 71–73, 124, 175, 205). Apart from the need for a way to reconcile these characterizations, the effect is to construe practices typical of oral manuscript culture *ad hoc* as a narrowly early Christian phenomenon. Much closer to the mark, therefore, is the analogy that Ehrman posits between interpretive scribal transformations and the active interpretation that always accompanies the reading of a text (Ehrman 1993, 31, 280; 2005, 216–17). What Ehrman characterizes as the "*unique* hermeneutical enterprise" of Christian scribes in physically transforming their texts (Ehrman 1993, 280, emphasis original), however, should be recognized as a typical tradent activity of scribes.

The work of Robbins, Parker, and Ehrman illustrates the difficulty that even cutting-edge gospels scholarship faces in escaping from print assumptions. This essay, following analytical approaches pioneered by Werner Kelber, has focused upon the convergence of orality, writing, and memory in the operations of scribal transmission. It has argued that the origins and transmission of the written gospel tradition are best viewed in light of the scribal tradent competence that was a feature of oral-manuscript culture. More specifically, the active manuscript transmission of early Christian scribes should be seen as the continuation of the cultural memory project initiated by the compositional activity of the Evangelists, with the *mouvance* dynamism of the written gospel tradition abating as the project developed in historically contingent and contested ways toward explicit canonization (see Kirk 2007). Along this course, the gospels' manuscript tradition comes to bear in its visible marks the memory of its reinscriptions down through the historical and cultural contexts of early Christianity.

11

THE ORAL-SCRIBAL-MEMORIAL ARTS OF COMMUNICATION IN EARLY CHRISTIANITY

WERNER H. KELBER

There is . . . a lag of well over a millennium between the time the numerical grid was certainly in use for "dividing" Scripture, and its first complete appearance on a physical page. It is clear in this instance that people had laid out the Bible on a grid in their memories for over a thousand years before they bothered to express that grid in writing, and for at least four hundred years before they thought it important even to suggest it in their scholarly citational habits.
—*Mary Carruthers (1990, 99)*

It has been murmured of late, however, that a great famine has arisen in that land and that historical criticism is in dire want.
—*Stephen Moore (1989, xiv)*

But memory is of the past.
—*Aristotle (De memoria et reminiscentia 449b15)*

We have not been sufficiently aware of the depth to which technology has penetrated the psyche.
—*Walter Ong (1992, 204)*

The whole modern method of historical research is founded upon the distinction between original and derivative authorities.
—*Arnaldo Momigliano (1950, 286)*

Prologue

There are times when we allow ourselves to be persuaded that the history of humanistic scholarship is one of systematic growth in knowledge and steady advances in intellectual comprehension. In the discipline of biblical studies, the discovery of new manuscripts, the application of hitherto unused methodologies, and the impact of electronically facilitated research tools all seem to promise a measurable increase in information and a continual progression in scholarly apprehension. Yet lurking beneath the relative calmness of this image is the actuality of academic debates over ideas, concepts, methods, and, always, interpretations—a world that represents a far less tranquil picture of the history of scholarship. The receptionist history of academic works in biblical studies, for example, is curious and complex, nourished not simply by the power of logic but often by deep-seated passions and strong polemical charges. Genuine breakthrough books can be marginalized because their very novelty runs counter to conventional approaches, while other studies take center stage despite the fact that their iterative character is immediately recognizable to those who are familiar with the history of biblical scholarship. In the course of this process, sometimes a work assumes an importance entirely unexpected by its author. When I wrote *The Oral and the Written Gospel* (*OWG*) in the early 1980s, I was making strenuous mental efforts to chart a course that I hoped would yield new insights into biblical texts and their modes of transmission/performance. But I did not anticipate, and could not have anticipated, the kind of sustained responses—positive, lukewarm, hesitant, and negative—that the book has received over the past quarter of a century.

Contextualizing a New Approach

At the end of his very generous and incisive introductory chapter to this book, Tom Thatcher states that *OWG* "initiated a project ... much larger than the vision of its own author" (see p. 25 above). Indeed. But the verb "initiate" needs to be contextualized with a measure of circumspection. Reflection on the numerous articles, monographs, journals, regular program units at the national meetings of the Society of Biblical Literature (SBL), and conferences that have dealt with what I have come to refer to as orality–scribality–memory studies of the Bible suggest that *OWG* has not been the single, generative force in a growing debate on the verbal arts in the early Christian culture of communications. Humanistic scholarship, like most textual traditions, does not proceed from single points of origin, with knowledge developing in a tight genealogical stemma system of transmission. Fresh approaches are always already interwoven with textures larger than the so-called "new." My own thinking was, and continues to be, deeply influenced by Albert Lord, Eric Havelock, Walter J. Ong, Mary Carruthers, John Miles Foley, and Ruth Finnegan, among others—all humanists of uncommon erudition and originality. Moreover, many of those who are now actively engaged in the study of the ancient Christian communication environment received inspiration less from my work and more from disciplines such as classics, Ancient Near Eastern history, African studies, sociology, Slavic scholarship, rhetoric, Judaic studies, sociology, medieval studies, comparative literature, and folkloristics. My assessment of my own contribution is that I have raised the problem of what Foley aptly termed "an inadequate theory of verbal art" with particular force and persistence over the years, alerting my colleagues in biblical studies to the textual, typographical bias inherent in much of our historical and interpretive work and drawing scholars from a variety of disciplines into the discussion (see Foley 1991, 5). In doing so, I have sought to give the discipline of biblical scholarship a much needed intellectual breadth while at the same time informing humanists outside the guild of the work that is being done in our circle.

To date, six volumes of *Semeia* have been devoted to the developing scholarship on orality, textuality (which I prefer to call "scribality"), and memory. *Semeia* 39, *Orality, Aurality and Biblical Narrative* (1987), edited by Lou H. Silberman, offered initial responses to some of the implications raised by *OWG*. A more wide-ranging discussion of orality–scribality issues was subsequently put forward in *Semeia* 65, *Orality and Textuality in Early Christian Literature* (1995), edited by Joanna Dewey. In 2003-2004, Jonathan Draper edited a two-volume set of essays that applied the oral–scribal approach to the South African and the ancient Jewish/Greco–Roman cultures, respectively. *Semeia* 46, *Orality, Literacy, and Colonialism in South Africa* (2003) illuminated how both the print Bible and text-based literacy functioned as media of control, administered by colonial authorities on the premise that Africans speak while the colonialists write. The companion volume, *Orality, Literacy, and Colonialism in Antiquity* (2004), explored the complex relationship between texts and oral discourse in ancient colonial settings, ranging from Homer, Plato, and Mithras to Hebrew and Christian Scripture and the rabbinic traditions. Social and cultural memory theory was the topic of *Semeia* 52, *Memory, Tradition, and Text* (2005), edited by Alan Kirk and Tom Thatcher. This volume outlined a comprehensive research agenda for the study of the memorial and commemorative impulses that empowered the synoptic tradition, the Q discourses, the narrative gospels, Paul's recollection of Jesus sayings, Hebrews, and the *Gospel of Thomas*. The two introductory essays in particular have had a formative influence on my memory work. Finally, in 2006, Richard Horsley edited *Semeia* 60, *Oral Performance, Popular Tradition, and Hidden Transcript in* Q. This volume developed an oral apperception of Jesus' speeches paralleled in Matthew and Luke and explored their social and political implications from anthropological and social science perspectives.

At present, the SBL is sponsoring three program units that address aspects of orality–scribality–memory studies. Since 1983, The Bible in Ancient and Modern Media Section has explored biblical materials in media other than silent print, including oral and electronic performances. The SBL group Mapping Memory: Tradition, Texts, and Identity seeks to restore memory to its historical position in the early Christian culture of communication and studies ways in which memory theory can be fruitful for understanding Christian commemorative processes. More recently, the SBL consultation Orality, Textuality, and the Formation of the Hebrew Bible has begun to examine how oral–scribal–memorial research might inform our understanding of the formation of the Hebrew Bible and, consequently, our interpretation.

I single out three monographs that have had an especially profound impact on my thinking. There is first the book that a distinguished colleague once called one of the most important humanistic monographs published in the 20th century: Jan Assmann's *Das kulturelle Gedächtnis* (1992). In this study the author explored the role of memory in the construction of cultural and political identities in the Mediterranean civilizations of ancient Egypt, Israel, and Greece with particular attention to the verbal arts. In a productive interfacing of memorial and chirographic forces, Assmann argued, these three civilizations generated political identities that embarked upon world history with hugely innovative cultural projects—ancient Egypt constituting the first world-empire state, Israel making the decisive move from temple rituals toward a canonized body of texts, and Greece harnessing the chirographic medium into a tool for the evolution of thinking. Although regrettably not translated, the book is, in my view, basic for an adequate comprehension of memorial dynamics in the formation of human culture. Without a solid grasp of Assmann's work our application of memory theory to biblical texts will always remain somewhat shaky. The second book is David Carr's *Writing on the Tablet of the Heart* (2005), an exceedingly ambitious study which examined ways in which people in Ancient Near Eastern civilizations worked and lived with texts, or, more precisely, in which chirographic activities and their written products functioned—orally, scribally, memorially—in largely educational contexts. The third book is Martin Jaffee's *Torah in the Mouth* (2001), which surveyed the nature of scribal culture in Second Temple Judaism and developed a concept of rabbinic culture as an oral-performative tradition.

Contesting the standard scholarly concept of a specifically Pharisaic claim on the Oral Torah, the author explicated the workings of the rabbinic textual transmission as processes of compilation and oral mediation (reoralization), viewing tradition not as an entity of the past but as revelation extending into the present by continuously infusing new life into it.

OWG and all of my subsequent work exists in and resonates with the intellectual context provided by this stream of publications and conference events, including many others not mentioned above. Not surprisingly, there is a sense in which the author of *OWG* has lost control of his book as it has become immersed in the public domain of what appears to be a growing and deepening discussion. Others have taken interpretive control of the book—accentuating, connecting, discounting, modifying, and deleting aspects and, in the process, situating it within a scholarly environment both different from and so much larger than the initial authorial context. This is, of course, a hermeneutical experience shared by all authors, but it is felt with particular keenness in the case of a book as widely deliberated as *OWG*. But it is precisely this widening nexus of scholarly interactions and my own participation in it that has allowed me to refine, modify, and correct my own thinking, hopefully carrying forward our understanding of the oral–scribal–memorial culture of early Christianity and advancing our critical reflection on the historical paradigm that is informing all academic work on the Bible.

OWG was written with the intent to raise consciousness about the "Gutenberg Galaxy" within which, I felt, much of biblical scholarship was being conducted. My thinking at the time was that I was dealing with what John Miles Foley has rightly called a "blind spot" (Foley 2002, 28), which, if corrected, would restore historical criticism to its genuine objective of being truly historical. It is not that I think I was incorrect in diagnosing the problem. The recent application of oral–scribal–memorial approaches, both to the Hebrew Bible and to the rabbinic tradition, has been encouraging. But the conceptual flaws that I sought to expose now appear more deep-seated and intractable than I had ever imagined. I now realize that the issue is not simply one of filling in a missing link—be it the oral dimension or the dynamics of memory—so that the historical-critical paradigm can carry out its assigned intellectual mission more strictly in keeping with the ancient culture of communication. Far from being superficial, the blind spot and the conceptual flaws that go with it reach to the core of the historical methodologies that govern our approaches to biblical texts.

In numerous writings over the past twenty-five years I have frequently expressed my profound admiration for the immensity and profundity of the philological, historical, and hermeneutical investigation of the Bible and of the cultures that produced it. Without a doubt, the reproduction, translation, exposition, and exploration of the Bible is the largest textual enterprise in Western history. The academic study of the New Testament alone, the critical exploration of its texts and of Christian origins, stands as a monument to Western intellectual history and to the liberal ethos of the Enlightenment—even though there exists in North America virtually no public consciousness of it. But the more I recognized that the print Bible (in whatever language) and our daily interaction with printed scholarly literature has served as a filter for the ways we view the ancient communication conditions of speaking, writing, and remembering, the more Walter Ong's dictum about the interiorization of technology rang true to me. Media technologies, Ong argues, produce something in the sensible world outside us but also affect the way our minds work. While external effects and changes brought about by media are often recognizable, we are not sufficiently aware of the depths to which technologies have penetrated the human psyche. Writing, print, and electronics are very much an "interiorized phenomenon, something registering inside man" (Ong 1992, 193). Benefitting from Ong's model, I became increasingly conscious of the fact that print was the medium in which modern biblical scholarship was born and raised and from which it had acquired its formative intellectual habits, its methodological tools, and, last but not least, its theories about the behavior of texts.

To explore the roots of historical criticism, I have been familiarizing myself with the eighteenth- and early-nineteenth-century German philological, historiographical, and hermeneutical tradition. Like many others, I had assumed that the key to understanding the genesis and rationale of the historical method lay in the German humanistic scholarship of the period roughly from 1750 to 1850. Once my awareness was raised about the implications of the typographical medium in the formation of the historical method, however, my attention was directed much further back, to Renaissance humanism. I owe much of my knowledge of that period to Anthony Grafton, the Princeton historian who, in a series of meticulously researched monographs, has shed brilliant light on the world of scholarship ranging from the Renaissance up to scientific modernity. The humanists of the fifteenth and sixteenth centuries seized upon the vast manuscript tradition of antiquity, collecting, classifying, prioritizing, and scrutinizing it for the purpose of reconstructing the classical heritage. They were in the habit of expounding the ancient texts in line-by-line and even word-by-word commentaries whose sheer volume exceeded the texts themselves.

Situating themselves in a textual universe, they perfected a methodological treatment of texts that strongly enforced their idea of classical antiquity as a dominantly textual one. Perhaps we could even say that humanism discovered that history belongs to the domain of literature. In any case, it was Renaissance humanists, not German philologists, who developed the scientific approach to ancient texts, laying the foundations of text criticism, source criticism, paleography, and, of course, philology.

Grafton himself made few references to the invention of printing and did not seem to acknowledge connections between typography and the humanistic project. This topic, however, has been explored by Elizabeth Eisenstein (1979) in her well-known work on the cultural implications of print technology. Eisenstein has brought "the unacknowledged revolution" into the limelight, illuminating the impact of printing and its importance as an agent of change in European history (Eisenstein 1979, 3–42). Aided by the scholarship of Grafton and Eisenstein, I could see a highly productive historical alignment between the forces of Renaissance humanism, the typographic invention, and rising Protestantism in generating a cultural environment in which the historical-critical paradigm arose and matured. Martin Luther, a deeply appreciative beneficiary of the new medium, lived from 1483 to 1546. Joseph Scaliger, one of the foremost figures of humanism and a convert to Huguenot Protestantism, flourished from 1540 to 1609. By 1450, Gutenberg's press was most likely in operation, and around 1454 or 1455 his forty-two-line version of the Vulgate saw the light of print. "By 1500, one may say with some assurance that the age of the scribes had ended, and the age of printers had begun" (Eisenstein 1979, 167). These dates provide a grid for a period in European history when a religious revolution that sought to break with a medieval past, an ideational revolution that labored to retrieve the distant classical past, and the so-called *modus modernus* of the communications revolution joined hands to nourish a pre-modern and developing modern culture that laid the groundwork for the historical-critical paradigm. This, broadly speaking, is the historical context that produced the methodological tools and intellectual habits that have shaped our sense of the nature and behavior of texts, and that have guided our professional examination of the print Bible to this day.

A few of the more salient features that typify print technology and its appropriation of texts may be cited here. The duplicative effects of printing gave rise to multiple copies of fully identical books, vastly enhancing the availability of texts and facilitating ease of access. The humanists were awash in printed texts as no scribal expert prior to the invention of this new technology ever was. Typographic fixity, moreover, reified verbal communication and conveyed a sense of verbal permanence that had not been experienced before. The sense of verbal objectivity that the printed book insinuated was highly favorable to the idea of a "standard" or "original" text versus "derivatives" or "variants." All these experiences fed into the humanistic strategy of establishing the reliability of sources, sorting out the true from the false, identifying forgeries, marginalizing secondary texts and eliminating erroneous ones. "[T]he revival of the classical heritage," Grafton has observed, "involved not only the discovery of what was lost but the expunging of what was false" (Grafton 1991, 162). To further that end, the humanists practiced a genealogical method that sought, where possible, to identify a textual archetype in relation to which other texts could be marked as secondary or simply ignored. Arnaldo Momigliano has incisively identified historical criticism's intense focus on the principle of textual prioritizing, differentiating between the original text and derivative texts. This focus, in turn, encouraged a fascination with what Paul Ricoeur has termed the "idol of origins" (Ricoeur 2004, 170). It manifested itself in the search for the original text that held supremacy in a textual hierarchy. Last but not least, the hierarchical organization of texts fostered a tendency to imagine tradition on the model of linear sequentiality and often along the straight line of an evolutionary ascent.

Knowledge of the past had to rest on a firm documentary foundation, and the truth about the past found its fulfillment in documentary proof. Something of a documentary frenzy had taken hold of the human sciences, or better, the human sciences became decidedly textual sciences. In this way, Renaissance humanism shaped its project within a textual universe that operated on an intrinsically textual and increasingly typographical rationality. In a world of this kind, where documents related to other documents or to literary sources of documents, memory was decidedly marginalized. Print effectively diminished reliance on the *ars memorandi*, and memory, viewed by the ancients as a centralizing authority of civilized life, was gradually written out of existence by a scholarship that was increasingly dominated by the print medium. Nor was there much, if any, room for the human voice. Where texts seemed to be derived from texts and communicated back to back with other texts, the oral component was superfluous, irrelevant even. The archival mentality parted company with the hearsay of oral testimony.

The more I became aware of the "Gutenberg Galaxy" and historical criticism's deep indebtedness to fifteenth- and sixteenth-century cultural, religious, and media history, the more I sensed that I was by no means merely dealing with a "blind spot" but rather with a form of Gutenberg and post-Gutenberg intellectualism that was patently culture bound and specifically media bound. Perhaps we may eventually come to see that historical criticism is not the kind of objective force, based on an unerring rationality, that we often imagine it to be but rather a phase in the receptionist history of the Bible.

From Documentary to Oral–Scribal Sensibilities

The repeated deliberations I have devoted to form criticism have grown out of my interest in oral discourse and tradition. Anyone who is inquisitive about matters relating to orality and the Bible is bound to pay attention to the discipline that was designed to come to terms with oral tradition. Beginning with *OWG* and following with a number of articles, I have concerned myself with the theoretical implications and practical results of form criticism.

From my examination of the history, theory, and application of form criticism, I draw five general conclusions. First, while the discipline was from its inception subject to numerous unfavorable judgments, the most vocal objections pertained to the historical skepticism that it exhibited toward the Jesus tradition. The form-critical premise of early Christian productivity in the formation of Jesus materials (*Gemeindebildungen*), and the resultant disconnection of Jesus from the early church, has met with widespread and continuous disapproval. The core issue, on this view, is the historicity of faith. Second, following the discipline's peak phase from the 1920s to roughly the 1960s, flaws have steadily been exposed, more conspicuously perhaps in Anglo–American scholarship but persistently in Europe as well. One sometimes has the impression that form criticism has been dying a slow death for some time even though many of its basic assumptions still guide our handling of biblical texts. Third, to my knowledge, there does not exist at present a systematic treatment of the historical roots, linguistic premises, practical results, and demise of form criticism. This must come as a surprise in view of the fact that, for the longest part of the twentieth century, form criticism was the dominant methodological approach to gospels and tradition. Fourth, in a perceptive review of Bultmann's *Geschichte der synoptischen Tradition,* Samuel Byrskog has written that the "fundamental problem with Bultmann's method is not its inherent skepticism toward the historicity of the tradition. . . . Rather, what is essentially problematic is precisely that his method does not work as a tool of historical inquiry" (Byrskog 2003, 55). This is precisely the point. The form-critical method, as it was conceptualized by Bultmann, is historically unworkable. Fifth, to the best of my knowledge, prior to my work form criticism had never been scrutinized exclusively from the angle of orality. None of the large-scale investigations—Erich Fascher's 1924 book and Reiner Blank's 1981 study, for example—chose to make oral discourse and performance a major focus of their critical deliberations. This, too, is surprising, since the explication of oral tradition was the declared objective of form criticism. The reason, I think, is that the minds of the form critics, no less than those of their critical reviewers, have been so dominated by literary, textual perspectives that the oral dimension never came into view.

It is, I think, fair to say that my analysis is the first of its kind that has strictly focused on the issue of whether form criticism has kept faith with its mission to explicate the history of the pre-literary, oral tradition of the gospels. If my assessment has turned out to be uncommonly critical, it is because I have concerned myself with the core theses of form criticism's work on oral tradition, all of which I found to be lacking in historical feasibility. Altogether, over the years I have problematized eleven aspects of form criticism, which I shall briefly summarize here in bulleted form.

- First, the use of *form* in the discipline's designation conjures up the notion of visually objectifiable items residing in literary texts. Recognizing the visual base of the key concept, one cannot help but wonder whether form criticism has not operated from the start with an ill-conceived understanding of the nature of speech. Performance, not form, is the central feature of oral tradition, and form criticism would have been well advised to commence its project as performance criticism.
- Second, the form-critical practice of detaching assumed oral items from the gospel texts raises the question whether "detachable speech" can have validity in oral theory. Oral discourse is uniquely dependent upon concrete social contextuality. To detach words from what is already a second level of narrative emplotment and to examine them in isolation will not give us oral tradition but a studied abstraction.
- Third, form criticism's search for "the original" form of sayings and stories misconceived the nature of oral verbalization. At least since the work of Albert Lord, it has to be understood that, in oral discourse, "each performance is 'an' original, if not 'the' original" (Lord 2000, 101). Oral tradition, therefore, is constituted by plural originals, not by singular originality.
- Fourth, almost from its inception, form criticism turned itself into an auxiliary discipline at the service of the quest for the historical Jesus. True to the calling of its mission, form criticism should have

developed a model of oral tradition, of the oral–scribal dynamics in the tradition and, last but not least, of the role of memory. Infatuation with the mistaken notion of the "original saying" has seduced form criticism to divert its attention away from oral tradition and toward the historical quest.

- Fifth, the form-critical premise that characteristic forms of speech correspond to distinct social settings is not an issue in current oral theory. Holly Hearon, in her essay in this volume, has demonstrated "the ubiquity of storytelling in the ancient Mediterranean world" and the difficulty of assigning to it a single form, content, context, or purpose (quote p. 94 above). Clearly, the interrelationship between oral and social life cannot be comprehended in the simple rules devised by form criticism.
- Sixth, it is strange to see the discipline embarking upon its exploration of oral tradition with a declaration of the irrelevance of any formal distinction between oral and literary communication. Did the form critics truly believe they could achieve their objective without articulating a formal theory of oral discourse? Even if one postulates oral–scribal interactions, as I think we should, one has to remember that the distinctive character of these interfaces remains unrecognized without a prior grasp of oral versus literary dynamics.
- Seventh, by design, form criticism operated with a model of linear transmission processes. The linearity of tradition, while orally unworkable, has had a strong hold on our imagination, in part because it is visually imaginable. Oral words, however, spring to life in specific performance circumstances, and they leave no enduring traces except in the minds and memory of hearers.
- Eighth, over the years, I have been surprised to discover how many colleagues are aware of the evolutionary implications of form criticism's linear model of tradition. That the discipline subscribed to the premise of a tradition moving incrementally and in stages is now widely recognized. I have raised evolutionary gradualism to the level of theoretical prominence because of its amazingly powerful influence not only on form criticism but on the historical paradigm in general. Yet, biological sciences aside, gradual evolutionism rarely, if ever, works in cultural, let alone communications, history.
- Ninth, form-critical evolutionism entails an element of determinism, of inevitability even, viewing the final form of the gospels almost exclusively as a result of innate tendencies in the tradition. On that model, tradition was assumed to have smoothly run into written

gospel, or better still, tradition was thought to have transformed itself into written gospel. In either case, the relationship between tradition and gospel was judged unproblematic, the former defining both the form and content of the latter. Although once again a visually appealing theory, evolutionary gradualism is an abstraction and not grounded in linguistic, let alone social, actualities. Oral tradition inextricably ties in with social context, and the social variables and, above all, the social circumstances surrounding the gospels' composition, rather than oral causalities inherent in tradition, harnessed tradition into gospel narrativity.

- Tenth, on all counts, the form-critical model suggests that the written gospel is a product of tradition and not really a composition in its own right. That the gospel could be in tension with tradition, embedded in tradition and yet embarked upon shaping a new vision, is not thinkable in form criticism.
- Eleventh, and finally, the central object of the form-critical mission is subject to review: the existence of a pre-gospel oral tradition that many of us have long taken for granted. Among those working in orality–scribality studies, this model is no longer widely shared. The Q discourses alone, which existed in scribal form although most likely in variant versions, militate against the notion of a pure oral tradition. Nor should one forget that Paul is perfectly capable of quoting Jesus sayings in 1 Corinthians. In the Ancient Near Eastern and Mediterranean worlds of communication, pure oral tradition, untouched by scribality, was no more the rule than pure scribality reveling in the realm of intertextuality and uninfluenced by oral performative dynamics.

Clearly, orality–scribality studies have moved from a unilateral to an interactive model. Does this mean that form criticism was right after all in leveling the difference of oral versus scribal dynamics? Not in the least. It rather suggests that, in addition to using historically unworkable tools and methods in the study of oral tradition, form criticism also applied itself to an ill-defined project.

When I published *Mark's Story of Jesus* in 1979, I was unaware that I had written one of the first books in modern biblical scholarship that attempted to grasp the full sequential story line of a gospel. The short answer to the question of why I had ever aspired to comprehend the gospel's narrative whole is that I had passed from historical to form criticism and from there to redaction and on to narrative criticism. At least, this is the way that the rise of narrative criticism from the 1960s onward is conventionally reported. It was gradually and over a period of years that I came to realize that biblical narrative has been the cause of great difficulties in biblical interpretation. Certainly in the modern period, literary criticism, in the sense of an exploration of narrative and rhetorical strategies, did not come naturally to biblical studies. The story of the successive rise of source, form, redaction, and literary criticism is overly simplistic, covering up more than it illuminates.

Among historical developments and scholarly experiences that were instrumental in shaping my attitude toward biblical narrative, though mostly after the publication of *Mark's Story of Jesus* (1979), three rather different phenomena come to mind. My direct interest in the gospel narratives and what I like to refer to as *narrative causalities* stems, to a fair extent, from media sensibilities. Along with many others, I was conscious of, and troubled by, the fragmenting force of our conventional commentaries. Mary Carruthers reports that for "well over a millennium" the memorial apperception of the Bible had habitually divided biblical texts into short units for ease of memorization, ritualization, and recitation (Carruthers 1990, 99). Thus, a memorial grid had long been operative in the appropriation of biblical texts, including the gospel narratives. But when the memorial grid was objectified as a numerical grid, initially in medieval manuscripts and subsequently in the print Bible, the resultant chapter-and-verse format proved destructive to any sense of narrative form and coherence. I shared with all my colleagues who worked in narrative criticism the desire to overcome the deleterious effects of our standard commentary format.

The second phenomenon took the form of a book that proved crucial in alerting me to theological impediments to narrative interpretation: Hans Frei's *The Eclipse of Biblical Narrative* (1974). In this, his *magnum opus*, Frei painstakingly documented the inability of scholars and theologians of the eighteenth and nineteenth centuries to capture the shape and intrinsic logic of biblical narrative. Even though the term "eclipse" conjured up the myth of a once ideal origin, when narrative was rendering a world at once real and meaningful, Frei admirably succeeded in diagnosing the malaise of an escape from narrative. A central motivating force in the separation of meaning from narrative form was, in Frei's words, the "factuality" or "positivity of revelation" (Frei 1974, 54, 255). Rationalists and supernaturalists alike aspired to disrobe the narrative in pursuit of the real, full presence. Whether biblical narrative was considered to have been constructed on the logic of history, in which case its significance rested in external events, or whether it was reduced to ideas or ethical counsel, meaning was held to be separable from the narrative plot. The common rationale among biblical scholars and theologians at that time was that form was an impediment to the attainment of full, revelatory meaning, be it historical or ideological. Frei's work left a deep impression on my thinking and sensitized me to formidable problems that were associated with narrative interpretation. Specifically, *Eclipse* made me aware of the extent to which classic theological ideas still had a hold on my own reading of the gospels. This is a point that has been reinforced by Richard Horsley in his contribution to the present volume and in some of his previous publications. I am now aware how much more difficult it is than I had imagined to take narrative seriously as narrative and to read it in the context of Israel's political, cultural history.

A third phenomenon that may have exercised a subtle influence on my thinking about narrative is a particular attitude symptomatic of the "New Criticism." In what I think is the best book on the recent literary criticism of the gospels, Stephen Moore has recognized new-critical undercurrents in the resurgence of interests in narrative—although these are largely unacknowledged drifts below the surface of our academic work (Moore 1989, 3–68). The New Criticism, which lasted from roughly the late 1930s through the 1950s, postulated the creed of the holistic nature of literature, poetic works in particular but narrative as well. Its premise was that literature has its own distinct properties, a life of its own, as it were. In asserting and practicing a view of literature "as an entity complete in itself, with elements fused by the 'pressure of the total context' into a unique artifact," the New Criticism claimed to be truly objective in its orientation toward the interior landscape of texts (Poland 1985, 80). As Moore saw it, the view of gospel narrative offered by the recent literary criticism of the gospels "has invested heavily but not exclusively in the idea of textual unity" (Moore 1989, xv).

Traditionally, the New Criticism has been traced back to Coleridge and Kantian aesthetics. But there is a media dimension to this twentieth-century attitude toward texts as well. Walter Ong has linked the closed, text-bound thinking characteristic of the New Criticism with the technologizing impact of print (Ong 1982, 160–61). It could be argued that the printed page, by virtue of its uniquely systematic spatial organization and finality of precision, eventually came to insinuate the notion of a perfectly unified textual whole not only in terms of form but of content as well. Centuries of the interiorization of print culture had made it artistically desirable and academically acceptable to view texts as autonomous worlds. In Ong's words, the "New Critics have assimilated the verbal art work to the visual object-world of texts" (Ong 1982, 160). Even though the numerical grid of the print Bible discouraged narrative reading, the steady working with typographically constructed texts had the effect of encouraging interpreters in subtle ways to think of narrative as an interiorly fully unified object. While my reading of the gospels has always explored both synchronic and diachronic potentialities, viewing these texts both as mirror and as window, it is also true that narrative unity and strenuous efforts to fit the narrative puzzles into a coherent whole was one of my overriding interpretive concerns. One should not underrate the role of print and the seductive perfection of the printed page in making us believe that the perfectly constructed print format is the carrier of a perfectly unified content.

I read and interpreted Mark's gospel as a piece of literature that was the product of rather sophisticated scribal activities, although nourished by substantial oral traditions. As I saw it, the narrative was dramatically and rhetorically so well constructed that I could only imagine it as the result of deliberate chirography. I was, moreover, so struck by the oddness of the narrative, especially in its characterization of the role of the disciples, Jesus' family, and prophetic personalities, that I viewed it as a text intent on gaining control over a prior identity, which I identified as an oral identity. At the time of the writing of *OWG*, I was entirely aware of challenging form criticism's evolutionary model of tradition with a revisionist model of the gospel. In different words, I discerned a clear logical connection between my deconstruction of form criticism and my construction of gospel narrativity.

In a departure from literary criticism, a series of studies have now appeared that propose an oral identity of the gospel. Among others, Pieter Botha (1991), Richard Horsley (2001), Whitney Shiner (2003), and above all Joanna Dewey (1989; 1991; 1992; 1994b; 2004) have offered readings of Mark as an oral text. Since Dewey has closely engaged my own interpretation in her piece in this volume, I will confine my response to this entire line of discussion to three critical points she has raised: the oral style of Mark, Mark's rejection of oral authorities, and the written nature of Mark's passion narrative. This last issue, concerning the passion narrative, I will discuss below under the heading "Memory and Manuscript." Here, I wish to confirm Dewey's observation that our readings of Mark are agreed on a fair number of substantive issues. Nonetheless, our disagreements bear on interpretive questions that are fundamental to a comprehension of the gospel.

Mark's gospel, Dewey suggests in her essay in this book, "is basically an oral narrative built on oral storytelling, employing an oral style, and plotted according to oral conventions" (see p. 72 above). In response, my initial questions are as follows: Granted that the Gospel of Mark, like much ancient writing, was intended to be recycled into oral performance, is it oral-traditional literature in the sense conjectured by Albert Lord? That is to say, is the Gospel of Mark a transcript of oral performances? Lord's proposal to this effect has not met with much, if any, approval by biblical scholars, although admittedly his exposition of the gospels as oral-traditional literature was not the best that could be made. Or is the Gospel of Mark "oral" in the sense that it is the product of mental composition and dictation? Or, when we speak of "oral plotting," do we mean that Mark grew out of the chirographic activities of an oralist scribe who wrote the text while hearing it? In other words, the oral gospel model raises intricate compositional questions that need to be addressed. Just as source critics ought to have given account of how their assumed textual manipulations were scribally, orally, memorially, technically workable, so do those of us who plead for an oral emplotment of the gospel need to explain the latter's compositional feasibility in the ancient media world.

The key question is whether the Gospel of Mark is as oral a narrative as Dewey has proposed. In *The Passion in Mark* (Kelber 1976), a volume of essays on that gospel's passion narrative, the contributors demonstrated how numerous major and minor themes from chapters 1 through 13 converge in the passion narrative (chapters 14–16). Do we not see here the beginnings of a circumspectly drawn literary construction? Are there not interconnections between parts, and arching thematic constructions that have an overriding effect on oral units? In short, is it truly conceivable that the Gospel of Mark's scribal composition did not take advantage of some potentialities inherent in the chirographic medium? Could we agree, perhaps, on viewing the gospel as a classic oral–scribal media mix?

A second set of issues revolves around the narrative role assigned to the disciples, the family of Jesus, and prophetic personalities. I have identified these three groups respectively as "the principal oral authorities" (Kelber 1983, 98), "oral representatives" (Kelber 1983, 98), and "spokesmen and spokeswomen on behalf of the tradition" (Kelber 1983, 103). I have sought to demonstrate that in the logic of Mark's narrative all were subject to severe criticism and renounced. Dewey writes that these three groups were "each critiqued in various ways . . . for *different* reasons, none specifically to do with oral authority" (see p. 77 above, emphasis in original). On the first point, I agree entirely. I think I have interpreted the disciples, the family, and prophets, and the objections raised against them painstakingly in their respective narrative contexts. The concept of oral authority was meant to suggest that the narrative depicted each of these three groups as playing a crucial role in the representation of Jesus and/or the continued existence of his message. Are not the disciples consistently placed in auditive immediacy of Jesus and privileged to witness his words and actions so as to be able to function as carriers of his mandate? Can we assume that Mark was unaware of the crucial role the family of Jesus played in the formative stage of the movement? The ending of Mark, one of the most intriguing literary endings of any piece in Western literature, seems to me to delegate to Mary the all-decisive role of tradent of the resurrection. The non-communication of the message to the disciples is as shocking an ending as there can be. I do not wish to blunt the sharp edge of that ending, as all subsequent tradition has done. As for the prophets, were they not utilizing the *ego eimi* style of self-presentation for the purpose of impersonating Jesus and speaking on his authority?

To be sure, much depends on exegetical detail, and here Dewey and I are in substantial disagreement. Yet even if one cannot follow my interpretation of a repudiation of these oral authorities, should it not give us pause for deep reflection to observe that, sociologically speaking, substantive negativity is expressed toward the legitimately appointed authorities, the hereditary authorities, and the charismatic authorities? One simply cannot think of Mark's narrative as a foundational story in the conventional sense. Is it conceivable that the model of tradition's evolutionary ascent into a narrative that secures apostolic transmission of the message is still, subliminally, working on our minds? My argument was, and is, that Mark, living under the impact of the catastrophe of 70 C.E., facilitated a *Traditionsbruch,* a rupture with tradition—a premise that Dewey basically accepts. Under those circumstances, tradition could no longer serve automatically as a basis, and those who could be expected to be the carriers of tradition had become problematic. Composing a narratively generated return to the foundational figure, Mark dissociated himself from the first-level bearers of tradition, writing a second-level foundation story in ways that explained the present demise and offered a way into the future. Finally, if I understand Dewey correctly, she suggests that in oral performance the ancient hearers would not understand the fate of the disciples as one of rejection, because, in the ancient agonistic climate, the polemical tone of Mark would have lost some of its effectiveness (see p. 74 above). I tend to think that the receptionist history of the discipleship theme is one of growing domestication. For hearers who lived in the aftermath of the catastrophic events, Mark's narrative must have had a powerfully relevant impact. The longer ending took the edge off Mark 16:8, because it was understandably perceived to be an offensive proposition. Even though in the Gospel of Matthew (16:16-19) Peter plays a thoroughly ambiguous role, he is nonetheless elevated to foundational significance in the church. Acts 1:21-22 is well on the way toward developing the classic concept of the apostolic eyewitnesses.

Memory and Manuscript

Memory entered my work on tradition and written gospels in the 1990s, and in 2001 I published the first of a series of articles on that topic. It was roughly in that period that I was also alerted to recent developments in textual criticism that facilitated new insights into ancient scribal activities. Unlike the form-critical inquiries, the recent text-critical explorations operated with data that are subject to objective papyrological verification. On the matter of memory, my indebtedness is, again, primarily to Assmann, whose *Das kulturelle Gedächtnis* (1992) has remained a source of continuous inspiration. Additionally, I cannot think of a more incisive and comprehensive introduction to the significance of memory for biblical studies than the above-mentioned *Semeia* volume on *Memory, Tradition, and Text* (2005), edited by Kirk and Thatcher. On the matter of text criticism, David Parker and Eldon Epp have opened my eyes to the remarkable scribal fluidity of Jesus materials. The integration of memorial and textual dynamics into the body of my previous work has now moved me in a direction where I feel that a more thoroughgoing reconceptualization of the early Jesus tradition, based on our understanding of the oral–scribal, memorial, and narratological interfaces, is possible.

At no place is the post-Gutenberg intellectualism of our historical scholarship of the Bible more palpable than in the virtual deletion of memory, *fons et origo* of ancient civilizations. The marginalization of memory that began in Renaissance humanism has now effectively reached its apex in the historical-critical paradigm. In our scholarly pursuits, memory is for the most part a phenomenon without history. As mentioned before, historical criticism, far from being the paragon of unfailing rationality, reveals itself as the culmination of a long history of the transformation of biblical texts that stretches from their oral and papyrological beginnings all the way to their typographic apotheosis in print culture. The one noteworthy exception to the *damnatio memoriae* in our scholarly pursuits is Birger Gerhardsson's classic work *Memory and Manuscript* (1961), whose enviable title I had the audacity of using as a heading for this section of my essay. Unlike the form critics, Gerhardsson fully recognized the central significance of memory and placed it at the heart of the synoptic tradition.

Irrespective of whether one agrees with his particular model of memory, he rightly took exception to a commonly held concept of tradition that operated entirely without memory. I turned to memory because I found it ever more difficult to imagine the oral–scribal materials and dynamics of the early tradition without the operational role of memory. Furthermore, I came to realize that cultural memory was a great explanatory force in clarifying gospel composition. It is vastly superior to Bultmann's awkward use of myth and both supplements and transcends our narrative comprehension. Undoubtedly, as long as our thinking moves within a tight web of intertextualities, we do well without memory. But the more my thinking shifted from documentary sensibilities to *composition in writing* and *composition in performance*, the more I felt that I was in need of a concept such as *composition in memory*.

In my work on memory, an often elusive and sometimes fuzzy concept, I took pains to attain conceptual transparency. Seeking to define the force of memory in tradition and gospel, I differentiated "memorization" from "remembering." *Memorization* suggests the instruction of knowledge by way of ceaseless repetition, a minimal accommodation to audiences and a passive notion of tradition. *Remembering*, on the other hand, thrives on compositional inventiveness, responds to social contexts, and facilitates an active notion of tradition. Mindful of Aristotle's dictum that memory is always of the past, I contrasted *repetition* with *recollection* to clarify the memorially generated relations between past and present. "Memorization" connotes the repetitive side of memory that resurrects the past so as to transplant it into the present. "Remembering" entails the recollective side of memory that reconstructs the past so as to harmonize it with the present. My own work has been partial toward the recollective side of remembering, although I have recognized that a balanced approach between these two properties of memory may at times be advisable. As noted above, Assmann's concept of *Traditionsbruch* proved especially helpful in crafting a new model of the relation between written gospel and tradition. Last but not least, I have learned from Assmann to grasp the Jesus figure, cast into various narrative roles, as an *Erinnerungsfigur* who operates as carrier of accessible values and memorable virtues so as to be able to serve as a focus of identity. In all my memory work, I continue to be conscious of Assmann's statement, "Man muss sich darüber klarwerden, dass Erinnerung nichts mit Geschichtswissenschaft zu tun hat" (Assmann 1992, 77).[1] From this, I concluded that the posture of remembering assumed by the gospels has nothing to do with historiography.

From the beginning, memory was instrumental in Jesus' very own language. As it has come down to us through the medium of tradition, his speech still manifests itself as a conspicuously rhythmic, formulaic diction composed in memorially usable patterns. As such, it is fully representative of the *ars memoriae* that was expected to facilitate remembering in the oral processing of knowledge and wisdom. It might be observed that this aspect of Jesus' language is well known and scarcely in need of further attention. And yet, I have been surprised that the form critics did not pay attention to this feature with any degree of specificity. Exploration of the oral-performative force of Jesus' speech would inescapably have alerted them to the power of memory.

Few developments in biblical studies have left as deep an imprint on my thinking as the phenomenon that I have referred to as the Copernican revolution in textual criticism. Parker's *The Living Text of the Gospels* (1997) induced me to turn my attention to text criticism, and Epp's SBL presidential address (Epp 2004) strongly reconfirmed my growing interest in one of our subdisciplines that I had habitually left to the specialists. Initiated by Parker and Epp, a fundamentally new attitude toward the scribal legacy of the New Testament is now being cultivated. Instead of evaluating available scribal products for their usability in the construction of a *textus receptus,* the new attitude sees to it that every available scrap of scribal evidence is taken seriously on its own terms and as a component of a rich and variegated tradition. This has the potential of transforming text criticism from a discipline intent on securing the standard text to one that examines the tradition.

The new text criticism is still very much in its infancy, but I view it as a promising development that has a chance of replacing the defunct form criticism. Not least, text criticism, unlike form criticism, has the advantage of working with hard data. We have scarcely begun to assimilate these data that are being presented to us by the new text criticism. Unless significant evidence to the contrary is forthcoming, we will henceforth have to proceed on the premise that the scribal tradition of Jesus sayings was characterized by an astounding fluidity. Significantly, the written tradition of Jesus sayings demonstrated a higher degree of variation in the early period, being "at its most fluid in the first century of its existence" (Parker 1997, 200). Instead of operating with a model of initial foundational stability followed by dispersion and variability, we may need to think with Parker of "initial fluidity followed by stability" (Parker 1997, 70).

While direct copying and unintentional changes did take place in the early phase of the Jesus tradition, these scribal procedures by no means typify the whole picture. According to Parker, intentional variations—sometimes small, sometimes significant, but cumulatively consequential—dominated the scribal dynamics. The phenomenon of textual pluriformity—the existence of more than one copy and often more than one version of a given Jesus saying—was far from being exceptional. I was all the more struck by Parker's observations because Eugene Ulrich (1998; 1999) had drawn similar conclusions from his study of the Dead Sea Scrolls. As far as the Hebrew texts that eventually evolved to canonical status are concerned, their observed pluriformity at Qumran is such that the existence of the Masoretic text, the normative text of the Hebrew Bible, cannot be assumed any time prior to 100 C.E. Both in the early Jesus tradition and in the textual tradition of what came to be the Hebrew Bible, scribal pluriformity was a phenomenon *sui generis*.

The more I looked at the textual evidence displayed by Parker and Epp, the more I noticed how closely the behavior of these scribal traditions corresponded with oral phenomenology. As I began to ponder the scribal evidence from perspectives developed in my work on the oral performance tradition, I was venturing into a terrain that lay beyond the scope of the text critics. It seemed to me that we were dealing with scribal traditions that were (as yet) not hemmed in by firm boundaries and confined to fixed content. The sense of verbal permanence assumed by typography was not what characterized early scribality. As was the case in oral tradition, criteria for originality and authorship seemed far more relaxed. Orality's propensity, moreover, to conduct itself in plural and varying renditions had been sustained in the textual tradition. Instead of fixation on the one original saying, this tradition was comfortable with multiple and variable versions, each of which claimed authority at one point. In analogy to oral performance, the scribal tradition moved with the flux of time by way of social adaptation, thus keeping itself alive by staying relevant.

These insights on scribal tradition have now been developed in Alan Kirk's masterful contribution to this present volume. Adopting Paul Zumthor's term *mouvance* (1990, 207–8), Kirk states that "dynamism was a core feature of ancient manuscript tradition" which, not unlike the oral performance tradition, sustained itself through "contemporizing enactment in recitation and transcription" (see pp. 225–26 above). Defining scribes in that media environment "narrowly as 'copyists' . . . gives them short shrift," Kirk rightly observes (see p. 220 above). It is quite possible, I think, that our conventional view of scribes exclusively as textual experts has been unduly influenced by the concept of medieval, monastic scribes and by ubiquitous images depicting them in the process of copying texts. In the ancient world, they were tradents more than mere copyists. Standing at the interface of oral–scribal dynamics, the scribes were the guardians of the cultural legacy in a culture where memory "played the major operational role" (see p. 218 above). For whether they copied what lay before them, or activated what they remembered, or reactivated an existing scribal version, they grasped scribal products both as visual and as voiced entities. In all instances, memory "lay at the core of the scribal ethos" (see p. 219 above). In this sense, one may speak of a memorially empowered tradition that operated by no means simply as a transmission of texts but as a functioning social memory—for example, as a continuous process of commemorative activities.

These interfacing dynamics of orality–scribality, memory, and narrativity converged in the composition of Mark's passion narrative. Until very recently, that story has been the prerogative of historical criticism. These are some of the principal issues that have occupied the historical approach: the judicial legality of the trial; the historicity of the law (or convention) of amnesty; the relationship between this story and the Last Supper tradition in Paul and the synoptic narratives; discrepancies between the synoptic and Johannine chronologies; determination of the date of Jesus' death; the literary relationship among the three synoptic stories; the relationship between the passion in Mark and the *Gospel of Peter*; the existence of a pre-Markan passion narrative; the compositional history of Mark's passion story; ideational shifts in the assumed compositional history from a Jewish toward a Gentile oriented text, from a martyrological toward a theological interpretation, and from historical reporting toward legendary embellishments. Overall, this is an approach that seems unfeelingly barren, largely devoid of religious sensitivities and a symptom of the "great famine" in the land of historical criticism invoked by Stephen Moore in an epigraph to this piece.

My own work on Mark's passion narrative proceeded from the issue of trauma. As controlled as the plot appears on the surface, it struggles with the dreadful task of absorbing Jesus' execution, the destruction of the temple (a theme closely intertwined with Jesus' own story), and the demise of the disciples, which reaches its tragic point of culmination in the passion. Mark's passion narrative, I wrote in *OWG*, "is laden with death, for it is really a story about three deaths" (Kelber 1983, 185). It is, I should add, a story about death and not death and resurrection. I suggested that the work of mourning requires, above all, distance—geographical, chronological, psychological, and also media distance. On the latter point, my argument was that the story about death stands in need of the distance provided by writing to assimilate the traumas. One writes about what one is reluctant to speak.

Joanna Dewey and also Tom Thatcher and Chris Keith in their respective pieces in this volume have contested my media thesis on the passion narrative. "[T]he narration of Jesus' crucifixion may have fit better in oral narrative than in writing," Dewey observes (see p. 81 above), and Keith and Thatcher state that "[V]iolent events, like Jesus' crucifixion, traumatize group memory to such an extent that memorialization is necessary almost immediately" (see p. 204 above). In response to these objections, I wish to draw attention to the fact that my argument about the scribally generated distance from the events grew out of my objection to a well-known form-critical thesis about the genesis of the passion narrative. The remarkable narrative coherence of the passion narrative, so the common reasoning, suggested an early written composition, and early authentication implies close proximity to history. My understanding was, and is, that narrative coherence is an index of narratological competence and has little to do with an early date for the composition. I felt obliged to refute an argument that lay at the basis of the theory of an early, written passion narrative. Dewey, Thatcher, and Keith may well be right that Jesus' execution was talked about more frequently than I thought. But I want to sustain sensitivity to the severe challenges the crucifixion posed for any language, oral or written. The crucifixion forces questions about the limits of representation and the transference of a traumatic death into the arena of language. In that regard, I am surprised that we have not attended more closely to the Last Supper tradition both in Paul and in the gospels (Kelber 1983, 194–95). Is it not interesting that Jesus' death is the event that requires ritualization? Is the act of gross violence in need of a special mediation just because one cannot live with and communicate the unvarnished, unedited terror? Ritualization makes the death event personally accessible without reviving realistic aspects of the execution. Thatcher and Keith emphasize the necessity for memorialization in cases of exceptional violence. Citing Michael Schudson (1989, 110), they point to Americans facing up to slavery and Germans to the Holocaust. But how long, I ask, did it take for these atrocities to become part of national consciousness? Slavery, it is fair to say, did not enter into the collective memory of North America until far into the twentieth century. In the case of the Holocaust, there was absolutely no "immediate" response following World War II. It is now widely acknowledged that the cataclysmic event did not fully enter into national consciousness in Germany until the so-called *Historikerstreit,* a public debate initiated by the historian Ernst Nolte—ironically with the intent to stifle memory of the Holocaust—and the philosopher Jürgen Habermas, who opposed him. They were rapidly joined by scores of other intellectuals. It happened in 1986 and 1987—roughly forty years after the end of World War II. And that in the modern communications age!

In my view, the Markan passion narrative may be seen as a commemorative text, with three memory strategies in operation. Benefitting from the insights of Arthur Dewey (2005), I have learned to discern the work of memory in the places it builds to provide a habitat for what is to be remembered. One such memory place—"a place to put things," as Dewey calls it in his article for this volume (see p. 189 above)—is the "Tale of the Persecution and Vindication of the Innocent One," which, it is agreed, supplies the core of the passion narrative. I assume that this widely dispersed and tradition-honored tale was accessible to Mark orally. Following Dewey, I came to understand Mark's memory bed as a device to bring the unthinkable event into accord with a familiar, almost normative pattern. In other words, one can say that the theme of the Innocent Sufferer "normalizes" Jesus' death. A second memory strategy is what Alan Kirk (2005, 194), relying on Barry Schwartz (1991, 225–32), has called interpretive "keying," whereby familiar, even archetypal, language is reclaimed to serve as a key to understanding the excesses of violence within established frames. From the perspective of "keying," the scriptural citations (above all, Psalm 22), paraphrases, and images on which the passion narrative is constructed convert Jesus into a socially and memorially accessible *Erinnerungsfigur.* A third device of memory is evident in Mark's linkage of the anti-temple motif with Jesus' death. So densely is the temple motif integrated into the narrative about Jesus that interpreters rarely step back to reflect on Mark's constructive achievement. Yet, to our knowledge, Mark was the first Christian who faced up to the two principal traumas suffered in the early period: the death of Jesus and the destruction of the temple. The principal mechanism of the explanatory powers of memory was to link and subtly synchronize these two traumas and thereby construct a rationale for the hitherto unconnected events. Jesus anticipated, even precipitated, the temple conflagration, and in part it was in the process of his mission against the temple that he was destroyed himself. The integration of narrative thinking, oral–scribal sensitivities, and memory theory places our understanding of the passion story on a new footing.

Epilogue

These summary reflections on my scholarly development are of necessity constructed from a retrospective vantage point. The same can be said of Thatcher's sensitive assessment of my work in his introduction to this volume. Retrospectivity is the gesture common to memory, to historiography, as well as to reconstructions of the past that are being pursued under the influence of memory. In my own case, this recollective posture carries with it the almost irresistible temptation to view my writings as an intrinsically coherent and logically developing project—the kind of neat continuum that hindsight excels in creating. In reality, each step I have taken came about for its own set of reasons and circumstances and not as part of a premeditated master plan. Thatcher's advantage in surveying my work is twofold: he is an astute reader of virtually all of my publications, and at the same time he is distanced from my writings in ways I could never hope to be. This sense of detachment has mitigated the subjective components implicit in all gestures of restrospectivity and, combined with his thorough familiarity with my scholarship, he has produced an exceptionally comprehensive and insightful understanding of my intellectual profile and scholarly project.

I was intrigued to read in Thatcher's introductory chapter that my work has "gradually taken the form of a media history of Christian origins" (see p. 2 above). I would probably prefer to say that over the decades my scholarship has grown into its own phenomenology of the verbal arts. But it is true that I have in fact moved the modalities of media and sensibility to media dynamics to the center of my scholarly thought, seeking to apprehend the Christian tradition, especially in its initial phase, as a history of communicative processes. Still, the term "media" tends to be surrounded with an aura of intellectual superficiality and is open to misperceptions. The rationale for media explorations will, therefore, have to be clarified with some care. Two issues in particular come to mind: media blindness and media determinism.

It has been my contention over the years that modern biblical scholarship, like many humanistic disciplines, has by and large been blind to the role and power of media, both with regard to ancient dynamics of communication and in relation to its own typographic captivity. For some time now, evidence has been accumulating that attests to the essentially performative character of Ancient Near Eastern and Mediterranean handwritten papyri, scrolls, and even codices. In very large measure, ancient writings functioned in the praxis of oral performance and not as freestanding, literary icons. I have, therefore, come to think of the biblical texts, both in their Jewish and Christian provenance, as voiced texts that were meant to come to life in an oral biosphere and that were in turn variously affected by their oral performance/transmission. And the more I became persuaded that we are dealing with something of a scriptural orality operative in a dominantly memorial culture, the more I was struck by the degree to which academia is held captive by a predominantly print-oriented mode of thinking. Of the many examples I have provided of what is, in my view, a typographic more than an oral-scribal rationality, the most conspicuous seem to be the project of form criticism, the persistent focus on the assumed textual archetype and the *ipsissimum verbum*, and the gaping lacuna caused by the near total *damnatio memoriae* of memory itself as an analytical category. On the other hand, the demise of form criticism (though as yet rarely acknowledged or systematically assessed), text criticism's refocusing from textual originality to textual multiformity, and the beginnings of an awareness of the role of memory in tradition are some of the developments that are bound to have far-reaching consequences for our understanding of the message of the historical Jesus, the nature of tradition, the relation of gospels to tradition, and Christian origins in general.

Jan Assmann, while keenly aware of and refreshingly candid about the blindness of humanistic scholarship with regard to the material significance of writing, has likewise reminded us that a media-sensitive hermeneutic runs the risk of unwisely reducing complex operations of meaning construction monocausally to what he has termed *Mediendeterminismus* (Assmann 1992, 25). If media blindness is a characteristic feature of the historical paradigm, media determinism can prove problematic for a strictly media-oriented model that reifies the successive stages of orality, chirography, typography and electronics. The perils of media determinism are all the more acute if one perceives media or communications history apart from, or in opposition to, a history of ideas that focuses on ideational content immaterially lodged in and perceived by the mind, and without regard to its somatic, material base and social engagement.

As my interests shifted from the narrative logic of the gospels to a more focused thematization of media modalities, I began to explore features such as oral compositioning and performance and the dynamics of oral tradition with a view toward the relation between gospel and tradition. I now look upon *OWG* as a product of that phase when I was operating, as neophytes in the field are likely to do, with a relatively simple concept of media, exhibiting a tendency to think in terms of pure forms. And yet, *OWG* succeeded beyond my expectations in reigniting the oral–scribal issue in biblical scholarship. Over the years, however, my media paradigm has undergone unmistakable complexification. Increasingly aware of the uneven, fluctuating and polymorphic nature of the ancient verbal arts, my conceptualizations have grown to encompass phenomena such as oral–scribal interfaces, multiple oral originals, recitation and repetition, the social, even political role of ancient scribes, textual performance and the formation of cultural identity, and now always memory. In short, I came to understand that all media are, by definition, mediating forces that variously interface with a people's historical experiences. I therefore concede a measure of fictionality to the fourfold media typology of orality, chirography, typography and electronics, because in ordinary media life these modes of communication run together and manifest themselves in mutual re-absorptions.

The transformative powers of media are most conspicuous at historic threshold events in Western history, such as the alphabetic revolution in ancient Greece around 700 B.C.E. (as demonstrated by Havelock), the fifteenth century shift from script to print (as documented by Eisenstein), and the arrival of the electronic media that we are experiencing in our own time. In each case, scarcely a single sphere of human activity was, and is, left untouched. These dramatic occurrences aside, communications in the ancient oral–scribal world should be viewed as a phenomenon of media interconnecting with other media, with social life, and with human consciousness. Situated in an oral biosphere, writings re-absorbed, reinforced or deconstructed commonplace traditions. The connection with social life is never more unmistakable than in the oral medium, because all living discourses, like all re-oralized scripts, were intertwined with, and indeed dependent on, the human lifeworld. In a culture where scripts were physical objects as much as items of recitation, dictation and memorization, writing and scriptural orality exhibited powers of psychological and cognitive penetration that deeply registered in minds and hearts. As the scrolling experience mutated into the page-turning experience of the codex, untapped potentials of the page were released, potentials that culminated in such literary accomplishments as Eusebius' canon tables and Origen's *Hexapla*, stunning philological achievements that exploited the devocalized page for purposes of referencing and comparison.

When, therefore, I seek to reconstruct early Christianity as a communications history, I aspire to discover a model that, far from media determinism, conceptualizes the interfacing of language and thought, memory and social life. The communications world that I am seeking to reconstruct has no counterpart in today's world and is, I should like to claim, entirely different from much of current biblical scholarship and its indebtedness to the deeply interiorized and quasi-hypnotic powers of print. At the least, I have awakened sensibility toward the ancient arts of communication, a sensibility that lets us discern a hitherto unexplored set of connections and causalities between texts and speaking, social and mental life. At the most, I have taken steps in paving the way toward a new paradigm for biblical studies.

NOTES

Chapter 1: Beyond Texts and Traditions (Thatcher)

1. Reviewers have typically praised *OWG* for its emphasis on new models of oral tradition, its provocative perspective on the relationships between written gospels and oral traditions, and its thorough critique of the inadequacies of form criticism and the Jesus quests. The book has typically been criticized for its peculiar readings of key themes in Mark, its overemphasis on the fixed nature of ancient texts, alongside an inadequate model of textual composition, and its insistence that larger, coherent narratives of Jesus' life and death did not exist in the oral period before the composition of written gospels (see Boomershine 1985; Brodie 1984; Culpepper 1984; Dunn 1986; Hurtado 1989, 48–49; Kloppenborg 1986). Daniel Patte's comments epitomize the consensus position: "These [Kelber's] points shatter fundamental assumptions of New Testament studies. The book's major contribution is to lead readers to a new perception of the relation between oral and written gospel. Its reading is a must. But because it is a pioneering, seminal work, this book calls for refinements. To make his case, Kelber overstates it sometimes and could not perceive all the implications of certain observations" (Patte 1985, 136).

2. It should be stressed that Kelber's interests are not limited to the period of Christian origins, nor to orality/literacy studies. Several of his more notable essays interact with developments in the Medieval and Renaissance periods, and his methods of analysis draw on literary theory, linguistics, philosophy, psychology, and sociology. The presentation here focuses on those aspects of Kelber's research that are most relevant to problems in early Christianity.

3. It should be noted that Kelber's research has focused almost exclusively on media that shape thought by managing the transmission of words. This interest is reflected in the title of his forthcoming work *Words in Time, Words in*

Space. Other media that have significantly impacted Christian thought and identity—including most notably liturgy, ritual, and iconography—have not yet received sustained treatment in his work.

4   Kelber has also reflected briefly on the hermeneutical implications of electronic media, which potentially represent a fourth phase in the church's media history. In a recent article, he notes that "Mein Beitrag ist von dem Bewusstsein geprägt, dass in der westlichen Welt, und zunehmend auf globaler Ebene, eine technisch-kulturelle Umstrukturierung in Gang gekommen ist, welche an die mit der Erfindung des Print-Mediums im 15. und 16. Jahrhundert verbundenen revolutionären Umbrüche im religiösen, sozialen und politischen Leben der westlichen Geschichte erinnert." (Author's translation: "My study is shaped by a consciousness that in the Western world, and increasingly on the global level, a technological-cultural restructuring is underway which calls to mind the revolutionary change in the religious, social, and political life of Western history associated with the invention of print media in the fifteenth and sixteenth centuries.") Like print, the hermeneutics of video, computers, and the Internet have created new possibilities for thought and discourse and, thus, new modes of reality construction (Kelber 2004a, 153–54). At present, however, the long-range impact of electronic technologies on religious consciousness cannot be determined.

5   Kelber borrows the term "oral synthesis" from the writings of psychologist John Carothers, as appropriated and developed by Walter Ong (see Kelber 1983, 19 n 179, 40).

6   Consequently, any attempt to identify the "original version" of an oral story is doomed from the start. "Approach tradition with an exclusive interest in historical originality and you have misunderstood the operations of tradition altogether" (Kelber 2005, 238). Indeed, "the notion of 'the original form' is a phantom of the literary—not to say typographic—imagination and incompatible with oral hermeneutics" (Kelber 2005, 231).

7   Author's translation: "distance, alienation, and a deferring of the signification process are inseparably intertwined in the textualization of oral tradition." Kelber insists that this distinction remains relevant even though ancient books were generally published orally. "It is, however, one thing to concede that speech and writing rarely exist in distinctly separate domains and quite another to imply that a text, just like speech, is also oral authority" (Kelber 1997, xxiv).

8   In the introduction to the 1997 Indiana University Press edition of *OWG*, Kelber confesses that "I was not, at the time of writing the book [1983], fully conscious of *composition in dictation,* and I was only dimly aware of *cultural memory*" (xxiii; emphasis original). This statement reflects the fact that the field of social/cultural memory studies did not gain significant momentum in North America until the late 1980s.

9   Kelber suggests that the motif of "esoteric secrecy"—including the synoptic parable theory (Mark 4), Johannine misunderstanding and irony, and Jesus'

resurrection appearances to select disciples in the *Gospel of Thomas* and the *Apocryphon of James*—was also a form of early Christian mnemotechnique. By focusing on a small and select group of remembrancers, secrecy reduces the inevitable contamination that accompanies the distribution of information. "The precious data are withheld from the public and guarded by the circle of initiates so as to protect them against corruption by dissemination" (Kelber 1988b, 6–7).

10 Author's translation: "When the words of the Lord were understood as a life-giving authority grounded in the living Christ, Jesus' long-past earthly existence and death, as well as a future resurrection of the faithful and all eschatology, had lost their meaning."

11 Kelber tends to associate Paul more closely with Q than with Mark on the basis of the Apostle's media preferences and apparent disinterest in stories about Jesus' life and death (see 1983, 148, 166–67, 198–99, 209, 213–14; 1987b, 109). Responding to the thesis that Mark's narrative is essentially an expansion of 1 Corinthians 15:1-8, Kelber insists that "no evidence has been introduced to demonstrate how Paul's oral creeds and oral gospel could have given rise to Mark's written gospel" (1983, 214, 190–91).

12 Even the summary of Paul's *kerygma* at 1 Corinthians 15:1-8 reflects the logic of orality. The basic structural outline of Christ's death and resurrection responds to "the deepest instincts of oral wisdom": "contrasts and antitheses, contending principles and parties aid in the memorization of knowledge." The deep structure of Paul's gospel is "a product of mnemonic, oral dynamics: it is eminently memorable, repeatable, and orally usable" (Kelber 1983, 148).

13 Heading is quoted from Kelber 1983, 91.

14 Author's Translation: "In terms of the intention of the gospel texts, one scarcely has to do with an original and faithful rendition of oral traditions. In the transposition into the scribal medium, one may rather suspect a deliberate distancing from oral interests, perhaps even a correction of oral hermeneutics."

15 The thesis that the Gospel of Mark is radically at odds with its preceding tradition is one of the most persistent—and most often criticized—themes in Kelber's research. On Mark's exclusion of sayings materials, see Kelber 1983, 207–9. On Mark's negative portrait of the disciples, Jesus' family, and charismatic prophets, see Kelber 1974, 113–16, 144–47; 1976, 47–60; 1979, 67–70, 75–80, 85–87, 93–95; 1983, 96–104, 125–30, 209; 1997, xxiv–xxvi. On the logic of Mark's exclusion of a resurrection account, see Kelber 1983, 100–101. Overall, "Mark's writing is fueled with a passion to disown the voices of his oral precursors"; more eloquently, "Mark, the storywriter, suffers and accomplishes the death of living words for the purpose of inaugurating the life of textuality" (1983, 104, 131).

16 Author's translation: Overall, "the Johannine sayings of the Lord distinguish themselves largely through a pneumatic–oral mode of operation"; indeed, "words are valued here [in the Fourth Gospel] primarily for efficacy and less

as bearers of ideas or information." One could, therefore, fairly say that the Johannine Jesus speaks "like an early Christian prophet."

17 Overall, in the Fourth Gospel, "In dem Maß wie bei Polycarp der Rückgriff auf das eine Wort einer Kritik an den vielen Worten gleichkam, so ist auch der ins Metaphysische gerückte Logos bei Johannes dazu bestimmt, der Flut der Logoi und ihrer Autonomie Einhalt zu gebieten" (Kelber1988a, 38). Author's translation: "To the extent that, with Polycarp, the [John's] recourse to the single Word amounted to a critique of the many words, so is the metaphysically elevated *Logos* in John calculated to stem the tide of words and their autonomy."

18 In the same vein, the modern typographic mentality utterly fails to comprehend the mindset of Paul. "It requires a strenuous act of historical imagination to recall that the Paul of the first century did not write but dictated his letters, that all his writings, including the most intricate theological arguments in Galatians and Romans, were mentally composed, and that large segments of his arguments are structured according to the conventions of Jewish–Hellenistic rhetoric" (Kelber 2002a, 73).

19 Kelber's most sustained attempt to contextualize Crossan's research in the larger history of scholarship appears in a paper delivered at K.U.Leuven in 1994, "Theological Refutation, Linguistic Dilemma, and Ethical Validity of the Search for the Historical Jesus" (Kelber 1994b). A revised version of this paper will appear as chapter two of Kelber's forthcoming *Words in Time, Words in Space*.

20 Author's translation: "Were one to take it [the principle of equiprimordiality] seriously, it would have fatal consequences for the endless search for the *ipsissima vox* of Jesus or, as it were, the *ipsissima structura* of his words."

21 Kelber insists that Matthew and Luke's appropriation of Q "is not the product of oral dynamics" and therefore cannot be cited as a precedent for the operations of oral tradition (Kelber 1995b, 148).

22 Even before the publication of *OWG*, Kelber's research was characterized by an emphasis on the unique narrative dynamics of each gospel (see Kelber 1976; 1979). This approach is particularly evident in Kelber's essays on the Gospel of John, which play on the tensions between John's *Logos* Christology and other features of his narrative, such as irony and characterization (see especially Kelber 1990; 1996).

Chapter 3: Oral Performance and Mark (Horsley)

1 The following is a cursory summary of some key points in David Carr, *Writing on the Tablet of the Heart* (2005) and further explorations in Richard Horsley, *Scribes, Visionaries, and the Politics of Second Temple Judea* (2007).

2 The belief that J, E, D, and P existed as written texts/sources prior to the composition of the books of the Pentateuch may be another product of print culture. But even if they did exist in written form, these sources would presumably have been known in memory by the scribes who composed Genesis, Exodus, and the other relevant texts.

3   Most of these connective devices disappear in modern translations, which attempt to transform the gospel narrative into good print-culture prose style.

Chapter 4: The Gospel of Mark as Oral Hermeneutic (J. Dewey)

1   Although I have certainly been influenced by others' responses to Kelber and by others' work on Mark, I am focusing in this article on Kelber's work. I am indebted to David Rhoads for his helpful suggestions on this essay.
2   My own supposition is that the Gospel of Mark originally ended at 16:8 with the oral performer concluding with something such as, "Whoever has ears to hear, let them hear."
3   That they were specifically Christian rather than Jewish proclaimers, however, is by no means certain.
4   In regard to Mark 13:14, I assume that "Let the reader understand" is not an address to the reader of Mark's gospel, but possibly to the public reader of Daniel's "abomination of desolation." See also Bultmann 1964. In a personal communication, David Rhoads has suggested to me that these words may be an aside to the performer and thus were not meant to be performed at all.
5   When biblical storyteller Dennis Dewey performs the Gospel of John, he omits considerable dialogue and monologue material in order to keep the story moving.
6   In a 2005 article, Kelber restated this triad but changed the last from the failure of the disciples to "the cessation of a generation of memories and memory carriers" (Kelber 2005, 244).
7   Mark may have known Q traditions, or both Q and Mark may have been drawing on common oral traditions.
8   It is not clear to me that these passages are meant to refer to resurrection appearances or to the *parousia* rather than simply to a return to the place of the in-breaking of God's kingdom. It is interesting to note that no titles are used in these prophecies. "Son of Humanity," used elsewhere both in the context of resurrection and of *parousia*, is notably absent.

Chapter 5: Storytelling in Oral and Written Media Contexts (Hearon)

1   Other Greek words referenced in this study include φιλομύθος, φιλομυθέω, μυθοποιός, λογοποιός, δρᾶμα, διηγέομαι; Latin words include *fabula, fabulatoribus, anilibusque fabulis, aretalogos, sermonem*. I am indebted to my research assistant, Connie Bandy, for her work in identifying language related to orality and in working with the *Thesaurus Lingua Grecae* to identify primary sources for consultation.
2   All quotes from Theon are taken from the translation by George A. Kennedy in *Progymnasmata: Greek Textbooks of Prose Composition and Rhetoric* (2003). All other ancient works are cited from the respective Loeb editions, unless otherwise indicated. See the Works Cited for full citation information.

3   Throughout this essay, the Greek or Latin words for "story" are included in parentheses when they actually appear in the primary source. Translators often add the word "story" for clarity when they believe the relevant terms are implied by the literary context.
4   Theon also offers examples of "narration of the mythical sort" (Plato) and those of "the factual sort" (Herodotus and Thycydides; Theon, *Progymnasmata* 62).
5   "The studied simplicity of stories is designed to meet the needs of oral expediency and social identification more than historical accuracy" (Kelber 1983, 71).
6   See, for example, Mark 5:16; 6:14; 8:27; 9:38; 14:67. Although the word "story" does not occur in these contexts, storytelling activity is implied.
7   Ἐπόπται is used for "eyewitnesses" only here in the New Testament; so also αὐτόπται in Luke 1:1.
8   The term ἱστορία does not occur in the New Testament.
9   Theon himself argues against making too much of distinctions between stories. "Those who say that some involve mute beasts, others human beings, some are impossible, others capable of being true, seem to me to make a silly distinction" (Theon, *Progymnasmata* 73).
10 William Harris asserts that even the romances had a limited reading audience (Harris 1989, 228).
11 Rosenberg observes that even in literate cultures values and attitudes are transmitted orally, through face-to-face contact (1987, 5).
12 One could argue that the distinctions being drawn here are subtle. Clearly, some written texts are viewed as the possession of a community rather than of an author—the Hebrew Scriptures are a prime example. Yet, as written texts, the Scriptures are not dependent upon oral circulation within the community for their existence. Further, access to these written texts would be mediated by a reader. Certainly, many people would have known passages of the Scriptures from memory, but this would be dependent, in part, upon what they had heard in readings or retellings of Scripture.
13 While worship may be supposed to be one of those contexts, there may have been others. In addition, it is difficult to assess what status was ascribed to the gospels at this early date.
14 Although the individual storytellers are not identified, the process is by no means "anonymous" (Kelber 1983, 28). The story is likely to have spread not from stranger to stranger but from known person to known person.
15 Kelber observes that "what is transmitted orally . . . is never all the information available, but only . . . [w]hat lives on in memory . . . what is necessary for the present life" (Kelber 1983, 14).
16 "Stock features are combined and reshuffled in endless variations, one theme is substituted for another, the order of sequence is changed, features are adopted from related or unrelated materials, and variant compositions are forever in the making. . . . [I]t can show infinite flexibility in modeling a message so as to make it compatible with social needs" (Kelber 1983, 29–30).

17 Foley emphasizes that "memory in oral tradition is emphatically not a static retrieval mechanism for data" but rather a "kinetic, emergent, creative activity" that is explicitly "linked to performance (Foley 2006a, 84; see also Rosenberg 1987, 87). Nonetheless, Kelber draws attention to the importance of patterning for facilitating retention and transmission of oral story (Kelber 1983, 27, 51). On memory, see also Shiner 2003, 104–107.

18 In contrast, Pliny says that Marcus Regulus was never able to learn even his written speeches by heart (Pliny, *Letters* 4.2.1). Apparently not everyone was gifted with a good memory.

19 "[T]he forgetting or rejection of a message is as much to be expected as its remembrance and transmission" (Kelber 1983, 28).

20 For example, when a history book omits certain significant events or persons that are unknown to the reader, he or she will not detect that omission. However, there may be a secondary social impact in the way the reader now remembers the historical narrative.

21 Kelber writes that, "even if the gospel was meant to be recited or read aloud, its writing was nonetheless done in the absence of hearers" (1983, 115). Precisely to what degree a gospel writer might be accountable to an audience is difficult to assess.

Chapter 6: Vice Catalogues as Oral-Mnemonic Cues (Draper)

1 Although van de Sandt and Flusser do not, in fact, take the Arabic *Vita Shenoudi* seriously as a witness in their textual reconstruction. In my opinion, however, it is closer to the main textual tradition than they allow.

2 The various mnemonic devices, such as necklaces, body incisions, wood carving, and the memory board, all draw on the same mnemonic system of reference. So, for instance, the "nkaka" pattern recurs in all forms of mnemotechnique and is symbolically related to the royal residence.

3 I am grateful to Thomas Q. Reefe for permission to include this image and to Mary Nooter Roberts for her assistance in securing permission. For further discussion of Luba memory boards, see Roberts and Roberts 1996, 140–42.

4 Following the text of *Syntagma* for convenience. These two texts are essentially recensions of the same redaction of the Two Ways.

5 VitSh has *fasaqa,* perhaps, "Do not commit grave sins." I am grateful to Gerhard van Gelder at St. John's College, Oxford, for his assistance with the Arabic text.

Chapter 7: Human Memory and the Sayings of Jesus (DeConick)

1 I am indebted to many people for their help in preparing this article. Benjamin Brochstein, a graduate student at Rice University, generated the computer tabulation of all the data for the pilot experiments. Thomas Mings and Megan Sheeley, Religious Studies majors at Rice University, entered the data into Brochstein's tabulation program. I also wish to extend my thanks to

Professor Jean Pretz, a cognitive psychologist whose faculty appointment is in the Department of Psychology at Illinois Wesleyan University. Professor Pretz consulted with me, helping me establish controls and setting up the pilot experiments discussed in this chapter. My secretary at Illinois Wesleyan University, Regina Linsalta, transcribed all the audio recordings and written responses into anonymous data. In the final year of my appointment at Illinois Wesleyan University, I was awarded a grant to subsidize and support the pilot experiments.

2   The number eighteen represents a revision of their earlier suggestion, sixteen; cf. McIver and Carroll 2002 with McIver and Carroll 2004.

3   See especially Poirier 2004, whose main objections appear to me to relate to McIver's application of the research data to the biblical sources, rather than to the experiment itself.

4   Cf. John 2:13-22; 15:20; 16:4; Acts 20:35; Jude 17-18; 2 Peter 3:2; *Ap. Jas.* 2.7–16; 1 Clem. 13.1–2, 46:7–8; Polycarp *Phil.* 2.3; Papias in Eusebius, *Hist. eccl.* 3.39.3–4, 3.39.15–16; Ps. Clem. *Rec.* 1.23; Clement of Alexandria *Strom.* 1.1.

5   Since their subjects were unable to produce a string longer than fifteen words in sequence, McIver and Carroll initially reported that copying was indicative of sixteen or more words in sequence (2002, 680). In a later republication and revision of the same article, they revised this number without explanation to eighteen or more (2004, 1264–65).

6   McIver and Carroll allow for the possibility of verbatim reproduction of proverbs without access to a written source because they can cite contemporary examples of this phenomenon in traditional societies. But their own research data does not support this conclusion, since none of their subjects were able to reproduce the test proverb verbatim in the long-term reproduction experiment.

7   Matthew 10:21-22//Mark 13:12-13; Matthew 11:25-30//Luke 10:21-24; Matthew 24:45-51//Luke 12:41-48; Matthew 3:1-12//Luke 3:1-20; Matthew 24:15-28//Mark 13:14-23; Matthew 11:1-19//Luke 7:18-35; Matthew 22:41-46//Mark 12:35-37.

Chapter 8: The Gospel of Trajan (A. Dewey)

1   This representation of Trajan was replaced with a statue of Saint Peter in the late sixteenth century, as depicted in Figure 1. My thanks to Ken Overberg for permission to use the photos that appear in this essay.

Chapter 9: The Scar of the Cross (Keith and Thatcher)

1   In Kelber's view, this conclusion is consistent with the fact that the literary style of Mark's passion narrative does not betray oral techniques of composition. Mark's written account of Jesus' death is tightly plotted and includes a number of geographical and chronological markers that "distinguish it from

the more thoroughly episodic story of life." While form critics had appealed to this fact as evidence that Mark's narrative is based on a much older account, one that had matured over time and developed a fixed form, Kelber contends that the "devices that foster narrative competence" in Mark's passion story all "thrive under textuality" and are unlikely to have originated in an oral milieu (Kelber 1983, 187–88).

Chapter 10: Manuscript Tradition as a Tertium Quid (Kirk)

1 "Tradition und Interpretation sind untrennbar miteinander verknüpft" (Author's translation: "Tradition and interpretation are inseparably bound together"; Assmann 1992, 175).
2 Carr (2005) construes scribal curricula of memorized classical texts somewhat monocausally as a hegemonic strategy of elites and tends to overlook the pragmatic exigency of the cultivation of cultural identity.
3 Research in the cognitive science of memory posits a "phonological loop" in short-term memory: in reading, written words are typically "heard" and held in short-term memory as auditory traces (Baddeley 1999, 51–53). The visual–spatial uniformities of modern printed texts are conducive to visual processing and so render the "phonological loop" less central to comprehension.
4 Hermas' copying of his visionary scroll "letter by letter, for I could not make out the syllables" (*Vision* II.i.4) may say more about his level of literacy than about scribal practice in general, as Metzger was inclined to think (Metzger and Ehrman 2005, 23n29). Junack estimates the length of the scribal phrase-units as "etwa zwischen 15 und 60 Buchstaben ... also 5 bis 12 Wörter bzw. 10 bis 25 Sprechsilben" (Author's translation: "somewhere between 15 and 60 letters ... so 5 to 12 words or 10 to 25 phonetic units"; 1981, 290).
5 "[T]he manuscript still participates with other scripta of the 'same' text in a system of differences" (Dagenais 1994, 129).
6 Assmann comments: "Das Berufsethos der Schreiber–Tradenten begreift das Geschäft der Überlieferung in den Kategorien rechtförmiger Verbindlichkeit. Tradieren heißt *eine Verpflichtung gegenüber dem Text eingehen, die den Charakter einer vertragsartigen Bindung hat*" (Author's translation: "In the occupational ethos of the scribe-tradent the duty of the transmission of tradition was understood in terms of a legal obligation, as undertaking a solemn, contractually binding obligation with respect to the text"; 1992, 104). On this point see also Junack 1981, 292–93; Veldhuis 2003, 22.
7 "Ben Sira's instruction is full of calls to 'listen' and 'hear' the instruction. . . . Yet the book itself witnesses to Ben Sira's use of writing to pass his instruction to 'future generations' (24:33–34; cf. 39:32)" (Carr 2005, 208).
8 The existence of writing as an external arrangement of signs was a factor in the twelfth-century scholastic emphasis on the primacy of the literal meaning, that is, a reading "strictly tied to the properties of the text," and the corresponding attempts to establish standard texts influenced Renaissance

9   Scribal re-performances of tradition, including those that lead to the issuing of expanded or otherwise significantly modified editions of texts, are themselves similarly strategic responses to a widening gulf between an authoritative text and the present realities of the tradent community. Van der Toorn argues along these lines in reference to the four editions of Deuteronomy (2007, 145–49), and there are many other examples that could be cited.
10 Carr observes the textual standardization of particularly ancient cultural texts in Mesopotamia and Egypt and at Qumran (2005, 44, 78–79, 235–36).
11 Like Ehrman, Kannaday offers insightful descriptions of scribal reperformances of manuscript tradition but lacks a model that can fully clarify the dynamics at work.

Chapter 11: The Oral–Scribal–Memorial Arts of Communication (Kelber)

1   "One must be clear that memory has nothing to do with historiography" (my translation).

WORKS CITED

Achilles Tatius. *Leucippe and Clitophon*. 1969. Translated by S. Gaselee. Loeb Classical Library (LCL). Cambridge: Harvard University Press.

Alexander, Loveday. 1998. "Ancient Book Production and the Circulation of the Gospels." Pages 71–111 in *The Gospels for All Christians: Rethinking the Gospel Audiences*. Edited by Richard Bauckham. Grand Rapids: Eerdmans.

Allport, Gordon W., and Leo Postman. 1947. *The Psychology of Rumor*. New York: Holt.

Apuleius, Lucius. *The Golden Ass: Being the Metamorphoses of Lucius Apuleius*. 1977. Translated by W. Adlington et al. LCL. Cambridge: Harvard University Press.

Arnal, William E. 2001. *Jesus and the Village Scribes: Galilean Conflicts and the Setting of Q*. Minneapolis: Fortress.

Aristotle. *On Memory and Recollection*. In *Aristotle on Memory*. 1972. Translated and edited by Richard Sorabji. Providence: Brown University Press.

———. *The Poetics*. 1932. Translated by W. Hamilton Fyfe. LCL. Cambridge: Harvard University Press.

Assmann, Jan. 1992. *Das kulturelle Gedächtnis: Schrift, Erinnerung und politische Identität in frühen Hochkulturen*. Munich: C. H. Beck.

———. 1999. *Fünf Stufen auf dem Wege zum Kanon: Tradition und Schriftkultur im frühen Judentum und seiner Umwelt*. Münstersche Theologische Vorträge. Münster: Lit Verlag.

Assmann, Jan. 2000. *Religion und kulturelles Gedächtnis: zehn Studien.* Munich: Beck.

———. 2006. "Form as a Mnemonic Device: Cultural Texts and Cultural Memory." Pages 67–82 in *Performing the Gospel: Orality, Memory, and Mark.* Edited by Richard A. Horsley, Jonathan A. Draper, and John Miles Foley. Minneapolis: Fortress.

Baddeley, Alan D. 1995. "The Psychology of Memory." Pages 3–25 in *Handbook of Memory Disorders.* Edited by Alan D. Baddeley, Barbara A. Wilson, and Fraser N. Watts. New York: Wiley & Sons.

———. 1999. *Essentials of Human Memory.* East Sussex: Psychology Press.

Bailey, Kenneth E. 1991. "Informal Controlled Oral Tradition and the Synoptic Gospels." *American Journal of Theology* 5:34–54.

———. 1995. "Middle Eastern Oral Tradition and the Synoptic Gospels." *Expository Times* 106:363–67.

Baltzer, Klaus. 1971. *The Covenant Formulary.* Philadelphia: Fortress.

Bar-Ilan, Meir. 1992. "Illiteracy in the Land of Israel in the First Centuries C.E." Pages 2.46–61 in *Essays in the Social Scientific Study of Judaism and Jewish Society.* 2 vols. Edited by Simcha Fishbane, Stuart Schoenfeld, and Alain Goldschläger. Hoboken, N.J.: KTAV.

Barrett, C. K. 1957. "Myth and the New Testament." *Expository Times* 68:345–48.

Bartlett, Frederic C. 1932. *Remembering: A Study in Experimental and Social Psychology.* Cambridge: Cambridge University Press.

Basgöz, İlhan. 1975. "The Tale-Singer and His Audience." Pages 143–203 in *Folklore: Performance and Communication.* Edited by Dan Ben-Amos and Kenneth S. Goldstein. The Hague: Mouton.

Bauckham, Richard. 2006. *Jesus and the Eyewitnesses: The Gospels as Eyewitness Testimony.* Grand Rapids: Eerdmans.

Bäuml, Franz H. 1984. "Medieval Texts and the Two Theories of Oral-Formulaic Composition: A Proposal for a Third Theory." *New Literary History* 16:31–49.

Beard, Mary, ed. 1991. *Literacy in the Roman World.* Journal of Roman Archaeology Supplementary Series. Ann Arbor: Journal of Roman Archaeology.

Beit-Arié, Malachi. 2000. "Publication and Reproduction of Literary Texts in Medieval Jewish Civilization: Jewish Scribality and Its Impact on the Texts Transmitted." Pages 225–47 in *Transmitting Jewish Traditions: Orality, Textuality, and Cultural Diffusion.* Edited by Yaakov Elman and Israel Gershoni. New Haven: Yale University Press.

Belleza, Francis. 1981. "Mnemonic Devices: Classification, Characteristics, and Criteria." *Review of Educational Research* 51:247-75.

Blank, Reiner. 1981. *Analyse und Kritik der formgeschichtlichen Arbeiten von Martin Dibelius und Rudolf Bultmann.* Basel: F. Reinhardt.

Bonanno, George A. 1990. "Remembering and Psychotherapy." *Psychotherapy* 27:175-86.

Boomershine, Thomas E. 1985. Review of *The Oral and the Written Gospel: The Hermeneutics of Speaking and Writing in the Synoptic Tradition, Mark, Paul, and Q. Journal of Biblical Literature* 104:538-40.

Botha, Pieter J. J. 1991. "Mark's Story as Oral Traditional Literature: Rethinking the Transmission of Some Traditions about Jesus." *Hervormde Teologiese Studies* 47:304-31.

Boyarin, Daniel. 1993. "Placing Reading: Ancient Israel and Medieval Europe." Pages 10-37 in *The Ethnography of Reading.* Edited by Jonathan Boyarin. Berkeley: University of California Press.

Brodie, Thomas L. 1984. Review of *The Oral and the Written Gospel: The Hermeneutics of Speaking and Writing in the Synoptic Tradition, Mark, Paul, and Q. Catholic Biblical Quarterly* 46:574-75.

Bruner, Jerome, and Carol Fleisher Feldman. 1996. "Group Narratives as a Cultural Context of Autobiography." Pages 291-317 in *Remembering Our Past: Studies in Autobiographical Memory.* Edited by David C. Rubin. Cambridge: Cambridge University Press.

Bultmann, Rudolf. 1958. *Jesus and the Word.* Translated by Louise Pettibone Smith and Erminie Huntress Lantero. New York: Charles Scribner's Sons.

———. 1962. "The Study of the Synoptic Gospels." Pages 11-76 in *Form Criticism: Two Essays on New Testament Research.* Rudolf Bultmann and Karl Kundsin. Edited and translated by Frederick C. Grant. New York: Harper.

———. 1963. *History of the Synoptic Tradition.* Rev. ed. Translated by John Marsh. New York: Harper & Row.

———. 1964. ἀναγινώσκω/ἀνάγνωσις. *Theological Dictionary of the New Testament* 1.343-44.

Burton-Christie, Douglas. 1997. "Oral Culture and Biblical Interpretation in Early Egyptian Monasticism." *Studia Patristica* 30:144-50. Edited by Elizabeth A. Livingstone. Leuven: Peeters.

Byrskog, Samuel. 2002. *Story as History, History as Story: The Gospel Tradition in the Context of Ancient Oral History.* Leiden: Brill.

———. 2003. "The History of the Synoptic Tradition." *Journal of Biblical Literature* 122:549-55.

Carr, David M. 2005. *Writing on the Tablet of the Heart: Origins of Scripture and Literature.* New York: Oxford University Press.
Carruthers, Mary J. 1990. *The Book of Memory: A Study of Memory in Medieval Culture.* Cambridge Studies in Medieval Literature. Cambridge: Cambridge University Press.
———. 1998. *The Craft of Thought: Meditation, Rhetoric, and the Making of Images, 400–1200.* Cambridge: Cambridge University Press.
Casey, Edward S. 1987. *Remembering: A Phenomenological Study.* Bloomington: Indiana University Press.
Ceci, Stephen J. 1995. "False Beliefs: Some Developmental and Clinical Considerations." Pages 91–125 in *Memory Distortion: How Minds, Brains, and Societies Reconstruct the Past.* Edited by Daniel L. Schacter. Cambridge: Harvard University Press.
Chaytor, Henry J. 1945. *From Script to Print: An Introduction to Medieval Vernacular Literature.* Cambridge: Cambridge University Press.
Clanchy, M. T. 1993. *From Memory to Written Record: England 1066–1307.* 2nd ed. Oxford: Basil Blackwell.
Clement of Alexandria. *Christ the Educator.* 1982. Translated by G. W. Butterworth. LCL. Cambridge: Harvard University Press.
———. *Exhortation to the Greeks.* 1982. Translated by G. W. Butterworth. LCL. Cambridge: Harvard University Press.
———. *Miscellanies.* 1982. Translated by G. W. Butterworth. LCL. Cambridge: Harvard University Press.
———. *Salvation of the Rich Man.* 1982. Translated by G. W. Butterworth. LCL. Cambridge: Harvard University Press.
Collins, John J. 1995. *The Scepter and the Sword: The Messiahs of the Dead Sea Scrolls and Other Ancient Literature.* New York: Doubleday.
Colwell, Ernest C. 1952. *What Is the Best New Testament?* Chicago: University of Chicago Press.
———. 1969. *Studies in Methodology in Textual Criticism of the New Testament.* Grand Rapids: Eerdmans.
Cooper, Craig. 2007. *Politics of Orality.* Vol. 6 of *Orality and Literacy in Ancient Greece.* Leiden: Brill.
Corbier, Mireille. 1991. "L' écriture en quête de lecturs." Pages 99–118 in *Literacy in the Roman World.* Edited by Mary Beard. Journal of Roman Archaeology Supplementary Series. Ann Arbor: Journal of Roman Archaeology.
Cribiore, Raffaella. 2001. *Gymnastics of the Mind: Greek Education in Hellenistic and Roman Egypt.* Princeton: Princeton University Press.

Crosby, Ruth. 1936. "Oral Delivery in the Middle Ages." *Speculum* 11:88–110.

Culpepper, R. Alan. 1984. Review of *The Oral and the Written Gospel: The Hermeneutics of Speaking and Writing in the Synoptic Tradition, Mark, Paul, and Q*. *Review and Expositor* 81:136–38.

Dagenais, John. 1994. *The Ethics of Reading in Manuscript Culture: Glossing the* Libro de buen amor. Princeton: Princeton University Press.

Danker, Frederick William. 2000. *A Greek–English Lexicon of the New Testament and Other Early Christian Literature*. Chicago: University of Chicago Press.

DeConick, April D. 2005. *Recovering the Original Gospel of Thomas: A History of the Gospel and Its Growth*. Library of New Testament Studies. New York: T & T Clark.

———. 2006. *The Original Gospel of Thomas in Translation, with a Commentary and New English Translation of the Complete Gospel*. Library of New Testament Studies. New York: T & T Clark.

Derrenbacker, Robert A., Jr. 2005. *Ancient Compositional Practices and the Synoptic Problem*. Bibliotheca ephemeridum theologicarum lovaniensium. Leuven: Leuven University Press.

Dewey, Arthur J. 2002. "2 Corinthians 5: Translation Issues." *Forum* 5:149–57.

———. 2005. "The Locus for Death: Social Memory and the Passion Narratives." Pages 119–28 in *Memory, Tradition, and Text: Uses of the Past in Early Christianity*. Semeia Studies. Edited by Alan Kirk and Tom Thatcher. Atlanta: Society of Biblical Literature.

Dewey, Joanna. 1980. *Markan Public Debate: Literary Technique, Concentric Structure, and Theology in Mark 2:1–3:6*. Society of Biblical Literature Dissertation Series. Chico, Calif.: Scholars Press.

———. 1989. "Oral Methods of Structuring Narrative in Mark." *Interpretation* 53:332–44.

———. 1991. "Mark as Interwoven Tapestry: Forecasts and Echoes for a Listening Audience." *Catholic Biblical Quarterly* 52:221–36.

———. 1992. "Mark as Aural Narrative: Structures as Clues to Understanding." *Sewanee Theological Review* 36:45–56.

———. 1994a. "Mark." Pages 2.470–509 in *Searching the Scriptures: A Feminist-Ecumenical Commentary*. 2 vols. Edited by Elisabeth Schüssler Fiorenza with Shelly Matthews. New York: Crossroad.

———. 1994b. "The Gospel of Mark as Oral/Aural Event: Implications for Interpretation." Pages 145–63 in *The New Literary Criticism and the*

New Testament. Edited by Elizabeth Struthers Malbon and Edgar V. McKnight. Sheffield: Sheffield University Press.

Dewey, Joanna, ed. 1995a. *Orality and Textuality in Early Christian Literature*. Semeia Studies. Atlanta: Scholars Press.

———. 1995b. "Textuality in an Oral Culture: A Survey of the Pauline Traditions." Pages 3–66 in *Orality and Textuality in Early Christian Literature*. Edited by Joanna Dewey. Semeia Studies. Atlanta: Scholars Press.

———. 1996. "From Storytelling to Written Text: The Loss of Early Christian Women's Voices." *Biblical Theology Bulletin* 26:71–78.

———. 2001. "Let Them Renounce Themselves and Take up Their Cross: A Feminist Reading of Mark 8:34 in Mark's Social and Narrative World." Pages 23–36 in *A Feminist Companion to Mark*. Edited by Amy-Jill Levine. Sheffield: Sheffield Academic Press. This article was reprinted in *Biblical Theology Bulletin* 34:98–104.

———. 2004. "Mark—A Really Good Oral Story: Is That Why the Gospel of Mark Survived?" *Journal of Biblical Literature* 123:495–507.

Dewey, Joanna, and Elizabeth Struthers Malbon. 2009. *The Gospel of Mark*. In *A Theological Bible Commentary*. Edited by Gail R. O'Day and David L. Petersen. Louisville, Ky: Westminser John Knox.

Dibelius, Martin. 1971. *From Tradition to Gospel*. Translated by Bertram Lee Wolf. Greenwood, S.C.: Attic. This translation was made in collaboration with Dibelius from the 2nd edition of *Die Formgeschichte des Evangeliums* (1933).

Dio Cassius. *Roman History*. 1970. Translated by E. Cary. LCL. Cambridge: Harvard University Press.

Dio Chrysostum. *Discourses*. 1985. Translated by H. Lamar Crosby. LCL. Cambridge: Harvard University Press.

Doane, Alger N. 1991. "Oral Texts, Intertexts, and Intratexts: Editing Old English." Pages 75–113 in *Influence and Intertextuality in Literary History*. Edited by Jay Clayton and Eric Rothstein. Madison: University of Wisconsin Press.

———. 1994. "The Ethnography of Scribal Writing and Anglo-Saxon Poetry: Scribe as Performer." *Oral Tradition* 9:420–39.

Dowd, Sharyn, and Elizabeth Struthers Malbon. 2006. "The Significance of Jesus' Death in Mark: Narrative Context and Authorial Audience." *Journal of Biblical Literature* 125:271–97.

Downing, F. Gerald. 1996. "Word Processing in the Ancient World: The Social Production and Performance of Q." *Journal for the Study of the New Testament* 64:29–48.

Draper, Jonathan A. 1995. "Barnabas and the Riddle of the *Didache*." *Journal for the Study of the New Testament* 58:89–113.

———, ed. 2003. *Orality, Literacy, and Colonialism in Southern Africa*. Semeia Studies. Atlanta: Society of Biblical Literature.

———, ed. 2004. *Orality, Literacy, and Colonialism in Antiquity*. Semeia Studies. Atlanta: Society of Biblical Literature.

Dunn, James D. G. 1986. "The Spoken Word versus the Written Word." *Interpretation* 40:72–75.

———. 2000. "Jesus in Oral Memory: The Initial Stages of the Jesus Tradition." Pages 287–326 in *The Society of Biblical Literature Seminar Papers* 39. Atlanta: Scholars Press.

Ehrman, Bart D. 1993. *The Orthodox Corruption of Scripture: The Effect of Early Christological Controversies on the Text of the New Testament*. New York: Oxford University Press.

———. 1995. "The Text as Window: New Testament Manuscripts and the Social History of Early Christianity." Pages 361–79 in *The Text of the New Testament in Contemporary Research: Essays on the* Status Quaestionis. Edited by Bart D. Ehrman and Michael W. Holmes. Grand Rapids: Eerdmans.

———. 2005. *Misquoting Jesus: The Story Behind Who Changed the Bible and Why*. San Francisco: HarperSanFrancisco.

Eisenstein, Elizabeth L. 1979. *The Printing Press as an Agent of Change: Communications and Cultural Transformations in Early-Modern Europe*. Cambridge: Cambridge University Press.

Eliot, T. S. 1943. *Four Quartets*. New York: Harcourt Brace.

Elman, Yaakov. 1975. "Authoritative Oral Tradition in Neo-Assyrian Scribal Circles." *Journal of the Ancient Near Eastern Society of Columbia University* 7:19–32.

Ephrat, Daphna, and Yaakov Elman. 2000. "Orality and the Institutionalization of Tradition: The Growth of the Geonic Yeshiva and the Islamic Madrasa." Pages 107–37 in *Transmitting Jewish Traditions: Orality, Textuality, and Cultural Diffusion*. Edited by Yaakov Elman and Israel Gershoni. New Haven: Yale University Press.

Epp, Eldon Jay. 1999. "The Multivalence of the Term 'Original Text' in New Testament Textual Criticism." *Harvard Theological Review* 92:245–81.

———. 2004. "The Oxyrhynchus New Testament Papyri: 'Not without honor except in their own hometown'?" *Journal of Biblical Literature* 123:5–55.

Euripides. *Fragments*. 1992. In *Select Papyri III: Poetry*. Translated by Denys L. Page. LCL. Cambridge: Harvard University Press.

Eusebius. *The Ecclesiastical History*. 1953. Translated by Kirsopp Lake. LCL. Cambridge: Harvard University Press.

Fantham, Elaine. 1999. "Two Levels of Orality in the Genesis of Pliny's *Panegyricus*." Pages 221–37 in *Signs of Orality: The Oral Tradition and Its Influence in the Greek and Roman World*. Edited by E. Anne Mackay. Leiden: Brill.

Fascher, Erich. 1924. *Die formgeschichtliche Methode, eine Darstellung und Kritik, zugleich ein Beitrag zur Geschichte des synoptischen Problems*. Zeitschrift für die Neutestementliche Wissenschaft und die Kunde der älteren Kirche. Giessen: A. Töpelmann.

Finnegan, Ruth. 1977. *Oral Poetry: Its Nature, Significance, and Social Context*. Cambridge: Cambridge University Press.

———. 1988. *Literacy and Orality: Studies in the Technology of Communication*. Oxford: Basil Blackwell.

———. 1992. *Oral Traditions and the Verbal Arts: A Guide to Research*. New York: Routledge.

Fishbane, Michael. 1985. *Biblical Interpretation in Ancient Israel*. Oxford: Clarendon.

———. 1989. "From Scribalism to Rabbinism: Perspectives on the Emergence of Classical Judaism." Pages 64–78 in *Garments of Torah: Essays in Biblical Hermeneutics*. Bloomington: Indiana University Press.

Floyd, Michael H. 2000. "'Write the Revelation!' (Hab 2:2): Re-examining the Cultural History of Prophecy." Pages 103–43 in *Writings and Speech in Israelite and Ancient Near Eastern Prophecy*. Edited by Ehud Ben Zvi and Michael H. Floyd. Society of Biblical Literature Symposium Series. Atlanta: Society of Biblical Literature.

Foley, John Miles. 1990. *Traditional Oral Epic: The Odyssey, Beowulf, and the Serbo-Croatian Return Song*. Berkeley: University of California Press.

———. 1991. *Immanent Art: From Structure to Meaning in Traditional Oral Epic*. Bloomington: Indiana University Press.

———. 1995. *The Singer of Tales in Performance*. Bloomington: Indiana University Press.

———. 1999. *Homer's Traditional Art*. University Park: Pennsylvania State University Press.

———. 2002. *How to Read an Oral Poem*. Urbana: University of Illinois Press.

———. 2006a. "Memory in Oral Tradition." Pages 83–96 in *Performing the Gospel: Orality, Memory, and Mark*. Edited by Richard A. Horsley, Jonathan A. Draper, and John Miles Foley. Minneapolis: Fortress.

———. 2006b. "The Riddle of Q: Oral Ancestor, Textual Precedent, or Ideological Creation?" Pages 123–140 in *Oral Performance, Popular Tradition, and Hidden Transcript in Q*. Edited by Richard A. Horsley. Semeia Studies. Atlanta: Society of Biblical Literature.

Fraade, Steven D. 1999. "Literary Composition and Oral Performance in Early Midrashim." *Oral Tradition* 14:33–51.

Frei, Hans W. 1974. *The Eclipse of Biblical Narrative: A Study in Eighteenth- and Nineteenth-Century Hermeneutics*. New Haven: Yale University Press.

Gamble, Harry Y. 1995. *Books and Readers in the Early Church: A History of Early Christian Texts*. New Haven: Yale University Press.

———. 2004. "Literacy, Liturgy, and the Shaping of the New Testament Canon." Pages 26–29 in *The Earliest Gospels: The Origins and Transmission of the Earliest Christian Gospels—the Contribution of the Chester Beatty Gospel Codex P45*. Edited by Charles Horton. Journal for the Study of the New Testament Supplement Series. New York: T & T Clark.

Georgi, Dieter. 1991. *Theocracy in Paul's Praxis and Theology*. Minneapolis: Fortress.

Gerhardsson, Birger. 1961. *Memory and Manuscript: Oral Tradition and Written Transmission in Rabbinic Judaism and Early Christianity*. Translated by Eric J. Sharpe. Grand Rapids: Eerdmans.

Goodman, Martin. 1983. *State and Society in Roman Galilee, A.D. 132–212*. Totowa, N.J.: Rowman & Allenheld.

———. 1994. "Texts, Scribes, and Power in Roman Judaea." Pages 99–108 in *Literacy and Power in the Ancient World*. Edited by Alan K. Bowman and Greg Woolf. Cambridge: Cambridge University Press.

Goody, Jack. 1998. "Memory in Oral Tradition." Pages 73–94 in *Memory*. Edited by Patricia Fara and Karalyn Patterson. Cambridge: Cambridge University Press.

Grafton, Anthony. 1991. *Defenders of the Text: The Traditions of Scholarship in an Age of Science (1450–1800)*. Cambridge: Harvard University Press.

Grant, Frederick. 1957. *Ancient Roman Religion*. New York: Liberal Arts Press.

Green, William Scott. 1989. "Writing with Scripture: The Rabbinic Uses of the Hebrew Scripture." Pages 7–23 in *Writing with Scripture: The Authority and Uses of the Hebrew Bible in the Torah of Formative Judaism*. Edited by Jacob Neusner. Minneapolis: Fortress.

Greenstein, Edward L. 1993. "Misquotation of Scripture in the Dead Sea Scrolls." Pages 1.71–83 in *The Frank Talmage Memorial Volume*. 2 vols. Edited by Barry Walfish. Haifa: Haifa University Press.

Hägg, Thomas. 1983. *The Novel in Antiquity.* Berkeley: University of California Press.

Haines-Eitzen, Kim. 2000. *Guardians of Letters: Literacy, Power, and the Transmitters of Early Christian Literature.* Oxford: Oxford University Press.

Halbwachs, Maurice. 1992. *On Collective Memory.* Edited and translated by Lewis A. Coser. Chicago: University of Chicago Press.

Hanks, W. F. 1989. "Texts and Textuality." *Annual Review of Anthropology* 18:95–127.

Harris, William V. 1989. *Ancient Literacy.* Cambridge: Harvard University Press.

Havelock, Eric A. 1963. *Preface to Plato.* Cambridge: Harvard University Press.

———. 1976. *Origins of Western Literacy.* The Ontario Institute for Studies in Education Monograph Series. Toronto: Ontario Institute for Studies in Education.

Hearon, Holly E. 2004. *The Mary Magdalene Tradition: Witness and Counter-Witness in Early Christian Communities.* Collegeville, Minn.: Liturgical Press.

Hearon, Holly E., and Linda M. Maloney. 2004. "Listen to the Voices of the Women." Pages 33–52 in *Distant Voices Drawing Near: Essays in Honor of Antoinette Clark Wire.* Edited by Holly E. Hearon. Collegeville, Minn.: Liturgical Press.

Hezser, Catherine. 2001. *Jewish Literacy in Roman Palestine.* Texte und Studien zum antiken Judentum. Tübingen: Mohr-Siebeck.

Himbaza, Innocent. 2002. "Le Décalogue du Papyrus Nash, Philon, 4QphylG, 8QPhyl3 et 4Qmez." *Revue de Qumran* 79:411–28.

Homer. *The Iliad.* 1999. Translated by A. T. Murray and William F. Wyatt. LCL. Cambridge: Harvard University Press.

Horsley, Richard A. 1984. "Popular Messianic Movements around the Time of Jesus." *Catholic Biblical Quarterly* 46:471–93.

———. 1985. "'Like One of the Prophets of Old': Two Types of Popular Prophets at the Time of Jesus." *Catholic Biblical Quarterly* 47:435–63.

———. 1987. *Jesus and the Spiral of Violence: Popular Jewish Resistance in Roman Palestine.* San Francisco: Harper & Row.

———. 1995. *Galilee: History, Politics, People.* Valley Forge, Penn.: Trinity Press International.

———. 2000. "The Kingdom of God and the Renewal of Israel: Synoptic Gospels, Jesus Movements, and Apocalypticism." Pages 303–44 in *The Encyclopedia of Apocalypticism.* Vol. 1: *The Origins of Apocalypticism in Judaism and Christianity*. Edited by John J. Collins. New York: Continuum.

———. 2001. *Hearing the Whole Story: The Politics of Plot in Mark's Gospel*. Louisville: Westminster John Knox.

———, ed. 2006. *Oral Performance, Popular Tradition, and Hidden Transcript in Q*. Semeia Studies. Atlanta: Society of Biblical Literature.

———. 2007. *Scribes, Visionaries, and the Politics of Second Temple Judea*. Louisville: Westminster John Knox.

Horsley, Richard A., with Jonathan A. Draper. 1999. *Whoever Hears You Hears Me: Prophets, Performance, and Tradition in Q*. Harrisburg: Trinity Press International.

Horsley, Richard A., Jonathan A. Draper, and John Miles Foley, eds. 2006. *Performing the Gospel: Orality, Memory, and Mark*. Minneapolis: Fortress.

Horsley, Richard A., and John S. Hanson. 1985. *Bandits, Prophets, and Messiahs: Popular Resistance Movements at the Time of Jesus*. Minneapolis: Winston.

Hunter, Ian M. L. 1984. "Lengthy Verbatim Recall (LVR) and the Mythical Gift of Tape-Recorder Memory." Pages 425–40 in *Psychology in the 1990s*. Edited by Kirsti M. J. Lagerspetz and Pekka Niemi. Advances in Psychology. Amsterdam: North-Holland.

———. 1985. "Lengthy Verbatim Recall: The Role of the Text." Pages 207–36 in *Progress in the Psychology of Language*. Edited by Andrew W. Ellis. Hillsdale, N.J.: Lawrence Erlbaum.

Hurtado, Larry W. 1989. "The Gospel of Mark in Recent Study." *Themelios* 14:47–52.

Ignatius. *Correspondence*. 1959. Translated by Kirsopp Lake. LCL. Cambridge: Harvard University Press.

Jaffee, Martin S. 1994. "Writing and Rabbinic Oral Tradition: On Mishnaic Narrative, Lists, and Mnemonics." *Journal of Jewish Thought and Philosophy* 4:123–46.

———. 1999. "Oral Tradition in the Writings of Rabbinic Oral Torah: On Theorizing Rabbinic Orality." *Oral Tradition* 14:3–32.

———. 2000. "The Oral-Cultural Context of the Talmud Yerushalmi: Greco–Roman Rhetorical Paideia, Discipleship, and the Concept of Oral Torah." Pages 27–73 in *Transmitting Jewish Traditions: Orality, Textuality, and Cultural Diffusion*. Edited by Yaakov Elman and Israel Gershoni. New Haven: Yale University Press.

———. 2001. *Torah in the Mouth: Writing and Oral Tradition in Palestinian Judaism 200 B.C.E.–400 C.E.* Oxford: Oxford University Press.

Josephus. *Against Apion*. 1976. Translated by H. St. J. Thackeray. LCL. Cambridge: Harvard University Press.

———. *Antiquities of the Jews*. 1998. Translated by H. St. J. Thackeray. LCL. Cambridge: Harvard University Press.

———. *Jewish War*. 1976. Translated by H. St. J. Thackeray. LCL. Cambridge: Harvard University Press.

———. *The Life*. 1966. Translated by H. St. J. Thackeray. LCL. Cambridge: Harvard University Press.

Junack, Klaus. 1981. "Abschreibpraktiken und Schreibergewohnheiten in ihrer Auswirkund auf die Textüberlieferung." Pages 277–95 in *New Testament Textual Criticism: Its Significance for Exegesis. Essays in Honor of Bruce M. Metzger*. Edited by Eldon Jay Epp and Gordon Fee. Oxford: Clarendon.

Kannaday, Wayne C. 2004. *Apologetic Discourse and the Scribal Tradition: Evidence of the Influence of Apologetic Interests in the Text of the Canonical Gospels*. Society of Biblical Literature Text-Critical Studies. Atlanta: Society of Biblical Literature.

Karnetzki, Manfred. 1956. "Textgeschichte als Überlieferungsgeschichte." *Zeitschrift für die neutestamentliche Wissenschaft und die Kunde der älteren Kirche* 47:170–80.

Keith, Chris. 2006. "The Role of the Cross in the Composition of the Markan Crucifixion Narrative." *Stone Campbell Journal* 9:61–75.

Kelber, Werner H. 1974. *The Kingdom in Mark: A New Place and a New Time*. Philadelphia: Fortress.

———. 1976. "The Hour of the Son of Man and the Temptation of the Disciples (Mark 14:32-42)." Pages 41–60 in *The Passion in Mark: Studies on Mark 14–16*. Edited by Werner H. Kelber. Philadelphia: Fortress.

———. 1979. *Mark's Story of Jesus*. Philadelphia: Fortress.

———. 1983. *The Oral and the Written Gospel: The Hermeneutics of Speaking and Writing in the Synoptic Tradition, Mark, Paul, and Q*. Bloomington: Indiana University Press.

———. 1987a. "Biblical Hermeneutics and the Ancient Art of Communication: A Response." Pages 97–105 in *Orality, Aurality, and Biblical Narrative*. Edited by Lou H. Silberman. Semeia Studies. Atlanta: Scholars Press.

———. 1987b. "Narrative as Interpretation and Interpretation of Narrative: Hermeneutical Reflections on the Gospels." Pages 107–33 in *Orality, Aurality, and Biblical Narrative*. Edited by Lou H. Silberman. Semeia Studies. Atlanta: Scholars Press.

―――. 1988a. "Die Fleischwerdung des Wortes in der Körperlichkeit des Textes." Pages 31–42 in *Materialität der Kommunikation*. Edited by Hans Ulrich Gumbrecht and K. Ludwig Pfeiffer. Suhrkamp-Taschenbuch Wissenschaft. Frankfurt: Suhrkamp.

―――. 1988b. "Narrative and Disclosure: Mechanisms of Concealing, Revealing, and Reveiling." Pages 1–20 in *Genre, Narrativity, and Theology*. Edited by Mary Gerhart and James G. Williams. Semeia Studies. Atlanta: Scholars Press.

―――. 1990. "In the Beginning Were the Words: The Apotheosis and Narrative Displacement of the Logos." *Journal of the American Academy of Religion* 58:69–98.

―――. 1995a. "Language, Memory, and Sense Perception in the Religious and Technological Culture of Antiquity and the Middle Ages." *Oral Tradition* 10:409–50.

―――. 1995b. "Jesus and Tradition: Words in Time, Words in Space." Pages 139–67 in *Orality and Textuality in Early Christian Literature*. Edited by Joanna Dewey. Semeia Studies. Atlanta: Scholars Press.

―――. 1996. "Metaphysics and Marginality in John." Pages 1.129–54 in *What Is John? Readers and Readings of the Fourth Gospel*. 2 vols. Edited by Fernando Segovia. Society of Biblical Literature Symposium Series. Atlanta: Scholars Press.

―――. 1997. "Introduction." Pages xix–xxxi in *The Oral and the Written Gospel: The Hermeneutics of Speaking and Writing in the Synoptic Tradition, Mark, Paul, and Q*. Voices in Performance and Text. Bloomington: Indiana University Press.

―――. 1999. "The Quest for the Historical Jesus from the Perspectives of Medieval, Modern, and Post-Enlightenment Readings, and in the View of Ancient, Oral Aesthetics." Pages 75–115 in *The Jesus Controversy: Perspectives in Conflict*. John Dominic Crossan, Luke Timothy Johnson, and Werner H. Kelber. Harrisburg: Trinity Press International.

―――. 2002a. "The Case of the Gospels: Memory's Desire and the Limits of Historical Criticism." *Oral Tradition* 17:55–86.

―――. 2002b. "Memory's Desire or the Ordeal of Remembering. Judaism and Christianity." *International Readings on Theory, History, and Philosophy of Culture* 12:181–207.

―――. 2004a. "Geschichte als Kommunikationsgeschichte: Überlegung zur Medienwissenschaft." Pages 153–68 in *Konstruktion von Wirklichkeit: Beiträge aus geschichtstheoretischer, philosophischer, under theologischer Perspektive*. Edited by Jens Schröter and Antje Eddelbüttel. New York: Walter de Gruyter.

Kelber, Werner H. 2004b. "The Theological Refutation, Linguistic Dilemma, and Ethical Validity of the Search for the Historical Jesus." Paper presented at K.U.Leuven, 29 April 2004. Leuven, Belgium.

———. 2005. "The Works of Memory: Christian Origins and Mnemohistory—A Response." Pages 221–48 in *Memory, Tradition, and Text: Uses of the Past in Early Christianity*. Edited by Alan Kirk and Tom Thatcher. Semeia Studies. Atlanta: Society of Biblical Literature.

———. 2006. "The Generative Force of Memory: Early Christian Traditions as a Process of Remembering." *Biblical Theology Bulletin* 36:15–22.

———. 2007. "The Bible as Media History." Paper presented at the University of Glasgow, 8 March 2007. Glasgow, Scotland.

Kennedy, George A. 2003. *Progymnasmata: Greek Textbooks of Prose Composition and Rhetoric*. Society of Biblical Literature Writings from the Greco-Roman World. Atlanta: Society of Biblical Literature.

Kirk, Alan. 2005. "The Memory of Violence and the Death of Jesus in Q." Pages 191–206 in *Memory, Tradition, and Text: Uses of the Past in Early Christianity*. Edited by Alan Kirk and Tom Thatcher. Semeia Studies. Atlanta: Society of Biblical Literature.

———. 2007. "Tradition and Memory in the *Gospel of Peter*." Pages 133–56 in *Das Evangelium nach Petrus: Texte, Contexte, Intertexte*. Edited by Tobias Nicklas and Thomas Kraus. Berlin: Walter de Gruyter.

Kirk, Alan, and Tom Thatcher, eds. 2005. *Memory, Tradition and Text: Uses of the Past in Early Christianity*. Semeia Studies. Atlanta: Society of Biblical Literature.

Kloppenborg, John S. 1986. Review of *The Oral and the Written Gospel: The Hermeneutics of Speaking and Writing in the Synoptic Tradition, Mark, Paul, and Q*. *Toronto Journal of Theology* 2:149–51.

———. 1992. "Literary Convention, Self-Evidence, and the Social History of the Q People." Pages 77–102 in *Early Christianity, Q, and Jesus*. Edited by John S. Kloppenborg with Leif E. Vaage. Semeia Studies. Atlanta: Scholars Press.

Koester, Helmut. 1990. *Ancient Christian Gospels: Their History and Their Development*. Philadelphia: Trinity Press International.

Loewe, Raphael. 1969. "The Medieval History of the Latin Vulgate." Pages 102–54 in *The West from the Fathers to the Reformation*. Vol. 2 of *The Cambridge History of the Bible*. 3 vols. Edited by Geoffrey W. H. Lampe. Cambridge: Cambridge University Press.

Loftus, Elizabeth F. 1998. "Imaginary Memories." Pages 135–45 in *Theories of Memory II*. Edited by Martin A. Conway, Susan E. Gathercole, and Cesare Cornoldi. Hove, East Sussex: Psychology Press.

Loftus, Elizabeth F., Julie Feldman, and Richard Dashiell. 1995. "The Reality of Illusory Memories." Pages 47–68 in *Memory Distortion: How Minds, Brains, and Societies Reconstruct the Past.* Edited by Daniel L. Schacter. Cambridge: Harvard University Press.

Longinus. *On the Sublime.* 1939. Translated by W. Hamilton Fyfe. LCL. Cambridge: Harvard University Press.

Longus. *Daphnis and Chloe.* 1978. Translated by George Thornley et al. LCL. Cambridge: Harvard University Press.

Lord, Albert. 2000. *The Singer of Tales.* 2nd ed. Edited by Stephen Mitchell and Gregory Nagy. Harvard Studies in Comparative Literature. Cambridge: Harvard University Press.

Lowenthal, David. 1985. *The Past is a Foreign Country.* New York: Cambridge University Press.

Lurie, Alison. 1990. *Don't Tell the Grown-ups: Subversive Children's Literature.* Boston: Little, Brown.

MacDonald, Dennis Ronald. 1983. *The Legend and the Apostle: The Battle for Paul in Story and Canon.* Philadelphia: Westminster.

Mack, Burton L. 1988 *A Myth of Innocence: Mark and Christian Origins.* Minneapolis: Fortress.

Malina, Bruce J. 1994. "'Let Him Deny Himself' (Mark 8:34 & Par): A Social Psychological Model of Self-Denial." *Biblical Theology Bulletin* 24:106–19.

Malkki, Liisa H. 1995. *Purity and Exile: Violence, Memory, and National Cosmology among Hutu Refugees in Tanzania.* Chicago: University of Chicago Press.

Mandel, Paul. 2000. "Between Byzantium and Islam: The Transmission of a Jewish Book in the Byzantine and Early Islamic Periods." Pages 74–106 in *Transmitting Jewish Traditions: Orality, Textuality, and Cultural Diffusion.* Edited by Yaakov Elman and Israel Gershoni. New Haven: Yale University Press.

McDonnell, Myles. 1996. "Writing, Copying, and Autograph Manuscripts in Ancient Rome." *Classical Quarterly* n.s. 46:469–91.

McIver, Robert K., and Marie Carroll. 2002. "Experiments to Develop Criteria for Determining the Existence of Written Sources and Their Potential Implications for the Synoptic Problem." *Journal of Biblical Literature* 121:667–87.

———. 2004. "Distinguishing Characteristics of Orally Transmitted Material When Compared to Material Transmitted by Literary Means." *Applied Cognitive Psychology* 18:1251–69. This is a revision and republication of McIver and Carroll 2002 (see above).

Metzger, Bruce M., and Bart D. Ehrman. 2005. *The Text of the New Testament: Its Transmission, Corruption, and Restoration*. 4th ed. New York: Oxford University Press.

Miller, P. H. 1998. "Contemplating Fuzzy-Trace Theory: The Gist of It." *Journal of Experimental Child Psychology* 71:184–93.

Momigliano, Arnoldo. 1950. "Ancient History and the Antiquarian." *Journal of the Warburg and Courtauld Institute* 13:285–315.

Moore, Stephen D. 1989. *Literary Criticism and the Gospels: The Theoretical Challenge*. New Haven: Yale University Press.

Morgan, Teresa J. 1998. *Literate Education in the Hellenistic and Roman Worlds*. Cambridge: Cambridge University Press.

Neal, Arthur G. 1998. *National Trauma and Collective Memory: Major Events in the American Century*. Armonck, N.Y.: M. E. Sharpe.

Nissinen, Martti. 2000. "Spoken, Written, Quoted, and Invented: Orality and Writtenness in Ancient Near Eastern Prophecy." Pages 235–71 in *Writings and Speech in Israelite and Ancient Near Eastern Prophecy*. Edited by Ehud Ben Zvi and Michael H. Floyd. Society of Biblical Literature Symposium Series. Atlanta: Society of Biblical Literature.

Nkindi, J. Kawende Fina, and Guy de Plaen. 1996. "Body Memory. Part II: Pearls of Wisdom." Pages 92–97 in *Memory: Luba Art and the Making of History*. Edited by Mary Nooter Roberts and Allen F. Roberts. New York: The Museum of African Art.

O'Keefe, Katherine O'Brien. 1990. *Visible Song: Transitional Literacy in Old English Verse*. Cambridge: Cambridge University Press.

Olson, David R. 1994. *The World on Paper: The Conceptual and Cognitive Implications of Writing and Reading*. Cambridge: Cambridge University Press.

Ong, Walter. 1967. *The Presence of the Word: Some Prolegomena for Cultural and Religious History*. New Haven: Yale University Press.

———. 1971. *Rhetoric, Romance, and Technology: Studies in the Interaction of Expression and Culture*. Ithaca: Cornell University Press.

———. 1982. *Orality and Literacy: The Technologizing of the Word*. New York: Methuen.

———. 1992. "Technology Outside Us and Inside Us." Pages 1.189–208 in *Faith and Contexts*. 4 vols. Edited by Thomas J. Farrell and Paul A. Soukup. Atlanta: Scholars Press.

Ovid. *Metamorphoses*. 1977. Translated by Frank Justus Miller. LCL. Cambridge: Harvard University Press.

Papias. *Fragments of Papias and Quadratus*. In *Apostolic Fathers*, vol.

2. 2003. Translated by Bart D. Ehrman. LCL. Cambridge: Harvard University Press.

Parker, David C. 1997. *The Living Text of the Gospels*. Cambridge: Cambridge University Press.

Parks, Ward. 1987. "Orality and Poetics: Synchronic, Diachronic, and the Axes of Narrative Transmission." Pages 511–32 in *Comparative Research on Oral Traditions: A Memorial for Milman Parry*. Edited by John Miles Foley. Columbus: Slavica.

———. 1991. "The Textualization of Orality in Literary Criticism." Pages 46–66 in *Vox Intexta: Orality and Textuality in the Middle Ages*. Edited by A. N. Doane and Carol Braun Pasternack. Madison: University of Wisconsin Press.

Parry, Milman. 1971. *The Making of Homeric Verse: The Collected Papers of Milman Perry*. Edited by Adam Parry. Oxford: Oxford University Press.

Patte, Daniel. 1985. Review of *The Oral and the Written Gospel: The Hermeneutics of Speaking and Writing in the Synoptic Tradition, Mark, Paul, and Q*. Journal of the American Academy of Religion 53:136–37.

Pelling, C. B. R. 1979. "Plutarch's Method of Work in the Roman *Lives*." Journal of Hellenic Studies 99:74–96.

Pervo, Richard. I. 2006. *Dating Acts: Between the Evangelists and the Apologists*. Santa Rosa, Calif.: Polebridge.

Philo. *Embassy to Gaius*. 1962. Translated by F. H. Colson. Cambridge: Harvard University Press.

Plato. *Gorgias*. 1991. Translated by W. R. M. Lamb. LCL. Cambridge: Harvard University Press.

———. *Laws*. 1967. Translated by R. G. Bury. LCL. Cambridge: Harvard University Press.

———. *Phaedo*. 1960. Translated by Harold North Fowler. LCL. Cambridge: Harvard University Press.

———. *Phaedrus*. 1960. Translated by Harold North Fowler. LCL. Cambridge: Harvard University Press.

———. *Philebus*. 1975. Translated by Harold North Fowler. LCL. Cambridge: Harvard University Press.

———. *Protagoras*. 1962. Translated by W. R. M. Lamb. LCL. Cambridge: Harvard University Press.

———. *Republic*. 1980. Translated by Paul Shorey. LCL. Cambridge: Harvard University Press.

———. *The Statesman*. 1990. Translated by Harold North Fowler and W. R. M. Lamb. LCL. Cambridge: Harvard University Press.

Plato. *Timaeus*. 1966. Translated by R. G. Bury. LCL. Cambridge: Harvard University Press.

Pliny. *Letters and Panegyricus*. 1972. Translated by Betty Radice. LCL. Cambridge: Harvard University Press.

Plutarch. *The Education of Children*. 1969. Translated by Frank Cole Babbitt. LCL. Cambridge: Harvard University Press.

———. *On the Fame of the Athenians*. In *Moralia*, vol. 4. 1969. Translated by Frank C. Babbitt. LCL. Cambridge: Harvard University Press.

———. *Theseus*. In *Parallel Lives,* vol. 1. 1959. Translated by Bernadotte Perrin. LCL. Cambridge: Harvard University Press.

Poirier, John C. 2004. "Memory, Written Sources, and the Synoptic Problem: A Response to Robert K. McIver and Marie Carroll." *Journal of Biblical Literature* 123:315–22.

Poland, Lynn M. 1985. *Literary Criticism and Biblical Hermeneutics: A Critique of Formalist Approaches*. American Academy of Religion Academy Series. Chico, Calif.: Scholars Press.

Quintilian. *Orations*. 1980. Translated by H. E. Butler. LCL. Cambridge: Harvard University Press.

Rainey, Anson F. 1969. "The Scribe at Ugarit." *Proceedings of the Israel Academy of Sciences and Humanities* 3:126–46.

Reynolds, Leighton D., and Nigel G. Wilson. 1991. *Scribes and Scholars: A Guide to the Transmission of Greek and Latin Literature*. 3rd ed. Oxford: Clarendon.

Rhoads, David, Joanna Dewey, and Donald Michie. 1999. *Mark as Story: An Introduction to the Narrative of a Gospel*. 2nd ed. Minneapolis: Fortress.

Ricoeur, Paul. 2004. *Memory, History, Forgetting*. Translated by Kathleen Blamey and David Pellauer. Chicago: University of Chicago.

Robbins, Vernon K. 1991. "Writing as Rhetorical Act in Plutarch and the Gospels." Pages 142–68 in *Persuasive Artistry: Studies in New Testament Rhetoric in Honor of George A. Kennedy*. Edited by Duane F. Watson. Journal for the Study of the New Testament Supplement Series. Sheffield: Sheffield Academic Press.

———. 1993. "Progymnastic Rhetorical Composition and the Pre-Gospel Traditions: A New Approach." Pages 111–47 in *The Synoptic Gospels: Source Criticism and the New Literary Criticism*. Edited by Camille Focant. Bibliotheca ephemeridum theologicarum lovaniensium. Leuven: Leuven University Press.

Roberts, Mary Nooter, and Allen F. Roberts, eds. 1996. *Memory: Luba Art and the Making of History*. New York: The Museum of African Art.

Roediger, Henry L., and Kathleen B. McDermott. 2000. "Distortion of Memory." Pages 149–62 in *The Oxford Handbook of Memory*. Edited by Endel Tulving and Fergus I. M. Craik. Oxford: Oxford University Press.

Rordorf, Willy. 1996. "An Aspect of the Judeo-Christian Ethic: The Two Ways." Pages 148–64 in *The Didache in Modern Research*. Edited by Jonathan A. Draper. Leiden: Brill.

Rosenberg, Bruce A. 1987. "The Complexity of Oral Tradition." *Oral Tradition* 2:3–90.

Royse, James R. 1979. "Scribal Habits in the Transmission of New Testament Texts." Pages 139–61 in *The Critical Study of Sacred Texts*. Edited by Wendy Doniger O'Flaherty. Berkeley Religious Studies Series. Berkeley: Graduate Theological Union.

Rubin, David C. 1995. *Memory in Oral Traditions: The Cognitive Psychology of Epic, Ballads, and Counting-Out Rhymes*. Oxford: Oxford University Press.

Sachs, J. S. 1974. "Memory in Reading and Listening to Discourse." *Memory and Cognition* 2:95–100.

Saldarini, Anthony J. 1988. *Pharisees, Scribes, and Sadducees in Palestinian Society*. Wilmington: Michael Glazier.

Sanders, James A. 1999. "The Scrolls and the Canonical Process." Pages 2.1–23 in *The Dead Sea Scrolls after Fifty Years: A Comprehensive Assessment*. 2 vols. Edited by Peter W. Flint and James C. VanderKam. Leiden: Brill.

Schacter, Daniel L. 1995. "Memory Distortion: History and Current Status." Pages 1–43 in *Memory Distortion: How Minds, Brains, and Societies Reconstruct the Past*. Edited by Daniel L. Schacter. Cambridge: Harvard University Press.

Schäfer, Peter. 1986. "Research into Rabbinic Literature: An Attempt to Define the *Status Quaestionis*." *Journal of Jewish Studies* 37:139–52.

———. 1989. "Once again the *Status Quaestionis* of Research in Rabbinic Literature: An Answer to Chaim Milikowsky." *Journal of Jewish Studies* 40:89–94.

Schudson, Michael. 1989. "The Present in the Past versus the Past in the Present." *Communication* 11:105–13.

———. 1992. *Watergate in American Memory: How We Remember, Forget, and Reconstruct the Past*. New York: BasicBooks.

Schwartz, Barry. 1991. "Collective Memory and Social Change: The Democratization of George Washington." *American Sociological Review* 56:221–36.

Schwartz, Barry. 2000. *Abraham Lincoln and the Forge of National Memory.* Chicago: University of Chicago Press.

Schweitzer, Albert. 1913. *Geschichte der Lebenjesuforschung.* Tübingen: J. C. B. Mohr.

———. 1931. *Die Mystik des Apostels Paulus.* Tübingen: J. C. B. Mohr.

Scott, Bernard Brandon, and Margaret E. Dean. 1993. "A Sound Map of the Sermon on the Mount." Pages 726–39 in *Society of Biblical Literature Seminar Papers* 32. Atlanta: Society of Biblical Literature.

Scott, James C. 1977. "Protest and Profanation: Agrarian Revolt and the Little Tradition." *Theory and Society* 4:1–38, 211–46 (2 parts).

Sedgwick, W. B. 1947. "Oral Transmission in Ancient Times." *Folklore* 58:288–91.

———. 1990. "Reading and Writing in Classical Antiquity." *Contemporary Review* 135:90–94.

Segal, Eliezer. 2004. "Anthological Dimensions of the Babylonian Talmud." Pages 81–107 in *The Anthology in Jewish Literature.* Edited by David Stern. Oxford: Oxford University Press.

Shiner, Whitney. 2003. *Proclaiming the Gospel: First-Century Performance of Mark.* Harrisburg: Trinity Press International.

Silberman, Lou H., ed. 1987. *Orality, Aurality and Biblical Narrative.* Semeia Studies. Atlanta: Scholars Press.

Small, Jocelyn Penny. 1997. *Wax Tablets of the Mind: Cognitive Studies of Memory and Literacy in Classical Antiquity.* New York: Routledge.

Snyder, H. Gregory. 2000. *Teachers and Texts in the Ancient World: Philosophers, Jews, and Christians.* New York: Routledge.

Stahl, Sandra Dolby. 1989. *Literary Folkloristics and the Personal Narrative.* Bloomington: Indiana University Press.

Starr, Raymond J. 1987. "The Circulation of Literary Texts in the Roman World." *Classical Quarterly* n.s. 37:213–23.

Stock, Brian. 1983. *The Implications of Literacy: Written Language and Models of Interpretation in the Eleventh and Twelfth Centuries.* Princeton: Princeton University Press.

Strabo. *Geography.* 1969. Translated by Horace Leonard Jones et al. LCL. Cambridge: Harvard University Press.

Strack, Hermann L., and Günter Stemberger. 1996. *Introduction to the Talmud and Midrash.* 2nd ed. Translated and edited by Markus Bockmuehl. Minneapolis: Fortress.

Suetonius. *Augustus.* In *Lives of the Caesars.* 1989. Translated by J. C. Rolfe. LCL. Cambridge: Harvard University Press.

Sweeny, Armin. 1987. *A Full Hearing: Orality and Literacy in the Malay World.* Berkeley: University of California Press.

Thatcher, Tom. 2006. *Why John Wrote a Gospel: Jesus—Memory—History.* Louisville: Westminster John Knox.

Theon. *Progymnasmata.* In *Progymnasmata: Greek Textbooks of Prose Composition and Rhetoric.* Translated with introductions and notes by George A. Kennedy. Society of Biblical Literature Writings from the Greco-Roman World. Atlanta: Society of Biblical Literature, 2003.

Thomas, Rosalind. 2003. "Prose Performance Texts: *Epideixis* and Written Publication in the Late Fifth and Early Fourth Centuries." Pages 162–88 in *Written Texts and the Rise of Literate Culture in Ancient Greece.* Edited by Harvey Yunis. Cambridge: Cambridge University Press.

Tov, Emanuel. 1998. "Scribal Practices Reflected in the Texts of the Judaean Desert." Pages 1.402–29 in *The Dead Sea Scrolls after Fifty Years: A Comprehensive Assessment.* 2 vols. Edited by Peter W. Flint and James C. VanderKam. Leiden: Brill.

Turner, Victor. W. 1967a. "Betwixt and Between: The Liminal Period in *Rites de Passage.*" Pages 93–111 in *The Forest of Symbols: Aspects of Ndembu Ritual.* Victor W. Turner. Ithaca: Cornell University Press.

———. 1967b. "Symbols in Ndembu Ritual." Pages 19–47 in *The Forest of Symbols: Aspects of Ndembu Ritual.* Victor W. Turner. Ithaca: Cornell University Press.

———. 1969. *The Ritual Process: Structure and Anti-Structure.* Chicago: Aldine.

Ulrich, Eugene. 1998. "The Dead Sea Scrolls and the Biblical Text." Pages 1.79–100 in *The Dead Sea Scrolls after Fifty Years: A Comprehensive Assessment.* 2 vols. Edited by Peter W. Flint and James C. VanderKam. Leiden: Brill.

———. 1999. *The Dead Sea Scrolls and the Origins of the Bible.* Grand Rapids: Eerdmans.

Van de Sandt, Huub, and David Flusser. 2002. *The Didache: Its Jewish Sources and Its Place in Early Judaism and Christianity.* Compendia rerum iudaicarum ad Novum Testamentum. Minneapolis: Fortress.

Van der Toorn, Karel. 2000. "From the Oral to the Written: The Case of Old Babylonian Prophecy." Pages 219–34 in *Writings and Speech in Israelite and Ancient Near Eastern Prophecy.* Edited by Ehud Ben Zvi and Michael H. Floyd. Society of Biblical Literature Symposium Series. Atlanta: Society of Biblical Literature.

———. 2007. *Scribal Culture and the Making of the Hebrew Bible.* Cambridge: Harvard University Press.

Vansina, Jan. 1965. *Oral Tradition: A Study in Historical Methodology.* Translated by H. M. Wright. Chicago: Aldine.

———. 1985. *Oral Tradition as History.* Madison: University of Wisconsin Press.

Vanstiphout, H. 1995a. "Memory and Literacy in Ancient Western Asia." Pages 4.2181–96 in *Civilizations of the Ancient Near East.* 4 vols. Edited by Jack M. Sasson. New York: Scribners.

———. 1995b. "On the Old Babylonian Eduba Curriculum." Pages 3–16 in *Centres of Learning: Learning and Location in Premodern Europe and the Near East.* Edited by Jan Willem Drijvers and Alasdair A. MacDonald. Brill Studies in Intellectual History. Leiden: Brill.

Veldhuis, Nick. 2003. "Mesopotamian Canons." Pages 9–28 in *Homer, the Bible, and Beyond: Literary and Religious Canons in the Ancient World.* Edited by Margalit Finkelberg and Guy G. Strousma. Jerusalem Studies in Religion and Culture. Leiden: Brill.

Vermès, Géza. 1997. *The Complete Dead Sea Scrolls in English.* New York: Penguin.

Wibbing, Siegfried. 1959. *Die Tugend- und Lasterkataloge im Neuen Testament und ihr Traditions-geschichte unter besonderer Berüchsichtigung der Qumran-Texte.* Beihefte zur Zeitschrift für die neutestamentliche Wissenschaft. Berlin: Walter de Gruyter.

Williams, Ronald J. 1972. "Scribal Training in Ancient Egypt." *Journal of the American Oriental Society* 92:214–21.

Wire, Antoinette Clark. 2002. *Holy Lives, Holy Deaths: A Close Hearing of Early Jewish Storytellers.* Society of Biblical Literature Studies in Biblical Literature. Atlanta: Society of Biblical Literature.

Xenophon. *An Ephesian Tale.* 1989. In *Collected Ancient Greek Novels.* Edited by B. P. Reardon. Berkeley: University of California Press.

Yamagata, Naoko. 2005. "Plato, Memory, and Performance." *Oral Tradition* 20:111–29.

Yerushalmi, Josef Hayim. 1989. *Zakhor: Jewish History and Jewish Memory.* New York: Schocken Books.

Youtie, Herbert C. 1971. "*Agrammatos*: An Aspect of Greek Society in Egypt." *Harvard Studies in Classical Philology* 75:161–76.

Zerubavel, Yael. 1995. *Recovered Roots: Collective Memory and the Making of the Israeli National Tradition.* Chicago: University of Chicago Press.

Zumthor, Paul. 1990. *Oral Poetry: An Introduction.* Translated by Kathryn Murphy-Judy. Theory and History of Literature. Minneapolis: University of Minnesota Press.

CONTRIBUTORS

Werner H. Kelber was formerly Isla Carroll and Percy E. Turner Professor of Biblical Studies and Director of the Center for the Study of Cultures at Rice University. He is the author of numerous papers, articles, and books on media culture, with particular attention to the interfaces between orality, scribality, and print in Western intellectual history. His major works include *Mark's Story of Jesus* (1979) and *The Oral and the Written Gospel* (1983). He is currently working on a collection of essays and a forthcoming two-volume study entitled *Words in Time, Words in Space*.

Tom Thatcher is Professor of Biblical Studies at Cincinnati Christian University. His research interests focus on ancient Christian media culture, Jesus Studies, and the Johannine Literature. He is the author/editor of numerous books and articles, including *The Riddles of Jesus in John: A Study in Tradition and Folklore* (2000), *Why John Wrote a Gospel: Jesus–Memory–History* (2006), *Jesus the Riddler* (2006), and *Memory, Tradition, and Text: Uses of the Past in Early Christianity* (with Alan Kirk; 2005). He currently serves as co-chair of the Mapping Memory Group in the Society of Biblical Literature.

Richard A. Horsley is Distinguished Professor of Liberal Arts and the Study of Religion at the University of Massachusetts, Boston. His wide-ranging research interests highlight the social contexts of the ministries of Jesus and Paul and the development of early Jesus traditions. He is the author/editor of numerous books, including *Hearing the Whole Story: The Politics* *of Plot in Mark's Gospel* (2001), *Oral Performance, Popular Tradition, and Hidden Transcript in Q* (2006), *Performing the Gospel: Orality, Memory, and Mark* (with Jonathan A. Draper and John Miles Foley; 2006), and *Scribes, Visionaries, and the Politics of Second Temple Judea* (2007).

Joanna Dewey is Harvey H. Guthrie, Jr. Professor Emerita of Biblical Studies at Episcopal Divinity School (Cambridge, Massachusetts). Her research interests focus on the Gospel of Mark and its oral media environment. Her many books and articles include *Mark as Story* (with David Rhoads and Donald Michie; 1999) and *Orality and Textuality in Early Christian Literature* (editor; 1994). She has long been a leading voice in the Society of Biblical Literature, including service as Chair of the Bible in Ancient and Modern Media Section from 1992-1996.

Holly E. Hearon is Associate Professor of New Testament at Christian Theological Seminary (Indianapolis, Indiana). Her research interests highlight the lives and experiences of early Christian women, relationships between early Christianity and formative Judaism, and the place of the Gospels in ancient media culture. She is the author of *The Mary Magdalene Tradition* (2004) and editor of *Distant Voices Drawing Near* (2004), as well as numerous papers and articles. She currently serves on the steering committees of the Bible in Ancient and Modern Media Section (Chair) and the Mapping Memory Group in the Society of Biblical Literature.

Jonathan A. Draper teaches in the School of Religion and Theology at the University of Kwazulu-Natal (South Africa). His research interests encompass a wide range of topics relating to the media environment of Christian origins, including Historical Jesus Studies, orality/literacy interfaces, and non-canonical Christian literature. He is the author/editor of numerous studies, including *The Didache in Modern Research* (1996), *Whoever Hears You Hears Me* (with Richard Horsley; 1999), and the acclaimed Semeia Studies volumes *Orality, Literacy, and Colonialism in Southern Africa* (2003) and *Orality, Literacy, and Colonialism in Antiquity* (2004).

April D. DeConick is Isla Carroll and Percy E. Turner Professor of Biblical Studies at Rice University. Her research explores the various ways that Jesus traditions developed in competing sectors of the early church. She is the author of numerous books and articles on non-canonical early Christian literature, including *Seek to See Him: Ascent and Vision Mysticism in the*

Gospel of Thomas (1996), *Voices of the Mystics: Early Christian Discourse in the Gospels of John, Thomas and Other Ancient Christian Literature* (2001), *Recovering the Original Gospel of Thomas* (2005), and *The Original Gospel of Thomas in Translation: With a Commentary and New English Translation of the Complete Gospel* (2006). Her current research projects focus on Gnostic spirituality and mysticism in the New Testament Gospels.

Arthur J. Dewey is Professor of Theology at Xavier University (Cincinnati). He is a former chair of the Bible in Ancient and Modern Media Section in the Society of Biblical Literature and a founding member of the Jesus Seminar, and the author of numerous articles, papers, and books on Jesus, Paul, and ancient Christian media culture, including *Spirit and Letter in Paul* (1996).

Chris Keith is Assistant Professor of Biblical Studies at Lincoln Christian College and Seminary. A recent graduate of the University of Edinburg, his research highlights the Johannine Literature, social memory theory, and the textual history of the New Testament.

Alan Kirk is Associate Professor of Religion at James Madison University. His research interests focus on memory, orality, and the history of Gospels traditions. He is founder of the Mapping Memory Group in the Society of Biblical Literature, and is co-editor of *Memory, Tradition, and Texts: Uses of the Past in Early Christianity* (with Tom Thatcher; 2005). He is the author of *The Composition of the Sayings Source: Genre, Synchrony, and Wisdom redaction in Q* (1998) and numerous articles and papers on the early Christian literature and its media culture.

INDEX OF BIBLICAL BOOKS AND OTHER ANCIENT WORKS

Note: Biblical books are listed in alphabetical, rather than canonical, order.

1 Clement, 192, 270n4
1 Corinthians, 16, 62, 77, 199, 246, 265n11, 265n12
1 Enoch, 56
1QHodayot, 55
1QS (Community Rule), 54–55, 111, 133
1 Samuel, 61
1 Thessalonians, 102
1 Timothy, 93, 94, 192
1, 2 Chronicles, 222–23

2 Corinthians, 15, 182, 192–194
2 Peter, 93, 99, 270n4
2 Samuel, 61
2 Thessalonians, 93
2 Timothy, 93, 192

4Q169, 213
4QPs[b], 221

11Q, 213

Acts of the Apostles, 76, 78, 121, 131, 192, 199, 214, 252, 270n4

Aeneid, 183–84, 188
Against Apion, 52, 94, 99
Antiquities of the Jews, 52
Apocryphon of James, 14, 264–65n9, 270n4
Augustus (in *Lives of the Caesars*), 95, 96, 101

b. Berakhot, 53
Beowulf, 49
Bereshit Rabba, 227

Canones Ecclesiasticae, 119, 124–25
Christ the Educator, 95
Commentarii Traiani, 189–90
Community Rule, *see* "1QS"
Constitutiones Apostolicae, 119, 127–31

Daniel, 56, 267n4
Daphnis and Chloe, 90, 91, 94, 96, 98, 99, 100, 106
Deuteronomy, 53, 56, 63, 126, 272n9
Didache, 111–12, 114–17, 119–23, 123–27, 131–33

299

Discourses (Dio Chrysostom), 91–92, 96
Doctrina apostolorum, 111, 119, 123–27, 132–33

Ecclesiastical History (Eusebius), 92, 100, 104, 270n4
Eclogues (Virgil), 183
Education of Children, 97
Embassy to Gaius, 52
Ephesian Tale, 96, 106
Epistle of Barnabas, 11, 119, 123–27, 131, 132–33
Euripides, *Fragments*, see "*Fragments* (Euripides)"
Exhortation to the Greeks, 95, 98, 99
Exodus, 55–57, 61, 121, 266n2

Fame of the Athenians, 91
Fides Nicanae, 111, 112, 119, 121, 127–31
Fourth Eclogue, *see* "*Eclogues* (Virgil)"
Fragments (Euripides), 102, 107

Galatians, 15, 43, 77, 192, 213 266n18
Genesis, 57, 266n2
Geography (Strabo), 92, 95, 96, 97, 98, 99
Golden Ass, 93, 94, 96, 97, 98, 100, 101, 106
Gorgias, 94, 97
Gospel of Peter, 197, 256
Gospel of the Hebrews, 92
Gospel of Thomas, 2, 14, 16–17, 19, 40, 41, 143, 144, 145, 146, 147, 149, 150, 151, 152, 153, 156–57, 158, 159, 161, 162–63, 164–65, 166–67, 170, 171, 172, 175–76, 179, 237, 264–65n9

Habakkuk, 54
Hebrews, 215, 237
Hermas *Vision*, 271n4

Iliad, 49, 81

Infancy Gospel of Thomas, 143, 144, 145, 148, 149, 150, 151, 152, 153, 154–55, 156, 157, 160, 166, 167–69, 171, 173–75
Isaiah, 52, 56–57, 61–62, 69–79, 226

Jeremiah, 223
Jewish War, 50, 107
John (Gospel of), 14, 15, 18–19, 24, 31, 33, 36, 37, 40–41, 93, 100, 106–7, 108, 197, 198, 266n17, 266n22, 267n5, 270n4
Joshua, 55
Jude, 270n4

Lamentations Rabbati, 223, 227
Laws (Plato), 96, 98, 106
Letters (Pliny), 90, 95, 96, 97–98, 100, 101, 102, 103, 104, 107, 268n18
Leucippe and Clitophon, 91, 94–95, 97, 98, 99, 105, 106
Leviticus, 57
Life (Josephus), 134
Luke, 18, 19, 20, 24, 37, 38, 39, 40–41, 77, 78, 79, 80, 82, 92, 97, 98, 100, 108, 156, 166, 179, 193, 233, 238, 266n21, 268n7, 270n7

Malachi, 61
Manual of Discipline, *see* "1QS"
Mark, 12–13, 17–18, 19, 23, 24, 25, 29, 30, 31–33, 35–36, 37–39, 40–41, 45, 47–48, 49, 51, 57, 58, 59, 60–63, 63–70, 71–87, 92, 93, 100, 107, 179, 194–96, 197–99, 200, 201, 202–4, 205, 207, 212, 213, 214, 231, 249–52, 256, 258, 263n1, 264n9, 265n11, 265n15, 267ch.4n1, 267ch.4n2, 267n4, 267n7, 268n6, 270n7, 270–71n1
Matthew, 17–19, 20, 24, 38–41, 77–78, 79, 85, 93, 107, 114, 156, 161, 166, 179, 233, 238, 252, 266n21, 270n7
Megillah, 53

Metamorphoses, 96, 98, 102, 104, 105, 106, 107
Miscellanies (Clement of Alexandria), 94, 98, 99

Nehemiah, 61

On Memory, 206, 235
On the Sublime, 95
Orations (Quintillian), 104

Phaedo, 91, 98
Phaedrus, 99
Philebus, 103
Philippians (Polycarp), 270n4
Pliny's *Letters*, *see "Letters* (Pliny)"
Poetics, 92, 94
Progymnasmata (Theon), 90, 91, 94, 96, 101, 104, 268n9
Protagoras, 96
Proverbs, 56
Psalms, 52, 55, 61, 63, 82, 205, 214, 258
Pseudo-Clementine *Recognitions*, 270n4

Q, 2, 14, 15, 16–17, 18–19, 39, 41, 49, 50, 57–59, 77, 78, 79, 80–81, 85, 194, 202, 203, 231, 237, 246, 265n11, 266n21, 267n7

Republic, 91, 96, 97, 98, 106
Res Gestae, 183, 184–85, 188–89, 195
Revelation, 114
Roman History (Dio Cassius), 99
Romans, 192, 266n18

Salvation of the Rich Man, 91, 95, 103
Secret Gospel of Mark, 35
Statesman, 95
Stromata, 270n4
Syntagma Doctrinae, 111, 112, 119, 121, 127–31, 269n4

Theseus (in *Parallel Lives*), 97–98
Timaeus, 94
Titus, 93, 99, 192

Vita Shenoudi, 111, 112, 127–31, 269 ch.6n1, 269n5

Wisdom of Jesus ben Sirach, 56, 59, 271n7

Zechariah, 56, 61

INDEX OF AUTHORS

Note: page numbers in **bold font** *include discussion of the author's work (beyond citation of her/his publications).*

Achilles Tatius, 91, 95, 98, 106
Alexander, Loveday, 217, 224
Allport, Gordon W., 140
Apuleius, 93, 94, 96, 98, **100–1**, 106
Arnal, William E., 50
Aristotle, 90, 92, 94, 206, 235, 253
Assmann, Jan, **12**, 38, 216, 218, 219, 222, 226, 228, 229, **238**, 252, **253**, **260**, 271n1, 271n6

Baddeley, Alan D., 145, 221, 271n3
Bailey, Kenneth E., **136**, 155
Baltzer, Klaus, 55
Bar-Ilan, Meir, 2
Barrett, C. K., 93
Bartlett, Frederic C., **139–41**, 179
Basgöz, Ilhan, 79
Bauckham, Richard, 90, **179**
Bäuml, Franz H., 219
Beard, Mary, 50
Beit-Arié, Malachi, 228
Bellezza, Francis, **117**
Blank, Reiner, 244
Bonanno, George, 210

Boomershine, Thomas E., 37, 263n1
Botha, Pieter J. J., 249
Boyarin, Daniel, 53
Brodie, Thomas L., 263n1
Bruner, Jerome, 218
Bultmann, Rudolf, 21, **22–24**, 47, **177**, **243**, 253, 267n4
Burton-Christie, Douglas, 112
Byrskog, Samuel, 90, **243**

Carr, David M., 49, 102–3, 108, 217, 218, 219, 220, 221, 224, 227, 228, **238**, 266n1, 271n2, 271n7, 272n10
Carroll, Marie, **137**, **145**, **151**, 155, **178–79**, 270n2, 270n3, 270n5, **270n6**
Carruthers, Mary J., 186, 189, 218, 219, 220, 224, 226, 235, 236–37, 247
Casey, Edward, 216
Ceci, Stephen J., 138
Chaytor, Henry J., 215, 217, 220, 221, 224, 229
Clanchy, M. T., 49, 217, 220, 227
Clement of Alexandria, 90, **91**, 92, 94, 95, 98–99, 103, 270n4

Index of Authors

Collins, John J., 59
Colwell, Ernest C., 220, 221, 228, 230
Cooper, Craig, 113
Corbier, Mireille, 217, 220
Cribiore, Raffaella, 217, 218, 219
Crosby, Ruth, 217
Culpepper, R. Alan, 263

Dagenais, John, 220, 222, **225**, 226, 227, **229–30**, 271n5
Danker, Frederick, 91
Dashiell, Richard, 138
Dean, Margaret E., 122
DeConick, April D., 25, 177
de Plaen, Guy, 119
Derrenbacker, Robert A., Jr., 218
Dewey, Arthur J., **25**, 193, 194, 258
Dewey, Joanna, **25**, 64, 72, 73, 74, 75, 76, 83, 84, 85, 86, 98, 237, **249–51**, **257**
Dibelius, Martin, 47, **199–203**, 206, 214
Dio Cassius, 90, 99
Dio Chrysostom, 91–92, 96
Doane, Alger N., 215, 216, 217, 220, 222, 225, 226, 230
Dowd, Sharyn, 83
Downing, F. Gerald, 36
Draper, Jonathan A., 25, 48, 59, 82, 90
Dunn, James D. G., **40**, 263n1

Ehrman, Bart D., 215, 221, 227, 230, **232–34**, 271n4, 272n11
Eisenstein, Elizabeth L., 224, 225, 229, **241**, 261
Eliot, T. S., 181
Elman, Yaakov, 220, 229
Ephrat, Daphna, 229
Epp, Eldon Jay, 34, 42, 230, 252, **254–55**
Euripides, 102, 107
Eusebius, 92, 100, 104, 261, 270n4

Fantham, Elaine, 217
Fascher, Erich, 244
Feldman, Carol Fleisher, 218

Feldman, Julie, 138
Finnegan, Ruth, 46, 86, 113, 216, 217, 236–37
Fishbane, Michael, 222, 223, 224, 225, 228
Floyd, Michael, 224
Flusser, David, **111–12**, **269ch.6n1**
Foley, John Miles, 30, 35–36, 48, 85, **114–16**, 131, 136, 216, 218, 222, 229, 236–37, 239, 269n17
Fraade, Steven D., 218, 219
Frei, Hans W., 24, **247–48**

Gamble, Harry Y., 102, 220, 224
Georgi, Dieter, 192
Gerhardsson, Birger, 21, **22–24**, 219, 222, **252–53**
Goodman, Martin, 52
Goody, Jack, 145
Grafton, Anthony, **240–42**
Grant, Frederick, 182, 183
Green, William Scott, 53
Greenstein, Edward L., 221

Hägg, Thomas, 92
Haines-Eitzen, Kim, 222, 224, 227, 229, 232, **233**
Halbwachs, Maurice, 206
Hanks, W. E., 216
Hanson, John S., 59
Harris, William V., 2, 50, 102, 112, **268n10**
Havelock, Eric A., **31–32**, 46, 79, 136, 236–37, 261
Hearon, Holly E., 25, 90, 93, 95, 106, 108, 245
Hezser, Catherine, 2, 50
Himbaza, Innocent, 221
Horsley, Richard A., 25, 48, 49, 54, 58, 59, 60, 68, 70, 90, **237–38**, **248**, 249, 266n1
Hunter, Ian M. L., **140**, 145
Hurtado, Larry W., 263n1

Ignatius, 94, 99, **192**

Jaffee, Martin S., 49, **54**, 216, **219**, 220, 226, 227, **238–39**
Josephus, **10**, **50–51**, **52**, **57**, **90**, **94**, **99**, **107**
Junack, Klaus, 220, **271n4**, 271n6

Kannaday, Wayne C., **232**, **272n11**
Karnetzki, Manfred, 230
Keith, Chris, **25**, 208, **257**
Kelber, Werner H., **1–26**, **27–43**, **45–64**, **66–70**, **71–87**, **89–90**, **97**, 99, **100**, 101, 103, 104, **105–6**, 107, 108, 109, **113–14**, 117, **136–37**, **181**, **197–98**, **200–5**, 206, **212–14**, **215**, **216**, 217–18, 219, 222, 232, 234, 250, 256, 257, 263n1, **263n2**, **263n3**, **263–64n4**, **264n5**, 264n6, 264n7, 264n8, 264–65n9, 265n10, **265n11**, 265n12, 265n13, **265n15**, 266n17, 266n18, 266n19, 266n21, **266n22**, 267ch.4n1, **267n6**, 268n5, 268n14, 268n15, 268n16, 269n17, 269n19, 269n21, **270–71n1**
Kennedy, George A., 267ch.5n2
Kirk, Alan, **25**, 48, **208**, 210, 212, 213, 234, **237**, **252**, **255–56**
Kloppenborg, John S., 50, 263n1
Koester, Helmut, **183**

Loewe, Raphael, 226, 228, 271–72n8
Loftus, Elizabeth F., 138
Longinus, 95
Longus, 91, 96, 98, 99, 100, 106
Lord, Albert, 35, **37**, 46, 136, 236–37, 244, **250**
Lowenthal, David, 206
Lurie, Alison, 86

MacDonald, Dennis Ronald, 93
Mack, Burton L., 83
Malbon, Elizabeth Struthers, 75, 83

Malina, Bruce J., 76
Malkki, Liisa H., **208–10**
Maloney, Linda M., 109
Mandel, Paul, 219, 223, **227**, 229
McDermott, Kathleen B., 138, 139
McDonnell, Myles, 224, 231
McIver, Robert K., **137**, **145**, **151**, 155, **178–79**, 270n2, 270n3, 270n5, **270n6**
Metzger, Bruce M., 221, 227, 271n4
Michie, Donald, 75
Miller, P. H., 153
Momigliano, Arnoldo, 235, 242
Moore, Stephen D., **33**, 235, **248**, 256
Morgan, Teresa, 217

Neal, Arthur G., 207, 208
Nissinen, Martti, 216
Nkindi, J. Kawende Kina, 119

O'Keefe, Katherine O'Brien, 49
Olson, David R., 216, 217, 219, 229, 271–72n8
Ong, Walter, **27**, 35, **36**, 46, 49, 79, 80, 83, 105, 136, 151, 235, 236–37, **240**, **248–49**, 264n5
Ovid, 94, 96, 98, 102, 104, 105, 106, 107

Papias, 92, 98–99, 100, 102, 104, 270n4
Parker, David C., **34**, 42, 82, 114, 215, 230, **231–32**, 233, 252, **254–55**
Parks, Ward, 216
Parry, Milman, 35, 46, 136
Patte, Daniel, 263n1
Pelling, C. B. R., 218
Pervo, Richard, 78
Philo, 52
Plato, **31–32**, 46, 90, 91, 94, 95, 96, 97, 98, 99, 103, 106, 112, 237, 268n4
Pliny, 90, 95, 96, 97–98, 100, **101–2**, **103**, 194, 105, 107, **108**, 269n18
Plutarch, 91, 97, 98, 178, 192
Poirier, John C., 270n3
Poland, Lynn M., 248

Postman, Leo, 140

Quintilian, **104**

Rainey, Anson F., 218
Reynolds, Leighton D., 218, 226
Rhoads, David, 74, 75, 267n1, 267n4
Ricoeur, Paul, 147, 242
Robbins, Vernon K., 178, 215, **230–31**, **233–34**
Roberts, Allen, **117**, 269n3
Roberts, Mary Nooter ("Polly"), **117**, 269n3
Roediger, Henry L., 138, 139
Rordorf, Willy, 131
Rosenberg, Bruce, 268n11, 269n17
Royse, James R., 221
Rubin, David C., **140–41**, **151**

Sachs, J. S., 145
Saldarini, Anthony J., 60
Sanders, James A., 223
Schacter, Daniel L., 138
Schäfer, Peter, 222, 223, 225, **227**
Schudson, Michael, 207, 208, 257
Schwartz, Barry, **210–11**, 258
Schweitzer, Albert, 42, **43**
Scott, Bernard Brandon, 122
Scott, James C., 57
Sedgwick, W. B., 100, 217
Segal, Eliezer, 224
Shiner, Whitney, 102, 249, 269n17
Silberman, Lou H., 237
Small, Jocelyn Penny, 217, 218, 220
Snyder, H. Gregory, 219
Stahl, Sandra Dolby, 95
Starr, Raymond J., 224, 231
Stemberger, Günter, 226

Stock, Brian, 217
Strabo, 90, 92, 95, 96, 97, 98, 99
Strack, Hermann L., 226
Suetonius, 95, 96, **101**, 192
Sweeny, Armin, 217, 218, 220

Thatcher, Tom, 37, 73, 206, **257**, **259**
Theon, 90, 91, 94, 96, 101, **104**, 268n4, **268n9**
Thomas, Rosalind, 217
Tov, Emanuel, 225
Turner, Victor W., 115, 116

Ulrich, Eugene, 52, **223**, 227, 229, 255

Van de Sandt, Huub, **111–12**, **269ch.6n1**
Van der Toorn, Karel, 217, 218, 220, 221, 223, **227–28**, 272n9
Vansina, Jan, 93, 112–13
Vanstiphout, H., 216, 218, 223
Veldhuis, Nick, 271n6
Virgil, 183–84, 188

Wibbing, Siegfried, 133
Williams, Ronald J., 218
Wilson, Nigel G., 218, 226
Wire, Antoinette Clark, 90, 93, 94, 95

Xenophon, 96, 106

Yamagata, Naoko, 221
Yerushalmi, Josef Hayim, 212
Youtie, Herbert C., 50

Zerubavel, Yael, **211–12**
Zumthor, Paul, 216, 224, **225**, 255

INDEX OF SUBJECTS

Note: see the Index of Authors to locate sustained discussions of an individual author's work. Greek terms are listed before English; German and Latin terms are alphabetized with English.

ἐπόπται ("witnesses"), 93, 268n7
εὐαγγέλιον ("gospel"), 181–83, 185, 192, 194; *see also* "gospel"; "gospel of Rome"
ἱστορία ("history"; "historical narrative"), 90, 91–92, 268n8
λόγος ("word"; "discourse"; "story/account"), 90, 91–92, 93, 94, 99; *see also* "Christology, *Logos* (Gospel of John)"
μῦθος ("myth"; "story"), 90, 91–92, 93, 94, 96–97, 98, 99, 103, 106, 107

9/11 attack, 198, 207, 209
70 C.E., *see* "Jerusalem, destruction of (70 C.E.)"

additions (in memory), 156, 157–61, 162–63, 164–65, 166, 167–69, 170, 172–74, 177, 178, 179
adversarial plotting, *see* "agonistic tone (of oral narrative)"
Aeneas, 183, 185, 188, 190

agonistic tone (of oral narrative), 11, 38, 74–75, 251; *see also* "oral narrative style"
Agrippa (Herod), 99
Aland's *Synopsis*, 20
Alexander the Great, 183, 190
Anglo-American approach to tradition, 35–36
Antipas (Herod), 58, 66, 81
anti-Semitism, 13–14
aphorism (oral form), 4–5, 59, 137, 176
apocalypticism, 59
apophthegms, 82
Apostolic Decree (Acts 15), 121, 131
applicability (aspect of oral performance), 11
Ara Pacis, 183–84, 188
articulatory loop, 145, 220–21, 271n3
Athens, 61
audience (of oral performance or recited text), 4–5, 6, 7–8, 8–10, 11, 13, 14, 15, 18, 21–22, 28, 37, 43, 48, 49, 73, 74, 75, 78, 79–80, 81, 84–85,

Index of Subjects 307

86, 87, 96, 97, 101–2, 108, 109, 116, 140, 253, 269n21
Augustine, 85
Augustus (Emperor), 95, 96, 101, 182–84, 185, 188, 189, 190, 194
authorities (traditional), *see* "oral authorities (in Christian tradition)"
authors (relationship to audiences and texts), 7–8, 9, 12, 20, 35–37, 39, 99–100, 101–2, 105, 223–24, 229–30, 255
authors vs. scribes, *see* "scribes, vs. authors"
authorship, notion of, *see* "authors"

Bar Kokhba, 193
Bartlett, Frederic, memory experiments, 139–40
Beelzebul controversy (Mark 3), 64, 67
Bible in Ancient and Modern Media Section (Society of Biblical Literature), 239
biographical apophthegms, 82
biosphere (speech context), 4, 5–6, 7–8, 13, 14, 15, 22, 28, 79, 260, 261
book culture, *see* "manuscript culture"
books (vs. orality), 2, 3, 9, 12, 19–20, 31–33, 43, 52–54, 61–63, 89, 114, 229, 264n7; *see also* "chirographs"; "print (mechanical type)"; "scrolls"; "writing"
"boy and dolphin" story (Pliny), 102, 103, 105, 107
bridal chamber, *see* "Virgin Proverb"
Burundi genocide, 198, 208–10

Caesar, *see* "Augustus (Emperor)" or "Julius Caesar"
canon[ization] (authority of), 10, 38, 43, 74, 141, 193, 216, 230, 232, 234, 238, 255, 261, 271–72n8
catechesis, 112, 115, 116, 117, 119, 127, 131

chain types, *see* "memory chains"
chains (in Mark's narrative), 65–68
chapter and verse mentality, *see* "numerical grid approach to texts"
characters/characterization, 5, 65, 74, 79, 94–95, 249
chiasm, 64–66, 116
chirographs, 3, 9–10, 19–20, 27–29, 107, 109, 216, 217–18, 219–20, 222–23, 224–25, 226–27, 238, 249, 250, 260–61; *see also* "scrolls"; "writing"
Christian origins (study of), 2–3, 14, 19, 22, 71, 198, 201, 202, 206, 240, 259, 260, 263n2
Christology, 17, 49, 59
 -oral vs. written, 6, 82–84, 202–4, 205, 265n12
 -*Logos* Christology (Gospel of John), 19, 266n17, 266n22
Cleave the Wood Saying (*Infancy Gospel of Thomas* 10.1–2), 143–44, 152, 153, 154–55, 157, 166, 175; *see also* "Foot Miracle"; "miracle stories, preservation of"
closings (of remembered stories), *see* "openings and closings (of remembered stories)"
codex, 193, 261
cold memory, *see* "memory, cold memory"
collective memory, *see* "memory, social memory"
Column of Trajan, *see* "Trajan's Column"
commemorative narrative, 211–12, 213
conflict, *see* "agonistic tone (of oral narrative)"
Constantine, 233
continuity (in tradition), *see* "uniformity (in tradition)"
controversy stories, *see* "pronouncement stories"

copying (of manuscripts), 36, 136–37, 145, 153, 155, 171, 175–76, 179, 201, 227–28, 230–31, 232–33, 254–55, 256, 270n5, 271n4; *see also* "scribes, copyists"
copyists, scribes as, *see* "scribes, copyists"
counterform to oral speech (writing as), 24, 25, 71–72, 73, 79, 84, 87, 204; *see also* "writing, opposed to orality"
covenant renewal theme, 54–55, 59, 65–66, 68, 70
cross, *see* "crucifixion"
crucifixion, 12, 13, 62, 70, 81, 82, 84, 199, 202, 203, 204–5, 213–14, 257; *see also* "passion narrative(s)"
cultural identity, *see* "identity (social)"
cultural memory, *see* "memory, social memory"
cultural texts, 218–19; *see also* "canon[ization], authority of"

damnatio memoriae, 252, 260; *see also* "forgetting (aspect of memory)"
David (King), 58–59, 61
Dead Sea Scrolls, 10, 47, 52–53, 67, 223, 255; *see also* "Qumran"
death of Jesus, 13, 16–17, 18–19, 35, 48, 62, 72, 73, 79–85, 197–98, 199, 200–5, 206, 207, 212–14, 256–58, 263n1, 265n11, 265n12, 270–71n1; *see also* "crucifixion"; "passion narrative(s)"
deletions (in memory), 156–57, 158–60, 162–63, 164–65, 167–69, 177, 178, 179
Derek Erets, 111–12, 133
Dewey, Dennis, 267n5
Dialogue Gospels, *see* "Sayings Gospels (genre)"
disciples of Jesus (as oral authorities), 17–18, 30, 32, 73–75, 76–77, 78, 80, 249, 250–52, 256, 265n15, 267n6

documents, *see* "print (mechanical type)"
"dolphin and boy" story (Pliny), 102, 103, 105, 107
dominical sayings, *see* "sayings of Jesus (traditional)"

echo chamber (of social memory), 181–82, 188–89, 192, 196
"eclipse of biblical narrative," 24, 247–48
Egypt, 50, 98, 100, 112, 238, 272n10
electronic media (hermeneutics of), 261, 264n4
Elijah, 66
emperor worship, 182, 186, 189–91
emplotment, *see* "narrativity"; "plot (element of narrative)"
ending of Mark's Gospel, 70, 74, 76, 84–85, 251–52, 267ch.4n2
equiprimordial(ity), 5, 7, 8, 19, 21–22, 23, 42, 200–1, 214, 266n20
Erinnerungsfigur ("memory figure"), 13, 253, 258
eschatological discourse (Mark 13), 76–77, 78–79, 81, 83, 84; *see also* "prophets, as oral authorities"
esoteric secrecy, *see* "secrecy motif"
Eucharist, 83, 199, 211, 256–57
"evolutionary ascent" model of tradition, 2, 20–21, 22–24, 41–42, 72, 198, 200–2, 242, 245–46, 249, 251
evolutionary gradualism, *see* "'evolutionary ascent' model of tradition"
Exodus (the), 60
exorcism (stories), 64–66, 67, 85, 203
extraordinary individual (in Roman propaganda), 188–92, 193–96; *see also* "propaganda (Roman)"
Ezra, 61–62

false Christs (Mark 13), *see* "prophets, as oral authorities"

Index of Subjects 309

false memories, 138, 179
false prophets (Mark 13), *see* "prophets, as oral authorities"
family of Jesus (as oral authorities), 17–18, 30, 72–73, 75–76, 77–78, 249–51, 265n15
feeding stories, 60, 65–66, 83–84
field (in oral register), 116–17
folkloristics, 46, 144
Foot Miracle (*Infancy Gospel of Thomas* 10.1-2), 143–44, 145, 148, 149–50, 151–53, 157, 160, 166, 167–69, 173–74, 175; *see also* "Cleave the Wood Saying"; "miracle stories, preservation of"
forgetting (aspect of memory), 12, 105–6, 109, 138, 189, 207, 260, 269n19; *see also* "memory, instability of"
form criticism, 2, 21, 22, 24, 33, 45, 46–47, 49, 58–59, 108, 177, 198–99, 202, 243–47, 249, 252, 254, 257, 260, 263n1, 270–71n1
forms (in oral tradition), 24, 33, 47, 48, 56–57, 58, 67, 81–82, 108, 111–12, 139, 141, 155, 199–200, 202–3, 244; *see also* "form criticism"
frameworks of memory, *see* "memory, frameworks of"
fundamentalism, 29
fuzzy trace theory, 153

Galilee, 49–50, 57–58, 59–61, 63, 67–68, 69, 70, 74, 84, 107
Gemma Augustea, 183–84, 190
genocide, *see* "Burundi genocide"
genre, 16–19, 40–41, 81, 92, 94, 112–13, 140, 143, 194, 197–98, 202–4, 217
-memory/transmission and, 151–52, 156, 157, 166, 226
Gerasene demoniac (Mark 5), 67
gist memory, 153, 176, 178
Good Samaritan (parable of), 6, 22, 97
gospel (oral proclamation of Jesus), 15–16, 23, 36, 42, 43, 48, 57, 58–59, 60, 63, 75, 82, 113, 114, 192, 194, 199, 215, 265n11, 265n12; *see also* εὐαγγέλιον; "Jesus tradition"
gospel of Rome, 182–85, 192
gospel of Trajan, *see* "'gospel' of Rome"
Gospels, relationship to oral tradition, 2, 10, 11–12, 13–14, 17–19, 20–21, 23–25, 33–34, 36, 37, 41–42, 72, 86, 100, 102–3, 107–8, 109, 179, 246, 249–52, 253, 260, 263n1; *see also* "Narrative Gospels"; "Sayings Gospels (genre)"
Gospels parallels/harmonies, 20, 39–40
"Great Divide" (between orality and writing), 27, 29–32, 37–39, 47–48
Greek Two Ways, *see* Two-Ways tradition
grid approach to texts, *see* "numerical grid approach to texts"
group identity, *see* "identity (social)"
Growing Seed (parable of), 69
Gutenberg, 9, 28, 241, 242–43
"Gutenberg Galaxy," 46, 239, 242

Hadrian (Emperor), 192
healing (stories), 64–67, 83–84, 92, 94, 195, 203
Hellenistic Christianity, 36, 177
Hellenistic Judaism, 43, 266
hermeneutics of orality, *see* "orality, hermeneutics of"
hermeneutics of writing, *see* "writing, hermeneutics of"
Herod Agrippa, 99
Herod Antipas, 58, 66, 81
Herodian(s), 50, 60, 65, 68
Hiroshima (bombing of), 208
Historical Criticism, 29, 46, 235, 239–43, 256
Historical Jesus, 17, 42–43, 198
-quest for, 2, 21–22, 42–43, 58–59, 244–45, 263n1

Historikerstreit, 258
history (nature of), 25
Holocaust, 198, 207, 211, 257–58
homeostatic balance, *see* "oral synthesis"
Homer, 36, 45, 46, 218, 229, 237
"Homeric question," 36
hot memory, *see* "memory, hot memory"
humanism, *see* "Renaissance humanism"
Hurricane Katrina, 209–10
Hutu nation, *see* "Burundi genocide"

identity (social), 8, 12–13, 47, 59, 72, 89, 97, 106, 109–10, 204, 207–10, 210–12, 216, 224, 228, 238, 249, 253, 261, 263–64n3, 271n2
illiteracy, *see* "literacy, rates (ancient world)"
images and themes (retention of in memory), 144, 152–55
imagination (affect on memory), 138–39, 140
imitation (rhetorical strategy), *see* "*mimesis*"
Innocent (Righteous) Sufferer motif, 13, 82, 258
interference effect, 138
intertext[uality], 48, 201, 246, 253
intrinsic causation (in tradition), 22–23, 24
inventio, 186, 189
ipsissima verba/structura, 21, 22, 113, 260, 266n20; *see also* "Historical Jesus, quest for"
Isaiah scroll, 226
"it is written" formula, 61–62

J, E, D, P, 266n2
James, Apostle, 14, 75–76; *see also* "disciples of Jesus (as oral authorities)"
James, brother of Jesus, 75, 77; *see also* "family of Jesus (as oral authorities)"

Jar Parable (*Gos. Thom.* 97), 143, 145, 147, 149, 152–53, 156–57, 159, 161, 164–65, 171, 172, 175–76
Jerusalem, 50, 57, 58, 60, 61, 62, 64, 65, 67, 68, 107
-destruction of (70 C.E.), 12–13, 38–39, 72–73, 204, 229, 251
Jesus quest, *see* "Historical Jesus, quest for"
Jesus research, *see* "Historical Jesus, quest for"
Jesus tradition, 6, 12, 14–15, 16–17, 20, 21–22, 23–24, 107–8, 111–12, 136–37, 138–39, 141, 145, 153, 155, 177, 178, 194–95, 201–2, 205–6, 243–44, 246, 252
Jews, 13–14, 43, 50, 52, 60, 94, 99, 107, 199, 211
John, Apostle, 64, 76, 91, 95, 103
John the Baptist, 66, 80–81, 107
John F. Kennedy, 207–8, 210
Joseph ben Eliezer, 228
Joshua, 58–59
Judea, 49–51, 52–53, 54–58, 59–63, 67–68, 107
Julius Caesar, 189–90

Kennedy assassination, 207–8, 210
keying (memory strategy), 13, 80, 198, 204, 205, 210–14, 258
kingdom of God/Heaven, 65, 69–70, 74–75, 76, 78, 80, 83–84, 87, 135, 143, 152, 156, 161, 171, 176, 212, 267n8
kinship groups, 76, 107
korban, 63, 66, 68

Last Supper traditions, *see* "Eucharist"
Law (of Moses), 32, 50–51, 52, 54, 61–62, 114; *see also* "Torah"
-Paul's view of, 15–16, 43
letters (ancient), 100–1
literacies, *see* "literacy, nature/kinds of"
literacy
-interfaces with orality, 9, 12–13, 16,

Index of Subjects   *311*

29–32, 47, 48, 49–50, 61–62, 99–101, 107–9, 112–14, 197, 215–18, 223–24, 237, 245–46, 249–50
-nature/kinds of, 50–55, 60–62, 220, 268n12
-rates (ancient world), 2, 29, 31, 43, 50–51, 57, 95–96, 112, 232, 268n10, 271n4
literacy and social position, *see* "writing, and social position/structure"
literalism, 29, 271–72n8
literate culture, 79, 268n11
locus of memory, *see* "memory places"
Logos Christology (Gospel of John), *see* "Christology, *Logos* (Gospel of John)"
long ending of Mark, *see* "ending of Mark's Gospel"
long-term memory, *see* "memory, long-term"
Lord's Prayer, 116
Lottery Ticket (parable of), 135–36
LTM (long-term memory), *see* "memory, long-term"
Luba nation, 117–19
lukasa (Luba memory board), 118–19, 121–22, 269n2, 269n3
Luther, Martin, 241
LXX, *see* "Septuagint"

Maidens and Lamps (parable of), 161
manuscript culture, 9, 25, 28, 89, 218, 220–21, 226–27, 229, 232–33, 234, 261; *see also* "print culture"
manuscript *mouvance*, *see* "*mouvance*"
manuscripts, *see* "books (vs. orality)"; "chirographs"; "scrolls"
Mapping Memory Group (Society of Biblical Literature), 238
Marcion, 192–93
martyrdom motif, 13, 83, 256
Mary (mother of Jesus), *see* "Mother of Jesus"
Masada, 211

Masoretic Text, 10, 126, 223, 255
master commemorative narrative, 211–12, 213
materiality of writing, *see* "writing, written words as things"
McGowan, Alec, 79
mechanical type, *see* "print (mechanical type)"
media blindness, 259–60
media determinism, 259, 260–61
media history, 14, 19, 259, 264n4
Mediendeterminismus, 260–61
memorial culture, 24, 36, 218, 239, 256
memorization, *see* "rote memorization/copying"
memory, 23, 36, 40, 91, 107, 136–38, 235, 237–38, 245, 259, 260–61
-cold memory, 11–12, 13, 19, 24, 71–72
-frameworks of, 10–11, 13, 104, 105, 117, 206, 209–10, 212–14, 218, 228; *see also* "memory, social memory"
-gist, 153, 176, 178
-hot memory, 11–14, 19, 23–24, 71–73
-instability of, 138–40, 142, 155–76, 179; *see also* "forgetting (aspect of memory)"
-long-term, 143–44, 144–55, 155–76, 178
-moral formation and, 218–19
-performance memory, 9–11, 25, 103–4, 114–15, 116, 117–19, 119–21, 122, 123, 141, 186, 189, 254, 264–65n9, 269n2, 269n17; *see also* "oral narrative style"
-reading and, *see* "reading and memory"
-recall, 10–11, 40, 101, 104, 117–19, 136, 138–40, 142–45, 151, 152–53, 155–57, 161, 171, 175, 177–79, 205–6, 253, 270n6; *see also* "memory, long-term"; "memory,

short-term"; "verbatim memory/recall"
-scribal, 54–57, 215, 217, 218–20, 220–24, 227–28, 229, 234, 236, 252–58, 266n2
-short-term, 143–44, 144–55, 155–76, 177–78, 230, 271n3
-social memory, 10–14, 25, 45, 48, 51, 53–58, 59, 61–63, 66, 67–68, 71–73, 84, 89, 103–5, 181–82, 186, 189, 194, 197, 198, 204, 205–6, 218, 229, 238, 264n8, 268n12
-stability of, 136–37, 140–41, 142, 144–55
-texts/manuscripts and, 49, 50–51, 55, 61–63, 87, 98–99, 103–5, 109, 112, 114–15, 117, 126–27, 138, 140–41, 217, 218–19, 220–24, 229–30, 236, 238–39, 242, 245, 252–58
-violence and, 13, 84, 197, 198, 204, 207–10, 211–12, 212–14, 257–58
memory and writing, *see* "memory, texts/manuscripts and"
memory board, *see* "*lukasa*"
memory buttons, *see* "memory pegs"
memory chains, 117–19, 121, 122–23
memory distortion, *see* "forgetting (aspect of memory)"; "memory, instability of"
memory pegs, 117–19, 121–23, 126–27
memory places, 13, 186, 189, 258
memory scars, 207–8, 210
messianic movements (ancient), 58–59, 196
metonymic reference, 116
mimesis (element of rhetoric), 73, 74, 75, 97–98, 186, 188
miracle stories, preservation of, 33, 127, 143–44, 145, 148, 149–50, 151–53, 155, 157,160, 166, 167–69, 171, 173–74, 175; *see also* "Cleave the Wood Saying"; "Foot Miracle"

Mishnah, 93, 226; *see also* "rabbis/rabbinic tradition"
mnemotechnique, *see* "memory, performance memory"
mode (in oral register), 116–17
monasticism, 112, 131, 228, 255
moral formation and memory, *see* "memory, moral formation and"
Moses, 59–60; *see also* "Law (of Moses)"
Mother of Jesus, 75–76; *see also* "family of Jesus (as oral authorities)"
mothers (as storytellers), 97–98, 107
mouvance, 225–29, 234, 255–56
Myra inscription, 183
myth plot structure, 211–13
multiformity (in tradition), *see* "memory, instability of"; "variability (in tradition)"
multiple attestation (criterion of), 21
Mustard Seed (parable of), 69

narrative chains (in Mark), 65–68
Narrative Criticism, 33–34, 35, 42, 74, 246–49, 266
Narrative Gospels, 12–13, 14, 17–19, 20, 24, 33–34, 39, 72, 85, 100, 182, 194–96, 203–4, 212, 237, 246–49, 260, 263n1, 265n11, 266n22, 270–71n1; *see also* "narrativity (hermeneutics and rhetoric of narrative)"
narrative style, oral, *see* "oral narrative style"
narrativity (hermeneutics and rhetoric of narrative), 5, 10, 12–13, 20, 23–24, 33–34, 41, 71, 72, 74, 77, 81–82, 85, 188–89, 200–4, 205, 207, 212, 237, 244, 246–51, 256–58, 260, 270–71n1
New Criticism, 248–49
nkaka memory pattern, 269n2
Noachide commandments, 119, 121, 132
nuclear scripts, 209–10, 213
numerical grid approach to texts, 45, 235, 247, 249

Index of Subjects 313

openings and closings (of remembered stories), 144, 151–52, 166, 177
oral authorities (in Christian tradition), 30–31, 72, 73–78, 86, 249, 250–52; *see also* "disciples of Jesus (as oral authorities)"; "family of Jesus (as oral authorities)"; "Mother of Jesus"; "prophets (early Christian), as oral authorities"
oral biosphere, *see* "biosphere (speech context)"
oral Christology, *see* "Christology, oral vs. written"
oral narrative style, 4–5, 11, 32–34, 48, 59, 63–66, 72, 73–75, 78–79, 81–82, 83–85, 200, 202–4, 249, 254, 270–71n9; *see also* "memory, performance memory"
oral register, 115–17
oral synthesis, 4, 6, 7, 264n5
oral-traditional culture, 9, 31, 151, 197, 202, 231
orality
  -hermeneutics of, 2–3, 4–5, 6–8, 10, 13–14, 15–17, 18, 21–22, 25, 76–77, 78, 79–85, 103–6, 114–16, 202–3, 206, 215–16, 244
  -spoken words as events, 4–5, 7, 8, 27–28, 103, 216, 245
orality/literacy interfaces, *see* "literacy, interfaces with orality"
Orality, Textuality, and the Formation of the Hebrew Bible Consultation (Society of Biblical Literature), 238
"original" form/meaning/text/version
  -oral sayings/tradition, 5, 10, 20–23, 42, 52–53, 69, 112–14, 177, 200–1, 244–45, 255, 261, 264n6; *see also* "equiprimordiality"
  -text/manuscript, 7–8, 10, 34, 46, 52–53, 86–87, 114, 220, 225–29, 230–33, 235, 242, 254, 260; *see also* "*mouvance*"
Oxyrhynchus papyri, 38

Paleography, 241
Papias, 92, 98, 100, 102, 104, 270n4
Parable of the Lottery Ticket, 135–36
parables, 6, 22, 42–43, 49, 64, 65, 67–68, 68–70, 78–79, 137, 142–43, 203
  -parabolic plot of Mark, 29–30, 68–70
  -preservation in tradition, 144–45, 152–53, 156–57, 161, 171, 172, 175–76, 179
parables discourse (Mark 4), 65, 69, 78–79, 264–65n9
parabolic plot, 29–30, 68–70
paraphrase (in memory), 155–56, 175–76, 178
passion narrative(s), 13, 48, 61, 80–84, 194–96, 197–205, 206–7, 212–14, 249–50, 256–58, 270–71n1
passive role of Evangelists, 20–21, 22–24, 47, 72, 198, 200, 203–5, 253
Paul, Apostle, 1–2, 49, 62, 76, 77, 102, 103, 133, 182, 183, 199, 256, 257
  -heroization of, 192–94
  -legends about, 192
  -media preferences, 14–16, 25, 42–43, 192, 203, 265n11, 265n12, 266n18
Paul's "two craters," 43
Pauline scholarship, 43
peasants (ancient Jewish), 50, 57–58, 60, 61, 67, 69
peg types, *see* "memory pegs"
Pentateuch, 52–53, 61, 228, 266n2
Performance Criticism, 74, 79, 83
Peter, Apostle, 36, 64, 74, 75, 77–78, 107, 252, 270ch.8n1
Pharisees, 50, 57, 59, 60, 62–63, 68
  -characters in the Gospels, 65–66, 68
philology, 241
phonological loop, *see* "articulatory loop"
pietas (piety), 183–84, 185, 188, 190
Plato, 31–32, 46, 112, 237

plot (element of narrative); see also "narrativity"
-narratives/Gospels, 24, 63–66, 68–70, 72, 74–75, 244, 248, 256
-oral, 5, 11, 63–66, 72, 74–75, 80, 82, 94, 200, 202, 249–50, 270–71n1
-parabolic plot (of Mark), 68–70
plurality (aspect of oral speech), see "memory, instability of"; "variability (in tradition)"
Polycarp, 266n17, 270n4
preachers/preaching, early Christian, 1, 3, 6, 11–12, 14–16, 197, 199, 201, 202; see also "gospel (oral proclamation of Jesus)"; "Jesus tradition"
presence, hermeneutics of, see "orality, hermeneutics of"
Priene inscription, 182–83, 192
print (mechanical type), 3, 9, 20, 28–29, 86, 225, 229, 241–42, 264n4
print culture, 46–48, 49, 50, 51, 53, 60, 69, 215, 218, 220, 231, 248, 252, 266n2, 267ch.3n3
print mentality, see "typographical mentality"
proactive interference, 221
pronouncement stories, 6, 59, 60, 67–68, 231
propaganda (Roman), 182–83, 184–85, 188, 194
prophetic movements (messianic), 57–58
prophetic speech, see "prophets, early Christian"
prophets, 89, 109, 194
-ancient Jewish, 57, 80, 81–83
-early Christian, 14–18, 37, 197, 203, 249–50
-as oral authorities, 17–18, 30, 72, 73, 76–78, 203, 249, 250–251, 266n15
Protestant Reformation, 28
proverbs, 56, 59, 65, 142; see also "Virgin Proverb"

-preservation in tradition, 136, 144–45, 146, 149–50, 151, 152–53, 154–55, 156–57, 161, 162–63, 166, 170–71, 175–76, 177, 179, 270n6
public reading, see "reading (public)"

Qumran, 47, 53–54, 55, 111, 221, 223, 228, 255, 272n10; see also "Dead Sea Scrolls"
quotations of Scripture, 60–63

rabbis/rabbinic tradition (ancient), 22, 49, 52–55, 111–12, 227, 237–39; see also "*Derek Erets*"; "Mishnah"; "Talmud"
reading (public), 1–2, 3, 9, 16–17, 30, 43, 48, 49, 51, 52, 53–54, 56, 71, 76, 85, 86, 96, 98, 101–3, 108, 112, 114, 115, 117, 217, 259–60, 267n4, 268n12, 269n21, 271n3
reading and memory, 142–43, 145–51, 153–76, 177–79, 217–19, 271n3
recall, see "memory, recall"
recitation (of manuscripts), see "reading (public)"
Red Riding Hood, 6
Redaction Criticism, 33, 194; see also "Two/Four Source Theory"
Reformation, 28
Regulus, 104, 269
relatedness effect, 138
Renaissance humanism, 240–42, 252
renewal theme, see "covenant renewal theme"
resurrection narratives, 18, 32, 62, 75, 77, 82, 84–85, 256–57, 264–65n9, 265n12, 267n8, 268n12
retention of images and themes, see "images and themes (retention of in memory)"
Rhetorical Criticism, 34
Richard de Fournival, 217
Righteous Sufferer motif, 13, 82, 258

Index of Subjects 315

ritual[ization], 36, 54–55, 115–17, 119, 183, 211, 238, 247, 257, 263–64n3
ritual elder, 115
Roman propaganda, *see* "propaganda (Roman)"
Rome/Romans, 13, 51, 59, 68, 70, 75, 110, 182–85, 192
rote memorization/copying, 22–23, 218, 231, 253

"sandwich" pattern (in Mark), 64, 66
sayings collections/Gospels (early Christian), 14, 16–19, 37, 39, 41–42, 77, 183, 194–96, 202–4
sayings of Jesus (traditional), 4, 10, 11, 14–15, 16, 21–22, 32, 33, 34, 40–42, 49, 52–53, 59, 72, 78–79, 86, 113–14, 135, 137, 141, 155, 178, 183, 194–95, 200, 201, 203, 232, 237–38, 244, 246, 254, 265n15, 265n16; *see also* "Jesus tradition"
Scaliger, Joseph, 241
scars (on memory), 207–8, 210
scenic duality, 11
scribal culture, 55, 136–37, 231, 238–39, 261
scribal memory, *see* "memory, scribal"
scribality, 9–10, 25, 34, 36, 71, 79–80, 82–84, 136–37, 144, 236–40, 246, 255–56; *see also* "chirographs"; "literacy, interfaces with orality"; "scribes"; "Textual Criticism"
scribes, 9, 28, 36, 49, 50, 82, 230, 231–32, 241; *see also* "memory, scribal"; "scribality"
-ancient Jewish, 46, 50–58, 62, 266n2
-characters in Gospels, 64–66, 67–68, 75
-copyists, 220–21, 224, 227–28, 230–31, 232–33, 254–56
-tradents, 220–24, 227–28, 233, 234, 255–56, 261
-vs. authors, 223–24, 230–31

Scripture, 13, 48, 51–53, 82, 98, 127, 199, 204–5, 213, 237; *see also* "Torah"
-authoritative status of, 3, 16, 61–63, 141, 232, 268n12
scrolls, 36, 50–57, 61–62, 185, 193–94, 218–19, 226, 259, 261, 271n4; *see also* "books (vs. orality)"; "chirographs"; "Dead Sea Scrolls"; "scribes"
-Trajan's Column as scroll, 186–89
sea crossings (in Mark), 60, 65–66, 83
Sea of Galilee, 60
secrecy motif, 18, 264–65n9
Semeia (Studies) (journal/series), 237–38, 252
Septuagint, 10, 32, 126
sequenced verbal agreement, 144–51, 178–79
short-term memory, *see* "memory, short-term"
"single originals," 34; *see also* "'original' form/meaning/text/version"
social biosphere (of speech), *see* "biosphere (speech context)"
social identity, *see* "identity (social)"
social memory, *see* "memory, social memory"
social position, *see* "writing, and social position/structure"
Society of Biblical Literature (SBL), 40, 236, 238, 254
Son of Humanity, *see* "Son of Man sayings"
Son of Man sayings, 65, 73–74, 76–77, 78, 80, 82–83, 267n8
Song of the Vineyard (Isaiah 5), 67, 69–70; *see also* "Tenants (parable of)"
sound maps, 122–23
Source Criticism, 2, 21, 22–23, 24, 35, 79, 230, 241, 250; *see also* "Two/Four Source Theory"
sources (written), *see* "Source Criticism"
Sower/Soils (parable of), 6, 68
speech, *see* "orality"

standardized texts/versions, 10, 209–11, 229, 254, 271–72n8, 272n10; *see also* "canon[ization] (authority of)"
STM (short-term memory), *see* "memory, short-term"
storytelling (ancient),
  -in Christian communities, 102–3, 107–8
  -functions of, 96–99, 101, 106
  -New Testament references to, 92–94, 95, 97, 98, 100, 106–7, 107–8
  -personal stories, 94–95, 106
  -social class and, 95–96, 102, 109–10
  -social contexts of, 106–7, 108
  -terms for, 91–94
  -topics of, 94–95, 106–7
  -written stories, 99–107
style of oral narrative, *see* "oral narrative style"
synagogues, 80, 98
synonym shifts (in memory), 158–60, 162–63, 164–65, 166–69, 171, 175, 178, 179, 221
Synopsis of the Four Gospels (Kurt Aland), 20
Synoptic Problem, 39–41, 137, 178–79; *see also* "Two/Four Source Theory"

Talmud, 53, 224, 229; *see also* "rabbis/rabbinic tradition"
Tenants (parable of), 64, 68, 69–70, 81
tenor (of oral register), 116–17
textintern, 216
Textual Criticism, 9–10, 25, 34, 35, 45, 52–53, 192–93, 230–34, 241, 250, 252–56, 260
textuality, 1–2, 6–10, 20, 24–25, 100, 229, 237–38, 265n15, 270–71n1; *see also* "scribality"; "writing, hermeneutics of"
Textus Receptus, 10
Thecla, 93

themes, retention of in memory, *see* "images and themes (retention of in memory)"
"threes," *see* "triad pattern"
Tiberius (Emperor), 184
Torah, 49–54, 63, 238–29; *see also* "Law (of Moses)"
tradents, scribes as, *see* "scribes, tradents"
traditio, 225
tradition (oral), *see* "orality, hermeneutics of"; "Jesus tradition"
traditional authorities, *see* "oral authorities"
Traditionsbruch ("break in tradition"), 12–13, 38, 73, 77, 218, 251–53
traditum, 223, 225, 225
Trajan (Emperor), 182, 185–88, 189–92
Trajan's Column, 185–92, 193, 194–95, 270n1
transcription, *see* "copying (manuscripts)"; "scribes, copyists"
trauma (and memory), *see* "memory, violence and"
triad pattern, 5, 64, 100
Tutsi nation, *see* "Burundi genocide"
the Twelve (Apostles), 64, 66, 74, 77–78, 89; *see also* "disciples of Jesus (as oral authorities)"
"two craters" (Paul's), 43
Two/Four Source Theory, 20, 23, 39–40
Two-Ways tradition, 111–12, 115–16, 119, 121–27, 131–33, 269n4
type (mechanical), *see* "print (mechanical type)"
typographical mentality, 19–20, 35, 36, 46, 112, 226–27, 229–30, 231–34, 237, 242, 259–60, 264n6, 266n18, 266n2

uniformity (in tradition), 5–6, 22, 202, 229; *see also* "memory, stability of"
University of Glasgow, 9–10

variability (in tradition), 5–6, 10, 19, 42, 71, 140, 216–17, 226, 254, 268n16; *see also* "memory, instability of"

variants (textual), 5, 7, 8, 21, 34, 52, 62, 67, 108, 113–14, 121, 131, 140–41, 220–21, 225, 227, 229, 232, 242, 246, 268n16

verbatim memory/recall, 40, 136, 140, 145, 151, 153, 155, 175, 177–79, 270n6; *see also* "memory, recall"

vice catalogues/lists, 116, 119, 121–23, 127, 131, 133

violence (and memory), *see* "memory, violence and"

violence ratio theorem, 209–10, 212

Virgin Proverb (*Gos. Thom.* 75), 143, 144–45, 146, 149–50, 153, 154–55, 161, 162–63, 170–71, 175–76

Vulgate, 29, 226, 228, 241

"wax tablet" model of memory, 205–6, 220

Wedding Banquet (parable of), 161

"Whoever Hears/Receives You Hears Me" saying, 15

"word processing," 36, 39

World Trade Center, 198, 207, 209

worship, 62, 98, 182, 199, 268n13; *see also* "emperor worship"

writers, *see* "authors"

writing, hermeneutics of, 2–3, 6–10, 11–12, 14, 15–17, 18–19, 28–29, 32, 79–80, 82–83, 86–87, 103–6, 108–9, 216–18, 239–40, 264n7, 269n21
 -opposed to orality, 1–2, 7, 17–19, 24, 28–29, 38–39, 41, 71–72, 73, 79, 84–87, 197, 203–4, 245–46, 249, 265n15, 266n17
 -and social position/structure, 50–51, 52, 55–56, 57–58, 60, 61–63, 102, 108–9, 113, 271n2
 -written words as things, 7, 8, 28–29, 103, 216–18, 241–42

writing and memory, *see* "memory, texts/manuscripts and"

Wyschogrod, Edith, 13